THE ACT IN CONTEXT

The Canonical Papers of Steven C. Hayes

Steven C. Hayes, Editor

Routledge
Taylor & Francis Group
NEW YORK AND LONDON

First published in paperback 2024

First published 2016
by Routledge
605 Third Avenue, New York, NY 10158

and by Routledge
4 Park Square, Milton Park, Abingdon, Oxon OX14 4RN

Routledge is an imprint of the Taylor & Francis Group, an informa business

Publisher's Note
The publisher has gone to great lengths to ensure the quality of this reprint but points out that some imperfections in the original copies may be apparent.

Library of Congress Cataloging-in-Publication Data
Hayes, Steven C.[Papers. Selections]Acts in context : the canonical papers of Steven C. Hayes / Steven C. Hayes.
pages cm
Includes bibliographical references and index.
1. Context effects (Psychology) 2. Cognitive therapy.
3. Behavior therapy. 4. Psychotherapy. I. Title.
BF315.2.H39 2015
150.19'43—dc23
2015019895

ISBN 13: 978-1-13-881860-6 (hbk)
ISBN 13: 978-1-03-292196-9 (pbk)
ISBN 13: 978-1-31-574513-8 (ebk)

DOI: 10.4324/9781315745138

Typeset in Abode Caslon
by Apex CoVantage, LLC

To Steven Joseph Pistorello-Hayes—my last child:

Suffering is ahead for you, due to life itself. It is painful to know I cannot completely prevent it. The same will be true of your children, for you, and of their children, for them.

I can hope, however, that something in this book, and the work and community it is part of, will be of use to you, even just a little. And I can hope that in some tiny way it puts things into the culture that will be there to help your children, and your children's children, even though they are unlikely ever to know who we were, nor our role in what was there for them.

Peace, love, and life, my sweet boy.

I love you always,

Dad

"Steve Hayes is one of the most original thinkers in modern psychology. His ideas not only revolutionized behavior analysis and clinical practice but also have the potential to shake up the realm of cognitive science. This book offers a unique opportunity to (re)discover some of his most fascinating work."

—**Jan De Houwer, PhD**, Professor of Psychology, Ghent University

"Few people are as creative and insightful as Steven Hayes in making sense of human complexity and helping people move forward in positive ways. This book chronicles the development of a great mind."

—**Kelly D. Brownell, PhD**, Dean, Sanford School of Public Policy, Professor of Psychology and Neuroscience, Duke University

"In this remarkable collection of profound insights, Steven Hayes laid the foundation of some ground-breaking new therapeutic approaches, including but not limited to, Acceptance and Commitment Therapy. Hayes' work shows incredible breadth and depth, ranging from theories of verbal relations and behavior analysis to issues on epistemology, spirituality, and evolution. Whether you agree with him or not, his thinking has been and will continue to be the inspiration of generations of future scholars, researchers, and clinicians. His thinking targets the essential questions about applied behavioral sciences with the goal to improve the human condition. Thank you, Steve."

—**Stefan G. Hofmann, PhD**, Professor of Psychology, Department of Psychological and Brain Sciences, Boston University; Author, *An Introduction to Modern CBT: Psychological Solutions for Mental Health Problems*

"Steve Hayes has dedicated his life to maximising human potential for a rich and meaningful life. This book will give you fascinating insights into that lifelong journey. Although these papers are technical in nature, and therefore somewhat demanding, this is a really worthwhile and meaningful read. If you are interested in the evolution of ACT and RFT, and the science and philosophy underpinning them, then it is well worth investing your time and energy to read and absorb these landmark scientific papers. A must for all ACT and RFT completionists."

—**Russ Harris**, Author, *The Happiness Trap*

THE ACT IN CONTEXT

The Canonical Papers of Steven C. Hayes is a compilation of his most pivotal articles written from 1982–2012. Through these selected papers, Hayes again revisits the theoretical struggles between behavioral and cognitive-behavior theories, taking us from the 1980s into present day, discussing the breakthroughs and follies. Using this as a focus point, he discusses the tradition of behavior analysis and its difficulties in addressing human language and cognition. Moving forward into the 90s, he chronicles the changes in a behavioral approach that emerge from a contextual perspective on human cognition, and lays out the foundation for a contextual behavioral science approach that he argues is more likely to lead to an understanding of human action and an alleviation of human suffering. Although the articles have previously been published, they have been edited and compiled to ensure this branch of research is clear to the modern audience. The compilation was chosen by Dr. Hayes to enhance his vision for a functional contextual approach to complex human behavior.

Steven C. Hayes, PhD, is a Nevada Foundation Professor at the Department of Psychology at the University of Nevada. An author of over 38 books and 550+ scientific articles, his career has focused on analyzing the nature of human language and cognition, and applying this knowledge to understanding and alleviating human suffering.

The *World Library of Mental Health* celebrates the important contributions to mental health made by leading experts in their individual fields. Each author has compiled a career-long collection of what they consider to be their finest pieces: extracts from books, journals, articles, major theoretical and practical contributions, and salient research findings.

For the first time ever the work of each contributor is presented in a single volume so readers can follow the themes and progress of their work and identify the contributions made to, and the development of, the fields themselves.

Each book in the series features a specially written introduction by the contributor giving an overview of his career, contextualizing his selection within the development of the field, and showing how his own thinking developed over time.

Rationality and Pluralism—The Selected Works of Windy Dryden
By Windy Dryden

The Price of Love—The Selected Works of Colin Murray Parkes
By Colin Murray Parkes

Attachments: Psychiatry, Psychotherapy, Psychoanalysis—The Selected Works of Jeremy Holmes
By Jeremy Holmes

Passions, Persons, Psychotherapy, Politics—The Selected Works of Andrew Samuels
By Andrew Samuels

Towards a Radical Redefinition of Psychology—The Selected Works of Miller Mair
Edited by David Winter and Nick Reed

Living Archetypes—The Selected Works of Anthony Stevens
By Anthony Stevens

Soul: Treatment and Recovery—The Selected Works of Murray Stein
By Murray Stein

A Developmentalist's Approach to Research, Theory, and Therapy—The Selected Works of Joseph Lichtenberg
By Joseph D. Lichtenberg

CONTENTS

A Note About Changes in the Included Articles xi
Steven C. Hayes

Functional Foundations of a Contextual Behavioral Approach: Professional and Personal History xiii
Steven C. Hayes

SECTION 1—ORIGINS AND ASSUMPTIONS 1

Planting the Seeds of Contextual Behavioral Science 3
Fredrick Chin and Steven C. Hayes

1 **Rule-Governed Behavior: A Potential Theoretical Framework for Cognitive-Behavioral Therapy** 7
Robert D. Zettle and Steven C. Hayes

2 **Falsification and the Protective Belt Surrounding Entity-Postulating Theories** 38
Steven C. Hayes

3 **Making Sense of Spirituality** 42
Steven C. Hayes

4 **Finding the Philosophical Core: A Review of Stephen C. Pepper's *World Hypotheses*** 57
Steven C. Hayes, Linda J. Hayes, and Hayne W. Reese

5 Mentalism, Behavior-Behavior Relations, and a Behavior-Analytic View of the Purposes of Science 78
Steven C. Hayes and Aaron J. Brownstein

6 Analytic Goals and the Varieties of Scientific Contextualism 100
Steven C. Hayes

7 Behavioral Epistemology Includes Nonverbal Knowing 117
Steven C. Hayes

SECTION 2—PRINCIPLES AND STRATEGIES 127

Cognition, Assessment, and Psychopathology: Basic Behavioral Principles and Applied Model 129
Fredrick Chin and Steven C. Hayes

8 Verbal Relations and the Evolution of Behavior Analysis 132
Steven C. Hayes and Linda J. Hayes

9 The Treatment Utility of Assessment: A Functional Approach to Evaluating Assessment Quality 160
Steven C. Hayes, Rosemery O. Nelson, and Robin Jarrett

10 Experiential Avoidance and Behavioral Disorders: A Functional Dimensional Approach to Diagnosis and Treatment 171
Steven C. Hayes, Kelly G. Wilson, Elizabeth V. Gifford, Victoria M. Follette, and Kirk Strosahl

SECTION 3—CLINICAL METHODS AND DEVELOPMENTAL VISION 205

Acceptance and Commitment Therapy, Relational Frame Theory, and a Contextual Behavioral Science Approach 207
Fredrick Chin and Steven C. Hayes

11 Acceptance and Commitment Therapy, Relational Frame Theory, and the Third Wave of Behavioral and Cognitive Therapies 210
Steven C. Hayes

12 Buddhism and Acceptance and Commitment Therapy 239
Steven C. Hayes

13 **Acceptance and Commitment Therapy: Model, Processes, and Outcomes** 249
Steven C. Hayes, Jason Luoma, Frank W. Bond, Akihiko Masuda, and Jason Lillis

14 **Contextual Behavioral Science: Creating a Science More Adequate to the Challenge of the Human Condition** 280
Steven C. Hayes, Dermot Barnes-Holmes, and Kelly G. Wilson

Epilogue
Looking to the Future of ACT, RFT, and Contextual Behavioral Science 319
Steven C. Hayes and Fredrick Chin

Index 323

A NOTE ABOUT CHANGES IN THE INCLUDED ARTICLES

The opening chapter, the section introductions, and the epilogue are new to this book. Everything else was in the original articles except for corrections of typographical errors, or modifying improper verb tense and the like, updating "in press" references to their published versions, and adding chapter page ranges, which was not required long ago.

It was hugely tempting to change things: in hindsight wordings were awkward, and arguments were poorly stated. Some points have proven to be less central; some terms have changed. For example, in Relational Frame Theory (RFT) the "transfer of stimulus functions" became the "transformation of stimulus functions." It would distort history too much to change such things, and I did not, but readers need to be aware of the time in which each piece was written and take care not to treat older pieces as current ones.

Readers also need to know that some things in some articles are not here. All abstracts were eliminated because there are section introductions that make sense of the articles, and given that chapters do not have abstracts while journal articles do, leaving them in created a needless inconsistency. Most authors' notes were removed (e.g., addresses for requests for reprints). Fredrick Chin and I worked together to shorten some articles so that more articles could be included. We tried to cut material that was redundant across articles, excessively referenced, or not central to the points at hand. For example, what was unique in Article 12 was the comparison of Acceptance and Commitment Therapy (ACT) and Buddhism. All of the material on ACT methods, RFT, and functional contextualism was cut because it is covered elsewhere. There was no attempt to cut material that was sloppy or that might be criticized.

The articles that were shortened beyond cutting abstracts or authors' notes are as follows (in articles with more than 2,500 words cut, the primary source(s) of those cuts are listed):

Article 1. Rule-Governed Behavior: A Potential Theoretical Framework for Cognitive-Behavioral Therapy—Shortened by 4,677 words. The cuts were focused largely on eliminating clarifying examples.
Article 4. Finding the Philosophical Core: A Review of Stephen C. Pepper's *World Hypotheses*—Shortened by 995 words.
Article 6. Analytic Goals and the Varieties of Scientific Contextualism—Shortened by 779 words.
Article 9. Treatment Utility of Assessment: A Functional Approach to Evaluating the Quality of Assessment—Shortened by 4,236 words. The main cuts were in the methodological typology of the kinds of research methods that could test treatment utility questions. A detailed system was described and examples given (those wanting to actually do treatment utility research may benefit by consulting the original article).
Article 10. Experiential Avoidance and Behavioral Disorders: A Functional Dimensional Approach to Diagnosis and Treatment—Shortened by 2,277 words.
Article 12. Buddhism and Acceptance and Commitment Therapy—Shortened by 3,704 words. The descriptions of ACT, RFT, and functional contextualism were cut.
Article 13. Acceptance and Commitment Therapy: Model, Processes, and Outcomes—Shortened by 3,024 words. We cut material on ACT, RFT, and definitions of third wave behavior therapy that we discuss in other articles in the volume. We also cut some of the details of the meta-analysis.
Article 14. Contextual Behavioral Science: Creating a Science More Adequate to the Challenge of the Human Condition—Shortened by 1,586 words.

Other than that, these articles are presented as they were, reflecting the development of a line of thought that we now call "Contextual Behavioral Science."

Steven C. Hayes
Reno, Nevada
January 2015

FUNCTIONAL FOUNDATIONS OF A CONTEXTUAL BEHAVIORAL APPROACH

Professional and Personal History

Steven C. Hayes, University of Nevada

This book is about the construction of a functional contextual approach in psychology and linking that approach to the other behavioral and life sciences. It is about human complexity, unpacked and opened to a pragmatic science of change.

The core idea inside pragmatism is behavioral function. Imagine a human being engaging in an action, any action. It does not matter what it is: raising a hand, making a statement, scratching a backside. If we ask you, the reader, "What is this person doing?" and the word *doing* is understood functionally, you will have to add something to this imaginary situation.

To accomplish this goal you cannot just list the form of the actions or describe them in molecular detail, because none of this tells you what the function is or how that function can be used to organize an ongoing behavioral stream into useful units. Action in a functional sense does not exist alone and cut off. It does not and cannot occur in a vacuum, as if a mere bundling of muscle twitches can tell us the nature of psychological events. To speak functionally you will have to add in the history of the person engaging in such actions and what occurred in the person's history before and after similar actions. You will have to examine the grit and grain of the current situation and what is similar between it and past situations. You will have to add in states of deprivation, aversive stimulation, or other motivational features of the current situation as they impact the individual and color what the environment affords.

As all of this is done, the action you are focusing on will begin to spread out across time and begin to penetrate the personal and situational context. You are not just looking at a hand being raised—perhaps you are looking at a person trying to gain permission to speak. You are not just looking at a person making a statement—you may be listening to a declaration of love and loyalty. And that backside being scratched is not just a response to an itch—it could rather be a humorous and loving imitation of a father long dead. And if all three occurred one after the other, you would need to repeat this entire process to create linkage to function at a higher level of organization, as individual actions became integrated episodes and sequences, now with a distinct history, meaning, and purpose in an even larger sense.

Function is woven into the fabric of lives. From a functional point of view psychological actions are historical, not in the sense of a dead history that must be repeated but in the way that the past informs, unfolds, and lives in the present moments of whole organisms. Such acts are situational, not as a mechanical reaction to the moment but as responses of an individual to an evolving set of opportunities. They reveal and create strands of history, meaning, and purpose in larger frames and sets, bringing actions together into repertories, episodes, and sequences that alter states of affairs, or for verbal human beings, that become integrated into stories and narratives that extend far into the future.

From the point of view of the person raising a hand, speaking, and scratching, these bits and pieces of living are part and parcel of commonsense purposive acts, so deeply so that if you asked this person "What are you doing?" she may not speak specifically of hands going up, or statement being made, or rear ends being touched. The response might dissolve these distinctions into action at a higher level of organization—more along the lines of "I'm sharing a funny story with my family about Dad. We lost him last year, and we are getting together on the anniversary of his death."

When function is the focus, the texture of action has no meaning if it loses contact with history and purpose. Ordinary people reveal their functional leanings in the natural narratives of their lives. There would usually be nothing surprising about the question "What are you doing?" and there are usually ready answers.

THE CONTEXTUALISM OF FUNCTIONAL ANALYSIS

For the functionally oriented analyst, however, life is much more difficult. It is difficult for two quite different reasons—one that is evident and one that is hidden.

Functional analysts know that they need to allow features of history and context to penetrate topographically constructed categories of action so that they can begin to answer a simple question like "What is that person doing?" in a functional way. That is hard and but its difficulty is known. It is clear that the interface between action and context is the only place the idea of function can be applied. That is why the core unit of pragmatic thinking in psychology is *the act in context*. But researchers realize it is by no means clear how best to categorize action from an ongoing stream, or how far and in what way to relate it to context. There seems to be nothing to prevent action from being as large as "everything" or as small as "nothing," or to prevent context from expanding into "everywhere" or "always" or shrinking into an instant.

Many pragmatic research traditions seem to dance around this difficulty, even though it is an obvious challenge to pragmatism. A researcher trying to understand how families deal with death would normally look at the episode involving the participant we have been unpacking and simply get on with it. Recordings could be made, questions could be asked, and categories could be applied. Measures could be taken across time and situation. For some, changes and challenges might even be put in place to see how systems are altered, testing the pragmatic impact of events in an analysis that can be manipulated. The researcher knows full well that it is hard to think functionally but hopes that empirical answers will be found anyway, and the best way to proceed is to proceed.

It is here that what is truly hard about functional thinking can explode onto the scene like a high school chemistry exercise gone awry. The researcher, too, is a behaving organism, with a history and set of purposes. If we are analyzing events functionally, how can we fail to address at least the key intended or experienced functions of analysis itself? What gave us the right to try to step out of this approach, as B. F. Skinner is famous for commenting, and now try to conduct analysis as if from the epicycle of Mercury?

Pragmatists have long seen the issue, but they often dodge it in exactly the way that our imaginary participant did. Our participant already knew that her father was dead when she raised her hand to gain the floor. She had the funny story in mind as she began to speak about her love for her father, or made her irreverent but loving imitation. When asked "What are you doing?" an answer came easily. The person did not need for the question to be asked in order to know what she was doing or to be able to tell the story. She just did it.

That is the usual approach in pragmatic research, beginning perhaps with William James who wrote an entire book on the utility of religious belief, without ever defining what kind of utility he himself was seeking in his psychology. A researcher trying to understand how families deal with death might simply move ahead without first doing a deep dive into what is meant by such words as *families*, *death*, or the all-important word *understand*. After all, the first two words could become clearer as the researcher focuses on the participants and their histories, goals, and purposes. But it is worth noticing that the same is not true of the last word. If the analysis seemed successful it might fit with the implicit purposes of "understanding" for the researcher, or it might not fit, but it will not tell the researcher what the intended purpose is or could be. Clarity about scientific goals requires researchers to focus on themselves and their own histories, goals, and purposes, and to acknowledge and take responsibility for the functions they seek for analysis itself.

I put you, the reader, in this exact situation moments ago as you read the first paragraph of this book. I asked you to think of what this person was doing. I did not stop to ask you to think of your own history and analytic purpose before even considering the question. And in all likelihood you did not think about these topics; you instead proceeded to the specific question I asked. The researcher who wanted to understand families and death likely did the same thing. And as Acceptance and Commitment therapists will know, that is exactly what clients do: they fail to focus on the functions they really seek, preventing them from escaping a system that has them entangled.

This raises the second issue—one that is both difficult and implicit. For a pragmatist, scientific action is functional, too, and thus must include the goals of the analyst. But when the history and goals of the analyst are included, shocking truths about pragmatism are immediately revealed: truth is local in the sense that it is inextricably bound to the purposes of the analysis, and thus whereas epistemology is key in pragmatism, it is silent by choice on ontological matters.

Two researchers could come to the issue of understanding how families deal with death and have different understandings in mind. One might want to appreciate the many historical and cultural elements that are part of human adjustment to loss. When the recordings are made, the questions asked, and the categories applied, the accomplishment of "understanding" might reveal itself in the ability to predict the course of events, or speak to and extend what is known already about cultural issues, or simply to have a sense of appreciation of the role and complexity of history. Another might wish to ameliorate cases of complicated grieving, and when the recordings are made, the questions asked, and the categories applied, the accomplishment of "understanding" might reveal itself in the ability to put changes in place that reduce the frequency and prevalence of this form of psychopathology. The categories and conclusions could be entirely different in these two situations, and in principle have almost nothing to do with one another. One person's understanding could be another person's incoherence. This is true because *there is nothing in pragmatism that guarantees that what is useful for one purpose is useful for another*. If action is functional then truth is as well, and although purposes can be acknowledged, owned, stated, or made more consistent, they cannot be justified. Justification is just another name for linkage to purpose. We can link purpose to larger purposes, but this process must end somewhere. Intended purposes need to be stated. Naked and in the wind.

When the pragmatist does this, he or she has immediately created a particular *form* of pragmatism. A flag has been planted, and others can come or walk away depending on the kind of knowledge they seek. Functional analysis thus ultimately demands not just an interest in context, but an interest in contextualism—the particular purposive context of the pragmatic analyst.

The history of thought shows that there is power in pragmatism for the behavioral and life sciences, but seeing that scientists, too, need to be thought of functionally is one of the most powerful moments the pragmatic journey foretells for the organization of these fields. Seeing the act in context, defined historically and situationally, as the core unit of behavioral science is just an outgrowth of taking a thoroughgoing functional approach. But once that unit is applied to knowledge seeking itself, something dramatic happens. The arrogance and certainty of commonsense categories drop away. It is no longer interesting to claim we "know" something if that way of speaking and thinking does not clearly lead to the accomplishment of the local purposes of knowledge. We cannot trust the simple categories provided by language itself are functional as measured against our local goals. But thinking of the scientists' own knowing as a pragmatic act means that nothing can be ruled out either—we cannot say, *a priori*, that *any* term is illegitimate—we have to see what it buys us to use it. This is tricky for scientists. It is tricky for clients, too. If therapists and scientists are going to guide others on this journey, it is one they have to take themselves.

As the articles in this volume will reveal (and thus there is no need to cite the sources here), this is the moment in which Skinner overthrows Watsonian behaviorism; this is the moment that goaded even Donald Campbell into refusing to apply evolution to his own analysis of evolution on the tortured grounds that doing so was solipsistic. This is also the very moment in which the core of a contextual behavioral science (CBS) approach forms. It is the moment too in which literal language transforms into functional processes in flight, and clinical battles with entangling thoughts and feelings shift into questions of what people really want out of their lives. It is the moment created by function radically and comprehensively applied.

THE HISTORY AND PURPOSE OF THIS BOOK

The full meaning and implications of what is being said will hopefully be clearer by the end of this book than they are likely to be right now. This introduction is designed to set the occasion for an exploration of a body of work, and in line with the theme of this introduction, the contextual factors associated with this book itself, as well as the life's work represented in its pages, are worthy of a brief analysis.

This introduction is being written by Steven C. Hayes. The book itself was assembled with the help of a person who will likely be his last student, Fredrick Chin. With your permission, in this introduction and in the section introductions and epilogue, words like *I*, *me*, or *my* refer to Hayes, whereas the word *we* refers to both Hayes and Chin (or at times to Contextual Behavioral Scientists as a group).

This book contains a set of canonical papers that have been selected so as to reveal the development of a line of thought. The general purpose of this line of thought is to create a behavioral science and a psychology more worthy of the challenge of the human condition. That is not a declaration of achievement—it is a declaration of purpose.

I have selected articles with the goal of casting light on a field. I asked for help from the CBS community, and several colleagues responded in detail (I appreciated the input and thank Niklas Torneke, Dennis Tirch, D.J. Moran, Patty Bach, James Hegarty, Scott Temple, Sandra Georgescu, and Brian Thompson). Several of the articles were then shortened to fit the current purpose, with Fred Chin's help (it is hard for me to see which of my words do not need to be said!). One article was rejected by Fred as redundant (I used him as test case for the impact of the book on readers relatively new to the work).

In a more specific sense, these articles reveal an approach that seeks the ability to predict and influence whole organisms interacting in and with a context considered historically and situationally and to do so with precision, scope, and depth. That sentence defines the psychological level of analysis and specifies the truth criterion of the philosophy of science that provides the foundation for the work: functional contextualism.

What happens when pragmatists embrace such purposes and then try to make clinical and other practical use of that combination? That is the story this volume tells, at least in part. It can only be in part because this line of thinking has become a communitarian endeavor and has a life of its own. It is a story still being written by many, and this volume is just one now largely historical strand inside of that larger fabric.

STEVEN C. HAYES: ACADEMICALLY AND PERSONALLY

Because a volume like this is a professional and personal one, it seems helpful to cover some professional and personal details. At the time of the writing of this introduction, I am 66 years old, and I am a Nevada Foundation Professor and Director of Clinical Training at the Department of Psychology at the University of Nevada. The usual short bio form of introduction says that I am an author of 38 books and over 540 scientific articles, and my career has focused on an analysis of the nature of human language and cognition and the application of this to the understanding and alleviation of human suffering. I allow myself to be described as the developer of Relational Frame Theory, an account of human higher cognition, although in fact it was developed with my colleague Aaron J. Brownstein (who would have been on the early articles about it, had he lived), and it was made into a viable research program by the efforts of Dermot Barnes-Holmes. I usually do not allow myself to be described as the developer of Acceptance and Commitment Therapy, a popular evidence-based form of psychotherapy that uses mindfulness, acceptance, and values-based methods. I use the term *co-developer* because although I started the ball rolling, my students and so many colleagues were central to the development of ACT over so many years that it seems rude and self-aggrandizing to grab at the word *developer*. I have been responsible for distinguishing functional contextualism from other forms of pragmatic thought; for helping to develop the psychological flexibility model and its elements; and for helping to create a knowledge development strategy and community under the rubric of Contextual Behavioral Science (CBS). I helped found the Association for Contextual Behavioral Science (ACBS), which is now (in early 2015) approaching 8,000 members worldwide.

I have been President of Division of Behavior Analysis of the American Psychological Association, the American Association of Applied and Preventive Psychology, the Association for Behavioral and Cognitive Therapy (ABCT), and ACBS. I was the first Secretary-Treasurer of the Association for Psychological Science, which I instigated (there is a story to be told there someday) and helped form. I served a 5-year term on the National Advisory Council for Drug Abuse in the National Institutes of Health. In 1992 I was listed by the Institute for Scientific Information as the 30th "highest impact" psychologist in the world. My work has been recognized by several awards including the Exemplary Contributions to Basic Behavioral Research and Its Applications Award from Division 25 of the American Psychological Association, the Impact of Science on Application Award from the Society for the Advancement of Behavior Analysis, and the Lifetime Achievement Award from the Association for Behavioral and Cognitive Therapy.

Those are the usual, mostly dry, academic details, presented in the usual way. But the heart of the matter is more personal, so some personal facts seem worth telling.

I came to psychology out of a yearning to mix bottom-up science with humanistic concerns. I made that decision in high school and never wavered. As a high school student my earliest substantive interest in psychology was Abraham Maslow. In the context of the suffering I saw in my family, I felt uplifted by the idea that life could be better and that fostering human growth and prosperity was part of our mission in the behavioral sciences.

I did my undergraduate degree at Loyola Marymount University (LMU) in Los Angeles (1966–1970) and quickly gravitated toward Irving Kessler, a psychology professor who became my mentor. Fresh from a dissertation on eye blink conditioning at the University of Southern California, he taught me that basic principles from the lab could inform our views of human complexity. One of the early behavior therapists in the area, he (surprisingly, in hindsight) let me (just a sophomore) sit in on clinical sessions with real clients while he was doing desensitization. I wrote my first undergraduate psychology paper in my sophomore year on applying exposure methods to emotions, not just to situations—an idea that would become central to ACT many years later. I was drawn to behavioral thinking, but only because I thought it could go to places like the ones Maslow wrote about.

I was a child of the 1960s: I sat on hippie hill in the pan handle of Golden Gate Park the "summer of love" in San Francisco; I consumed more hallucinatory drugs than was wise. Part of the counterculture, I was especially attracted to the utopian ideals of the time and to the importance of spiritual exploration. I was heavily influenced by Eastern thinking, particularly the writings of D.T. Suzuki and Alan Watts. I explored T-groups, Esalen, and Gestalt Therapy. I edited my college literary magazine.

My interests in spirituality, the arts and humanities, and science came together for me most powerfully in the work of B.F. Skinner. I read *Walden Two* in my junior year as part of the honors program. I bought into the idea that you could have a science that could move from animal learning to utopian thought. Reading Skinner's *Science and Human Behavior* was a kind of Zen exercise—his radical functionalism, I thought, changed the game of knowledge itself. I saw no contradiction between Skinner and Eastern thought or Maslow or Perls. Skinner appeared to me to provide a better means to these ends.

I became increasingly behaviorally oriented, even creating a rat lab at LMU, building the cages myself, and completing an honor's thesis comparing response prevention, shaping, and observation in the reduction of avoidance behavior in rats. I thought avoidance behavior made no sense, however, unless it was in conflict with approach contingencies, and this idea led to one of my first research papers.

It took three years to get into a doctoral program because the priest who headed my department thought I was a drug addict (I wasn't—just a relatively sane and cautious hippy). In the years after college I lived on an Eastern religious commune; I was an environmental activist and political organizer who disrupted Chamber of Commerce meetings and traded barbs with the mayor of San Diego. I thought if I didn't get into graduate school I'd become a politician, or perhaps a carpenter.

My communal living and activism background gave me a utopian vision and a missionary zeal. I saw in Skinner's work the possibility of developing a basic science that could transform the world by channeling such energies that could explain how to live together in peace, how to have relationships that worked, how to raise children, and how to prosper as individuals. I sought out behaviorally oriented departments and I finally landed as a doctoral student West Virginia University. WVU's Department of Psychology was (and remains to this day) one of the strongholds for functional thinking. The faculty I worked with were behavior analysts or cognitive behavior therapists, including John Cone, Rob Hawkins, Andy Lattal, Norm Cavior, John Krapfl, and Hayne Reese. Cone, Krapfl, Lattal, and Hawkins, in particular, saw Skinner as a radical functionalist who provided new ways to explore the world within, and to create a more prosocial world without.

I did my dissertation on energy conservation under John Cone. I had a lot of heart for environmentalism but was discouraged by the lack of interest in behavioral science by policy makers. My mission in psychology shifted from environmentalism to something else. It seems worth a more extended description.

In 1972 or 1973 the late Willard Day, founder and editor of the journal *Behaviorism*, visited the Department of Psychology at WVU. Willard was an incredibly charismatic person, with the kind of breadth of knowledge and intensity of intellect that could freeze a student in place much as a bright light can freeze an animal in the road. He gave a colloquium that day on the importance to a functional perspective of understanding verbal behavior "as it actually occurs; as it is actually displayed by human beings." I took him to mean by that phrase that we needed an analysis that was as useful in predicting and influencing this kind of behavior as direct contingency principles are in predicting and influencing other actions. He was not arguing that such an account existed; merely that it was essential to the very survival of functional behavioral thinking that such an account be brought into existence.

To explain why this colloquium thundered down upon me, you need to understand the mood of the times. Behavior analysis was just beginning to be felt as an applied force, but there were social and political problems everywhere to be seen. *The Journal of Applied Behavior Analysis* had launched only four or five years earlier. Behavior analysis seemed to many of those inside of it to be incredibly fresh and exciting. It was subtle and challenging—not at all like the cartoons that anti-behavioral people made of it. It had nothing to do with eliminating consideration of private experiences—rather it was focused on a functional understanding of these events. It had nothing to do with "muscle movements and glandular secretions"—what we call pejoratively called "squirts and jerks." It embraced all actions of whole organisms that were situated in history and circumstance. Willard had written (1969), for example, about how close behaviorism was to phenomenology, which spoke to some of my earliest interests in psychology. This was a naturalistic approach that had a chance to change the world and speak to the deepest challenges of the human condition.

At the same time, behavioral thinking was under attack. The movie *A Clockwork Orange* appeared in 1971, conflating behavior modification with involuntary aversion therapy. Skinner's *Beyond Freedom and Dignity* appeared during the same year and was widely misunderstood by those who failed to read it with care and understanding to be arguing that behavioral science needed to *eliminate* freedom and dignity in order to progress. Terms like *behavior modification* were attacked by national politicians on the grounds that they represented an attempt of the elite to install coercive control over others through mind control or even psychosurgery. Behaviorism was viewed by its enemies as a robot-like mechanistic approach that wanted to produce legions of compliant robots through brainwashing and conditioning.

To people like me, the ones who felt the beating heart of a naturalistic and functional new way forward that would speak to issues of love, community, compassion, and purpose, it all felt so desperately unfair. People did not understand. Psychosurgery? Aversive conditioning? Robots?

Willard's colloquium thundered down. Functional thinkers needed to explain how to *foster* freedom and dignity! Doing that meant we had to go beyond "mental way stations" that can block our ability to learn to live better lives and to find the contexts that support growth and prosperity. And to do that we needed to understand language *as it actually occurs*. The very survival of functional thinking and our role in promoting human progress was at stake.

I made a mental promise, sitting there listening to Willard. If it could be done, I would be part of it. There was a feeling in my stomach that clicked into place with that silent commitment, a fluttery feeling that said that this was a worthy challenge. This needed to be done. This was important. This was worth my life's moments.

That feeling never left me. I am slightly embarrassed to say (embarrassed perhaps because of the innocence of it, the vulnerability of it, the child-like yearning it reveals) it is a feeling sitting with me still, as I write this introduction sitting in my chair with a computer on my lap.

I learned to do therapy largely on internship, working with David Barlow in the first internship class at Brown University School of Medicine and being influenced by others at the internship who would go on to make a difference in the field, such as Kelly Brownell, Peter Monti, Toy Caldwell-Colbert, Carol Landau, and a few others (including a brief overlap with Neil Jacobson).

I settled into my first academic job at the University of North Carolina at Greensboro (UNC-G), exploring radically functional approaches to assessment with my colleague Rosemery Nelson-Gray and trying as best I could to understand the new and rising cognitive behavior therapy movement. I floundered in this effort to study human language. Every attempt to do so seemed on reflection to be better done with nonhuman animals. I played with the concept of rule-governed behavior, but progress was slow even if my energy was high.

And then my world collapsed.

As my academic department slid into decades of hyperconflict, I developed a panic disorder. Beginning in department meetings, in little more than a year's time my panic symptoms spiraled into near paralysis. I avoided travel, restaurants, open spaces, shopping malls, giving lectures, riding elevators, teaching classes, or making phone calls. The most basic functions seemed almost impossible. I remember looking at the seat belt announcements of an airline stewardess as if I was watching an Olympic athlete performing an impossible feat of psychological dexterity: she was talking in front of 120 people without any external signs of terror. How did she *do* that?!

I tried everything I knew to do to solve the problem of anxiety. Therapy. Drugs. Self-help from behavioral and cognitive behavioral psychology. I hid my dysfunction from everyone I could but still found myself in horrifying situations, such as lying on a bench outside of the National Air Museum unable to move as my young daughter for whom I was responsible, who was perhaps 9 or 10 at the time, anxiously asked me if I was dying.

It was only when I turned back to my Eastern training and to the human potential movement that I began to progress. I grasped tightly to the issue of *function*. How was I giving thoughts and feelings a function? I saw that my avoidance, entanglement, and attentional focus were making anxiety the center of my life. I learned to leap into openness through acceptance and defusion. That had a profound impact. I rediscovered a sense of self that was powerful in my hippy days and in my exploration of Eastern spiritual traditions but that I'd somehow lost touch with. I rediscovered there was a spiritual me, a transcendent sense of self, untouched by the terror. I found that values work and committed action creates a tangible sense of growth and direction. I challenged myself with commitments for no reason other than I said so. For example (one of several), I joyfully did not eat desert for a year—laughing all the way because I was doing it for no reason at all other than I said so. Ha, ha, ha! Some seemed to think I'd lost my mind, which I agreed with in a sense—but I'd also found myself. I tried these ideas with clients and they progressed, too. Rapidly. ACT became not just a way of working, but a way of life.

One step at a time, I came back. But I came back forever changed. I now knew, and I would never forget, that anytime, anywhere I could grind to a halt inside the "no" of avoidance and fusion. I knew that what I had experienced was a problem with how my mind worked, but I saw also that the hole I had stumbled into *was entirely based on normal cognitive processes*. All it took was high levels of anxiety (any new professor would have been terrified in those horrible department meetings, seeing full professors fight like animals) combined with a forceful "no" directed at anxiety itself. I'd stumbled on the key to panic, and there was nothing special about it. It was normal.

Fascinated, I looked again at Skinner's approach to language and cognition, and my own experiences showed the hole in knowledge that was buried deep inside that work. We will describe the hole in Section 1 of the book but the core was the fact that we had no sensible definition of verbal stimuli—we had no model of how words worked and why. We could not model the "no" I said to anxiety. I looked again at behavioral and cognitive therapy and saw holes there too: There was no account of how normal verbal/ cognitive processes gave rise to psychopathology, and consequently no appreciation for the powerful role of acceptance and mindfulness and values. All of these things needed to change. My mental promise to Willard clicked together with my mental promise to myself as I emerged from panic disorder.

I stumbled on the phenomena of "stimulus equivalence" and working with my colleague and lab partner, the late Aaron J. Brownstein, in a handful of days developed RFT. Aaron immediately said it was tight and right—which was critical because he was the best behavior analyst I had ever known and had become a father figure to me. The two of us laid out about 25 studies that needed to be done on it (almost all were later done, though most of them by other research teams).

I began to use, teach, and give workshops on Comprehensive Distancing (which later became ACT, so we will use that label here). It seemed profoundly useful personally and with clients, but professional interest initially was more one of curiosity than real interest. My students and I did several early studies, finding that ACT did unusually well as compared to the best available methods in the areas of depression, pain, and weight control.

After a sabbatical year with the basic behavior analyst Charles Catania, I escaped the corrosive turmoil of UNC-G and went to the University of Nevada in 1986 as Director of Clinical Training. At the same time, I stopped doing any outcome research on ACT at all. I did not begin again for 15 years.

I was acutely aware that these ideas were drawn as much from wisdom traditions and the human potential movement as they were scientific psychology. Today the idea of research on acceptance, mindfulness, and values is routine. At the time it seemed so far out of the mainstream as to be almost impossible. Behaviorists, I feared, would hate it. Cognitive behavior therapists, I knew, would be threatened by it. Empirical clinical psychologists, I suspected, would sneer at it. I knew ACT worked but I felt as though a much stronger foundation needed to be built.

Had I been more aware of the developments with Mindfulness-based Cognitive Therapy (MBCT) or Dialectical Behavior Therapy (DBT) (and so on) I might have moved ahead more quickly, but I thought we needed to have measures in hand of key processes, and components that were well defined and replicable. We needed a basic account that worked and basic assumptions that were solid. And to be honest I was not ready personally: I feared the crowds, and requests, and demands that seemingly lay ahead if we could pull this off. Popularizing ACT would have to wait.

Especially after marrying a well-known behavior analytic philosopher, Linda Parrot, I dove into philosophy of science issues that seemed needed to establish a firm footing for the work. Hayne Reese put me on to the work of Stephen Pepper, which helped a great deal. Working with key colleagues, especially Dermot Barnes-Holmes, I worked to turn RFT into an empirical research program. I worked on how to understand ACT theoretically and to assess its core processes. I conducted a 2-year training and evaluation program with Kirk Strosahl at Group Health of Puget Sounds. Kirk had been exposed to the work in 1986 at a key ACT workshop done at the University of Washington (others, such as Neil Jacobson and Patti Robinson, learned of ACT at that same workshop, which is famous in my mind also for the multiple anxiety attacks I had while giving the workshop). Students came with me or arrived at the University of Nevada, Reno (UNR) who pushed the ACT work forward, including several who would be important to the ACT community for many years going forward, such as Barbara Kohlenberg, Sue McCurry, Kelly Wilson, Jacqueline Pistorello, Liz Gifford, and many others (I apologize to those left off the list but since I've graduated 45 doctoral students in my life and all had a role, it cannot be helped). Colleagues at UNR became interested in ACT and shaped my thinking: Victoria Follette and Bill Follette.

After a decade of such work, in 1996 the core of the ACT model was presented in a major article (with Kelly, Liz, Victoria, and Kirk); in 1998 the first effectiveness trial appeared from the work done in Puget Sound with Kirk; in 1999 the first ACT book came out with Kirk and Kelly as coauthors; in 2000 the first randomized clinical trial on ACT of the modern era appeared from a team in the United Kingdom headed by Frank Bond; in 2003 the first international meeting on CBS occurred in Kinkoping, Sweden; in 2004 the first measure of experiential avoidance was published with Kirk and many others, and the first major article on the "third wave" came out as my president address for ABCT; in 2005 the first broadly focused ACT self-help book was published (*Get Out of Your Mind and Into Your Life*, Hayes & Smith, New Harbinger Publications, 2005), and I married Jacque Pistorello; in 2006 the first wave of national publicity hit with a major article in *Time Magazine* and ACBS was formed. ACT became the overnight success—that took 25 years to produce.

Someday the personal history of all of that may be told. Now is not the time. The purpose of this mix of personal and professional details is to place the current volume in a historical and purposive context: This book shows the journey of a man who came to make a difference but saw it nearly all taken away by a severe anxiety disorder. This book shows the intellectual journey of a man determined to change behavioral psychology and to put it back at the center of the field. This book is titled *The Act in Context* both because the functional situated act is the core of the work and because these articles are themselves acts that occur in a professional and personal context. My work is in part a path of personal transformation, and in part of an effort to transform a field. Through functional contextualism, RFT, psychological flexibility, ACT, and CBS, I have dedicated my life to creating a new form of behavioral psychology that can better empower human lives. This book tells part of that story in outline form in a way I hope will allow those interested in these topics to explore ACT, RFT, and CBS with a great sense of intellectual coherence, continuity, and zeal.

This work is about something—it has a history and purpose. I hope a few readers will share that feeling in their stomach that something important is at stake. As we members of the CBS community add our personal lives and interests, we grow and extend that history and purpose. This community of souls is the human context that will help determine whether CBS as an intellectual and practical line of work is worthwhile. Functionally speaking, of course.

Section 1

Origins and Assumptions

PLANTING THE SEEDS OF CONTEXTUAL BEHAVIORAL SCIENCE

Fredrick Chin and Steven C. Hayes
University of Nevada

Section 1 of the volume is about the origins and foundational assumptions of a contextual behavioral science approach. There are seven articles in this section: three were published in the 1980s; two in the 1990s; and one in 2004.

These articles describe an early attempt to understand cognitive processes using the direct behavioral principles available at the time, followed by a much later but very short piece that waives off falsificationism and entity postulating theories. In the gap between these two lies a question: How are we going to address the challenge of human language and cognition from a functional point of view? The answer implicit in what follows is this: First get your philosophical house in order. Get your assumptions clear, consistent, and known. The other pieces describe how that is done. They lay out the development of functional contextualism and its key characteristics as a modification of Skinner's radical behaviorism. They show a pivotal difference in the willingness of functional contextualists to consider the use of any term on pragmatic grounds, regardless of its literal status. They explicate a pragmatic truth criterion, explain the environmentalism of a functional contextual approach, and show how functional contextualism differs from other contextualistic approaches, primarily in its goals.

Section 1 is the longest of the three sections of the book and the least obviously connected to clinical matters. These articles are the most important in many ways, however, despite their obscurity. Without clarity about foundational assumptions, it is impossible to create a coherent and progressive research program that is as ambitious as contextual behavioral science.

Article 1— Rule-Governed Behavior: A Potential Theoretical Framework for Cognitive-Behavioral Therapy. The first item in Section 1 is an early attempt to understand cognitive behavior therapy by applying and expanding the traditional Skinnerian model of rule-governed behavior. The Zettle and Hayes (1982) chapter tried to demonstrate that behavioral ideas could be used to explain and to guide therapeutically significant processes of change in cognitive and behavioral psychotherapy. The chapter is an ambitious piece that had to reach beyond the existing empirical work in order to link rule formation and following to psychopathology and its amelioration. At its best, Zettle and Hayes's chapter shows that a bottom-up application of behavioral thinking to cognitive behavioral approaches was not that difficult to construct. Astute readers may recognize holes within this account, however. For one thing, it was impossible to define what a verbal antecedent was, and as a result the concept of rule-governed behavior itself was left hanging. In order to answer this question, it would become necessary to create a new basic behavioral theory of language and cognition, but that would happen only later as RFT emerged. The other quality of this chapter is that it does not tell you much about what to do differently. Part of that was deliberate since the piece explicitly assumed all of CBT is basically useful in order to set the foundation for an account. The social basis of cognitive change is noted and a few other such matters seem innovative, but there is a sense of reinventing the wheel. This was the last such effort—a new approach was needed. But it left us with some useful concepts that came to life later in ACT.

Article 2—Falsification and the Protective Belt Surrounding Entity Postulating Theories. This short article (Hayes, 2004) will not make full sense unless you first read Paul Meehl's classic article (1978) about the slow progress of soft psychology, but the general drift will be evident without doing so. Falsification is almost universally embraced by empirical clinical psychology, and Meehl's article is often used to justify this step. Hayes's 2004 article shows the flaws in Meehl's argument. In limited forms contextualists use falsification as well, but for them it is not the golden road to the Truth, and this article explains why. The problem is that the gap between terms and the conditions under which they are measured and applied can always be blamed for failures. That is especially true for entity postulating theories because the gaps there are very large. In functional contextualistic approaches the gap is usually small, as Meehl himself acknowledges, but when it is small, verification of extensions of functional models works as a test of conceptual quality. This piece explains why the twin steps of falsification and entity postulating theories are toxic to progress and outlines the alternative approach that CBS explores.

Article 3—Making Sense of Spirituality. This is widely considered to be the first article that foretells the development of ACT and RFT, and lays the foundation for the use of middle level terms in CBS. The key idea in Hayes (1984) is that naturalistic behavioral approaches need to take seriously the possibility that important phenomena are described by dualistic and mentalistic terms. Spirituality is the queen of such concepts, since it is distinguished in common usage from material events themselves. On analysis, the article argues that there is an important natural phenomenon addressed by the language of spirituality, and attempts to provide a contextual behavioral account. The article appeals to human perspective taking and describes a new approach to self and self-awareness. In doing so, it describes the nascent development of what will later be called deictic relational framing. The article tacitly demonstrates that the basic-applied relationship is bidirectional—that is, identifying applied problems that need to be solved can suggest basic processes as well as the reverse.

Article 4—Finding the Philosophical Core: A Review of Stephen C. Pepper's World Hypotheses. The next article (Hayes, Hayes, & Reese, 1988) explores the philosophical thought of Stephen C. Pepper and makes the case for behavior analysis as a contextualistic system. The article describes Pepper's four relatively adequate "world hypotheses" and uses a number of quotes of Skinnerian ideas to show that the expected features of contextualism can be found there. Pepper helps us understand why theoretical disagreements between contextual behavioral approaches and others persist: They are often disguised disagreements about philosophical assumptions. Pepperian thought has at least two immediate benefits for scientists: First, it reduces needless fighting since alternative worldviews are not "incorrect"—they are just different. Second, it helps develop a scientific program that emerges from and remains consistent with a set of philosophical assumptions. Both of these advantages have subsequently been explored in CBS.

Article 5—Mentalism, Behavior-Behavior Relations, and a Behavior-Analytic View of the Purposes of Science. This article (Hayes & Brownstein, 1986) shows that when the purpose of behavioral science is prediction and influence, environmentalism is necessary. It demonstrates the pragmatic problem that emerges from identifying actions as causal variables over other actions and proposes a contextual alternative: the use of contextual variables to alter the likelihood of behavior-behavior relations. This is the very basis of ideas that will later blossom in ACT, such as the use of defusion and experiential acceptance to deal with difficult thoughts and feelings. By focusing on the manipulable variables in the environment that alter not just action but also the relations of action to action, a pragmatic alternative to mental causality is constructed—a critical and necessary step for functional contextualists wanting to enter the lion's den of cognition and its role in other forms of action.

Article 6—Analytic Goals the Varieties of Scientific Contextualism. This chapter (Hayes, 1993) is the first to distinguish descriptive contextualism from functional contextualism. It argues that *a priori* verbal goals are necessary for contextualists to use successful working as a scientific truth criterion. Truth devolves into mere reinforcement without the addition of specific goals, and thus all operant behavior would be "true"—leading to an incoherent lack of precision. It also shows that there are at least two distinct families of contextualism based on their analytic goals.

Article 7—Behavioral Epistemology Includes Nonverbal Knowing. Finally, in order for successful working to be maintained as a truth criterion, it needs to be distinguished from correspondence-based truth. The problem is that referring to evidence to support pragmatic claims leads to an infinite regress of "how do you know?" and the very core of the defense of these knowledge claims seemingly rests upon a correspondence truth criterion. The solution to this paradox stands on nonverbal knowing as this chapter (Hayes, 1997) tries to show. As soon as this nonverbal knowledge is made verbal, defense of utility once again pulls toward an appeal to correspondence, but the same process allows the analyst to stay one step ahead of literal language. This is basically the same approach that is used by ACT therapists to defend workability over literal truth, ending (or at least pausing) in the silent knowing of "present moment" and "self-as-context" exercises, or the vitality of valued living itself. Thoughts that ask, "How do you know you're a good person? What if you're not?" at least temporarily lose their power in the space where verbal and nonverbal knowing interact—at the locus of experience in which all pragmatic working judgments transition into life itself.

REFERENCES

Hayes, S. C. (1984). Making sense of spirituality. *Behaviorism, 12*, 99-110.

Hayes, S. C. (1987). A contextual approach to therapeutic change. In Jacobson, N. (Ed.), *Psychotherapists in clinical practice: Cognitive and behavioral perspectives* (pp. 327–387). New York: Guilford.

Hayes, S. C. (1993). Analytic goals and the varieties of scientific contextualism. In S. C. Hayes, L. J. Hayes, H. W. Reese, & T. R. Sarbin (Eds.), *Varieties of scientific contextualism* (pp. 11–27). Reno, NV: Context Press.

Hayes, S. C. (2004). Acceptance and Commitment Therapy, Relational Frame Theory, and the third wave of behavioral and cognitive therapies. *Behavior Therapy, 35*, 639–665. doi: 10.1016/S0005-7894(04)80013-3

Hayes, S. C. & Brownstein, A. J. (1986). Mentalism, behavior-behavior relations and a behavior analytic view of the purposes of science. *The Behavior Analyst, 9*, 175–190.

Hayes, S.C., Hayes, L.J., & Reese, H.W. (1988). Finding the philosophical core: A review of Stephen C. Pepper's World Hypotheses. *Journal of the Experimental Analysis of Behavior*, 50, 97–111.

Meehl, P.E. (1978). Theoretical risks and tabular asterisks: Sir Karl, Sir Ronald, and the slow progress of soft psychology. *Journal of Consulting and Clinical Psychology, 46*, 806–834.

Zettle, R. D., & Hayes, S. C. (1982). Rule-governed behavior: A potential theoretical framework for cognitive-behavior therapy. In P. C. Kendall (Ed.), *Advances in cognitive-behavioral research and therapy* (pp. 73–118). New York: Academic.

ARTICLE 1

RULE-GOVERNED BEHAVIOR

A Potential Theoretical Framework for Cognitive-Behavioral Therapy

From Robert D. Zettle and Steven C. Hayes (1982). In P.C. Kendall (Ed.), *Advances in cognitive behavioral research and therapy* (pp. 73–118). New York: Academic.

The emergence and increasingly wide acceptance of cognitively based treatments are major developments in behavior therapy. In recent years there has been the formation of a new journal, *Cognitive Therapy and Research*, and a special interest group within the Association for Advancement of Behavior Therapy devoted to cognitive-behavioral therapy (Dowd, 1978), as well as the appearance of several major books in the area (Beck, Rush, Shaw, & Emery, 1979; Kendall & Hollon, 1979, 1981; Mahoney, 1974; Meichenbaum, 1977).

It is unclear which specific intervention procedures comprise cognitive-behavioral therapy (Wilson, 1978), but one suggested area in common is the commitment to behavioral methodology each reflects (Kendall & Hollon, 1979). Methodological rigor has often distinguished behavior therapy from other treatment approaches. In recent years, however, behavior therapy has increasingly neglected conceptual concerns (Hayes, Rincover, & Solnick, 1980). Cognitive-behavioral therapy, in particular, currently finds itself in the unfortunate position of a methodological movement without a firm conceptual foundation. Generally neglected altogether is the potential contribution that a radical behavioral analysis of cognitive-behavioral therapy might provide.

One reason for the relative neglect of radical behaviorism may be unfamiliarity with its view on private events and confusion over how it differs from other forms of behaviorism as a philosophy of psychology. Contemporary radical behaviorism (e.g., as reflected in the current writings of Skinner, Day, Catania, and others) is often confused with Watsonian behaviorism. For example, radical behaviorism is thought to represent the rejection of feeling, thinking, and other cognitive events (e.g., see Shevrin & Dickman, 1980). In fact, contemporary radical behaviorism incorporates these events as behavior—nothing more, but also, nothing less.

It is curious that methodological behaviorism, rather than radical behaviorism, has become a common ground for much of cognitive-behavioral therapy. Methodological behaviorism (as a philosophical position) has emphasized that, for methodological reasons, only publicly observable behavior can be considered as scientifically admissible. We can, however, generate "hypothetical constructs" which we infer based upon public events. Private events are thus relegated to a land of the hypothetical; never directly accessible and never, somehow, on a par with publicly observable organismic activity. Over time, the odious philosophical content of this position has seemingly faded from view for many cognitive-behavioral therapists and the words "methodological behaviorism" have come to mean simply "behavioral methodology," or for some "the scientific method," or even "empiricism."

The fact that radical behaviorism has been so ignored and misunderstood as it applies to cognitive behavior is due in part to radical behaviorists themselves. Much of the applied empirical work done by radical behaviorists has seemingly not required attention to the factors being examined by cognitive therapists.

Due largely to historical factors (Kazdin, 1978), applied work in a radical behavioral tradition has emphasized the manipulation of strong behavioral consequences with severely disturbed populations. Very few adult clinicians, for example, are radical behaviorists. A radical behavioral view of common clinical issues has thus been poorly developed or has been developed in a way that has not led to the needed research (e.g., Skinner's 1957 book on verbal behavior). Presently, it is sadly true that radical behaviorists have "consistently eschewed the analysis and modification of private events" (Wilson, 1978, p. 8).

The present article is a first attempt to provide a framework for cognitive-behavioral therapy (and semantic therapies more generally) in radical behavioral terms. As such, it is both general and speculative. Nevertheless, it is meant to be testable, modifiable, and clinically applicable. It is written in the hopes that cognitive-behavioral therapists might look anew at radical behaviorism as an approach within which to develop their field. It is also hoped that radical behaviorists will begin to study cognitive phenomena in a rigorous manner.

RADICAL BEHAVIORISM AND COGNITIVE PHENOMENA

It is not our intent to describe radical behaviorism in detail, but some generalities about cognitive phenomena are warranted. To the radical behaviorist, behavior is regarded as observable organismic activity. Private events are regarded as stimuli or behavior that can be observed by an audience of one. [Public observability is not regarded as essential for scientific analysis (see Skinner, 1945).] Private events are not given special status simply because of the audience size. This does not mean that thoughts do not have special roles to play (the current article argues that they do) but merely that privacy does not establish that status.

Because the position is functional, causal factors are reserved for those that can be shown directly to help predict and control behavior. It is recognized that behavior can influence other behavior and that behavior can influence the environment so as to influence other behavior ("reciprocal determinism"). Nevertheless, ultimately all "causes" are restricted to environmental events. Behavioral "causes" are not ultimately acceptable since no one can change behavior without changing its context (e.g., through instructions, drugs, consequences, settings).

Thoughts and feelings, then, are behavioral phenomena on an equal par with other behaviors. Like all behaviors they can enter into causal sequences, but cannot be accepted as the ultimate cause of other behaviors. If cognitive phenomena control other behavior, the task is to identify the environmental supports for such behavior-behavior relationships.

A concept of critical importance to this task is rule-governed behavior. All behavior is thought to be ultimately contingency shaped, but an important subset of this behavior is rule-governed behavior (Skinner, 1966, 1969, Chapter 6; Zettle, 1980b). Skinner (1969, p. 146) provides an interesting example. An outfielder moves to catch a ball. Following its trajectory, he moves under it and grasps it with his glove. This event is undoubtedly contingency shaped. The outfielder is simply responding, as he has done hundreds of times before, to the effects his behavior has on moving toward the ball. A dog can easily acquire the same behavior in the same way (e.g., in catching Frisbees). Contrast this with the ship captain moving to "catch" a descending satellite. The trajectory of the satellite is analyzed in detail. Mathematical models are consulted which take into account a host of factors such as wind speed and drag coefficients. Its place of impact is predicted and approached. This behavior is not controlled solely or directly by the past consequences of trying to catch satellites—it is controlled by rules. Unlike ball catching, this activity requires a verbal organism as host.

It is our view that the concept of rule-governed behavior, if expanded somewhat, can incorporate much or all of cognitive and semantic therapy without distorting its basic phenomena. It also points to several mechanisms of change as yet under investigated in the field. In the sections that follow, we will outline the essential characteristics of rule-governed behavior, identify some of its components and functional units, apply this to therapies developed by Ellis, Meichenbaum, and Beck, and point to some mechanisms of psychopathology and its treatment implied by this analysis.

DEFINITION OF RULES

Rules have been described by Skinner (1966, 1969) simply as "contingency-specifying stimuli." This definition is somewhat problematic. We are concerned that it is excessively narrow in some respects, and excessively broad in others. It also readily leads to confusion between rules and discriminative stimuli in general. Part of this confusion seems to result from the differing nature of their definitions. Essentially, Skinner's definition of rules as contingency-specifying stimuli is a topographical one whereas discriminative stimuli are defined functionally. Rules that are not followed can be readily distinguished from discriminative stimuli but confusion results when rules are followed.

It can be seen that all effective rules are discriminative stimuli, but not all discriminative stimuli are rules. What is crucial here is that rule-governed behavior involves two distinct sets of contingencies. One set of contingencies involves those related directly to the behavior of interest. The second set is verbal and somewhat independent of the first. This can be seen most readily when the two are in competition. For example, a person may be told "You are supposed to fast today." The effects of fasting itself may never have functioned as a reinforcer, and yet the person may follow the rule, for example, in order to avoid social sanctions for noncompliance. These dual contingencies are possible only in social organisms that can establish behavior that is effective solely through the mediation of others—that is, in verbal organisms. We will follow Skinner's definition of verbal behavior as "behavior reinforced through the mediation of other persons" (Skinner, 1957, p. 14).

The direct contingencies themselves, even if they are at times complex, are simply the controlling variables. Only verbal organisms can discern and differentially reinforce behavior because of its controlling variables. Thus, it is self-awareness, or contingencies about contingencies, that are the essential requirements for rule-governed behavior.

We are ready now to return to the definition. Rule-governed behavior is behavior in contact with two sets of contingencies, one of which includes a verbal antecedent. These verbal antecedents are rules. This definition has several advantages. It makes a clear distinction, as Skinner's does not, between rules and other complex antecedents such as modeling stimuli (e.g., see Skinner, 1969, p. 163). Further, it avoids the thorny problem of what it means to "specify" contingencies. It incorporates rules that, while verbal, do not clearly specify contingencies. As will be seen later, Skinner's definition applies most clearly to a subtype of rule-governed behavior proposed in the present system. Finally, it directs attention to the dual contingencies involved in rule-governed behavior.

COMPONENTS OF RULE-GOVERNED BEHAVIOR

Rule-governed behavior involves verbal antecedents, and different types of verbal behavior relate to different types of rules. To understand this, we will concentrate at first on rules given to a listener by another person. Three steps are involved in this sequence. First, the speaker speaks. The functional units involved have to do with the contingencies surrounding speaking. Second, the form of the verbal behavior itself must be considered. Finally, the listener listens and reacts in some way due to contingencies surrounding listening. Put another way, a complete analysis must incorporate functional units for the speaker, formal aspects of speech, and functional units for the listener.

Functional Units of Speaker Behavior

Skinner has developed several separate functional units for the speaker. While many of these units have implications for rule-governed behavior, the most important are tacts and mands. A tact is a verbal operant in which a response of given form is evoked or strengthened by a particular object or event or their properties (Skinner, 1957, pp. 81–82). Thus, it is under relatively tight stimulus control and is relatively insensitive to changes in states of deprivation or aversive stimulation impinging on the speaker. For example, I may say "that's a chair" when a chair is brought forth. This is probably a tact. It is if its emission is controlled by the chair itself. Importantly, a chair is a chair regardless of my needs or desires at the moment. Note that tacting is not the same as "naming" or "referring to." A mand, by contrast, is a verbal operant in which the response is under the control of conditions of reinforceability in the speaker (e.g., relevant conditions of deprivation or aversive stimulation) and of antecedents indicating an availability of a relevant consequence (Skinner, 1957, pp. 35–36). For example, a person enters a room and wanting to sit down says "a chair." A chair is then brought forth by a listener. Note that the mand is reinforced by characteristic listener-mediated consequences.

The listener usually relies very heavily on the form of speech in discerning the contingencies surrounding the listener's reaction to it. Thus, the formal units of speech are the major mode of interchange between a speaker and listener. The speaker speaks because there is a listener and vice versa.

Functional Units of Listener Behavior

Pliance. At least three main functional units can be discerned in the listener. One parallels the mand. We term it pliance, drawn from the word "compliance." Pliance is rule-governed behavior primarily under the control of apparent speaker-mediated consequences for a correspondence between the rule and the relevant behavior. The rule itself is termed a ply. A simple case is as follows. A thief says, "Your wallet or your life" and the person hands the thief the wallet, an apparent instance of pliance. It is pliance only if the listener is under the control of apparent speaker-mediated consequences for following the rule. This can be determined by the sensitivity the behavior shows to variables affecting apparent speaker-mediated consequences such as the ability of the speaker to monitor compliance, the ability of the speaker to deliver consequences, the importance of the consequences to the listener, and many others.

Tracking. A second unit of rule-governed behavior parallels the tact. We term it tracking, to suggest following a path. Tracking is rule-governed behavior under the control of the apparent correspondence between the rule and the way the world is arranged. The rule itself is termed a track. A simple case might be the advice "The way to get to Greensboro is to follow I-85." If the listener's behavior is brought under control of the rule because of an apparent correspondence between it and how actually to get to Greensboro, then this is tracking.

Tracking is sensitive to a host of variables affecting the apparent correspondence between the rule and natural contingencies and the importance of that correspondence. For example, tracking is influenced by the listener's history with similar rule givers, the correspondence between the rule and other rules or events in the listener's history, the importance of the consequence implied by the rule, and so on. Note that the speaker does not mediate compliance. Tracking would be as likely to occur if the rule is in a book as if it were given by an actual speaker (assuming similar histories in these two situations).

Augmenting. A third unit of rule-governed behavior does not clearly parallel units in the speaker. We term it augmenting, to suggest a changed or heightened state of affairs. Augmenting is rule-governed behavior under the control of apparent changes in the capacity of events to function as reinforcers or punishers. The rule is itself termed an augmental.

Several different functional units of speaker behavior can serve as augmentals. A particularly obvious one is the autoclitic. Autoclitics denote verbal behavior by a speaker which is based upon or depends upon other verbal behavior (Skinner, 1957, p. 315). Autoclitics of particular types are normally manipulated in composing poems and similar literary productions until the final verbal output has a certain emotional impact on the composer (Skinner, 1957, Chapter 14). Much of this effect may result from the ability of words to elicit conditioned emotional responses. A poem that generates a certain emotional reaction in its composer may be expected to have a similar impact on other listeners and thereby alter their capacity to find particular events reinforcing or punishing.

There are probably other units of rule-governed behavior, but the three main units above seem most distinct and useful. Note that each definition includes the word "apparent." This is simply to emphasize that rules are antecedent stimuli. The consequences that follow them affect their future value as antecedents, but not their present value. Their present value is determined by the history of the listener.

FORMAL ASPECTS OF SPEECH AND SPEAKER-LISTENER INTERACTIONS

Although there is a relationship between the speaker, the form of rules, and the listener, this relationship is not direct. Figure 1.1 shows the possible avenues

Functional unit of verbal behavior for the speaker	Apparent form	Functional unit of rule-governed behavior for the listener
Mand	Mand Form	Pliance
Tact	Tact Form	Tracking

→

Time

Figure 1.1 An outline of speaker-listener interchanges.

of interaction between a speaker and a listener considering only mands, tacts, pliance, and tracking. There are eight possible avenues. For example, a speaker may emit a tact, which appears to be a tact, and yet pliance may be produced. Suppose a parent upon reading a thermometer tells a child a tact: "It's cold outside." Though this may be a tact in tact form, it could lead to pliance. The child may put on a jacket, not because it is cold but because what is "heard" is "I'm demanding you put on a jacket, or else." This can be understood by examining Figure 1.2.

Speakers often deliberately manipulate the form of speech. For example, a parent tells a child "If you act like that, the neighbors won't like it." Though this is in tact form, it may actually be a mand (e.g., "cut it out"). We call these mands "Trojan tacts" because, like the Trojan horse, the tact form conceals their true nature.

To understand such maneuvers, a more detailed analysis of pliance and tracking is necessary. In particular, we need to describe the forms they can take and to account for why rules once followed are later abandoned. Pliance does not necessarily involve doing what one is told. The unit also incorporates doing the opposite, when the controlling variable is the avoidance of control by speaker-mediated consequences. Pliance is probably most often generated by mands in mand form.

In this situation, speaker-mediated consequences are delivered for behavior of value primarily to the speaker. If the speaker-mediated consequences are weak or aversive, the listener may begin to undermine apparent manding. In the present system, this can be termed counterpliance.

Tracking can also involve apparently contradictory listener behavior. Recall that tracking is controlled by the apparent correspondence between the rule and the way the world works. Suppose a listener learns that whatever a speaker says is usually wrong. The apparent correspondence between the rule and the world may be reversed and tracking may take on an apparently opposite form. An example is provided by one of our friends who, when playing volleyball, consistently calls balls that are just inside the line "out." If he shouts "out" everyone on his team knows to dive for the ball, because it probably is actually "in."

Speaker	Form	Listener(child)
Mand	Mand Form	Pliance (child puts on jacket because parent "demand" to do so)
Tact (Parent reads thermometer and realizes "it's cold outside." Parent states this.)	Tact Form ("It's cold outside.")	Tracking

Figure 1.2 An example of an interchange between a speaker and a listener. Note that the words "It's cold outside" are a tact from the point of view of the speaker and a ply from the point of view of the listener.

The conditions generating pliance or tracking also imply conditions for the termination of control by plys and tracks. Plys should lose control when the speaker cannot monitor the behavior and cannot or does not deliver the consequences, when the consequences are weakened relative to others (e.g., by changes in reinforceability), and other such factors. Tracks should lose control when they are tested and shown to be inaccurate, when the speaker is shown to be less credible, when other experiences or rules conflict with the track, when the consequences specified by the track lose their importance, and so on.

SELF-RULES

As already pointed out, rules that come to govern an individual's behavior can be formulated and issued either by himself or by another. The discussion thus far has been limited to instances of rule-governed behavior in which the speaker and listener are separate individuals. In the case of self-rules, the speaker and listener exist in the same skin. This complicates the analysis as the rules involved cannot be directly manipulated. It is especially difficult, for instance, to determine whether a particular self-rule governs behavior, or whether the rule is merely a collateral response. That is, both the rule and the behavior it appears to govern may be controlled by the same variables.

Formulation of Self-Rules

There appear to be at least two reasons why an individual whose behavior is already complying with a set of contingencies would formulate rules about these conditions. One reason may be described as being proximal and personal—a person may formulate rules "because he himself can then react more effectively either now or later when the contingency-shaped behavior has weakened" (Skinner, 1969, p. 159). In such instances, the same individual is thus both a rule formulator and rule follower and it is advantageous to specify the variables of which his behavior is a function.

A second account of why individuals formulate "self-rules" is more distal and appeals to the individual's social history. The formulation of rules is verbal behavior in the sense that it has a history of reinforcement exclusively through the mediation of other persons (Skinner, 1957). As Skinner (1969 and elsewhere) has emphasized, "self-awareness" which contributes to the formulation of "self-rules" is a function of one's interaction with a social environment.

As suggested earlier, self-awareness is often a prerequisite for rule-governed behavior. Self-awareness is induced by a verbal community repeatedly questioning its members about behavior they have already engaged in, are currently engaged in, and will engage in, and the variables of which their behavior is a function. The verbal descriptions that are supplied in response to such inquiries may subsequently come to exert control over the speaker's behavior.

The proper formulation of self-rules may be critical in the avoidance of psychopathology. For example, it is common to describe a relationship in ways that are untestable (e.g., "It is horrible not to be loved"). This will be analyzed in more detail shortly. For now, it should be clear that rule formulation is a major area of concern in self-rules.

Following of Self-Rules

A definition of rule-governed behavior offered earlier emphasized contact with dual contingencies, one of which is verbal in nature. By definition then, any instances of self-rule-governed behavior must also be affected by these two sets of contingencies. One contingency affecting self-rule-governed behavior is that following one's own rules may permit more efficient responding. The novice poker player may formulate rules of the game such as when to bet or pass on certain hands through the outcomes of his playing. He may subsequently recall these rules in future games and use them to guide his playing in a more efficient way than if he had not formulated any rules but merely allowed his behavior to be shaped by the natural contingencies of gambling. These natural contingencies and the rule both surround the card playing and are the dual contingencies required of rule-governed behavior. An ultimate appeal to social contingencies may be needed to account for many instances of self-rule following.

Even if rules do not lead to natural consequences that capture the behavior (e.g., unlike the card player previously), rule following may still occur due to social consequences. Self-rules which are only verbalized covertly may exert at least some control over behavior for both of these reasons.

Numerous theorists have sought to provide an alternative account of self-rule following by appealing to self-reinforcement (Bandura, 1976; Kanfer, 1970, 1971, 1977; Kanfer & Karoly, 1972; Mahoney, 1974; Thoresen & Mahoney, 1974). To summarize, it has been argued that individuals generate self-rules regarding their behavior and self-reinforce themselves for complying with such rules. Radical behaviorists, by contrast, have maintained that the procedure of reinforcing oneself for following self-rules may serve ultimately to cue the type of social and other reinforcement for self-rule following just discussed (Catania, 1975, 1976; Munt, Hayes, & Nelson, 1979; Rachlin, 1974; Rosenfarb, Hayes, & Zettle, 1981; Zettle, 1980b). Accordingly, an appeal to self-reinforcement in an account of why self-rules are followed merely diverts attention away from the ultimate social and other contingencies which must be analyzed in accounting for such behavior.

The allure of self-reinforcement as a variable controlling self-rule following is reduced upon considering an analysis of resolutions and other types of self-rules that are made public. While resolutions, plans, purposive statements, and other similar self-rules may be effective at the covert level as just seen, the power and saliency of social contingencies affecting rule following may be increased whenever such self-rules are made public. Skinner's analyses of resolutions are especially relevant in this regard.

We prepare aversive stimuli which will control our own future behavior when we make a resolution. This is essentially a prediction concerning our own behavior. By making it in the presence of people who supply aversive stimulation when a prediction is not fulfilled, we arrange consequences which are likely to strengthen the behavior resolved upon. Only by behaving as predicted can we escape the aversive consequences of breaking our resolution. As we shall see later, the aversive stimulation which leads us to keep the resolution may eventually be supplied automatically by our own behavior. The resolution may then be effective even in the absence of other people (Skinner, 1953, p. 237).

A "resolution" is a sort of mand upon oneself which masquerades as a tact. I am not going to smoke for the next three months is not a response to a future event. Its value in self-control lies in the fact that it can be made now when appropriate contingencies, possibly involving aversive events, are powerful, whereas "not smoking for three months" requires three months for its execution, during which time the underlying deprivation or aversive stimulation may change. The resolution creates a set of conditions under which smoking is particularly punished (as "breaking a promise") either by the speaker himself or by others. The effect is greater if the resolution is publicly announced or, better, conspicuously posted during the period in which it is in force (Skinner, 1957, p. 444).

As pointed out by Skinner, once an individual publicly states a rule about his future behavior as in making a resolution, he has made a social commitment. Accordingly, he is placing his self-rule following under the control of social contingencies whereby he may be punished for a discrepancy between his verbal and nonverbal behavior. Private commitments may function similarly. The fact that resolutions under some conditions may be an effective self-control procedure illustrates the dual contingencies surrounding such self-rule following. Resolutions about behavior which would result from natural contingencies are of little value. Their value lies in pitting social contingencies for following such self-rules against those naturally controlling the behavior resolved upon.

Functional Units of Self-Rule Following

Thus far, the formulation and following of self-rules have been considered with little regard to the form that self-rules may take and the functional units of behavior that they may control. This is a difficult task. Unlike public rules, self-rules do not permit clear distinctions between the rule giver and the rule follower.

Thus, the distinction between pliance and tracking is difficult to assess in self-rule following. For example, the presence of the speaker cannot be manipulated so as to test for pliance. We can, however, see points along the continuum which might be agreed to be instances of self-pliance or self-tracking. Self-tracking occurs when we act as if the rule is to be followed because it is a description of the state of affairs. Self-pliance occurs when we act as if the rule is to be followed simply because it has been formulated.

At first glance it would appear as though the type of rule and the type of rule-governed behavior would always be consonant in the case of self-rules: Tacts would generate self-tracking; mands would generate self-pliance. Unfortunately, this is not true and the resultant distortion of self-rule following turns out to be an essential concern of most cognitive therapies. For example, there are several ways that self-rules may be generated which appear to be tacts, but are not. One is an impure tact. An impure tact is verbal behavior that is controlled by a stimulus object or event as well as by consequences relevant to the speaker's current level of deprivation (Skinner, 1957). Impure tacts thus are functionally similar to mands in that they are at least partly controlled by levels of deprivation and aversive stimulation of the speaker. A pure tact, by contrast, is controlled by generalized reinforcement rather than by consequences relating to the speaker's current level of deprivation. Scientific laws provide one example of pure tacts. Another instance of pure tacts may be the probabilities of certain hands in poker paying off which a novice player may eventually formulate.

Another problem occurs when rules are in tact form, but are actually intraverbals. Tacts, recall, require the control by stimulus objects or their properties. Unlike mere naming, tacting requires a direct experiential base. For example, a person may say, "It is terrible to be embarrassed." This is not a tact, though it is in tact form. "Terrible" is not a stimulus object or property. It is logically derived (Skinner might call it an "intraverbal").

Self-augmenting also seems possible. Under certain conditions, speakers may attempt to induce particular emotional changes in themselves as an audience. This may be an effective means of self-control in some instances (Skinner, 1953, pp. 235–236). A woman who is somewhat ambivalent about having an abortion may, for example, repeat to herself poems, songs, or proverbs about death, which makes her "decision" in this matter an easier one to make.

RULE-GOVERNED BEHAVIOR AND COGNITIVE-BEHAVIORAL THERAPY

Our preliminary analysis of rule-governed behavior, though not exhaustive, and somewhat speculative, nevertheless provides some insights into current cognitive-behavioral interventions. Several current types of cognitive-behavioral therapy will be examined using this system: rational-emotive therapy (RET) (Ellis, 1962, 1973a,1973b), cognitive restructuring methods (Goldfried, 1979; Meichenbaum, 1977), and cognitive treatment of depression (Beck et al., 1979). While these particular treatments have sometimes been viewed collectively as examples of rational psychotherapy (Wilson, 1978) or cognitive restructuring therapies (Mahoney & Arnkoff, 1978), sufficient differences exist among their specific methodologies, techniques, and underlying theoretical and conceptual bases to make separate analyses of each meaningful. Separate analyses will be provided of each treatment as a therapeutic procedure and of its underlying conceptual basis. This appears to be meaningful, since treatment may be effective for reasons unrelated to those specified by a particular theory or view of psychopathology upon which it is based.

RET AND RULE-GOVERNED BEHAVIOR

Current Status

Outcome research on RET, with few exceptions (Moleski & Tosi, 1976; Wolfe, 1976), has been limited to unsystematic case studies and experimental analog investigations. In general, RET appears to lead to significant reductions in anxiety in comparison to attention-placebo and no-treatment control groups, but has been found to be less effective or no more effective than several other available procedures (DiLoreto, 1970; Germer, 1975; Jarmon, 1973; Karst & Trexler, 1970) in the treatment of anxiety. Some research suggests that other cognitive treatment procedures, differing from RET as it is usually practiced, may be more effective than RET in reducing anxiety (Germer, 1975; Kanter, 1976; Meichenbaum, 1972; Meichenbaum, Gilmore, & Fedoravicius, 1971—for a comprehensive review of the RET literature see Zettle & Hayes, 1980).

Rational-Emotive Theory

Ellis (1962, 1973a, 1973b) has consistently maintained that maladaptive emotional responses do not result directly from external situations, but are instead caused by irrational beliefs which clients hold about such situations. More specifically, according to Ellis (1973a), clients react to certain events at point A with any number of irrational beliefs, largely consisting of statements of should, ought, or must and often relating to personal worth. It is these responses at point B that, in turn, lead to anxiety and other maladaptive responses at point C. As a therapeutic procedure, RET basically attempts to initiate therapeutic change by replacing these irrational beliefs which are assumed to be the basis of psychopathology with alternative beliefs which are more rational in nature.

What particular thoughts comprise the universe of irrational beliefs appears to be somewhat unclear and arbitrary. In one of his earlier writings, Ellis (1962) listed 11 beliefs that comprise one's potential repertoire of irrational thoughts. The origin of irrational beliefs is also unclear. Ellis (1973a) has generally preferred a biological rather than a learning-based account for the origin of irrational beliefs, while other writers (DiGiuseppe, Miller, & Trexler, 1977) have suggested that irrational beliefs are acquired rather than inborn. Assuming that irrational self-statements are acquired, it is also unclear whether they are initially formulated by clients as self-rules, are rules originally issued by others which clients then follow, or are a combination of the two. Phenomenologically, irrational beliefs are self-rules. When irrational beliefs are originally formulated and issued by others, these original rule givers are unlikely to be in a position to exert any direct control over rule following. However, certain kinds of public rules (e.g., tracks) do not require presence of the rule giver. Thus, irrational beliefs are probably composed of both self-rules and public rules.

Irrational Beliefs as Rules. As already suggested, the irrational beliefs enumerated by Ellis may be regarded as rules. Essentially, rational-emotive theory maintains that maladaptive behavior is rule-governed. The majority of Ellis's irrational beliefs are in mand form. Autoclitics such as "should," "must," and "ought" are commonly used in conjunction with such mands, Several of Ellis's irrational beliefs are in tact form but do not actually tact the way the world is arranged. A tact, by definition, is experientially based and is therefore testable. Ellis says irrational beliefs "cannot be supported by any empirical evidence" (Ellis, 1973a, p. 57). In other words, they are not experientially based and testable: they are not tacts. Nevertheless, they may resemble tacts and may generate tracking. Nevertheless, clients may respond to irrational beliefs as if they were accurate and tested tracks. Recall that tracking is controlled by testing the relationship described, the credibility of the speaker, states of reinforceability, and so on. In this fact lies the destructive potential of tracks that are not tact based.

Behavior controlled by irrational beliefs may also be conceptualized in part as pliance. It seems plausible that particular histories of reinforcement for rule following may establish pliance as a response class under the control of rules which share certain formal characteristics—such as the use of "should" and similar autoclitics. If pliance in the past has been mediated through unescapable or unavoidable aversive control, current mands of particular forms may effectively control avoidance behavior (pliance).

This is troublesome when the self-plys are poor rules. Pliance is designed to produce insensitivity to the contingencies ("Just do as I say"). Sometimes this is helpful ("Don't touch a hot stove"); sometimes not. It depends on the situational appropriateness of the particular rule. Most "irrational beliefs" are clearly destructive when they are viewed as plys.

Rational-Emotive Therapy

Precisely what specific procedures and techniques comprise RET is somewhat unclear based on a reading of Ellis's writings. Following Ellis's (1980) recent attempt to differentiate RET from other cognitive treatments and his (1973b) description of RET as a "cognitive-emotive-behavioristic method of psychotherapy," we will attempt to delineate several of the key therapeutic components which are most relevant for our analysis.

Cognitive Components. The cognitive emphasis within RET essentially involves discrimination training, whereby clients are taught to differentiate between rational and irrational beliefs. After disputing and debating particular instances of irrational beliefs with clients, the therapist proceeds to instruct the client how logically and empirically to dispute such irrational self-statements and to replace them with ones of a rational nature.

Emotive Components. The emotive components of RET emphasized by Ellis largely deal with the verbal behavior of rational-emotive therapists toward their clients. In particular, Ellis recommends actively haranguing, persuading, and cajoling clients until they acknowledge irrational beliefs that are assumed to be the basis for their present difficulties.

Behavioral Components. RET, like many other types of behavioral treatments, incorporates homework assignments in which clients are required to engage in appropriate overt behaviors in situations that they find anxiety provoking. According to Ellis, such homework assignments are instrumental in assisting the client in interrupting and disputing irrational beliefs and are therefore regarded as "motor counterpropagandizing activities."

Rational-Emotive Therapist as a Rule Giver

All of the therapeutic components of RET just outlined place primary emphasis on the verbal behavior of rational-emotive therapists in their interactions with clients. While the other cognitive-behavioral approaches to be considered are also primarily "talking therapies" and therefore rely heavily upon verbal interactions between client and therapist as a medium of therapy, the role of the therapist as rule giver appears to be of relatively greater importance in the case of RET. Some rational beliefs which clients are taught appear to be quite similar to those they are designed to replace. A rational belief such as "I'm not worthless if I fail," like its corresponding irrational belief, does not tact any natural contingencies and also must be regarded as untestable. The distinction made between rational beliefs that "can be supported by empirical data and [are] appropriate to the reality that is occurring" and irrational beliefs that "cannot be supported by any empirical evidence" (Ellis, 1973a, p. 57) is thereby undermined. Thus, aspects of RET seem to challenge untestable tracks, but others simultaneously establish them.

The use of emotive components shows a similar pattern: Some of it seems behaviorally sensible, some of it is not. As discussed earlier, particular aspects of a speaker's behavior, such as the way and manner in which rules are stated, may be the important discriminative stimuli for rule following by a listener. Ellis encourages therapists to confront clients very directly. These statements may have an augmenting function. An aversive state is created in which clients are motivated to change their own talk.

Unfortunately, confrontation can have other outcomes. For example, it may model the opposite of the behavior desired in the client. Confrontational therapist verbal behavior consists primarily of mands, not tacts. To the degree that RET results in client behavioral change, it may often involve pliance rather than tracking. Changes in clients' self-verbalizations may at times be controlled by the mand "You shouldn't say 'shoulds' to yourself."

Confrontation by the therapist might also result in counterpliance and other attempts by clients to escape or avoid perceived aversive control (e.g., by dropping out). No studies have yet been done on this question. Others have expressed reservations about the effectiveness of this approach. As Mahoney (1974) has observed, "It may be more therapeutic to be gently directive in self-discovery exercises than to beat a client over the head with the salience of his irrationality" (p. 233).

Thus, RET may work (when it does) through two mechanisms. First, the client may abandon untested tracks and seek out new ones which are more accurate and testable. The use of homework may be particularly important in this latter regard. Second, RET may work by adding therapist rules. These may be essentially "irrational" as well, but may control more adaptive responding because the rules themselves are more adaptive. Changes in this case might be more limited, and might account for the equivocal results RET has achieved relative to other cognitive therapies.

COGNITIVE RESTRUCTURING AND RULE-GOVERNED BEHAVIOR

Current Status

Another popular cognitive-behavioral modification procedure is cognitive restructuring. Cognitive restructuring procedures, encompassing more specific treatments such as stress inoculation training and systematic rational restructuring, have been found to be effective in a variety of relatively specific, nondebilitating problem areas including test anxiety (Goldfried, Linehan, & Smith, 1978; Holroyd, 1976; Hussian & Lawrence, 1978; Meichenbaum, 1972), speech anxiety (Fremouw & Zitter, 1978; Meichenbaum et al., 1971), and the management of anger (Novaco, 1975, 1976, 1979) and pain (Meichenbaum & Turk, 1976; Turk & Genest, 1979). In addition, as previously pointed out, cognitive restructuring procedures in several studies have been found to be relatively more effective than rational-emotive-based treatments in the reduction of anxiety (Germer, 1975; Meichenbaum et al., 1971).

Importance of Self-Statements

Cognitive restructuring procedures seek to reduce anxiety by identifying negative self-statements and replacing them with alternative self-verbalizations more coping in nature (Meichenbaum, 1974, 1977). The results of a recent component analysis (Glogower, Fremouw, & McCroskey, 1978) suggest that knowledge and rehearsal of coping self-statements as replacements for negative thoughts are the primary components contributing to the effectiveness of the procedure. Given the important role that coping self-statements play in the efficacy of cognitive restructuring procedures, our analysis will focus on such coping self-statements and the types of negative self-statements they are designed to replace.

Based on their form, negative self-statements, such as "I'm making a fool of myself" or "My God, am I anxious!" have the appearance of tacts. However, as previously noted in the discussion of irrational beliefs, self-awareness of "making a fool of oneself" or "being anxious" is probably not verbal behavior under the control of environmental objects or events. Rather, negative self-statements generally appear to be verbal behavior under the control of other verbal behavior. For example, a client who, while giving a speech, observes that he has mispronounced a word or that his heart is beating faster than usual may then conclude, "I'm making a fool of myself" or "My God, am I anxious." Self-awareness of mispronouncing a word or the activity of one's heart refer to events and therefore can be conceptualized as tacts; the collateral verbal behavior that follows cannot. Therefore, undermining negative self-statements may be aimed at the weakening of untestable tracks.

Functions of Coping Self-Statements

Given the finding that negative self-statements may elicit emotional reactions (Rimm & Litvak, 1969; Rogers & Craighead, 1977; Russell & Brandsma, 1974), it seems conceivable that coping self-statements as conditioned emotional stimuli might serve a similar augmenting function in facilitating anxiety-relief. A series of investigations by Meichenbaum and Cameron (1972, 1974), incorporating coping self-statements with anxiety-relief procedures, however, has failed to provide definitive support for this conceptualization. A second function that coping self-statements might serve, in light of attentional interpretations of anxiety (Wine, 1971), is as distractors in diverting attention away from anxiety-eliciting cues.

Another potential function that coping self-statements might serve is a self-instructional one. This view has been supported by Kanfer, Karoly, and Newman (1975) in comparing the relative effectiveness of different rules in increasing darkness tolerance among children. Different groups of children who were fearful of the dark were instructed to engage in statements of a neutral nature, ones relating to competence, or statements about the dark itself. Children in the competence group, for instance, were asked to say, "I am a brave boy (girl). I can take care of myself in the dark," whereas subjects in the stimulus group were instructed in statements about the dark itself such as, "The dark is a fun place to be. There are many good things in the dark." The overall results were viewed from a self-control interpretation and indicated that the group instructed in competence statements was superior to the other two groups.

Thus, the competence group may have shown greater tolerance because the verbal controlling responses represented self-instructions to behave like a brave boy or girl, with the expectation of social approval and self-reinforcement based upon past encouragements to act competently (Kanfer et al., 1975, p. 257).

If coping self-statements do serve as self-instructions as Kanfer et al. suggest, it remains unclear whether they essentially function as plys or tracks. However, the finding that competence statements were more effective than statements about the dark itself and the appeal made to social factors in interpreting this outcome suggest that coping self-statements may often produce pliance rather than tracking. The statements of the children in the competence group appear to have served the same function as public resolutions about one's behavior or, alternatively, as mands issued by another speaker. In either case, the behavior of following such rules would be expected to be controlled in part by socially mediated consequences. For this reason, the statements of children in the competence group apparently resulted in pliance. By contrast, the statements of the factual group resemble tacts about the dark and would be expected to result in increased darkness tolerance to the extent that they were found to be accurate. When children tested such tracks by finding out that the dark is not "a fun place to be," the ability of such statements to control behavior could be greatly weakened.

Coping Self-Statements as Plys. The possibility that coping self-statements may primarily control pliance rather than tracking was evaluated recently by the authors (Zettle & Hayes, 1979). If coping self-statements are plys, they should be affected by the variables of which pliance is a function. For example, if they are plys the effectiveness of coping self-statements should vary to the degree that both the statements themselves and the behaviors to which they make reference are publicly accessible. Both conditions are generally met in clinical cognitive restructuring procedures. If, on the other hand, coping self-statements function as tracks, their effectiveness should presumably not be affected by whether or not they are stated publicly.

Speech-anxious college students were randomly assigned to either a control group or to one of two experimental groups. Control group subjects received no coping self-statements while subjects in both experimental groups selected a coping self-statement ("I can remain calm and relaxed by taking deep breaths and talking more slowly") from a bag supposedly (but not actually) containing many different statements. The two experimental groups differed only in the degree to which the coping self-statement which they were to use was apparently made known to the experimenter. Subjects in a social context group were asked to read out loud to the experimenter the coping self-statement they selected. Subjects in a private self-statement group received the same self-statement but merely read it to themselves (and thus believed the experimenter did not know their rule). Social context subjects thus made an overt purposive statement about their behavior during speeches while private condition subjects engaged in the same self-rule but at a completely covert level.

The results may be viewed as providing preliminary support for a rule-governed account of coping self-statements as plys. On self-report measures of speech anxiety, only the social context group showed improvement over the private condition and control groups. More specifically, subjects in the social context group reported feeling less anxious about their speeches and more helped by the procedure than those in the other two groups. The only difference among the groups on behavioral measures indicated that subjects in the social context group had followed the coping self-statement by talking more slowly. The coping self-statement was effective only when it was made public and thus appears to have functioned as a ply (under the control of the social consequences) rather than a track (under the control of the correspondence between the rule and the way the world is arranged).

Coping Self-Statements as Competing Rules. A final possibility is that coping self-statements function by replacing or competing with negative self-statements. There are some data (e.g., see Craighead, Kimball, & Rehak, 1979; Kendall, Williams, Pechacek, Graham, Shisslak, & Herzof, 1979) that suggest that an absence of negative self-statements is more important than the presence of positive self-statements in many clinical problems (see also Kendall & Hollon, 1981). Coping self-statements may work by competing with and replacing negative self-statements in some people. As analyzed earlier, negative thoughts are often destructive rules and clinical benefits from their elimination would be expected.

Implications for Treatment

Since pliance cannot be mediated by a rule giver unless the behavior to be engaged in is clearly specified, coping self-statements that more closely specify the relevant behavior should result in greater change than others which do so in a vague manner. For instance, a coping self-statement such as, "I can remain calm and relaxed by talking at a steady pace," should be more effective in reducing speech anxiety than one which merely states, "I can remain calm and relaxed." Since pliance also cannot be mediated unless the behavior specified by the rule can be monitored, coping self-statements should be most effective when they are public and when the therapist can directly observe the actions of clients in confronting and interacting with anxiety-provoking situations.

Thus, coping self-statements may operate primarily through the social influence that a therapist exerts over clients. They direct the behavior of clients toward a stimulus situation they might otherwise avoid. It seems probable that exposure by clients to anxiety-eliciting stimuli, an implicit component of pliance to coping self-statements, which following coping self-statements provides, is of considerable importance in any substantial reductions of anxiety that occur.

If the present analysis of coping statements is correct, this treatment approach should be most successful in relatively minor disorders, susceptible to social influence. Most of the studies to date have examined just such problems. A second implication is that more general disorders of rule formulation would not be treated. Essentially, the therapist is establishing a new set of rules to follow without attacking directly the formulation of self-rules. The effects, therefore, should be relatively specific. Indeed, the literature tends to confirm this (e.g., Hussian & Lawrence, 1978).

RULE-GOVERNED BEHAVIOR AND THE COGNITIVE TREATMENT OF DEPRESSION

Current Status

Perhaps one of the most highly regarded of the cognitive behavior therapies currently in use is Beck's cognitive treatment of depression. Its status can be accounted for by the success it has shown in the treatment of a highly prevalent and potentially life-threatening affective disorder.

Cognitive Basis of Depression

According to a cognitive view of depression, this affective disorder is "in part, a consequence of pervasive, negative misconstructions of objective experiences" (Hollon & Beck, 1979, p. 154). In particular, Beck (1967) has argued that depressed clients exhibit what he has labeled "the negative cognitive triad," consisting of a regard for themselves as defeated, deprived, or diseased; for their worlds as full of obstacles preventing the achievement of satisfactions; and for their futures as pessimistic, without any hope of improvement. More specific examples of the negative cognitive triad are detailed by Beck's classification of logical distortions, which characterize the thinking of depressed individuals:

- Selective abstraction (a stimulus set); forming a conclusion regarding a particular event on the basis of an isolated detail, while ignoring contradictory and more salient evidence.
- Arbitrary inference (a response set); drawing a conclusion in the absence of evidence.
- Overgeneralization (a response set); extracting a belief or rule on the basis of a particular event and applying that concept in an unjustifiable fashion to other dissimilar situations.
- Magnification (a response set); the overestimation of the significance or magnitude of undesirable consequent events.
- All-or-none thinking (a response set); the tendency to think in absolute terms. (Hollon & Beck, 1979, pp. 156–157)

According to a cognitive view of depression, such distorted thinking by clients not only results in a depressed affect but also leads to behavioral deficits commonly noted in depressed clients.

Problem of Inference. All types of cognitive behavioral treatments maintain that the disorders they deal with to a large degree are cognitively based, or stated somewhat differently, rule-governed. A problematic issue facing cognitive procedures is that clients are sometimes thought to be engaging in particular types of self-statements because their behavior is dysfunctional. Such inferences, however, are derived from the very behavior they attempt to explain.

Rules and Cognitive Distortions

As we have done throughout this article, we will assume that a cognitive view of depression is basically sound in order to offer a rule-governed account of this perspective. In this regard, the general classes of logical distortions Beck believes characterize the thinking of depressed clients may be conceptualized as disorders in rule formulation and rule following. For instance, errors in selective abstraction, arbitrary inference, and overgeneralization all suggest a tendency by depressive clients to formulate inaccurate and untestable rules. The rules that are formulated may have the form of tacts and clients track them as if they specified relationships among events in the environment. The rule following which is generated is insensitive to the natural consequences which are produced.

Cognitive Treatment of Depression

Beck's cognitive treatment of depression may be viewed as training clients to tact variables controlling their own behavior and subsequently to track such rules. Stated somewhat differently, the attempt is to replace inaccurate and untestable rules which may be contributing to a client's depression with rules that are controlled by events with which clients have direct contact. Behavior subsequently controlled by such rules may be viewed as tracking. It is relatively sensitive to the natural contingencies since they are described in the formulated rules.

Therapeutic Components

While Beck prefers to refer to his specific approach to the treatment of depression as cognitive therapy, he has emphasized its incorporation of both cognitive and behavioral components and its differentiation from cognitive-semantic approaches, such as RET, which rely more on semantic or persuasive techniques (Beck, 1964, 1967, 1970).

Cognitive Components: Training in Tact-Formulation. Beck has maintained that verbal interactions between client and therapist should be collaborative rather than persuasive and confrontational, as advocated by Ellis. In following such an approach, the therapist avoids issuing mands to clients. This decreases possible client counterpliance and increases the importance of tracking controlled by rules formulated in collaboration with the therapist. Such an approach in effect seeks to establish more accurate self-rule formulation in clients.

Specific cognitive techniques within Beck's approach, such as identifying automatic thoughts and evaluating thought content, constitute training in identifying specific depressive self-statements and formulating more accurate and testable rules. In this regard, Beck has emphasized the necessity of clients being able to "distance" themselves from their beliefs, or stated somewhat differently, being able to observe their own verbal behavior from the perspective of a listener. Over time, self-rules are often not viewed critically by the person formulating them. This has several destructive effects. For example, augmenting functions may occur automatically—in a sense, the person-as-listener may become needlessly emotionally invested in a particular view of things. Similarly, obvious impure tacts or intraverbals may be seen as tacts in a way they never would be for others' rules. Distancing allows self-rules to be viewed as behavior of an organism—not as literal reality or as the organism itself.

Behavioral Components: Training in Tracking. Beck has outlined several behavioral techniques, such as graded task assignment and activity scheduling, that comprise his cognitive therapy for depression. Of primary importance for the current analysis are homework assignments in which clients are essentially given an opportunity to "test out" specific hypotheses they have formulated from their beliefs. This strategy may be conceptualized as providing clients training in tracking. Clients are essentially encouraged to evaluate the accuracy of their rules, once they have been reformulated into testable hypotheses, in determining to what degree they actually specify relevant contingencies. Given the likelihood that the client's hypothesis is shown to be inaccurate, more accurate tracks can be formulated in their place. Hollon and Beck (1979) in commenting on this process have observed:

> The explicit disconfirmation of stated beliefs by means of direct, self-monitored experiences following from the client's own activities is followed by a discussion of the contingencies involved and the conclusions that can be drawn. Such a procedure involving both enactive and cognitive-symbolic components, is seen as the optimal paradigm for generating cognitive changes and for maximizing the generality of the behavioral procedures. Instead of "getting the client moving," such a combination increases the probability of the client's being able to challenge successfully anticipated nongratification or fantasized incompetence in future situations. Similarly, rather than simply mobilizing the client in the lace of negative expectations, the client is trained to evaluate systematically such predictions, putting the beliefs to an unbiased test, eventually learning that it is the negative expectations that are inaccurate. (pp. 184–185)

Given that the skills of tact formulation and tracking that clients acquire through cognitive therapy are likely to be sensitive to and be maintained by the natural contingencies surrounding important behavior, it is not surprising that any treatment gains would generalize and be maintained across time. Beck's approach, in comparison to the approach of Ellis and Meichenbaum, is probably most consistent with the approach implied by the conceptual system developed here.

RULE-GOVERNED BEHAVIOR AND PSYCHOPATHOLOGY

The purpose of the present article is to begin to develop rule-governed behavior as a theoretical framework for considering cognitive-behavioral therapy.

There is a danger that the analysis might become a mere post hoc explanation for established techniques. For example, Dollard and Miller's (1950) pioneering effort has been so regarded and its impact was less than its potential as a result. The present analysis, however, could conceivably form the basis of a more general approach to psychopathology and its treatment. While this is extremely speculative, some possible directions can be seen.

Mechanisms of Psychopathology

Pathological Rule Formulation. One general mechanism of psychopathology, according to a rule-governed analysis, is dysfunctional rule formulation. The most obvious examples involve self-rules. We are less likely to doubt ourselves than someone else. For this reason, inappropriate self-rules are likely to lead to rule following and maladaptive results.

One common error in rule formulation has been analyzed extensively above: the formulation of self-rules which appear to be based on tacts but are not. These self-rules are often based upon impure tacts or intraverbal behavior. Such rules generally are in tact form and may successfully produce tracking. Tracking under such conditions, however, is "blind" and may often appear insensitive to its natural consequences. Clinical manifestations of self-deception (Knapp, 1980) and rationalization (Zettle, 1980a) provide clear examples.

The destructive effect of tracking nontact rules depends heavily on the specific rule involved. The belief that "everyone loves me" may not be as destructive as "everyone must love me," even though both might be nonexperientially based. (The first statement could be a tact, although it is unlikely.) The tendency to formulate and track nonexperiential (nontact) rules, however, might be a general response class. If so, even harmless self-rules of this sort could be part of a generally maladaptive response pattern.

Other self-rules may function as plys. For example, the statement "I am going to exercise every day for a week" may be followed as if following it was due simply to its being said. In other words, the person may not be able to give reasons for doing it, but seems to be doing it "just because I said I would." Often these are stated publicly, thus engaging possible social consequences. These self-plys can be pathological under some circumstances. Unlike tracking, the whole purpose of pliance is to produce an insensitivity to immediate environmental contingencies. Pliance to public rules is often established when insensitivity is required (e.g., "Junior, don't touch the hot stove"). By adding in speaker-mediated contingencies for rule following, natural contingencies may be overridden. A similar process occurs with self-plys. If this is useful (in the exercise example it may well be), self-pliance is healthy. But it can be destructive when there is no need for insensitivity. For example, a person may follow the rule "I'm going to be a millionaire no matter what." If this produces emotional and interpersonal carnage, reevaluation of such a goal would be desirable, but may not occur. Thus, self-plys can be formulated pathologically if their precise content is destructive.

In addition to self-rules, the formulation of public rules can also be maladaptive. The verbal behaviors of the pathological liar, psychopathic con artist, sociopathic gang leader, or manipulative histrionic are examples. Such instances involve separate speakers and listeners and the rule-following behavior of the listener (e.g., the "easy mark" or the gang member) may also often be regarded as maladaptive.

Pathological Rule Following. There are two types of problems in maladaptive rule following. One involves "errors in translation" in verbal interactions between particular speakers and listeners. Specific aspects of a speaker's verbal behavior (e.g., tone of voice or use of certain words) may exert incorrect discriminative control over the listener—it is often difficult to know what a speaker is "really saying."

The slippage in this system can produce particular listener histories that will lead to serious difficulties. Since so much of our behavior is rule-governed, any unusual tendencies in discerning and following rules will radically alter a listener's world. For example, if the listener is unable to distinguish tacts from mands, possibly as a result of their historical similarity in form in the listener's world, he might be expected to respond to tacts issued by the speaker as if they were plys or vice versa. This would be most likely to occur with a specific speaker (with whom the listener has had this type of history) but generalization to other speakers might also occur. Such a person may seem to set up others in an authority role. Some may then follow these tacts as plys ("passive-dependency"), or attempt to undermine them ("passive-aggressive"). Any disorder in the tendency to interpret others would certainly have pervasive and profound effects, perhaps leading to typical patterns of maladaptive behavior which have traditionally been referred to as "personality disorders."

Even if rules are accurately discerned, a second type of problem is possible: They may be followed pathologically. For example, a person whose pliance has consistently been achieved through highly aversive means or to serve the whims of the speaker may tend later to show counterpliance in response to reasonable plys. The rebellious individual with "difficulty relating to authority" is an example. Similarly, a person exposed to an inconsistent or unpredictable environment may never learn to follow tracks well. The lower class individual who does not stay in school because "school doesn't really help you get a job—that's just jive" may be an example.

Similar difficulties can occur with self-rules. Inability to show proper self-pliance or tendencies to show self-counterpliance are common. For example, a person with a weight problem may say, "I won't eat for three more hours" and immediately be overwhelmed by hunger, unable to think of anything but food, and finally, give in and eat. This kind of self-defeating behavior may amount to a kind of self-counterpliance, quite similar to its public form. Others are simply unable to make commitments to themselves and to follow them.

This lack of self-pliance can be destructive when some insensitivity to immediate contingencies is needed in order to come under the control of more remote consequences. Persons with this difficulty are commonly said to be impulsive, untrustworthy, self-destructive, or lacking in self-control.

Mechanisms of Therapeutic Change

Formulating "Tactful" Tracks. As we have suggested, maladaptive tracking appears typically to result when the rules involved are not tacts. Accordingly, a general strategy for therapeutic change is to encourage clients to replace formulations about their behavior and its consequences which are intraverbals or impure tacts (e.g., "That's terrible!" "God, am I anxious!" "I can't do anything right!") with formulations that are restricted to tacts (e.g., "I received an F on my exam," "My palms are sweaty, "I completed three reports on time"). Any behavior controlled by such "tactful" tracks is apt to be more flexible and sensitive to its actual consequences. Such a strategy seems to underlie the success of Beck's cognitive treatment of depression and may be a major mechanism involved in insight-oriented psychotherapies (Zettle, 1980a), or in growth-oriented interventions such as est (cf. Baer & Stolz, 1978).

Other available treatments focus on instructing speakers to formulate tacts, as opposed to mands and intraverbals, in their interactions with certain listeners. "Communication training" for couples in marital therapy and Parent Effectiveness Training, for instance, may be conceptualized as employing this general strategy.

Formulating Plys. Behavior therapists have long emphasized the importance of proper client goal setting both for oneself and others. Issues such as specificity, immediacy, and discernibility in goals set may amount to training in proper ply formulation. These dimensions allow the individual to know when a ply has been met. In the case of self-plys, this may begin to expose the individual to the natural consequences of doing (or not doing) what you say you are going to do. These consequences may then capture and support self-pliance. In the case of public plys it may allow the individual to experience a more predictable world and may increase the likelihood of pliance.

Other aspects of ply formulation are also important. Every ply implies a state of reinforceability in the speaker. The rule itself should be in contact with the actual reinforcers. For example, the statement "I'm going to be a millionaire" is presumably based upon the apparent beneficial aspects of being rich. In fact, these aspects may not be reinforcers for a given individual. For that person, such a rule may not be desirable. Plys can also specify behavior not in the person's repertoire (or capable of becoming so). People with "unrealistic standards" show this pattern.

Rule Following. The treatment of disorders of rule following is not well advanced. Difficulties occur in two areas: failure to discern rules accurately and failure to follow rules. Errors in discerning rules are extraordinarily difficult to treat because the therapist's own verbal behavior is also likely to be misunderstood. One case occurs when tacts produce pliance or counterpliance. In such instances, the client may believe that the therapist has some personal stake in advice being offered. Some therapist strategies in this case might include (a) avoiding all statements in mand form (including autoclitics such as "must"), (b) discussing the potential confusion itself, (c) encouraging self-testing of apparent tacts, (d) encouraging more self-rule formulation and following, especially "tactful" tracks, (e) avoiding obvious differential reinforcement from the therapist for rule following (i.e., use "unconditional positive regard"), and (f) manding behavior opposite that desired, as in "paradoxical intention" (Frankl, 1960).

At times mands (perhaps in tact form) may produce tracking. This is likely to be reflected in things such as excessively moralistic behavior or in extreme conformity. In this case, confrontation might be useful, especially if it is paradoxical, so as to break down mand rule following. Training in self-rule formulation and following may also be helpful.

Disorders of rule following include such things as (a) showing excessive counterpliance to plys, (b) showing little or no pliance, (c) failing to track adaptive rules, and (d) tracking destructive rules. All of these can involve either public or self-rules. The general strategy in each case might be to arrange conditions in which a better history of successful rule following can be built. For example, the person showing little or no pliance may need at first to be in a restrictive environment in which pliance can be produced in response to reasonable demands. Gradually, social controls could be loosened as the successful results of pliance begin to take hold.

This article has attempted to argue that behaviorists should attend to the concept of rule-governed behavior and explore the potential relevance of Skinner's (1957) analysis of verbal behavior to the therapeutic environment. In our view, a more thorough understanding of rule-governed behavior in particular, and verbal behavior more generally, may help provide solutions to several thorny clinical problems and may expand the scope of behavior therapy. Areas such as personality disorders or psychological growth have hardly been touched by behaviorists—the present analysis suggests ways in which we may begin. Finally, the present analysis may offer an alternative conceptual framework for cognitive-behavioral therapy and semantic therapy more generally. Whether such a bold statement is justified will depend on future empirical and conceptual work on the concept of rule-governed behavior.

REFERENCES

Baer, D.M., & Stolz, S.B. (1978). A description of the Erhard Seminars Training (est) in the terms of behavior analysis. *Behaviorism*, *6*(1), 45–70.

Bandura, A. (1976). Self-reinforcement: Theoretical and methodological considerations. *Behaviorism, 4*(2), 135–155.
Beck, A.T. (1964). Thinking and depression: II. Theory and therapy. *Archives of General Psychiatry, 10*, 561–571.
Beck, A.T. (1967). *Depression: Clinical, experimental, and theoretical aspects.* New York: Harper.
Beck, A.T. (1970). Cognitive therapy: Nature and relation to behavior therapy. *Behavior Therapy, 1*, 184–200.
Beck, A.T. (1976). *Cognitive therapy and the emotional disorders.* New York: International Universities Press.
Beck, A.T., Rush. A.J., Shaw, B., & Emery, G. (1979). *Cognitive therapy of depression.* New York: Guilford.
Catania, A.C. (1975). The myth of self-reinforcement. *Behaviorism, 3*(2), 192–199.
Catania, A.C. (1976). Self-reinforcement revisited. *Behaviorism, 4*(2), 157–162.
Craighead, W.E., Kimball, W.H., & Rehak, P.J. (1979). Mood changes, physiological responses, and self-statements during social rejection imagery. *Journal of Consulting and Clinical Psychology, 47*, 385–396.
DiGiuseppe, R.A., Miller, N.J., & Trexler, L.D. (1977). A review of rational-emotive psychotherapy outcome studies. *The Counseling Psychologist, 7*, 64–72.
DiLoreto, A. D. (1970). A comparison of the relative effectiveness of systematic desensitization, rational-emotive and client-centered group psychotherapy in the reduction of interpersonal anxiety in introverts and extroverts (Doctoral dissertation, Michigan State University, 1969). *Dissertation Abstracts International, 30*, 5230A–5231A. (University Microfilms No. 70–9521).
Dollard, J., & Miller, N.E. (1950). *Personality and psychotherapy: An analysis in terms of learning, thinking, and culture.* New York: McGraw-Hill.
Dowd, E.T. (1978). *Cognitive Behavior Therapy Newsletter.* Association for Advancement of Behavior Therapy, *1*(1).
Ellis, A. (1962). *Reason and emotion in psychotherapy.* Secaucus, New Jersey: Stuart.
Ellis, A. (1973a). *Humanistic psychotherapy.* New York: McGraw-Hill.
Ellis, A. (1973b). Rational-emotive therapy. In R. Corsini (Ed.), *Current psychotherapies.* Itasca, Illinois: Peacock.
Ellis, A. (1980). Rational-emotive therapy and cognitive behavior therapy: Similarities and differences. *Cognitive Therapy and Research, 4*(4), 325–340.
Frankl, V.E. (1960). Paradoxical intention: A logotherapeutic technique. *American Journal of Psychotherapy, 14*, 520–535.
Fremouw, W.J., & Zitter, R.E. (1978). A comparison of skills training and cognitive restructuring-relaxation for the treatment of speech anxiety. *Behavior Therapy, 9*, 248–259.

Germer, W.A. (1975). Effectiveness of cognitive modification, desensitization, and rational-emotive therapy in the treatment of speech anxiety (Doctoral dissertation, University of Texas at Austin, 1975). *Dissertation Abstracts International, 36*, 907B-908B. (University Microfilms No. 75–16. 674).

Glogower, F.O., Fremouw, W.J., & McCroskey, J.C. (1978). A component analysis of cognitive restructuring. *Cognitive Therapy and Research, 2*(3), 209–223.

Goldfried, M.R. (1979). Anxiety reduction through cognitive-behavioral intervention. In P.C. Kendall & S.D. Hollon (Eds.), *Cognitive-behavioral interventions: Theory, research, and procedures* (pp. 117–52). New York: Academic Press.

Goldfried, M.R., Linehan, M.M., & Smith, J.L. (1978). The reduction of test anxiety through rational restructuring. *Journal of Consulting and Clinical Psychology, 46*, 32–39.

Hayes, S.C., Rincover, A., & Solnick, J.V. (1980). The technical drift of applied behavior analysis. *Journal of Applied Behavior Analysis, 13*, 275–285.

Hollon, S.D., & Beck, A.T. (1979). Cognitive therapy of depression. In P.C. Kendall & S.D. Hollon (Eds.). *Cognitive-behavioral interventions; Theory, research, and procedures* (pp. 153–204). New York: Academic Press.

Holroyd, K.A. (1976). Cognition and desensitization in the group treatment of test anxiety. *Journal of Consulting and Clinical Psychology, 44*, 991–1001.

Hussian, R.W., & Lawrence, P.S. (1978). The reduction of test, state, and trail anxiety by test-specific and generalized stress inoculation training. *Cognitive Therapy and Research, 2*(1), 25–37.

Jarmon, G.J. (1973). Differential effectiveness of rational-emotive therapy, bibliotherapy, and attention-placebo in the treatment of speech anxiety (Doctoral dissertation, Southern Illinois University, 1972). *Dissertation Abstracts International, 33*, 45108. (University Microfilms No. 73–6217).

Kanfer, F.H. (1970). Self-regulation: Research, issues, and speculations. In C. Neuringer & J.L. Michael (Eds.), *Behavior modification in clinical psychology* (pp.178–220). New York: Appleton.

Kanfer, F.H. (1971). The maintenance of behavior by self-generated stimuli and reinforcement. In A. Jacobs & L.B. Sachs (Eds.), *The psychology of private events* (pp. 39–61). New York: Academic Press.

Kanfer, F.H. (1977). The many faces of self-control, or behavior modification changes its focus. In R.B. Stuart (Ed.), *Behavioral self-management: Strategies, techniques, and outcomes* (pp. 1–. New York: Brunner/Mazel.

Kanfer, F.H., & Karoly, P. (1972). Self-control: A behavioristic excursion into the lion's den. *Behavior Therapy, 3*, 398–416.

Kanfer, F.H., Karoly, P., & Newman, A. (1975). Reduction of children's fear of the dark by competence-related and situational threat-related verbal cues. *Journal of Consulting and Clinical Psychology, 43*(2), 251–258.

Kanter, N.J. (1976). A comparison of self-control desensitization and rational restructuring for the reduction of interpersonal anxiety (Doctoral dissertation, State University of New York at Stony Brook, 1975). *Dissertation Abstracts International, 36,* 3611B. (University Microfilms No. 76–792, 392).

Karst, T. O., & Trexler L. D. (1970). Initial study using fixed-role and rational-emotive therapy in treating public-speaking anxiety. *Journal of Consulting and Clinical Psychology, 34,* 360–366.

Kazdin, A.E. (1978). *History of behavior modification: Experimental foundations of contemporary research.* Baltimore: University Park Press.

Kendall, P.C., & Hollon, S.D. (Eds.). (1979). *Cognitive-behavioral interventions: Theory, research, and procedures.* New York: Academic Press.

Kendall, P.C., & Hollon, S.D. (Eds.). (1981). *Assessment strategies for cognitive-behavioral interventions.* New York: Academic Press.

Kendall, P.C., Williams, L., Pechacek, T.F., Graham, L.E., Shisslak, C., & Herzof, N. (1979). Cognitive-behavioral and patient education interventions in cardiac catheterization procedures: The Palo Alto medical psychology project. *Journal of Consulting and Clinical Psychology, 47,* 48–59.

Knapp, T. (1980). Psychoanalysis, behavior analysis, and self-deception. In S.C. Hayes (Chair), *The baby and the bathwater: Radical behavioral interpretations of traditional clinical phenomena.* Symposium presented at the meeting of the Association for Advancement of Behavior Therapy, New York.

Mahoney, M.J. (1974). *Cognition and behavior modification.* Cambridge, Massachusetts: Ballinger.

Mahoney, M.J., & Arnkoff, D.B. (1978). Cognitive and self-control therapies. In S.L. Garfield & A.E. Bergin (Eds.), *Handbook of psychotherapy and behavior change* (2nd ed., pp. 689–722). New York: Wiley.

Meichenbaum, D.H. (1972). Cognitive modification of test anxious college students. *Journal of Consulting and Clinical Psychology, 39,* 370–380.

Meichenbaum, D.H. (1974). *Cognitive behavior modification.* Morristown, New Jersey: General Learning Press.

Meichenbaum, D.H. (1977). *Cognitive-behavior modification: An integrative approach.* New York: Plenum.

Meichenbaum, D.H., & Cameron, R. (1972). *An examination of cognitive and contingency variables in anxiety relief procedures.* Unpublished manuscript, University of Waterloo.

Meichenbaum, D.H., & Cameron, R. (1974). The clinical potential of modifying what clients say to themselves. *Psychotherapy: Theory, Research, and Practice, 11,* 103–117.

Meichenbaum, D.H., Gilmore, J.B., & Fedoravicius, A. (1971). Group insight versus desensitization in treating speech anxiety. *Journal of Consulting and Clinical Psychology, 36,* 410–421.

Meichenbaum, D.H., & Turk, D. (1976). The cognitive-behavioral management of anxiety, anger, and pain. In P.O. Davidson (Ed.), *The behavioral management of anxiety, depression, and pain* (pp. 1–34). New York: Brunner/Mazel, 1976.

Moleski, R., & Tosi, D.J. (1976). Comparative psychotherapy: Rational-emotive therapy versus systematic desensitization in treating stuttering. *Journal of Consulting and Clinical Psychology, 44*, 309–311.

Munt, E.D., Hayes, S.C., & Nelson, R.O. (1979, December). *The effects of immediate environmental factors on a self-reinforcement procedure designed to improve reading comprehension skill.* Paper presented at the meeting of the Association for Advancement of Behavior Therapy, San Francisco.

Novaco, R.W. (1975). *Anger control: The development and evaluation of an experimental treatment.* Lexington, Massachusetts: Heath.

Novaco, R.W. (1976). Treatment of chronic anger through cognitive and relaxation controls. *Journal of Consulting and Clinical Psychology, 44*, 681.

Novaco, R.W. (1979). The cognitive regulation of anger and stress. In P.C. Kendall & S.D. Hollon (Eds.), *Cognitive-behavioral interventions: Theory, research, and procedures* (pp. 241–285). New York: Academic Press.

Rachlin, H. (1974). Self-control. *Behaviorism, 2*, 94–107.

Rimm, D. C., & Litvak, S.B. (1969). Self-verbalization and emotional arousal. *Journal of Abnormal Psychology, 74*, 181–187.

Rogers, T., & Craighead, W.E. (1977). Physiological responses to self-statements: The effects of statement valence and discrepancy. *Cognitive Therapy and Research, 1*, 99–119.

Rosenfarb, I., Hayes, S.C., & Zettle, R.D. (1981, May). *Public versus private goal-setting and self-reinforcement of academic behavior.* Paper presented at the meeting of the Association for Behavior Analysis, Milwaukee.

Russell, P.L., & Brandsma, J.M. (1974). A theoretical and empirical integration of the rational-emotive and classical conditioning theories. *Journal of Consulting and Clinical Psychology, 42*, 389–397.

Shevrin, H., & Dickman, S. (1980). The psychological unconscious: A necessary assumption for all psychological theory? *American Psychologist, 35*, 421–434.

Skinner, B.F. (1945). The operational analysis of psychological terms. *Psychological Review, 52*, 270–277.

Skinner, B.F. (1953). *Science and human behavior.* New York: Free Press.

Skinner, B.F. (1957). *Verbal behavior.* New York: Appleton.

Skinner, B.F. (1966). An operant analysis of problem solving. In B. Kleinmuntz (Ed.), *Problem-solving: Research, method, and theory* (pp. 225–257). New York; Wiley.

Skinner, B.F. (1969). *Contingencies of reinforcement: A theoretical analysis.* New York: Appleton.

Thoresen, C.E., & Mahoney, M.F. (1974). *Behavioral self-control.* New York: Holt.

Turk, D. C., & Genest, M. (1979). Regulation of pain: The application of cognitive and behavioral techniques for prevention and remediation. In

P.C. Kendall & S.D. Hollon (Eds.), *Cognitive-behavioral interventions: Theory, research, and procedures* (pp. 287–318). New York: Academic Press.
Wilson, G.T. (1978). Cognitive behavior therapy: Paradigm shift or passing phase? In J.P. Foreyt & D.P. Rathjen (Eds.), *Cognitive behavior therapy: Research and application* (pp. 7–32). New York: Plenum.
Wine, J. (1971). Test anxiety and direction of attention. *Psychological Bulletin, 76*(2), 92–104.
Wolfe, J. L. (1976). Short-term effects of modeling/behavior rehearsal, modeling/behavior rehearsal-plus-rational therapy, placebo, and no treatment on assertive behavior (Doctoral dissertation, New York University, 1975). *Dissertation Abstracts International, 36*, 1936B–1937B. (University Microfilms No. 75–22, 937).
Zettle, R.D. (1980a). Insight: Rules and revelations. In S.C. Hayes (Chair), *The baby and the bathwater: Radical behavioral interpretations of traditional clinical phenomena*. Symposium presented at the meeting of the Association for Advancement of Behavior Therapy, New York.
Zettle, R. D. (1980b). *The role of rule-governed behavior in clinical phenomena*. Unpublished manuscript, University of North Carolina at Greensboro.
Zettle, R.D., & Hayes, S.C. (1979). *The effect of social context on the impact of coping self-statements*. Unpublished manuscript, University of North Carolina at Greensboro.
Zettle, R.D., & Hayes. S.C. (1980). Conceptual and empirical status of rational-emotive therapy, In M. Hersen, R.M. Eisler, & P. M. Miller (Eds.), *Progress in behavior modification* (Vol. 9, pp. 126–166). New York: Academic Press.

ARTICLE 2

FALSIFICATION AND THE PROTECTIVE BELT SURROUNDING ENTITY-POSTULATING THEORIES

From Hayes, S. C. (2004). *Journal of Applied and Preventive Psychology, 11*, 35–37.

This is a commentary on Meehl's 1978 article (see references). Full understanding will require that you read it but the main points can be appreciated without doing so.

Meehl's classic article (1978) is both brilliant and frustrating. On the one hand, he detects and illuminates the problems of soft psychology with incisiveness and a level of honesty that can only be described as brutal. On the other hand, he fails to appreciate his own role, in this article and others, in protecting failed theoretical approaches. From the vantage point provided by 25 years of distance it is more possible to see this problem. After the sense of intellectual awe wears off it is the contradictions that are most striking.

Meehl has always preferred "entity-postulating theories" as he says in several different ways in this article. He is a trained psychoanalyst. He has been through analysis himself. Although his best-known work to a general psychological audience is methodological and conceptual, his substantive theoretical and empirical work has emphasized one hypothesized entity after another.

The "slow progress" he is speaking of could hardly be more evident than in some of the research areas he prefers (e.g., psychoanalytic theories; personality theory). The methodological arguments he has made (such as the distinction between hypothetical constructs and intervening variables; the concept of nomological networks; the importance of falsification) need to be seen in that light. The paradox of this article and of Meehl's thinking more generally is that he has always been too intelligent to deny the problems presented by the kinds of theories he prefers, but has failed to view his theoretical preferences as a foundational problem. Rather, over the last 50 years his arguments and criticisms have paradoxically helped build the case for the kind of theoretical work that has produced the problems he laments. With his help psychology has constructed an intellectual protective belt around entity-postulating theories, and with the collapse of classic behaviorism, hardly anyone seems to have noticed.

In this article, Meehl carefully lays out some of the key conceptual and measurement difficulties that must be faced by "soft psychology," and rightly condemns the dominance of statistical inferential tests in our field, but then he suddenly (and without any real defense) lurches toward an embrace of falsificationism (p. 817). The present article is often cited as if it supports falsifiability, and Meehl himself seems to speak of it that way, but it emphatically does not. Indeed, a defense of Popper's *modus tollens* is barely mounted (p. 317) before Meehl appreciates its key logical flaw: tests of theories require auxiliaries and conditions that are themselves not tested (p. 818). Meehl notes that in the hard sciences this is not so much of a problem, because there is not a large gap between tested theories and the auxiliaries and conditions that go into the test. Meehl notes such is hardly the case in the soft sciences, which "makes it hard for us social scientists to fulfill a Popperian falsifiability requirement" (p. 819). The only solution Meehl is able to come up with in "defense" of falsifiability under these conditions is the empirical (not logical!) principle of the "very strange coincidence" (p. 821) between empirical observations and the "antecedently improbable observational patterns" (p. 821) suggested by a theory and loosely linked auxiliaries and conditions *precisely because they are loosely linked.*

There are two important things worth mentioning about this idea. First, this is not falsification: it is *verification.* Indeed, in case anyone doubts it, note that Meehl later comes to the same verification-based conclusion in the section on statistical inference, emphasizing that it is *"valuable to show approximate agreement of observations with a theoretically predicted numerical point value, rank order, or function form"* (p. 825; italics in the original). Second, once this argument is seen as a form of verification, it should also be noted that the loose link between theory and linked auxiliaries and conditions becomes a curse to the larger research program, not a secret source of logical strength as it might be in a specific study as Meehl (correctly) argues. The reason is this: poorly understood variability in auxiliaries and conditions can (and probably will) lead useful theories to fail to correspond to the data for reasons that have nothing to do with the theory. Stated another way, while Meehl is correct that verification can still work in the soft sciences based on the principle of a "very strange coincidence" if an analysis is specific and non-obvious, a *lack* of correspondence provides a weak guide in these circumstances because it may *not* be very strange or unexpected, even if the theory is in principle useful, if auxiliaries and conditions are poorly linked to the theory.

As a behavioral psychologist I do not find the collapse of falsification disturbing. Falsification is logically true only in an abstract and limited universe. In the real world it is both logically and psychologically false. The former is shown by Meehl, Lakatos, Kuhn, Feyerabend, and others. The latter is shown by behavioral psychology itself. Organisms, scientists included, work on the basis of consequences and thus it will always be the *achievement of consequences* that drives science. I believe that the goal of science is the construction of increasingly organized systems of verbal rules that allow analytic goals to be accomplished with precision, scope, and depth, and based on verifiable experience (Hayes, 1993). Scientific analyses that are high in precision and scope allow for the kind of broad and specific tests that lead to detection of a poor fit with the data, but that is not falsification in a technical sense: it is simply the conditions under which verification provides a particularly useful guide to a research program. For scientific analyses to have high precision and scope, however, there has to be a small gap between theory and the auxiliaries and conditions that allow them to be applied. And that is where the target paper fails us.

By their very nature, entity-postulating theories are loosely fitted to their assumptions and conditions, as Meehl himself argues. For example, Meehl notes that Skinner's more inductive approach "does not usually present us with the kind of evidentiary evaluation problems that we get with entity-postulating theories" (p. 824) and then goes on to the solutions he proposes for "those of us whose cognitive passions are incompletely satisfied by [such] theories" (p. 824). Why doesn't this very preference and sense of incomplete satisfaction need to be defended intellectually? Meehl does not say. Meehl notes that in the realm of replicable observations "Skinner is in better shape than Freud" (p. 813) and later agrees that the reasons for this might "mean that we could most profitably confine ourselves to low-order inductions, a (to me, depressing) conjecture that is somewhat corroborated by the fact that the two most powerful forms of clinical psychology are atheoretical psychometrics of prediction on the one hand and behavior modification on the others" (p. 829). But instead of following through with the implications of his own analysis, Meehl rejects more inductive approaches on the grounds that they do not have "the kind of conceptual richness that attracts the theory-oriented mind" (p. 829). In the extended addendum Meehl goes one step farther, explaining, "I cheerfully admit, in this matter, to the presence of a large distance between my subjective personalistic probability (based on my experiences as analysand and practitioner of psychoanalytic psychotherapy) and the present state of the 'intersubjective public evidence'" (p. 830).

As a human matter, it is hard to be cross with someone who "cheerfully" points to what may be "a terribly irrational leap of faith" (p. 831), but as a scientific matter, more is involved and more should be expected. Every intellectual criticism Meehl offers of soft psychology is made notably worse in the context of entity-postulating theories, and yet the only reasons Meehl offers for not abandoning them is he is "theoretically minded," he has "cognitive passions," and he has had personal experiences in analysis that he finds interesting. That is a defense that is as weak as his criticism of soft psychology is strong.

In the 25 years since this article first appeared, approaches to psychology that emphasize concepts that are tightly linked to their observations have continued to progress, slowly but surely. Many do not know this because these areas have fallen so far out of fashion. Areas that emphasize entity-postulating theories have continued to excite and then disappoint—a cycle that Meehl carefully documents. Many do not know this, because they are blinded by the excitement of the latest new thing. Unfortunately, this very article and others in this related line of reasoning have protected these latter approaches. Somehow the message that has come through is that with sufficient tough mindedness, entity-postulating theories can be constructed that will finally work. It is a perverse combination: the appearance of scientific rigor, vigorous criticism of the sad state of our field, and unexamined embrace of a form of theorizing that has never succeeded against either of these criteria.

Meehl's article still casts a challenging and harsh light on psychology but in the context of the 20 difficulties listed we now have 25 more years of experience leading to the conclusion Meehl refused to state in simple form: there are no scientific methods that can reliably provide entity-postulating theories with a route toward scientific success. Psychology should take a cleaner and more radical step than the one Meehl proposes: entity-postulating theories must themselves be questioned or even abandoned.

REFERENCES

Hayes, S.C. (1993). Analytic goals and the varieties of scientific contextualism. In S.C. Hayes, L.J. Hayes, H.W. Reese, & T.R. Sarbin (Eds.), *Varieties of scientific contextualism* (pp. 11–27). Reno, NV: Context Press.

Meehl, P.E. (1978). Theoretical risks and tabular asterisks: Sir Karl, Sir Ronald, and the slow progress of soft psychology. *Journal of Consulting and Clinical Psychology, 46*, 806–834.

ARTICLE 3

MAKING SENSE OF SPIRITUALITY

From Hayes, S.C. (1984). *Behaviorism, 12*, 99–110.

The purpose of the present paper is to attempt to analyze the distinction between matter and spirit from a behavioral point of view. I have three major reasons to attempt such an analysis. First, it is obvious that spiritual concerns exert an enormous influence over the behavior of many, if not most, of the members of our culture. Popular books on religion, mysticism, meditation, and spiritual growth are consistent sellers. Spiritual leaders are followed the world over. We spend billions of dollars each year on spiritual enhancement, from growth-oriented therapies to organized religion. Second, despite calls for a change in this area (Schoenfeld, 1979), there have been relatively few attempts to conduct behavioral theoretical analyses of such concerns. Those that have been done have largely focused on the development of superstition, or on the moralizing influence of organized religion (e.g., Skinner, 1953). While these are important topics, they are relatively easy to analyze in terms of principles of reinforcement or cultural survival. The matter/spirit distinction per se is more difficult to understand, but it is also more interesting in many ways. I intend to focus on the nature of the distinction as it is talked about in Western culture, while avoiding issues about the regulative, moralizing influence of organized religion. Third, I believe that a behavioral analysis of spirituality leads to important outcomes for a behavioral view of several other topics, including self-awareness and therapeutic processes.

BEHAVIORAL APPROACHES TO "NON-BEHAVIORAL" TERMS

When presented with terms like "spirit" there are several possible responses from behaviorists. One response is to reject them out of hand. In this approach, a behavioral perspective might first be said to have various characteristics. Behaviorism might be declared to be deterministic; materialistic, or monistic, for example. Since spiritual or dualistic terms literally contradict materialism, monism, and the like, they would be rejected as scientific or behaviorally illegitimate. While this is a logical response, it is not really a behavioral analytic response.

From a behavioral point of view, rejecting terms purely on the basis of their literal meaning has two problems. First, written or spoken words are the structural products of the functional behavior of speaking or writing. You can "understand" these very sentences even though you know very little or nothing about the contingencies causing them to be emitted. Your understanding of these products of behavior is due to a history provided by the verbal community for reacting to them in commonly agreed upon ways. For example, you can look words up in a dictionary and "find out what they mean" based solely on the form or structure of the words themselves. A structural analysis of these products of behavior is not the same as a functional analysis of the behavior of saying or writing them.

The behavioral analysis of language is based on understanding the behavior of speaking and listening by analyzing contingencies. Terms are to be understood by identifying the conditions under which they are used and the effects their use has. Literal meaning is part of this picture (because the socially established structure of language must participate in its function) but it is not synonymous with it. Thus, rejecting terms as irrelevant because they are "non-behavioral" when that is based purely on logical or literal inconsistency with behaviorism is itself non-behavioral—not because the logic is incorrect but because that kind of analysis is not a behavioral analysis.

There is a second and related problem with rejecting terms based on literal meaning. In a radical behavioral view terms have literal meaning only within the structure of language achieved by social agreement. Terms are recognized to "mean" things based in part upon their participation in equivalence classes (Sidman, 1971; Sidman & Cresson, 1973) established by the verbal community. Thus, for example, by agreement the term "matter" is not equivalent to "spirit." You cannot interchange the terms and secure reinforcement from the verbal community for doing so. In a behavioral view, however, public agreement is not a shortcut to the truth or validity of terms or observations (Skinner, 1945). We can all agree something is so, and it can nevertheless not be so. The scientific validity of observations depends not on agreement about them but upon the contingencies controlling the observations. There is little reason to suspect that public agreement within the behavioral verbal community ensures contact with the actual contingencies any more than does agreement within the mainstream culture.

For both of these reasons, argument by literal analysis is based on a non-behavioral view of the analysis of psychological terms. A behavioral analysis can be done of any term, even those which are literally incompatible with behaviorism (e.g., see Hayes & Maley, 1977). That is my purpose in this paper.

A second type of response behaviorists sometimes make to "non-behavioral" terms is more satisfactory, but is not always ultimately adequate. When confronted with the need to explain the use of difficult terms or rules, behaviorists often point to the immediate, social conditioning that gave rise to an individual's use of such terms or control by such rules. We might, for example, speak generally about how a child came to use the word "spirit" based on the contingencies exerted by family or church. More abstractly, we might wonder about the contingencies of cultural survival that might have supported the use of such terms. Both of these tacks are behaviorally sound, and in many cases may be fully adequate to the analytic demands of the situation. If, however, the term has tact properties, these two tacks are not adequate because we must then also understand the actual physical conditions that gave rise to the term.

SPIRITUALITY

An essential characteristic of much of verbal behavior is the way it is controlled by (and can form stimulus equivalence with) elements in the natural and social environment. Much of human verbal behavior is, to some degree, a tact. Under these conditions, understanding the stimulus situation is critical. To understand the term "apple" it is not enough to speak broadly about social conditioning or cultural survival. We must also deal with apples. To the extent that it is a tact, apples are a necessary precondition for the way we use the term "apples."

The same might be true in the matter/spirit distinction. Of course, behaviorists (while behaving as behaviorists) would not believe that dualism is literally true. The danger is to *presume* that, based solely on our agreement that dualism is incorrect, talk of spirituality cannot be a tact. This falls back into the trap of literality just discussed. The matter/spirit distinction either is in part a tact or it is not. Public agreement will not decide this for us. A primitive tribe may tact all airplanes as "God." The fact that this is in formal disagreement with our view does not make it any less a tact. Furthermore, were we to study this verbal community, we could not understand "God" without dealing with the physical phenomenon of airplanes.

Thus, a third approach is try more comprehensively to identify the sources of control over the origin of such talk—to identify the actual physical conditions under which such concepts and distinctions might arise and the functions they might serve. Looking for events that might have first supported the matter/spirit distinction seems especially reasonable when you realize that matter/ spirit distinctions are nearly universal in modern culture. How did it first come to be that matter was distinguished from spirit? If we can provide plausible physical stimuli that occasion the word "spirit," then it could be tact. If not, then this may be another mentalistic term that is due purely to social-verbal conventions. The strategy I intend to follow in this paper is to search for real, physical events that occasion the matter/ spirit distinction, while recognizing fully that simply because we have a term for something does not mean that it literally exists.

WHAT IS "SPIRIT"?

If you want to understand what a term "means" it is reasonable (though not ultimately satisfactory) to start with what social agreement has to say, that is, to look it up in the dictionary. As I've already discussed, any functional account must encompass a structural account, so formal definitions delineate what must be encompassed. The following definitions can all be found in the Oxford English Dictionary. The OED defines "spirit" as an "incorporeal or immaterial being" and as a "being or intelligence distinct from anything physical." In essence, then, spirit is said to be knowable but it is nevertheless said to be neither material nor physical. If you look up "matter" you will find that it is related to the word for timber or building materials. Matter is the "stuff of which a thing is made." So matter is "thing-stuff." A "thing" is defined as "that which is or may be an object of perception, thought, or knowledge." The word "object" comes from a word meaning "to throw." It is a "thing thrown down to the senses or the mind." We can go no further, because this definition refers us back to "thing." If we go back and pick up the word "physical" we find we can go no further there either. The word "physical" comes from a word for nature (thus the science of physics) and is defined as "of or pertaining to the phenomenal world of the senses; matter."

Putting these various definitions together, if we are to take the words literally, we are first looking for events that are not publicly observable. "Spirit," furthermore, could not be just any private event because it is not experienceable as a thing or object (as most private events surely are) though it must somehow be experienceable if the term is under the control of any event at all.

THE ANALYSIS

Where might we turn to begin to understand behaviorally such a strange concept as "spirit"? It seems illogical on the face of it, and certainly nothing like what we know in the world of behavior. That is the appearance, but I want to argue that it is not the truth. There is a behaviorally sensible event that corresponds quite well to the characteristics mentioned. To see it we will have to examine an obvious area: verbal behavior.

Let the word "seeing" represent all of the major things we do with regard to the world (feeling, moving, etc.). To non-verbal organisms there is just the world and seeing. Seeing is controlled entirely by the direct contingencies (of survival and reinforcement). Seeing is simply a response to these non-arbitrary contingencies.

With the advent of verbal behavior this changes. According to the traditional behavioral analysis, something else called, self-awareness or self-knowledge is added. Skinner has described it this way:

> There is a . . . difference between behaving and reporting that one is behaving or reporting the causes of one's behavior. In arranging conditions under which a person describes the public or private world in which he lives, a community generates that very special form of behavior called knowing. . . . Self-knowledge is of social origin. (1974, p. 30)

In other words, the verbal community establishes additional arbitrary contingencies for a behavior that is hard to imagine could emerge any other way: not only seeing but what we might call "seeing seeing" or self-knowledge. Supposedly this happens through such things as questions like "What happened to you yesterday? What did you see? What did you eat?" and so on. There emerges a generalized tendency to respond discriminatively to one's own behavior so as to establish a correspondence between it and verbal behavior and thereby give the verbal community access to what we see. As Skinner says, "It is only when a person's private world becomes important to others that it is made important to him" (Skinner, 1974, p. 31).

So far there is nothing here that truly smacks of spirituality. The world of the senses ("seeing") is explicitly what is *not* spiritual. It is thing-like in the sense that now we see this, now that, so there is a distinction between this and not-this. Such a distinction is the requirement for things to be things.[1] Seeing seeing is not quite as thing-like, but it is also experienceable as a thing. For example, we say that we are conscious, asleep, or hypervigilant. Our seeing seeing changes; it comes and goes. This quality of distinction within the world of seeing seeing means that it is experienceable as a thing, and thus (according to the dictionary) cannot be the stuff of which spirit is made.

What seems to have been missed in most behavioral accounts is that seeing seeing cannot be all there is to self-awareness. It is also critical to the verbal community that this behavior occurs from a given and consistent perspective, locus, or point of view. That is, we (the verbal community) must not only know that you see and that you see that you see, but that *you* see that you see. Reports of seeing (i.e., seeing seeing) must be from the point of view of you.

This behavior might emerge in several ways. First, words such as "here" and "there" are acquired which do not refer to a specific thing but to a relation to the child's point of view. For example, "there" is always anywhere else but "here" and "here" is always "from this locus or point of view." Second, children are taught to distinguish their perspective from that of others. Young children have a hard time with the issue of perspective. For example, young children seated across from a doll will, when asked, report that the doll sees what they are seeing. Gradually, however, a sense of perspective emerges. A child learns what he or she sees is seen from a perspective. Similarly, a young child, asked what she had for breakfast, may respond with what her brother actually ate, but an older child will not make such a mistake. Through correction ("No, that is what your brother ate. What did *you* eat?") a child must learn to see seeing from a consistent locus. Finally, it is also possible that a sense of locus emerges by a process of elimination or by metaphorical extension. Suppose a child can give correct answers to the question "What did you x?" where "x" is a wide variety of events such as eat, feel, watch, and so on. The events constantly change. In our terms, the seeing and the seeing seeing change. Only the locus does not. Thus, the one consistency between the word "you" in such questions and behavior is not seeing or seeing seeing but the behavior of seeing that you see from a particular locus or perspective. Thus, in some real sense, "you" *are* the perspective.

The behavior of seeing seeing from a perspective is a very odd behavior. For the person engaging in the behavior, it is not truly possible to see it as an object. It is only experienceable in its effects, the feelings associated with it, or as a kind of fleeting after-image when we attempt to grab it and look at it directly. If we were to see our own perspective (i.e., as an object) from what perspective would we see it?

An analogue to this issue (which is not directly the same thing, but may serve as a convenient metaphor) may help us see the issue. Consider the event of looking from one's eyes. It is impossible truly to look at looking from one's eyes where the object is the same as looking at the object. If you could leap aside yourself faster than the speed of light you would see yourself looking (as you might if you took a snapshot) but you would be doing so from a changed perspective. Your eyes would be elsewhere. If you look in a mirror you see yourself head on—you are essentially looking back at yourself—but what you are looking at is not the same perspective as looking *from* your eyes. No matter where you are, your eyes are there. You cannot truly see your perspective and at the same time view from that perspective. To see perspective, perspective must change. (This same basic issue has been widely discussed in the philosophy of science literature where philosophers have pointed out that the assumptions of a theory cannot themselves be explained by the theory.)

The sense of perspective or locus as a behavioral event is like that of the eye as a structural event. Most of you undoubtedly have experienced the phenomenon of talking, then suddenly seeing that you are talking, then realizing that in some sense *you* are seeing yourself talk. At that very instant, you realize that *you* are one step behind the *you* that saw yourself talking. This kind of tail chasing is as ultimately unsuccessful as it is fascinating. There simply seems to be no way to see your own seeing-from-perspective without doing so from a now-shifted perspective. This means that you-as-perspective is not itself fully experienceable as a thing or object by the person looking from that perspective.

The verbal community uses the word "you" in many ways, of course. Sometimes it means "you" as a physical system, such as "I saw you asleep yesterday." Most often, however, it seems explicitly to refer to you-as-perspective. Consider the following question: "If you lost your arms and legs, would you still be you?" Given one sense of the question ("You as a physical structure") the question could reasonably be answered "no." If the sense of the question, however, refers to the verbally established you-as-perspective, then the obvious answer is yes. In fact, our bodies change regularly, but we are still said to be the same person. The same principle applies to any aspect of ourselves that can be held as an object, such as our thoughts, emotions, behavioral predispositions, and so on. If you are asked to remember what it was like to be 10 years old—to remember looking out at the world at that age—and you are asked "Was that *you* then?" or "Deep down, is the *you* that is here now the *you* that was there then?" again the obvious answer is yes. Logically, this is not at all true in terms of you-as-object. Your thoughts are different, your body is different, your feelings are different, and so on. But now look at the previous sentence. Though it sounds normal, note that the "you" in this sentence refers to some sort of agent *independent* of all of the things about you. When I say "your body" it is as if you possess a body—not that you are your body. For a behaviorist (or any materialist) this seems literally impossible. The verbal community, however, is not making a scientific statement in such phrases. Rather the "you" referred to by the verbal community is seeing seeing from a set context. As long as this behavior itself does not change, you are still you. *What you* see will change radically—your body will age, your thoughts will change—but the locus or context of self-knowledge will not and cannot.

You have never seen seeing from a different perspective than your own. You can imagine what it might be like to do so (it may even be important to do this in order to acquire a sense of perspective), but even as you imagine this you see these imaginings from the self-same perspective. Thus, while the *content* of your life may change, *you-as-perspective* cannot[2] (parenthetically, this distinction is crucial to the procedure known as the est training which is where I first encountered it).

If it were allowed to do so, we could not get generally reliable answers to questions such as "What did you do yesterday'?" If you really could view events from a different locus, you would no longer *be* you. A verbal community that permitted anything else would collapse in chaos.

IMPLICATIONS FOR SPIRITUALITY

Spirit is defined as an "immaterial" being; and matter is the stuff of things. Spirit is thus a being non-experienceable as a thing. You-as-perspective seems to fit this definition rather well. As was argued earlier, the essence of a thing or object is "this—not that." To see a thing we must also see "not-thing." Thus, all things must be finite—they must have edges or limits. It is the edges or limits that allows us to see a thing. If a thing was absolutely everywhere, we could not see it as a thing. For the person experiencing it, you-as-perspective has no stable edges or limits—it is not fully experienceable as a thing. Perspective is precisely the aspect in which things are held. As soon as perspective is viewed as content from what perspective is it viewed? Perspective must move one step back. It seems plausible, then, that the matter/spirit distinction has as its source the content/perspective distinction established as a necessary side effect of language. Quite literally, it may be that verbal behavior gave humankind a soul.

The matter/spirit distinction is an ancient one, and originated long before a scientific perspective emerged. Rather than rejecting this distinction, the present analysis suggests that it is a very reasonable and sophisticated one—allowing us to use language in a situation where the normal use of language (to tact events that are experienceable as things) does not readily apply.

Obviously, the present analysis suggests that perspective is in fact a thing—it is a socially established behavior of importance to the verbal community. We can readily examine other people and see their "you-as-perspective behavior" as a thing. Even as we do this, however, we are observing this from our own you-as-perspective behavior, and *this* context or perspective is not experienceable as a thing by ourselves. Thus, you-as-perspective behavior can be a stable thing only when it is someone else being observed. For the person doing it, it is not observable and describable in the same way as all other events are observable and describable.

Talking in this way helps us understand some of the characteristics that are said to be part of the world of the spirit. Consider the characteristics of temporal immortality or physical infinity. This means undying; without limit or end; boundless. So far as you can directly know, you have never been anywhere you-as-perspective have not been. There is nothing you have ever done or experienced that you know about that wasn't known in the context called you. On experiential (not logical) grounds, so far as you know you have no limits and no end. At least you have never experienced any limits, or boundary, or end that you know about, by definition. If you know about it, you were there to know about it.

Other aspects of spirituality also become clear in the same way. It is commonly believed that the spiritual side of humankind participates in the divine. For example, humans are said to be made in the "image and likeness of God." Let us now examine the characteristics of a metaphysical God and see how this relates to you-as-perspective. Consider these terms that have been used to describe God.

Absolute, the One, Perfect Identity, Unity

You can directly experience no divisions in your own perspective. We do recognize, however, that others exist, so while we participate in or model ultimate unity, we don't usually claim it for ourselves. God's "Perfect Identity" is, in a sense, a logical extension of our own experience of ourselves as context or pure perspective.

Nothing/Everything

This more Eastern view of God is easily understandable in the same way. You are not experienceable as a thing. Therefore you are "no thing" (the word "nothing" was originally written as "no thing"). The only events which are without edges (they are not things) are nothing and everything. Experientially, we are everything/nothing.

Unchangeable, Eternal, Omnipresent

Since you-as-perspective can *hold* content but is itself not experienceable *as* content there is no thing about you-as-perspective to change. You have been you your whole life. You are everywhere you have ever been. The words listed are perfectly good ways of saying this. Obviously, however, we recognize logically that we do die and change; that we are here and not there. Thus there is a logically induced tension that makes it difficult really to accept what our experience tells us about you-as-perspective. God is an entity without any such contradictions.

Love

When people speak of "God as love" they usually are referring to a quality of a metaphysical God of absolute acceptance. In a sense, God is seen as the context of all contexts. Note that you-as-perspective is perfectly accepting of all content. Pain and pleasure is equally welcome. The fact that we don't like pain (and so on) is just more content that is also equally welcome. A metaphor for perspective might be a flat floor going in all directions endlessly. The floor will hold something ugly as well as it holds something beautiful. Love is a reasonably good word for this in our personal lives (when someone really accepts "who we are" completely), and by extension the context of all contexts is in its essence loving in this sense.

What I am claiming is that the qualities of a metaphysical God can be understood as a metaphorical extension of the experienced qualities of seeing-seeing-from-perspective behavior. If the soul is a by-product of language, then a metaphysical God is another, when viewed from this perspective.[3]

Previous behavioral analysis in the area of religion has tended to dwell on the moralizing aspects of religion, or the possible superstitious behavior that brings it about. Without the experience of our spiritual aspects (in the sense used here) such institutions may have developed anyway, but it seems their universality is more easily explained by a common original source. Advanced use of language, then, might set the stage for dualism, spirituality, *and* religion, by the inherent distinction or "dualism" of content and perspective. Most religions have mystical and spiritual traditions in addition to their moralizing and rule giving ones. Paradoxically, spirituality may be the *source* of many of these rules, in that it may be easier to contact the actual contingencies (and then generate rules about them) from a spiritual viewpoint—a topic to which I now turn.

WHY MIGHT SPIRITUALITY BE IMPORTANT?

It is one thing to provide, as I hope I have, a plausible behavioral account of the spirit/matter distinction. It is another to explain why this distinction should be the subject of so much attention. There are strong cultural traditions that support the search for our spiritual dimensions. Why might this be?

Perhaps one clue is that, from this analysis, only verbal organisms can establish a matter/spirit distinction. Yet this very verbal system creates other problems. There is a growing literature suggesting that verbal organisms make contact with the world in a very different way than do non-verbal organisms (Baron & Galizio, 1983; Hayes, 1989). One particularly intriguing finding is that control by rules or verbal stimuli produce an insensitivity to changes in the natural or direct contingencies (Hayes, Brownstein, Zettle, Rosenfarb, & Korn, 1986; Hayes, Greenway, Brownstein, Haas, Russell, Squittiere, Rosenfarb, Zettle, Herbert, Herbert, Meinhold, & Thompson, 1984; Matthews, Shimoff, Catania, & Sagvolden, 1977; Olson & Hayes, 1984; Shimoff, Catania, & Matthews, 1981). There may be several sources of control over this effect (Hayes et al., 1986), but the fundamental basis of the differences between control by verbal stimuli and control by non-arbitrary stimuli may be that rules have their discriminative or other effects based not just on direct training but also upon their participation in equivalence classes or other symbolic classes established by the verbal community (Hayes, 1989; Hayes, 1987; Hayes et al., 1986). In other words, when our behavior is controlled by rules it is controlled by the indirect effects of symbolic stimuli (or "concepts") *because* of their symbolic or conceptual nature. This is a fundamentally different kind of stimulus control and greatly increases the impact of the verbal community on our behavior, even when the direct contingencies would be more efficient in guiding our behavior. The resultant insensitivity to direct contingencies may produce great benefits to the culture but also great costs to the individual. Because of our verbal abilities, we are constantly analyzing, explaining, figuring out, and so on, even when the direct contingencies would more efficiently produce effective behavior. To take a trivial example, we may try to "figure out" how to hit a tennis ball and become so attached to these analyses that we have to take "Inner Tennis" lessons to learn to be quiet and just hit the ball. Rule-governed behavior thus may present a major impediment to direct contingency control.

Because verbal behavior, once established, requires no environmental support for its occurrence, there is little to stop the "internal dialogue"—that is, private speaking and listening. This means that rules will always be readily available to participate in the control of our behavior once we have acquired verbal behavior. If rules incur a significant cost in some areas, it is difficult to imagine how we might escape this form of verbal control. This seems frequently to be a central focus of psychotherapy.

Consider the following situation, which is drawn from a therapeutic package known as "comprehensive distancing" (Hayes, 1987; Hayes, Korn, Zettle, Rosenfarb, & Cooper, 1982). Imagine that I have you wired up to the world's best polygraph, and that there is absolutely no way that you can be anxious without me knowing it. Now suppose your task is simply to relax—to not be anxious. To help motivate you to perform this simple task I bring out a gun and explain that as long as you remain relaxed, you will not be shot. In such a situation it seems obvious that you will be anxious if you try not to be anxious. That is, following the rule "At all costs, I must not be anxious" is itself something to be anxious about. The anxiety is not just due to the gun, because the same reaction seems likely if you would lose a million dollars by getting anxious. The point is that following a rule is often counter-productive when it seeks to get rid of particular autonomic reactions, emotions, or thoughts: trying not to lose an erection is one of the surest ways to do so, trying not to think a thought automatically creates that thought, and so on (for a more complete analysis of this issue see Hayes, 1987). This seems to be very much the situation many clients are in—especially those clients dealing with unwanted emotions and thoughts (such as agoraphobics), who are caught in an often unsuccessful struggle to get rid of certain reactions deliberately (that is, by following a rule).

The problem is that it is nearly impossible in such a situation not to generate such a rule. Rule-governed behavior may be ineffective (even disastrously so) in this situation, but the rule is nevertheless present.

You-as-perspective, however, might provide a partial solution. From the perspective developed here, the socially created "you" is distinct from the content (e.g., private speech) within you. It seems more possible from this perspective to *see* a rule, without having to *follow* that rule. A metaphor I often use in therapy might help make the point. (The "copy theory" overtones of this example are due to its use clinically and should not be taken literally.) Imagine two people sitting in front of two identical computers. Given a particular set of programming, a given input will produce a given output. In this case, suppose the output shown on the screen is "Deep down you are a bad person." In one case let's imagine that the person sitting in front of the screen is well aware of the distinction between himself and the computer. When the read-out appears on the screen it may be interesting, something to consider, or something to show to others. It will probably not be something that has to be struggled with, covered up, followed, not followed, and so on. The second person, however, is completely absorbed by the screen. In fact, like a person totally involved in a movie, he has forgotten that there is a distinction between the screen and himself as observer of the screen. In this situation the read-out is probably much more impactful. It is something to be gotten rid of, denied, forgotten, believed, and so on. In other words, it will control a good deal of behavior.

Thus, it may be that destructive rule control can be undermined by distinguishing you-as-perspective from the content that is there. This is what is claimed by a variety of mystical writers, who term this aspect of self-awareness such things as "the observing self" (Deikman, 1982) or by religious leaders who distinguish between a person's *soul* and their body, behavior, thoughts, and so on. It has been said that "by dis-identifying with automatic sequences (of thoughts) we lessen their impact and provide free space in which to choose an appropriate response. . . . By identifying with the observing self, we can make a more realistic assessment . . . permitting more effective and creative behavior" (Deikman, 1982, p. 108). Despite the mentalistic language, the point is fairly clear. Control by self-rules can be weakened by viewing them from the point of view of you-as-perspective, and perhaps more creative (presumably contingency-shaped) behavior can then emerge.

Mystical traditions are explicitly oriented toward enhancing the distinction between the verbally held *content* in peoples' lives and the *context* of pure-perspective established in verbal organisms. Perhaps one way to think of this is to think of a second kind of contingency-shaped behavior. In nonverbal organisms, all behavior is contingency-shaped, either in the lifetime of the individual or the species. In verbal organisms, even originally contingency-shaped behavior can be described, labeled, rationalized, and so on. That is, events can enter into pre-existing symbolic (e.g., equivalence) classes established by the verbal community. These classes are often then available to control future behavior. Other behavior was rule-governed to begin with, in the sense that it was originally controlled by arbitrary stimuli organized into symbolic classes by the verbal community. Thus, in verbal organisms rules come to encompass a good deal of the available behavioral repertoire. Pure perspective-taking, however, does not involve taking a perspective in the sense of having an opinion. The behavior cannot enter into equivalence (or other symbolic) classes and still perform its function. Perspective-taking is not a symbolic activity. The behavior is *produced* by verbal behavior. It may be thought of as a second type of purely contingency-shaped behavior—but in this case the contingencies are those produced by the verbal community in the process of establishing self-awareness. Any procedure which breaks down the literal quality of rules will tend to enhance the salience of this second type of contingency-shaped behavior.

Consider the "concentrative meditation" characteristic of, for example, Transcendental Meditation, in which a mantra is repeated over and over again. As any intrinsic meaning in the content of the mantra collapses (by repetition and, perhaps, satiation) what is left is more context than content. In other types of meditation, more characteristic of the Buddhist tradition, a dispassionate observation of spontaneous thoughts is encouraged. In this case, rules appear but are not reacted to in any way—what might be thought of as a kind of extinction procedure for control by the literality of self-talk. Other examples can be given. Monks enter monasteries where talk is eliminated or greatly restricted. Other traditions encourage repeated rhythmic chanting. In no form of meditation, as that term is usually used, does the meditator engage in discursive, analytical thought (Deikman, 1982). Said in another way, none of these traditions encourage the individual to react to the qualities of terms established by their participation in equivalence classes, such as "meaning," "logic," or "reference." What is common to all these traditions is the selection of procedures that might weaken the literal quality and thus the rule-control exerted by self-talk while enhancing the salience of you-as-context.

It is remarkable how common this move to create a distinction between content and context is within psychotherapy. Beck has his "distancing" (Hollon & Beck, 1979), for example, and even Freud asked clients to adopt an attitude of "quiet, unreflecting self-observation" (in Strachey, 1964, p. 287). Thus, although the language differs greatly, Western psychotherapeutic thought has been guided (often not deliberately) by the content/context distinction.

Language has been said to have produced a "loss of innocence" in humankind. The story of Adam and Eve is perhaps a reflection of this thought. Spirituality is said by some to reestablish a kind of "experienced innocence." Like the Zen koan that asks "Does a dog have Buddha-nature?" we find that we cannot really go back, but that spirituality (you-as-context) offers one possible solution to the dilemma. Through a second type of contingency-shaped behavior, it may weaken automatic rule-control and allow the direct contingencies themselves to take more control. As one Eastern monk puts it, "When I am hungry, I eat; when I am tired, I sleep."

In summary, then, a behaviorally sensible interpretation of spirituality suggests not only a source, but also possible maintaining contingencies for a matter/ spirit distinction. It is possible to make an argument that in these perilous times we are even more in need of a kind of spirituality that will allow our behavior to come under more effective control by the direct contingencies. It is ironic, but science and materialism may provide a good rationale for the functional utility of aspects of the dualism it seeks to supplant.

NOTES

1 Hineline (1980) and others have warned that it is dangerous to view behavior as a thing. It is better considered as a verb than a noun. For our purposes, however, things are events that allow us to see that they are "this" and "not that." Running is not talking, for example, and in this sense even verbs are things. In general use, however, I would agree strongly with Hineline's analysis.

2 This distinction is crucial to the procedure known as the est training. Persons who have taken this training will recognize the intellectual debt the present argument owes to it, and I would like formally to acknowledge that debt.

3 This statement, and to some degree this entire paper, might be thought by some to be sacrilegious. It is not my interest, however, to say literally that God or spirit in a religious sense does not exist independent of humankind. To the contrary, God could have created the very mechanisms I am describing that make spirituality knowable. The paper is only meant to talk about spirituality within the game we call science.

REFERENCES

Baron, A., & Galizio, M. (1983). Instructional control of human operant behavior. *The Psychological Record, J3*, 495–520.

Deikman, A.J. (1982). *The observing self: Mysticism and psychotherapy*. Boston: Beacon Press.

Hayes, S. C. (1987). A contextual approach to therapeutic change. In N. Jacobson (Ed.), *Cognitive and behavioral therapists in clinical practice* (pp. 327–387). New York: Guilford.

Hayes, S. C. (Ed.). (1989). *Rule-governed behavior: Cognition, contingencies, and instructional control.* New York: Plenum.

Hayes, S.C., Brownstein, A.J., Zettle, R.D., Rosenfarb, I., & Korn, Z. (1986). Rule-governed behavior and sensitivity to changing consequences of responding. *Journal of Experimental Analysis of Behavior*, 45, 237–256.

Hayes, S. C., Greenway, D., Brownstein, A.J., Haas, J., Russell, F., Squittiere. D.C., Rosenfarb, I., Zettle, R.D., Herbert, J.D., Herbert. D.L., Meinhold, P., & Thompson, S.K. (1984, May). *Rules, multiples schedules, and extinction.* Paper presented at the Association for Behavior Analysis, Nashville.

Hayes, S.C., Korn, Z., Zettle, R.D., Rosenfarb, I., & Cooper. L. (1982, November). *Rule-governed behavior and cognitive behavior therapy: The effects of comprehensive distancing on pain tolerance.* Paper presented at the meeting of the Association for Advancement of Behavior Therapy, Los Angeles.

Hayes, S.C., & Maley, R.F. (1977). Coercion: Legal and behavioral issues. *Behaviorism, 5*, 95–97.
Hineline, P. (1980). The language of behavior analysis: Its community, its functions, and its limitations. *Behaviorism. 8*, 67–85.
Holton, S.D., & Beck, A.T. (1979). Cognitive therapy of depression. In P.C. Kendall & S.D. Hollon (Eds.), *Cognitive-behavioral interventions: Therapy, research, and procedures* (pp. 153–204). New York: Academic Press.
Matthews, B.A., Shimoff, E., Catania, A.C., & Sagvolden, T. (1977). Uninstructed human responding: Sensitivity to ratio and interval contingencies. *Journal of the Experimental Analysis of Behavior*, 27, 453–467.
Olson, T.W., & Hayes, S.C. (1984, May). *Effect of rule-specificity on sensitivity to changing contingencies.* Paper presented at the meeting of the Association for Behavior Analysis, Nashville.
Schoenfeld, W.N. (1979, September). *Religion and human behavior.* Invited address at the meeting of the American Psychological Association, New York.
Shimoff, E., Catania, A.C., & Matthews, B.A. (1981). Uninstructed human responding: Responsivity of low-rate performance to schedule contingencies. *Journal of the Experimental Analysis of Behavior, 36*, 207–220.
Sidman, M. (1971). Reading and auditory-visual equivalences. *Journal of Speech and Hearing Research*, 14, 5–13.
Sidman, M., & Cresson, O., Jr. (1973). Reading and cross-modal transfer of stimulus equivalences in severe retardation. *American Journal of Mental Deficiency*, 77, 515–523.
Skinner, B. F. (1945). The operational analysis of psychological terms. *Psychological Review, 52*, 270–277.
Skinner, B. F. (1953). *Science and human behavior.* New York: MacMillan.
Skinner, B. F. (1974). *About behaviorism.* New York: Knopf.
Strachey, J. (Ed). (1964). *77th standard edition of the complete psychological works of Sigmund Freud.* Vol 16. London: Hogarth Press.

ARTICLE 4

FINDING THE PHILOSOPHICAL CORE

A Review of Stephen C. Pepper's *World Hypotheses*

From Hayes, S.C., Hayes, L.J., & Reese, H.W. (1988). *Journal of the Experimental Analysis of Behavior, 50*, 97–111.

Behavior analysis has always had significant conflicts with other psychological perspectives. At their fundamental level, these conflicts are often philosophical, concerning such issues as the nature of the human and the purposes of science. Why are *these* the conflicts? What, if anything, can we do about them? Can we resolve them? Can we avoid them altogether by simply abandoning philosophy?

To answer these questions, we must be clear about the philosophy underlying behavior analysis compared to those of other perspectives. To be clear is difficult, however, because the assumptions and postulates of the position are not deliberately and unambiguously laid down. Fundamental assumptions, specific theories, and historical accidents are too often discussed concurrently and without adequate differentiation in behavior analytic expositions. Skinner's philosophical writings are especially prone to this difficulty, perhaps because he is so extensively involved with so many nonphilosophical aspects of the field.

In 1942 Stephen C. Pepper, a philosopher and aestheticist, published *World Hypotheses: A Study in Evidence*. His central insight was that philosophical systems cluster around a few core models, or "world hypotheses," drawn from common sense.

To make Pepper's position understandable, we must summarize some parts of the book fairly extensively. To show its value for a field he never analyzed, we must interpret it and extend it. Our purpose is not to promote the use of Pepper's conceptual categories per se; it is to use them to illuminate the conceptual categories of modern behavior analysis and of competing psychological systems.

THE NATURE OF WORLD HYPOTHESES

A world hypothesis is a model of the universe of observations and inferences. World hypotheses differ in scope (i.e., the range of events incorporated) and precision (i.e., the fewness of alternative interpretations made of the events incorporated), and their adequacy is a matter of the degree to which each obtains. Ideally, a world view has unlimited scope and is so precise that it permits one and only one interpretation of every event. In practice, all reasonably adequate current world views fall short of this ideal. Scope and precision tend to be inversely related: A model that specifies precisely how to interpret a given event will tend not to incorporate as many events as a model that permits viewing a given event in a number of different ways.

Pepper argued that each world hypothesis is autonomous. As an attempt to provide a complete view of the world, each world hypothesis creates its own field of play. Within that field of play "competing" world views can be interpreted but cannot compete directly. This argument anticipates the similar views of Kuhn (1962) among others (there are good reasons to believe that many of Kuhn ideas were derived from Pepper's work; Efron, 1980) and has several implications. First, using the categories of one world view to analyze and criticize another is illegitimate and inherently useless. Second, no world hypothesis can be strengthened by revealing shortcomings in another. The weakness of one world view in no way implies strength in another. Third, eclecticism, if it involves combinations of distinct world hypotheses, is inherently confusing. Each world hypothesis entails a different set of conceptual categories, many of which are mutually contradictory across different world hypotheses. No coherent combination of currently popular world views seems likely and none has yet succeeded. This does not mean that forms of integration are not possible, but if Pepper was correct, successful integration can come only by combinations based on yet another coherent world hypothesis. A single exception exists in strategic integrations of world views subordinated to a single world view. As discussed later, such an integration is possible in only one of the relatively adequate world views.

According to Pepper, world hypotheses are derived from "root metaphors." A root metaphor is a commonsense conceptualization of a domain, in accordance with which categorical concepts have been constructed. The root metaphor structures an understanding of the technical categories. A technical construct sustaining no conceptual contact with its underlying metaphor becomes empty and meaningless.

THE RELATIVELY ADEQUATE WORLD VIEWS

Pepper identified four relatively adequate current world hypotheses: mechanism, formism, organicism, and contextualism. Mechanism and formism are analytic: The whole is reducible to its parts. The parts are basic, the whole derived. Organicism and contextualism are synthetic: The whole is basic, the parts derived. Formism and contextualism are dispersive: Facts are related when they are found to be so, not by assumption. Chance, therefore, is not denied in these hypotheses. Mechanism and organicism are integrative: facts are related by assumption and order is categorical. As such, chance is denied. Dispersive world views tend to be higher in scope than in precision; integrative world hypotheses tend to be higher in precision than in scope.

Describing psychological systems in Pepper's terms organizes them into coordinated sets of related propositions and concerns. The likely conflicts between particular psychological systems may then be derived, and solutions to these conflicts proposed. For this reason, examining each of Pepper's four relatively adequate world views seems potentially worthwhile to an analysis of psychological systems.

Mechanism

The root metaphor of mechanism is the machine. Any commonsense machine is composed of discrete parts related to other parts in some systematic way. Relations among the parts do not change the nature of the parts, however, as the parts exist independently of those relations. Further, in any commonsense machine, some sort of force or energy is exerted on or transmitted through the system to produce predictable outcomes.

A simple example is the lever. A lever is composed of two discrete and independent parts—a lever and a fulcrum. When they are related in a particular way (e.g., the lever is placed on the fulcrum), a force exerted on one end of the lever produces a predicable effect at the other end according to the amount of force, length of the lever, placement of the fulcrum, and so on. In more complicated machines, the history of forces applied may also be relevant to the operation of the machine. In this context, history means that one part may not function until other parts have functioned, or that various parts have worn down. For example, a clock does not strike until the spring controlling the hour hand has been wound and has operated for a predetermined period of time.

According to the world hypothesis of mechanism, the entire universe is like a machine. Different machines yield different variants of mechanism. The hydraulic statuary of the Middle Ages leads to one theory, the computer model leads to another. Nonetheless, the key elements of commonsense machines and their means of operation are always present.

The machine metaphor extends to the knower as well as the known. The knower relates to the world by producing an internal copy of it, through mechanical transformation. This epistemological stance preserves both the knower and the known intact and basically unchanged by their relation—a requirement of mechanism. In some versions of mechanism, the internal copy is "mental"; in others it is "physiological." Regardless, the knower knows a copy of the world, not the world itself. Truth is a matter of how well the copy corresponds to the world, as evaluated by corroboration among independent knowers. Corroboration is required because the correspondence between the copy and the world cannot be observed directly.

Correspondence between what we say about the world and what we see in it is relatively trivial when the material described is immediately present. Correspondence of this limited kind is not adequate for the mechanist for several reasons. The mechanist's goal is to discover the parts and the relations among parts of the existent machine. Because mechanism is integrative, all the parts are assumed to fit together. Order is categorical. Thus, mechanists do not simply describe parts in the commonsense world; rather, they seek to discover the true nature of a given event by specifying what kind of part it really is and by placing it properly in the machine. Such a goal is aided by an *a priori* model or theory. Scientists cannot use the correspondence between a verbal construction of the machine and the facts as a test of the adequacy of the construction if the very same facts serve both as the source of the construction and as the means of its verification. Truth is best established by examining the correspondence between the verbal construction and a variety of new facts implied by the construction. In line with the integrative quality of mechanism, the more derived and indirect these predictions are, the better (Ericcson & Simon, 1984). Hypothetico-deductive research methodology exemplifies this logic and many mechanists gravitate toward it.

Formism

The root metaphor of formism is similarity. The kind of similarity implied here is the recurrence of recognizable forms: blades of grass, sheets of paper, rows of donuts, or the like. The position of immanent formism (one of two major variants) is as follows. The perception of any event involves contact with two aspects of that event—character and particularity—that are absolutely distinct but cannot be experienced independently. Character refers to the qualities and relations that are tied to a given object: This donut has the qualities of being soft, warm, and sticky; it has the relation of side-by-sidedness with the other donuts in this row. Theoretically, a given object may have an infinite number of characters.

A given character may occur in an infinite number of particulars. Still, this donut is this donut and no other. This donut is the particularization of a character, as well as the characterization of a particular. The donut involves the participation of one with the other.

A collection, or "class," of particulars participating in one or more characters is another categorical concept in formism. "Gorilla," for example, is neither a particular event, nor a character, nor a participation. It is all three together.

Certain characters that participate in a particular object lead us to identify that object as "gorilla." Each other object that is characterized in the same way is also a "gorilla," and all these objects considered together are the class "gorilla."

Systematic organizations of facts are not assumed by formists; hence principles of operation (such as "force") are not required to explain them. Indeed, if all facts were integrated by a set of formistic principles, then those facts would necessarily form a system (the integration itself) and formism would begin to have the character of mechanism. A causal law in formism is no more than a bridge from one set of characterized particulars to another. It is a form.

The truth criterion of formism, like that of mechanism, is correspondence. In formism, however, the simpler sense of this criterion (correspondence however derived) is adequate given its dispersive quality.

Organicism

The root metaphor of organicism is the process of organic development, as in living, growing, organic systems. In such systems, change is given and stability is to be explained. Versions of developmentalism that rely on stage models reflect this philosophy. For example, a person is assumed to move from one stage of growth to another in an orderly way. To explain the person's current stage we must explain the orderliness of changes from stage to stage. In other words, we must explain how the rules of change operate, assuming that change occurs according to rules of change that are themselves unchanging (Reese & Overton, 1970). The organicist notes "the steps involved in the organic process and . . . the principle features in the organic structure ultimately achieved" (Pepper, 1942, p. 281).

In organicism, the whole is not a synthesis of parts; the whole is basic, the parts meaningless except in the context of the whole. The organicist embraces teleology: "The structure achieved or realized is always the ideal aimed at by the progressive steps of the process" (Pepper, 1942, p. 281).

The truth criterion of organicism is coherence. When a network of interrelated facts converges on a conclusion, the coherence of this network renders this conclusion "true." All contradictions of understanding originate in incomplete knowledge of the whole organic process. When the whole is known, the contradictions are removed and the "organic whole . . . is found to have been implicit in the fragments" (Pepper, 1942, p. 283).

Epistemologically, organicists adopt constructivism. The knower actively construes the world—it is neither known directly nor mechanically transformed.

Contextualism

Contextualism is the most important world view for our purposes, so we here describe Pepper's analysis of contextualism in more detail. The root metaphor of contextualism is the ongoing act in context. Another term might be the historical act, but not as a dead description of a thing done. It is doing as it is being done, as in hunting, shopping, or making love.

Two fundamental categories of contextualism are "quality" and "texture." *Quality* is the experienced nature of an act; *texture* is the details and relations that make up its quality. In contextualism, even these categories might change (if they do) because nothing is final or ultimate about our knowledge of the world—not even that the world will stay the same. In our present epoch, however, all events have quality and texture.

Each category is defined in terms of other categories. Quality, for example, is made up of "spread" and "fusion." *Spread* refers to the extended present of an act in context. The past and future of an act exist in the ongoing act. The act spreads, as we say, both backward and forward.

Fusion refers to the integration of the textural details of a given event. Lemonade has the texture of water, lemons, and sugar. The quality of lemonade is a fusion of these distinct ingredients—so thoroughly so that the ingredients are difficult to analyze out. Cooking a meal is composed of many textural elements (e.g., picking up a pot, selecting ingredients, mixing the ingredients), all of which may be fused in the overall quality of cooking the meal. If one becomes more interested in the act of picking up the pot than in the act of cooking a meal, the fusion of the larger act dissolves. Picking up the pot becomes the experienced quality.

Texture is defined in terms of other categories, namely, "strands," "context," and "reference." *Strands* are the interconnections among the details of an act that directly contribute to its quality. *Context* is made up of the interconnections among strands, contributing indirectly to the quality of a given act. The two cannot be fully distinguished because each contributes to the nature of the other. As an example, a cook prepares a dessert. The details and relations of this act, that is, its texture, may be arranged in strands of various sorts. This act could comprise the strand we might call "entertaining a dinner guest," occurring in a context of the guest. It could be the strand we call "the performance of the cook" occurring in a context of other meals prepared by the cook. It could be the strand of "mixing in the eggs," occurring in a context of breaking the eggs, holding the bowl, and so on. The quality of the act in each case emerges in the interaction of the strand and its context.

The third category of texture, *reference*, is simply strands more intimately considered. Reference concerns the temporal relations or interconnections among the details of an act, specifically their point of initiation, course, and satisfaction. The concept of reference is worthy of note because it pertains to issues of similarity and novelty as contextualistically interpreted. Similarity, for example, is not a feature of events from a contextualistic standpoint: No two events in the world are inherently similar. Rather, similarity is an attribution made when different initiations converge on one satisfaction. Planting a garden and going to a restaurant, though formally dissimilar, are regarded as similar to the extent that they produce the same outcome, namely, sustenance.

The quality of an act is necessarily threatened by examining its texture because any given strand of that texture might be experienced as a quality in its own right. This circumstance is a consequence of the dispersive character of contextualism: The parts, being derived, may be derived in any number of ways. As such, the texture of this new quality might be examined, one of its strands experienced as a quality, and so on. Were analysis made for its own sake nothing would prevent this process from continuing ad infinitum. For the contextualist, however, analysis is always for some purpose.

The truth criterion of contextualism is successful working. Analyses are true only in terms of the accomplishment of particular goals. No postulational provision is made for the evaluation of the goals themselves. Truth may thus exist with regard to relatively trivial goals. This pragmatic view of truth is quite radically applied: "The quality of blowing your nose is just as cosmic and ultimate as Newton's writing down his gravitational formula. The fact that his formula is much more useful to many more people doesn't make it any more real" (Pepper, 1942, p. 251).

A powerful implication of this truth criterion is that on contextualistic grounds one can adopt the analytic strategy of an alternative world view in a given situation if doing so is useful toward some end. For example, a philosophical contextualist might adopt a mechanistic theory because it is useful in identifying ways of "controlling" behavior. Strategic integration of this sort does not violate Pepper's warning against the destructive effects of eclecticism, because no integration of the underlying root metaphors is implied. The machine metaphor is merely used in the service of a contextualistic agenda; and the truth of the analysis based on that usage is evaluated against a successful working criterion.

IMPLICATIONS FOR BEHAVIOR ANALYSIS

Pepper did not write *World Hypotheses* for psychologists, or even for scientists in general. Thus, the correspondence between his world views and philosophies underlying science is only approximate. Nevertheless, particular approaches to psychology do seem often to have the predominant character of one or another of Pepper's four relatively adequate world views.

Behavior Analysis as a Contextualistic System

The predominant character of behavior analysis, or at least what is central and distinctive about behavior analysis, is contextualistic. Among the particularly contextualistic features of behavior analysis are the concept of the operant, the criterion for truth or adequacy, the role of the scientist in scientific analysis, and the possibility of novelty.

The Concept of the Operant. Several characteristics of the operant correspond closely to the categorical concepts of contextualism. An operant is defined as a relation among behavior and stimulus events. The events participating in an operant cannot usefully be examined independently because their nature depends on their relations to the other participants. Similarly, for a contextualist, an act out of context is not an act, categorically speaking: "It is not an act conceived as alone or cut off that we mean; it is an act in and with its setting" (Pepper, 1942, p. 232).

Because context must be included in the analysis of an act, contextualists analyzing an act quickly find themselves outside the confines of the original event of interest (the act) and in the domain of other events (the context). "The quality of an event is the fused qualities of its strands, and the qualities of its strands come partly out of its context, and there we are outside of the event" (Pepper, 1942, p. 249). The parallels to behavior analysis are obvious. For example, "We cannot account for the behavior of any system while staying wholly inside it; eventually we must turn to forces operating upon the organism from without" (Skinner, 1953, p. 35).

Membership in an operant class in no way depends on the formal characteristics of the behavior involved. Responses share membership in an operant to the extent that they produce common effects on the environment: "The consequences define the properties with respect to which responses are called similar" (Skinner, 1953, p. 65). This type of classification corresponds precisely to the contextualistic conception of similarity as derived from "convergence of action on a single effect" (Pepper, 1942, p. 255).

An operant has no fixed boundaries. We might speak of the larger operant as a composition of smaller elements (in Pepper's terms, strands of texture), but speaking in this way does not exclude examining the elements as operants in their own right. Similarly, any aspect of a strand of texture may be examined and consequently become the quality of interest.

Finally, the behavior analytic view of behavior emphasizes the verb-like quality of all behavioral interactions (e.g., Hineline, 1980). This emphasis precisely parallels the root metaphor of contextualism.

The Criterion for Truth or Adequacy. As Pepper noted, "The analysis of an event consists in the exhibition of its texture, and the exhibition of its texture is the discrimination of its strands, and the full discrimination of its strands is the exhibition of other textures . . . and so on from event to event as long as we wish to go, which would be forever or until we got tired" (Pepper, 1942, p. 249). What saves contextualism from being paralyzed by its fluidity is its criterion for the adequacy of analysis, namely, successful working. Successful working always implies success with regard to the accomplishment of some potentially attainable goal. For this reason, the contextualist rather disparages analysis for analysis's sake. "Serious analysis for [the contextualist] is always either directly or indirectly practical. . . . If from one texture you wish to get to another, then analysis has an end, and a direction, and some strands have relevancy to this end and others do not, and . . . the enterprise becomes important in reference to the end" (Pepper, 1942, pp. 250–251). Likewise, Skinner commented: "It is true that we could trace human behavior not only to the physical conditions which shape and maintain it but also to the causes of those conditions and the causes of those causes, almost ad infinitum" but we need take analysis only to the point at which "effective action can be taken" (Skinner, 1974, p. 210). That point is the manipulable environment, because only there may successful working toward the behavior analytic goals of prediction and control be achieved and evaluated (Hayes & Brownstein, 1986).

Several behavior analytic positions are understandable in these terms. For example, behavior analysts object to analyzing private events as causes because an event "is useless in the control of behavior unless we can manipulate it" (Skinner, 1953, p. 34). Searching for private causes is thus a "tiresome and exhausting digression" (Skinner, 1953, p. 35) when considered in terms of the purposes of analysis.

The commitment of behavior analysis to successful working as a truth criterion is also demonstrated by repeated appeals to it in criticizing other positions. For example: "The objection to the inner workings of the mind is not that they are not open to inspection but that *they have stood in the way of the inspection of more important things*" (Skinner, 1974, p. 165, emphasis added), and "mentalism has obscured the environmental antecedents which would have led to a much more *effective* analysis" (Skinner, 1974, p. 165, emphasis added). Many such examples are available in the writings of Skinner and other behavior analysts. Skinner in particular has been explicit about this truth criterion: "[Scientific knowledge] is a corpus of rules for effective action, and there is a special sense in which it could be 'true' if it yields the most effective action possible. . . . [A] proposition is 'true' to the extent that with its help the listener responds effectively to the situation it describes" (Skinner, 1974, p. 235).

As previously mentioned, a contextualist can make use of the categorical structures of other world views without becoming philosophically eclectic. Behavior analysts have done just that on occasion, although very likely without full awareness, and much to the confusion of others. For example, Skinner has talked of humans as complex machines: "We have discovered more about how the living organism works and are better able to see its machine-like properties" (Skinner, 1953, p. 47). He did not become a mechanist thereby, because his world view and the truth criterion it entails are contextualistic, not mechanistic. He merely borrowed mechanistic models when doing so seemed useful.

The Role of the Scientist in Scientific Analysis. The importance of a scientific analysis of the behavior of the scientist has long been recognized within behavior analysis (Kantor, 1938; Skinner, 1945). Behavior analysts believe that scientists cannot stand apart from the world under analysis; they are, rather, a part of that world. Because analysis is itself an act in context "the contextualist . . . does not make any exceptions to his analysis of analysis, not even for that analysis itself" (Pepper, 1942, p. 252). The value of any analysis, even of contextualism itself, is to be determined by its usefulness in the accomplishment of some explicit purpose.

Behavior analysts acknowledge the fact that science is, among other things, the action of scientists—action meaningful only by reference to its context. Accordingly, science is not assumed by behavior analysts to be directed toward the attainment of ultimate knowledge. Ultimate knowledge is, by definition, context-free. As Kantor (1953, pp. 9–25) pointed out, science is the work of particular individuals working at particular times in particular places with particular materials for particular purposes. The products of scientists' actions bear the unavoidable stamp of those particulars and cannot thereby be presumed to characterize the universe. Pepper summarized the contextualistic view of science this way: "[Scientific] schemes, such as maps, diagrams, formulas, functional equations, and symbolic systems . . . have been developed on the basis of past social experience, and their status is a good deal like that of a social institution. . . . They constitute what is called 'the science' of a period, and change from period to period" (Pepper, 1942, p. 267).

The Possibility of Novelty. A central tenet of contextualism is the possibility of novelty. At first glance, this position seems to disqualify contextualism as a scientific philosophy. The position, however, is not that events *will* be novel, only that they *may* be. If order be found, so be it. The only evidence for true novelty, that is, the utterly uncaused event, is "an absence of any evidence to the contrary" (Pepper, 1942, p. 260); and by this criterion, true novelty has never been demonstrated. As far as successful working is concerned, then, the possibility of true novelty can be ignored: It makes no difference (until and unless it does.)

This aspect of contextualism does not seem to have obvious parallels in behavior analysis. Skinner, for example, has noted that while we may not be able to prove that behavior is "fully determined," the evidence points in this direction (Skinner, 1974, p. 189). The contextualistic concept of novelty does indeed show up in behavior analysis, though. Operant behavior is said to be "emitted," not "elicited." Its emission is "occasioned" by certain antecedent events, not "caused" by those events in the mechanistic sense of direct production. From a behavior analytic standpoint, prediction and control pertain not to instances but to classes of behavior. Consequently, no attempt need be made to predict specific instances of an operant at specific times (Skinner, 1938, pp. 10–12, although see Skinner, 1957, p. 28).

Mechanistic Elements of Behavior Analysis

Nonfunctional Definitions. To a contextualist, acts and their context are inseverable. The contextualist who loses sight of this interdependence loses contact with the quality of an act, which ultimately leads to the dissolution of the contextualistic perspective: "To think of contexts as existing in addition to or apart from practices is like imagining smiles alongside or beside faces" (Bhaskar, 1983, p. 87). Skinner has emphasized a similar point: "Neither [stimulus nor response] may be defined as to its essential properties without the other" (Skinner, 1938, p. 9).

The mechanist does not deny the behavior of the whole, but asserts that it is derivable from the behavior of the parts. The meaning of a part is its role in the behavior of the whole. This role can change as the whole changes. For example, the role of a cogwheel depends on whether it is part of a clock or being used as a fulcrum. A cogwheel is a cogwheel in either case, but the meaning of the part is defined by its potential functions in relation to the potential functions of the other parts of the whole.

Functional definitions of behavior can thus be incorporated into either world view. For the contextualist, they are incorporated as an extension of the basic root metaphor; for the mechanist, as a reference to the functions established among the parts of the machine.

Nonfunctional definitions of behavior can be readily incorporated into mechanism as a description of the parts themselves. For contextualists, however, nonfunctional definitions present more of a problem.

Consider the following nonfunctional definition of behavior: Behavior is muscle movements and glandular secretions. The root metaphor of contextualism is an act in context. Accordingly, the experienced quality of an act is dependent upon context. Consequently, a contextualist would be hard pressed to abide by the above definition of behavior without losing contact with the contextualistic root metaphor.

Such nonfunctional definitions occasionally show up in behavior analytic writing. To the extent that they reflect mechanistic thinking, they threaten the philosophical consistency of behavior analysis.

Reductionism. Reductionism applied to psychology holds that psychological events are reducible to neural or other biological events. This position is incompatible with contextualism, not because biological events are of no concern but because in reductionism the parts are primary and the whole derived.

In *Behavior of Organisms*, Skinner (1938, pp. 418–432) argued against the reduction of psychology to neural events, asserting the legitimacy of a science of behavior in its own right. This position is contextualistically sensible. If an analysis works at the level of the whole organism interacting in and with a context, then it works. Analyses at the level of parts of the organism interacting with other parts are "truer" than other analyses only in terms of particular goals.

Nevertheless, many behaviorists embrace biological reductionism. For example, some argue *a priori* that thoughts or feelings are "really" activities of the nervous system. Skinner himself has said: "(The physiologist of the future) will be able to show us how an organism is changed when exposed to contingencies of reinforcement" (Skinner, 1974, p. 215). If he meant that physiologists may someday be able to give psychologists the "real" explanation of reinforcement, then the statement is incompatible with contextualism, because it is based on the primacy of parts over wholes.

This does not mean that reductionism is always mechanistic, nor that all mechanists are reductionists. The assumption that the whole is reducible to its parts is categorical in mechanism; but the assumption that psychology is (in principle) reducible to biology, for example, is not required. A mechanical conception of thinking based on the metaphor of the brain as computer does not obligate a concern with neurology.

In contextualism, parts are abstractions, and therefore reduction of some parts to other parts is merely an analytic, conceptual tool. Reductionism of this kind does not imply that the whole is literally reducible to the parts because the parts do not exist independent of analysis. Reducing parts to other parts is a fiction that may be useful in a given instance. Thus, a contextualist might suggest a biological explanation for a psychological event if it is useful in understanding the whole. Mechanists may say similar things, but believe that the parts are real—the whole is the fiction. For the mechanist, the different scientific domains are hierarchically related and *must* fit together in an integrated and complete system of knowledge. Given this assumption, the reduction of one domain to another *is* the reduction of the whole to its fundamental parts (e.g., Bugelski, 1973, p. 62), and is thus mechanistic.

Causality. Some psychologists (e.g., Howard & Conway, 1987; Sarbin, 1986) believe that concern for efficient causality is mechanistic: "Efficient causality description is the goal for scientists working with one or another paradigm within the mechanist world view. Behaviorism and radical empiricism exemplify psychological and philosophical movements committed to this world view" (Sarbin, 1986, p. 6). Based on this belief and the behavior analytic adoption of efficient causality, some have concluded that behavior analysis is mechanistic (e.g., Howard & Conway, 1987).

Whether the behavior analytic treatment of causality is mechanistic depends on the purposes of this treatment and the criteria by which truth is determined. If one's goals are prediction and control, as are Skinner's, calling something a cause may be understood to mean that the analytic purposes of the scientist have been accomplished: prediction and control have been achieved. Such a pragmatic interest in efficient causality does not imply mechanism.

Mechanists are interested in the primary parts of a system, their relations, and the forces that make them operate. An interest in efficient causality may lead one to say that "*this* caused *that*." Such a causal statement is mechanistic only if it is an extension from a system of parts, relations, and forces.

Causal talk may carry certain philosophical assumptions with it, however, especially for those who have not carefully articulated their philosophical assumptions. "*This* caused *that*" may lead to the view that *this* and *that* are discrete parts that exist independently of their relation, or of the scientist's act of analyzing the whole into parts. The construction of independent parts invites commentary as to the "force" by which this caused that. Perhaps some contextualists embrace only descriptive forms of science (e.g., Rosnow & Georgoudi, 1986b) in an effort to avoid the seductive effects of causal analyses. If such seduction is likely, then behavior analysts must be especially aware of their philosophical assumptions if they are to retain their contextualistic stance.

Conflicts Between Behavior Analysis and Other Psychological Systems

According to Pepper, world views are orthogonal to each other and therefore cannot conflict. Apparent conflicts are really pseudoconflicts, wherein criticisms of one world view are made in terms of the categorical concepts of another. These kinds of conflicts are illegitimate and cannot be resolved; they can only be recognized. Some of the most persistent conflicts between behavior analysis and other psychological systems seem to fit this pattern.

Arguments Between Contextualists and Mechanists. When contextualists argue against mechanism, they are likely to question the "thingness" of the pieces of the mechanistic machine. They might ask: Are these things really concrete things? Can they really be known in isolation and is their nature really not changed by virtue of the relations into which they enter? Along these lines, a contextualist might attempt to show that the same pieces of the machine function differently given other histories or other contexts. To this challenge, a mechanist is likely to argue that historical and contextual arrangements of this sort change only the operation of the system, not the nature of its parts. For example, "The machine is built to execute an instruction only when it stands in a particular sort of relation to that instruction. . . . In human psychology, similarly, we assume that people are so constituted" (Stabler, 1984, p. 604). Contextualists, cognizant also of the quality of events and not just their textural details, might argue further that mechanistic theoretical structures prevent scientists from experiencing the world as it truly exists. Mechanists might answer that what is real or true is decided on other criteria. Finally, contextualists might attack whatever force is invoked to explain the operation of the machine, arguing that the force is inferred from the events it "explains" and is, thus, an instance of reification. From a mechanistic standpoint, however, a driving force of some sort is *necessary*; it is not a matter that depends on observation.

For their part, mechanists might attack contextualistic approaches on the grounds that they are vague and imprecise. The flexibility of possible units of analysis across various situations might be viewed as undisciplined thinking. Making a place for randomness might be seen as justifying ignorance. A mechanist might argue that contextualists are confused about the purposes of science and have no theory, at least no testable one. The post hoc quality of some contextualistic analyses might be cited to illustrate this inadequacy.

Most especially, mechanists might be disturbed by the pragmatic truth criterion contextualists invoke, asserting that contextualists are merely technicians, more interested in changing events than understanding them.

The arguments between behavior analysts and other positions seem to fit the pattern just described. For example, stimulus-response learning theory is a classic example of mechanism within psychology. It has all the components of a mechanistic system: stable pieces (e.g., stimulus objects), elaborate models of the structural relations of these pieces (e.g. Hull's *Behavior System*), and forces (e.g., drives) to activate the operation of the machine. Truth is assessed by correspondence.

Behavior analysts have criticized this stimulus-response formulation, adopting, instead, the concept of the operant and an emphasis on selection by consequences (Skinner, 1974, pp. 222–225). The specific objections to stimulus-response learning theory are exactly what might be expected were the argument made by contextualists against mechanism. The stability of the elements in stimulus-response theory was challenged by showing contextual limits on their application. The need for such elements was challenged by providing explanations derived more directly from the relations among contextual and behavioral events. The various forces were viewed as mere reification. The theorizing was challenged on the grounds that it takes the scientist away from the real world and amounts to vacant construction (e.g., Skinner, 1950).

More recent arguments of behaviorists against cognitive psychology can be seen as arguments of contextualists against mechanism. Not all cognitive theorizing is mechanistic (Piaget was an organicist, for example), but the kind built on computer models and computer simulation (e.g., Ericcson & Simon, 1984) is clearly so. Jenkins tried to develop cognitivism as a contextualistic position (1974) but without great success because the categorical concepts were simply borrowed from Pepper, without the development of an adequate psychological system per se. As with stimulus-response theory, mechanistic cognitivists are criticized by behavior analysts as building unnecessary theories: "We can avoid hypothetico-deductive methods . . . by formulating the data without reference to cognitive processes, mental apparatuses, or traits" (Skinner, 1984a, p. 523). The stability of their categories is challenged. Explanations in terms of context are offered.

For their part, many cognitivists do indeed see behavior analysis as vague and imprecise: "The concepts of 'behavior,' 'response,' and 'reinforcement' appear to be used so broadly that . . . there is hardly anything they do not seem to encompass. Skinner has stretched these notions" (Kochen, 1984, p. 600). Similarly: "Skinner's proposals have a fundamental limitation. They . . . simply are not sufficiently precise" (Scandura, 1984, p. 603). Behavior analysts are also said to have misunderstood the purpose of psychology as a science: "The success of the behaviorist enterprise would leave quite untouched the scientific problem of accounting for how we are capable [of behaving.] . . . Only an account of the machinery within the skin can explain behavior" (Marshall,

1984, p. 637). And, finally, many cognitivists see Skinner more as a technician than as a scientist: "Skinner's emphasis on control is wrong. . . . The emphasis should be on understanding" (Millward, 1984, p. 528).

The nature of the cognitivist's reply to behavioral criticism is also illuminating. Behavior analysts generally criticize mentalism on pragmatic grounds. A typical reply to this criticism is to deny a reliance on immaterial entities and processes: "mental processes are synonymous with brain processes" (Ellis & Hunt, 1983, p. 11). These replies are at times explicitly mechanistic: "Mentalists are neither vitalists nor physiologists, but rather engineers concerned with discovering the type of machine that is man" (Marshall, 1984, p. 637), and "[Behavioral criticisms are irrelevant to] a form of cognitivism that is not teleological but mechanistic" because the "basic analogy—the computer—does not involve purposes but only mechanistically determined programs" (Furedy & Riley, 1984, p. 625).

Arguments Between Contextualists and Organicists. Contextualists have different concerns with organicism. They might view the organicists' reliance on coherence as confusing the personal reactions of the scientist with the actual value of the scientific work. Likewise, the organicists' admission of final causes might be challenged by contextualists, and is likely to yield sputterings about circular reasoning. The embrace of constructivism might be criticized because it ignores the context in which such construction take place. Further, the organicists' explanation of events by an appeal to their orderly change is likely to be regarded a confusion of description with explanation.

The objections behavior analysts have to "developmentalism" show the nature of the last argument quite clearly. Skinner wrote that "developmental schedules are really schedules of changing environments . . . stages are changes in the way in which behavior acts upon and is reinforced by the (primarily social) environment" (Skinner, 1984b, p. 719). From Skinner's perspective, "We need to go beyond mere observation to a study of functional relationships" (Skinner, 1938, p. 8).

Behavior analysts have attempted to reveal the shortcomings of organicism by manipulating contextual variables that accelerate or delay transitions through developmental stages (e.g., accelerating the acquisition of Piaget's object constancy through direct training).

Organicists should be completely undaunted by such data, however, because they presume that organic elements are subject to interference and believe that rejecting final causes is failing to admit the obvious. The operation of a final cause on an acorn inevitably produces an oak tree. If an acorn is eaten by a pig, it is no longer an acorn and the final cause of an acorn cannot operate upon it.

Some organicists attribute to behavior analysts a belief in a passive organism, pushed and pulled by mechanical forces in the environment. Behavior analysts might reply that the "organism is not . . . passive in the sense of submissive" (Skinner, 1984b, p. 719) but such a reply would probably not alter the organicists' conclusion. The pragmatic truth criterion of behavior analysis might be seen as contributing nothing to intellectual coherence and therefore as unimportant to scientific understanding. Behavior analysts' interest in control might lead organicists to view behavior analysis as mechanistic (e.g., Howard & Conway, 1987).

Arguments Between Contextualists and Formists. A contextualist might accuse formists of engaging in analyses that are of no use. What good is mere classification of events or cataloging of relations among them? Does this kind of activity make a difference? If it did, the contextualist might be reassured, but only in that specific instance. Formists do not have practical usefulness as a goal of analysis in general. A contextualist might be concerned that the very ground of similarity, upon which formistic laws are built, is shaky. For the contextualist, similarity is a functional rather than formal affair.

For their part, formists might challenge contextualists on the arbitrariness of their decision as to what makes a difference. What right has a contextualist to proclaim that only relations serving their purposes are worthwhile? Formists might also be baffled by the contextualists' refusal to acknowledge immediately obvious similarities among things. Contextualist might be criticized for constructing similarities on the basis of only one small aspect of the situation.

As an example, some of the work on personality types is formistic. A personality type is identified; its characteristics are explored; and its relation to other personality types is articulated. From a formistic standpoint, the analysis need proceed no further, and often does not. Behavior analysts respond to this research as contextualists might be expected to respond. They question whether the "similar" events are really similar, applying the contextualistic concept of similarity as a test. This point is the core of Skinner's criticism of the "formalistic error" (Skinner, 1969, p. 89). Behaviorists also challenge the usefulness of this kind of research. To a behavior analyst relations among traits of personality cannot, in and of themselves, directly achieve behavior analytic purposes, because to achieve those purposes one must have access to the contextual variables of which the relations are held to be a function (Hayes & Brownstein, 1986).

Chomsky (1986) provides another example. Although he may be viewed as an organicist (Overton, 1984), he may also be categorized as a "transcendent formist." Plato, one of the original transcendent formists, used the idea of norms to explain how persons know so much even though their experiential basis for knowledge is small. Chomsky (1986) has explicitly dealt with one form of what he called "Plato's problem": how persons know so much about language even though their experiential basis for this knowledge is small. Preexisting and nonexperiential norms provide the answer: Language emerges according to a plan or norm housed in a language acquisition device in the "mind/brain," as he calls it (Chomsky, 1986). Underlying similarities in grammar occur as approximations to this norm. Behavior analysts question whether the regularities discerned by Chomsky are true (i.e., functional) regularities.

Dealing With Arguments Across World Views. The list of arguments mentioned above is not exhaustive. Moreover, many of the arguments are shared among world views. For example, organicists are as likely as mechanists to see contextualism as vague and imprecise. All others should agree that contextualists confuse technology with science. Most of this sort of overlap can be predicted from the dispersive and analytic qualities of the various world views. On issues relevant to the primacy of parts versus wholes, for instance, both formists and mechanists will disagree with contextualists.

The philosophical arguments between behavior analysts and other psychologists are pseudoconflicts among world views. Given that arguments of this sort are illegitimate and cannot be resolved, what can we do about them? Pepper suggested three legitimate courses of action, which behavior analysts can take. They can: (a) increase the precision and scope of behavior analysis and make these improvements evident; (b) analyze the precision and scope of other systems, when taken on their own terms and with relevance to their own purposes (but recognizing that if such an analysis reveals weaknesses, the strength of behavior analysis is in no way increased); and (c) clearly articulate the assumptions and purposes of behavior analysis and note the differences in the assumptions made by others. For example, one can quite legitimately describe a pragmatic truth criterion and explain how to proceed if such a truth criterion is adopted; one cannot legitimately insist that it be adopted.

Conflicts Within Behavior Analysis: The Costs of Conceptual Confusion

Scientific work always involves philosophical assumptions that influence the kinds of problems addressed, the methods employed for their solution, and the manner in which findings are interpreted. When properly articulated and organized into a postulational system, these assumptions serve as criteria against which the internal consistency and cross-disciplinary compatibility of a given scientific enterprise may be evaluated. Philosophical assumptions have their sources in cultural circumstances, and like those circumstances, they are not all of one piece. Unfortunately, philosophical assumptions do not cease their influence on scientific work simply because individual investigators are unaware of them. When philosophical assumptions are *not* properly articulated and organized into a postulational system, scientific formulations based on them tend to be inconsistent and confusing (Parrott, 1986).

If behavior analysis rests on an unsystematic mixture of mechanistic and contextualistic postulates, it is in danger of being replaced by more consistent and less confusing psychological systems. Contextualism allows the strategic use of categorical concepts from other world views subordinated to contextualistic criteria. Skinner can be thought of as a contextualistic philosopher who at times uses mechanistic theorizing. Although such strategic mixtures are consistent with contextualism, they carry with them notable hazards.

First, avoiding the philosophical implications of foreign concepts is difficult. The mechanistic elements of behavior analysis, in particular, may be erroneously taken to represent the philosophical basis of behavior analysis. This is extremely dangerous to behavior analysis because, as a mechanistic system, it is not very interesting. The analogy of the computer is far richer and more elaborate, for example. Inevitably, the more elegant form of mechanism will prevail.

Second, borrowing concepts must be compared to the usefulness of developing concepts from within a contextualistic world view. Prematurely using foreign concepts may delay more consistent and effective system building.

Third, strategic use of other world views can degenerate into undisciplined thinking. A mere reference to "successful working" is no justification for intellectual chaos. If foreign concepts are to be used, they must be used deliberately, and compared to the working of alternative domestic concepts.

These hazards may be minimized, if not altogether avoided, if behavior analysts clarify their philosophical assumptions. Pepper's analysis may be helpful for this purpose.

The Natural Allies of Behavior Analysis

If behavior analysis is, in principle, a contextualistic system, who are its natural allies? Many other scientific systems share contextualistic postulates, including some forms of evolutionary biology (e.g., Dawkins, 1982), cultural anthropology (e.g., Harris, 1979), Marxism, ethology, and psychobiology. Yet most contextualists think that behavior analysis is mechanistic; given the subtleties and inconsistencies of behavior analysis this is not difficult to understand.

Sharing the same world view does not mean that different theories will not conflict. Indeed, according to Pepper, all legitimate intellectual conflicts, like all forms of effective collaboration, occur among proponents of the same world view. Advocates of different world views will always either agree to disagree or will see each other as intellectual enemies. Thus, to the extent that behavior analysis is mistaken for a representative of a world view foreign to it, truly productive collaboration with other compatible scientific systems is impossible.

Because contextualism entails no stand on what the goal of analysis ought to be, any potentially attainable goal may be entirely consistent with contextualism. For example, many contextualistic findings are "specific, often taking the form of accounts justified by their coherence" (Fiske, 1988, p. 93). Nonetheless, successful working may be evaluated with respect to some scientific goals more readily than others. Success with respect to the goals articulated by behavior analysts, namely, prediction and control, is readily evaluated, at least in so far as these goals apply to concrete instances. Thus, these goals and contextualism seem especially harmonious (Hayes & Brownstein, 1986). In another sense, however, they are not. A constant threat is that analyses that help achieve these goals will be taken literally. When causes and effects are viewed as preexisting things in the world, the holistic quality of contextualism is threatened, and mechanism is but a short step away.

Other goals could also be completely consistent with a contextualistic world view. A contextualistic system directed toward goals other than prediction and control might appear alien or even hostile to behavior analysis (e.g., Rosnow & Georgoudi, 1986a), but it would be so only in the sense of being a rival. It would be a rival member of the same "family of theories," that is, theories derived from a single world view and therefore comparable with each other on empirical grounds (Reese & Overton, 1970.) The antipathy between psychobiology and behavior analysis may be partially understood in this manner because the behavior analytic goal of control is not embraced by most psychobiologists.

Behavior analysis is a contextualistic system. This conclusion significantly alters our view of what is central to behavior analysis and what is mere historical accident or theoretical preference. For example, when viewed as a contextualistic system, behavior-analytic emphases on functional definitions and a pragmatic truth criterion stand out in high relief. Pepper also provides guidance in difficult areas of system development. For instance, it becomes obvious that causal laws are ways of speaking, not representations of nature.

Behavior analysis is a position with a history of success in achieving its goals, but a position that fails to develop is a position that fades away (Reese, 1986). How can behavior analysis find its way, while retaining the useful qualities that made it what it is? Pepper shows behavior analysts what is truly unusual and important about their position. His book helps put behavior analysts' hands on the tiller of their philosophical vessel. It may steer better from there.

REFERENCES

Bhaskar, R. (1983). Beef, structure, and place: Notes from a critical naturalist perspective. *Journal for the Theory of Social Behaviour, 13*, 81–97.

Bugelski, B.R. (1973). *An introduction to the principles of psychology* (2nd ed.). Indianapolis: Bobbs-Merrill.

Chomsky, N. (1986). *Knowledge of language*. New York: Praeger.

Dawkins, R. (1982). *The extended phenotype*. New York: Freeman.

Efron, A. (1980). Pepper's continuing value. In A. Efron & J. Herold (Ed.), Root metaphor: The live thought of Stephen C. Pepper. *Paunch, Numbers 53–54*, 5–53.

Ellis, H.C., & Hunt, R.R. (1983). *Fundamentals of human memory and cognition* (3rd ed.). Dubuque, IA: Brown.

Ericsson, K.A., & Simon, H.A. (1984). *Protocol analysis: Verbal reports as data.* Cambridge, MA: MIT Press.

Fiske, D.W. (1988). Review of *Contextualism and Understanding in Behavior Science: Implications for Research and Theory.* R.L. Rosnow & M. Georgoudi (Eds.). *American Scientist, 76,* 93.

Furedy, J.J., & Riley, D.M. (1984). Undifferentiated and "mote-beam" percepts in Watsonian-Skinnerian behaviorism. *Behavioral and Brain Sciences, 7,* 625–626.

Harris, M. (1979). *Cultural materialism: The struggle for a science of culture.* New York: Random House.

Hayes, S.C., & Brownstein, A.J. (1986). Mentalism, behavior-behavior relations, and a behavior analytic view of the purposes of science. *The Behavior Analyst, 9,* 175–190.

Hineline, P.N. (1980). The language of behavior analysis: Its community, its functions, and its limitations. *Behaviorism, 8,* 67–85.

Howard, G.S., & Conway, C.G. (1987). The next steps toward a science of agency. *American Psychologist, 42,* 1034–1036.

Jenkins, J.J. (1974). Remember that old theory of memory? Well, forget it. *American Psychologist, 29,* 785–795.

Kantor, J.R. (1938). The nature of psychology as a natural science. *Acta Psychologica, 4,* 1–61.

Kantor, J.R. (1953). *The logic of modern science.* Bloomington, IN: Principia Press.

Kochen, M. (1984). Problem solving as a cognitive process. *Behavioral and Brain Sciences, 7,* 599–600.

Kuhn, T.S. (1962). *The structure of scientific revolutions.* Chicago: University of Chicago Press.

Marshall, J.C. (1984). Mechanism at two thousand. *Behavioral and Brain Sciences, 7,* 637.

Millward, R. (1984). Cognitive science: A different approach to scientific psychology. *Behavioral and Brain Sciences, 7,* 527–529.

Overton, W.F. (1984). World views and their influence on psychological theory and research: Kuhn-Lakatos-Laudan. In H.W. Reese (Ed.), *Advances in child development and behavior* (Vol. 18, pp. 191–226). New York: Academic Press.

Parrott, L.J. (1986). The role of postulation in the analysis of inapparent events. In H.W. Reese & L.J. Parrott (Eds.), *Behavior science: Philosophical, methodological, and empirical advances* (pp. 35–60). Hillsdale, NJ: Erlbaum.

Pepper, S.C. (1942). *World hypotheses: A study in evidence.* Berkeley: University of California Press.

Reese, H.W. (1986). On the theory and practice of behavior analysis. In H.W. Reese & L.J. Parrott (Eds.), *Behavior science: Philosophical, methodological, and empirical advances* (pp. 1–33). Hillsdale, NJ: Erlbaum.

Reese, H.W., & Overton, W.F. (1970). Models of development and theories of development. In L.R. Goulet & P.B. Baltes (Eds.), *Life-span developmental psychology: Research and theory* (pp. 115–145). New York: Academic Press.
Rosnow, R.L., & Georgoudi, M. (Eds.). (1986a). *Contextualism and understanding in behavioral science.* New York: Praeger.
Rosnow, R.L., & Georgoudi, M. (1986b). The spirit of contextualism. In R.L. Rosnow & M. Georgoudi (Eds.), *Contextualism and understanding in behavioral science* (pp. 3–22). New York: Praeger.
Sarbin, T.R. (1986). The narrative as a root metaphor for psychology. In T.R. Sarbin (Ed.), *Narrative psychology: The storied nature of human conduct* (pp. 3–22). New York: Praeger.
Scandura, J.M. (1984). New wine in old glasses. *Behavioral and Brain Sciences, 7*, 602–603.
Skinner, B.F. (1938). *Behavior of organisms.* New York: Appelton-Century-Crofts.
Skinner, B.F. (1945). The operational analysis of psychological terms. *Psychological Review, 52*, 270–276.
Skinner, B.F. (1950). Are theories of learning necessary. *Psychological Review, 57*, 193–216.
Skinner, B.F. (1953). *Science and human behavior.* New York: Free Press.
Skinner, B.F. (1957). *Verbal behavior.* New York: Appelton-Century-Crofts.
Skinner, B.F. (1969). *Contingencies of reinforcement: A theoretical analysis.* New York: Appelton-Century-Crofts.
Skinner, B.F. (1974). *About behaviorism.* New York: Knopf.
Skinner, B.F. (1984a). Methods and theories in the experimental analysis of behavior. *Behavioral and Brain Sciences, 7*, 511–523.
Skinner, B.F. (1984b). Reply to Catania. *Behavioral and Brain Sciences, 7*, 718–719.
Stabler, E.P., Jr. (1984). Rule-governed behavior in computational psychology. *Behavioral and Brain Sciences, 7*, 604–605.

ARTICLE 5

MENTALISM, BEHAVIOR-BEHAVIOR RELATIONS, AND A BEHAVIOR-ANALYTIC VIEW OF THE PURPOSES OF SCIENCE

From Hayes, S.C., & Aaron J. Brownstein, (1986). *The Behavior Analyst, 9*, 175–190.

Criticism of a behavioral approach to human behavior has been frequent since its inception. Recently, a type of criticism has emerged from knowledgeable critics suggesting that there is a more rapid path to the kinds of scientific knowledge sought by behaviorists (e.g., Keat, 1972; Wessells, 1981, 1982). Even individuals who formerly have been sympathetic to a behavior-analytic position have embraced this line of criticism. For example, Killeen has suggested that we need to "restore the excitement" in our field by admitting mentalism (Killeen, 1984).

Behaviorists would enthusiastically embrace this suggestion if the alternatives being proposed (e.g., Killeen's "emergent behaviorism," 1984) advanced the goals of science as seen by behavior analysts. Sadly, that possibility does not appear likely. Instead, the critics seem to be proposing a kind of science that is ill-suited to the scientific ends sought by behavior analysts. Although the criticisms may seem to be about scientific strategies or tactics, in actuality they concern the behavior-analytic view of scientific explanation itself.

The nature of the recent criticism suggests that it may be worthwhile to reexamine some of the philosophical underpinnings of a behavior-analytic view of science. Many of the points we hope to make have been made elsewhere, but the discussions have often been directed toward other specific concerns and have not always been interconnected or given a comprehensive rationale. Keystones of a behavior-analytic position can then appear to be dogmatic or arbitrary, rather than required for the intellectual integrity of the position.

Our starting point will be the primary purposes of science from a behavior-analytic viewpoint—prediction and control. We will attempt to show that an emphasis on prediction and control is not arbitrary in behavior analysis because it is a necessary part of successful forms of the philosophy that underlies behavior analytic theorizing. We will examine mentalism from several vantage points and show that regardless of its form, mentalism is necessarily counterproductive to the purposes of science embraced by behavior analysts. Mentalism can, however, contribute to the purposes of science as seen from other perspectives. We will examine a behavioral translation of some types of mental phenomena in terms of behavior-behavior relations, but warn against uses of the translation that also interfere with the accomplishment of prediction and control. We will then briefly examine several concepts within a behavioral perspective that are on a slippery slope to the same problem created by mentalism.

THE PURPOSES OF SCIENCE: PREDICTION AND CONTROL

When differences in goals are made evident, many arguments seem to dissolve. The goals of science from a behavior-analytic viewpoint have been quite explicitly stated: "We undertake to predict and control the behavior of the individual organism. This is our 'dependent variable'—the effect for which we are to find the cause" (Skinner, 1953, p. 35). It seems only fair to evaluate a position with respect to the goals it sets for itself, while recognizing of course that other purposes might be well served by different positions.

The Emphasis on Control

Prediction and control are the primary goals of behavior analysis (the goals of interpretation and explanation are discussed later). The behavioral approach places emphasis on the words "and control" in the phrase "prediction and control." Behavior analysis has sought an explanation of behavior in terms of events that are of a kind that at least potentially allows both prediction and control simultaneously. As we discuss below, some kinds of descriptions of events and relations can in principle only directly produce successful prediction and not control. Other kinds of descriptions of events and relations can allow both, in principle, though of course for practical reasons control may presently be impossible. Behavior analysis is committed to emphasizing this latter kind of analysis.

The importance of prediction and control as a guide to behavior-analytic theorizing cannot be overemphasized. It is the key to understanding many behavioral positions that might otherwise appear to be arbitrary. For example, behavior-analytic accounts of behavior are always ultimately to be cast in terms of "environmental variables" or "external variables": "Our 'independent variables'—the causes of behavior are the external conditions of which behavior is a function" (Skinner, 1953, p. 35). This position is not based on an *a priori* dictum that only what are commonly called "external variables" can possibly influence behavior. In a sense, the flow is in the opposite direction. If an event can in principle directly allow both prediction and control of behavior, then it deserves the name "environmental variable" or "external variable." This relation can be shown by the fact that, in behavior analysis, the words "external" or "environmental" do not always refer to the world outside the skin: rather they refer to the world outside behavior (most of which, of course, is outside the skin). For example, it is sometimes useful ("useful" in terms of prediction and control) to think of an "internal environment" influencing behavior.

An emphasis on "external variables" comes from the goals of science as viewed by behavior analysis. Seeking both prediction and control puts certain constraints on the kinds of statements of relations that are useful for the scientist. Only statements that point to events external to the behavior of the individual organism being studied can directly lead to prediction and control. The logic of this claim is as follows. Scientific statements, as Skinner pointed out, are not themselves the causes of the phenomena they encompass. Bodies do not fall, for example, because of the law of gravity. Rather humans can bring their behavior under the control of this verbal statement of a relation (i.e., this rule) and achieve certain ends. Thus, scientific rules help us accomplish particular ends by describing contingencies. They are rules for scientists, not rules for the world. Thus, scientists who seek prediction and control must rely on rules that start with the environment, in the sense of the "world outside of the behavior," because scientists are, and can only ever be, in other organisms' environment in this sense. Scientists cannot directly use a rule to control behavior unless it starts where the scientist is—in the potentially manipulable world outside of the behavioral system. If a scientific statement is used by the scientist to control phenomena but does not itself start from where the scientist resides, there must be some unspecified and unanalyzed link between the statement and the scientist's behavior. It may be useful, but it is necessarily incomplete in the sense that the rule itself did not specify whatever was done to control the phenomena of interest.

Why Prediction Must Be Included and Control Emphasized

Much of the confusion over a behavior-analytic perspective on the goals of science would have vanished had control alone been emphasized as the defining property of science. To the extent that control is pursued, it forces us to emphasize external variables that are functionally related to the behavior. Indeed, if the critics of a behavioral position were right and the emphasis on control represented merely an emphasis on technological advancement, there would have been no reason not to emphasize control alone as the issue. The criticism is a fairly common one. For example, Wessells (1981) objects to an emphasis on control, saying "the kinds of predictions one aims to make need not be dictated by the pragmatic desire to change behavior for the better" (p. 161). The concern over control, however, is not primarily with the development of technology, though the technological outgrowth of behavior analysis is impressive and a legitimate source of intellectual support for the position. At a theoretical level, the concern is primarily with the completeness of the account according to the scientific goals embraced by behavior analysis. A behavior-analytic position on the goals of science in turn derives its dignity from the necessary relation between these particular goals and the overall philosophical integrity of the worldview represented by behavior analysis (cf. Reese, 1984).

Behavior analysis is based on a pervasive use of a particular explanatory model: the "act in context." In behavior analysis, any event is to be understood and even defined through a contextual analysis. The three-term contingency of radical behaviorism is a dynamic spatiotemporal contextual unit—none of the terms can be defined independently of any of the others. Radical behaviorism is so thoroughgoing in its attempt to analyze context that even the behavior of scientists as they conduct contextual analyses is to be understood through more contextual analyses (Skinner, 1945).

The explanatory model of the "act in context" is shared by many perspectives on behavior, from certain forms of evolutionary biology (e.g., Dawkins, 1982), to some types of cultural anthropology (e.g., Harris, 1979), to Marxism. Because a basic explanatory model (or "root metaphor") is at the core of any well-integrated and consistent worldview, Pepper (1942) has suggested that all perspectives that rely on the "act in context" as an explanatory model be thought of as types of the worldview he calls "contextualism." According to Pepper (1942), the underlying "truth criterion" of contextualism is "successful working" or pragmatism. A term, concept, or statement of a relation is not true or false simply according to public agreement about the correspondence between it and other events, but according to the impact that the use of the term, concept, or statement has on dealing successfully with the phenomena of interest. Radical behaviorism clearly encompasses such a view (e.g., Skinner, 1945).

The nature of contextualism and of other worldviews, in Pepper's fullest sense, is a complicated topic. It would take us beyond the scope of this paper to defend fully the claim that behavior analysis fits all of Pepper's defining characteristics for contextualism (but see Hayes & Reese, in press). For our purposes, we will refer to behavior analysis as a type of contextualism only in the limited and uncontroversial sense of a view of the world consistently based on an analysis of the spatiotemporal context of acts, and driven by a pragmatic theory of truth.

The problem with the "act in context" as an explanatory model is that it does not and cannot specify the scope of the act or the context. Context can proceed outward spatially to include all of the universe. Context can proceed backward in time infinitely to include the remotest antecedent, or forward in time to include the most delayed consequence. The "act" in question can vary from the finest muscle twitch to the most elaborate and extended behavioral sequence. Consequently, in behavior analysis, an operant can be of almost any size and, in principle, can be influenced by contingencies that are extremely remote or indirect. Under such circumstances, one might ask how we are to know that a particular contextual analysis (in behavior analysis, a particular "contingency analysis") is adequate.

"Successful working" provides an answer to this question. An analysis need proceed only to the point at which successful action can be based on it. Successful action confirms the value of the analysis—it changes the indeterminate units of contingency analysis in the abstract into the determined units of a given instance of successful contingency analysis. In behavior analysis, the name for such successful working is "prediction and control." We know that a given event should be called a discriminative stimulus, for example, because the effects of doing so are that we can deal more successfully with the behavior of interest. While prediction alone provides some confirmation of the value of an analysis, only control "proves" that the units we have selected (the divisions we have made in context and behavior) are valid. One could ask, for example, how do we know that this is the relevant stimulus for this behavior? The answer is of the general form that when we change this stimulus (and not that stimulus), we get a change in this behavior (and not that behavior). Without manipulation, the units we select could be completely mistaken. Because the explanatory model in behavior analysis does not and cannot specify the precise nature of these units *a priori*, this would present a grave problem. Without manipulation, we could guess, for example, that event X is a discriminative stimulus, but instead it could be part of event Y and not a separate event at all, or it could covary with behavior due to coincidence, or the wrong construction could have been placed on the proper units of behavior and thus on its antecedents, and so on. It is primarily the confirmation of the validity of the units of the analysis that requires that control be emphasized in successful forms of contextualism.

An additional problem in behavior analysis (or any contextualistic perspective) is that even the behavior of a scientist analyzing behavior is itself behavior that can be analyzed. Contextual analysis can easily be paralyzed, however, by the need to analyze context, and then to analyze the context of the analysis of context, and so on ad infinitum. Prediction and control both confirm the value of the analysis and provide an endpoint to the need for analysis—it need continue only to the point at which prediction and control is possible in principle. Without control as an endpoint, behavior analysis could be caught up in an intellectual whirlpool of infinite regressions of ever more massive contextual analyses and would lose contact with "successful working" as its truth criterion. The argument can be made that the relative lack of empirical work springing from J.R. Kantor's extremely contextualistic view of psychology shows what can happen if contextualists let go of control as a primary goal of science. It is the successful operation of contextualism that pragmatically requires that control be emphasized—it is not a postulate of the philosophy.

If we have explained why control must be emphasized as a goal of science in behavior analysis, why should prediction be included at all as a goal? There are two reasons. First, prediction is pragmatically useful and thus naturally part of the truth criterion of contextualism. It would be arbitrary to exclude it. Second, control cannot be the only proximate outcome of successful science, because technical limitations often exist on our ability to manipulate events. Predictive relationships are not by their nature incomplete when prediction is based upon variables that are in the domain in which the potential for control exists because in principle they can provide a complete account. They take us outside the behavioral system. Whether they in fact do provide a complete account in a specific instance can be assessed as additional techniques allow direct manipulation and as additional knowledge creates networks of mutually supportive observations.

Critics of the goals of science embraced by behavior analysis have often misunderstood the basis for these goals and the integral role they play in behavior analysis. It is to such criticisms that we now turn.

THE BEHAVIOR-ANALYTIC VIEW OF EXPLANATION

Wessells (1981) has objected to the criterion of control by pointing out that "behavioral control can be achieved in the absence of explanation and vice versa" (p. 161). Astronomy is a commonly used example (Martin, 1978; Wessells, 1981) because we cannot test astronomical principles based on our ability to control cosmic events. The literal meaning of explanation comes from the same root as the word "plane"—literally, explanation means to lay out flat before us. According to the behavior-analytic position, "explanation" ultimately refers to prediction and control with adequate scope and precision. Thus, seen from the standpoint of behavior analysis, Wessell's statement is at least partially incorrect. We cannot have control in a sophisticated manner without what behaviorists take to be "explanation." With thorough and general control must also come prediction, and to a behaviorist, prediction and control of sufficient scope and precision is "explanation"—it is how behaviorists "lay out" behavioral systems. Control that is limited in scope and precision does not, of course, justify the term "explanation" and in that sense Wessell's observation seems obviously valid. The observation that pointing a gun at people and saying "Your money or your life" will often control monetary exchange is hardly an explanation of charitable giving. Such coercion fails as an explanation for monetary contributions in general because it has insufficient scope: a wide variety of instances are not encompassed by the "explanation."

Behavior analysts also agree that at times science can have explanation without control. Skinner uses the term "interpretation" to describe such cases. It occurs when a system can be thoroughly described, but for technical reasons control is not possible. Even then, behaviorists insist that an adequate explanation or interpretation be based on events that are of the same kind as those permitting control. As we have emphasized above, this insistence is not an arbitrary component of behavior analysis. It is also consistent with the strategy of the natural sciences under such circumstances. Modem astronomy, for example, is based fundamentally on the controlled observations of the physicist, and the observations are of the same kind. Someday we may even manipulate cosmic events. The limitations that occur in astronomy are technical, not problems with the kinds of events themselves.

The Mechanistic View of Explanation

This view of explanation can be contrasted with others that are popular in psychology. To put the best face on it from the point of view of behavior analysis, some forms of cognitivism are usefully considered as efforts to describe the structure of behavior (Catania, 1973). A description of the structure of behavior, however, is a description of the phenomena to be explained. Knowing the phenomena to be explained is vital, but it must not be mistaken for a contextual explanation of these very phenomena. The distinction is critical because if behavioral events are orderly, they themselves can allow prediction of behavioral phenomena, without ever going outside the particular behavioral system. This is not adequate behavior analytic explanation even though in a more limited sense it clearly can be useful. No amount of description of behavioral events will directly provide for control of behavioral events in the same individual. To think otherwise is to make the "structuralist error" (Skinner, 1974). We cannot control the behavior of an individual without considering events other than the behavior of that individual.

Thus, the cognitivist agenda does not necessarily meet the goals of science according to behavior analysis. Cognitivists themselves have no quarrel with this point: "Most [cognitive] investigators agree that their current theories are descriptive and that an explanatory theory, which would accommodate the effects of the environment, is a distal goal" (Wessells, 1982, p. 77). Just as it is unfair, however, to criticize behavior analysis without considering its goals and underlying philosophy, so too it is unfair to criticize cognitive perspectives in the same manner. Cognitivists do not believe that they are confusing description and explanation. Nor do they believe that the lack of concern for control is a weakness. They are correct in both instances, but only in the context of their own underlying philosophical position.

Most, though not all, forms of a cognitive account of behavior seem to be based on the worldview of mechanism (cf. Pepper, 1942). The fundamental explanatory model of mechanism is that of the machine. The type of cognitive theorizing that is based on computer metaphors and uses computer simulations to test the adequacy and operating characteristics of various theoretical models is obviously mechanistic in this sense. We will limit our discussion of cognitivism to this mechanistic variety. (Some forms of behaviorism are also mechanistic, but not radical behaviorism. A detailed discussion of this is beyond the scope of this paper, but see Hayes & Reese, in press.) In accord with its explanatory model, a mechanist shows no hesitation in explaining a behavioral system by specifying the component parts of its structure and the nature of its orderly operation; just as a person examining a car would readily explain its action by an appeal to its component parts (e.g., pistons, spark plugs) and structural organization (e.g., the spark plug wire is connected to the spark plug). In mechanism, each part can be described independently of the others and the nature of the parts does not change when they are combined into systems. The conditions that gave rise to this structure or the ways we can manipulate it are irrelevant to the description of the operation of the machine and predictions based on this description.

Mechanism has a correspondence-based truth criterion (Pepper, 1942). A term, concept, or statement of relation is true to the extent that we can agree that it corresponds with events. This presents particular restrictions to mechanistic theories. It would be improper to develop a description of a system based on close contact with it and then to treat this as an adequate theory of the system because obviously any detailed and careful description of events will be in close correspondence with these very same events. Correspondence can be used to test the adequacy of theories or concepts only by applying them to new situations, that is, by deductive prediction. The more abstract the relation between the original situation, the theory, and the new situation, the better (e.g., see Ericsson & Simon, 1984, on this point). When we can deductively predict with sufficient precision and scope, we have "explained" the phenomena according to a mechanistic account. The emphasis on hypothetico-deductive theorizing that exists in all mechanistic perspectives (e.g., most forms of cognitivism and S-R theory [stimulus-response theory]) is not arbitrary; it is integral to the functioning of the underlying worldview.

Thus, for mechanists, description and theoretical prediction form an adequate basis for explanation; in contrast, contextualists emphasize prediction and control. These differences about adequate scientific explanation correspond with differences about the goals of science according to the underlying worldview. Neither can be said to be "right" or "wrong" because any evaluation we can make about the adequacy of scientific goals must itself be in terms of some set of underlying values or goals. From the point of view of contextualism, all we can say is that these two views of science may be more or less useful for accomplishing particular ends, or that they might have this or that effect on the culture that supports them. Most behaviorists probably believe, of course, that a contextualistic perspective has positive consequences for scientific subcultures and perhaps the majority culture. Evaluating truth on the basis of consequences, however, is itself a distinctly contextualistic line to take. Few behaviorists would argue that behavior analysis is leading to better and better hypothetico-deductive theories. For a mechanist, this may show the inadequacy of behavior analysis. For a contextualist, it shows no such thing.

To summarize our main points so far: Prediction and control are reasonable goals for science. Together, they allow behavior analysis to progress efficiently, providing an adequate basis for scientific explanation according to a contextualistic perspective. Unlike prediction, control requires that we go outside of the behavioral system itself. Sometimes even when we do, control will be technically impossible. For the sake of a complete account, however, it is necessary that we explain behavior in terms of events that in principle allow both prediction and control. This requirement is not due primarily to a concern with technology. Rather, it is necessary for the successful working of the explanatory system used in behavior analysis. Other explanatory systems imply other kinds of scientific goals, and alternative practices can be defended on those grounds.

MENTALISM

An arena in which to examine the implications of the preceding analysis is the study of private events. Indeed, many of the objections to behavior analysis are usually cast in terms of private events and their investigation. The dominant alternative to a behavioral analysis of private events is mentalism. Objections to mentalism can be placed in two basic categories: metaphysical objections and metatheoretical objections. The metaphysical objections are directed at the concept of literal dualism and are shared by virtually all scientific perspectives. The metatheoretical objections have to do with the incompleteness of the account mentalism engenders when measured in terms of the goals of prediction and control. Our main point is that it is important not to confuse these two types of objections. Many of the behavior-analytic concerns with mentalism are metatheoretical objections driven by the goals of science embraced by behavior analysis, and these objections are by no means unique to the topic of mentalism. We show later that they apply to topics within behavior analysis itself.

The Scientific Unacceptability of Literal Dualism

Originally, psychology was the study of the soul. The Oxford English Dictionary (OED) defines "soul" as "the spiritual part of man." The OED defines "spirit" as an "incorporeal or immaterial being" and as a "being or intelligence distinct from anything physical." The word "physical" comes from a word for nature (thus the science of physics) and is defined as "of or pertaining to the phenomenal world of the senses; matter." Thus, if you take the words literally, "soul" and "spirit" are inherently dualistic terms because they oppose matter and nonmatter. We might label this "literal dualism." Literal dualism is the belief that there are two different essences in the world—one type exists in space and time, while the second type is nonspatiotemporal.

This type of literal dualism was to some degree transferred to the concept of "mind" and thus to its study. The OED defines "mind" as "the mental or psychical being or faculty." An elaborating definition explains that "mind" is "the seat of a person's consciousness, thoughts, volitions, and feelings; also, the incorporeal subject of the psychical faculties, the spiritual side of a human being; the soul as distinguished from the body. . . . Mental being; opposed to matter." The spiritual meaning of "mind" is also shown by the fact that God has long been referred to as "mind," as for example in the quote "That eternal infinite mind, who made and governs all things" (Locke, 1690). Thus, in lay terms, the essence of the mind is fundamentally different from the essence of the physical universe. "Mind" explicitly makes contact with a cultural tradition of literal dualism.

The objection to literal dualism is twofold. First, such a view is not scientifically tenable. This objection is shared by virtually all scientists, including cognitivists. By definition, nonspatiotemporal events cannot have form, mass, acceleration, beginnings, or ends. How they can be regarded as "events" in such a case is problematic. Any event that can be discerned is being observed in the world of space and time, and must in that sense be regarded as "physical." Literal dualism also raises the impossibly difficult issue of how nonspatiotemporal events can cause physical events to occur.

This argument is not about terms. If someone wanted to call all events "mental," there could be no objection, though it would distort our normal understanding of the term. The concern is more directed at literal dualism: "What is lacking is the bold and exciting behavioristic hypothesis that what one observes and talks about is always the 'real' and 'physical' world (*or at least the 'one' world*)" (Skinner, 1945, p. 276, emphasis added). As the last phrase in this quote shows, radical behaviorism is monistic, but not physicalistic in the sense of naive realism or related perspectives.

The second major objection to literal dualism is that it leaves a gap in the domain of science. Who is to predict and control mental events and relate them to behavioral events if they are not in the purview of science (Skinner, 1953, p. 258)? This objection is a metatheoretical one, and it applies equally forcefully to mentalistic theorizing that explicitly denies dualism.

Mental Physiology

For the above reasons, virtually all scientists avoid obvious forms of literal dualism in their scientific work. A variety of linguistic practices, however, have the same metatheoretical problems as literal dualism. One such practice is the creation of a pseudophysiological analysis to replaced literal dualism (Skinner, 1969, pp. 280–284).

It is very popular to use the word "mind" to mean "brain." Television shows or magazine articles on the action of the human brain, for example, are almost always said to be about "the human mind." Cognitive psychology has made no bones about the connection. A recent authoritative text on cognitive psychology asserted that in cognitive psychology "the contemporary view [is] that mental processes are synonymous with brain processes" (Ellis & Hunt, 1983, p. 11). Study of the brain and the nervous system is, of course, worthwhile and relevant to a behavioral analysis. But it is no less troublesome simply to substitute the word "brain" for "mind" and then to engage in precisely the same kinds of analyses as before.

Cognitivists use talk of the brain for two purposes. One is simply to claim that "mental functioning is not a mysterious, nonphysical event" (Ellis & Hunt, 1983, p. 7), that is, to emphasize the rejection of literal dualism. The second reason is more subtle. As we have described above, in the kind of hypothetico-deductive theorizing naturally promoted by mechanism, there is no requirement that terms used in the analysis of events refer to other events outside the original domain of interest. In order that there can be a proper division of labor among the sciences, however, scientists must take a complete scientific account to the point at which the determinants of a given phenomenon are themselves being analyzed by other scientists.

In psychology, contextualism naturally does this because it leads to the identification of events outside the behavioral system, as we have already discussed. These events are themselves to be explained by others. Behavior analysis, for example, does not attempt to understand how operant chamber key lights work. It is enough to know the conditions under which key lights can function as stimuli. The study of electrical lights is turned over to another science. Conversely, mechanism (though it need not do so) can leave a hole in the fabric of science because scientifically adequate analyses from this perspective can stay entirely inside the original domain. Behavioral events, or processes inferred from them can be explained by other behavioral events, or processes inferred from them. Although philosophically permissible in mechanism, this kind of circularity is intuitively unappealing, even to cognitivists.

By appearing to study brain processes, however, cognitive psychologists can identify causes that appear to go outside of the behavioral system itself. Cognitive psychology can superficially present itself under the umbrella of the neurosciences. If we actually understood how the structure of the nervous system was influenced by events, and exactly how any current structure produced behavior, we would indeed have one type of complete account (in fact, one quite comfortable to mechanists). But studying behavioral activity called "mental" is no more inherently a study of the brain than studying any behavioral activity. In order to maintain a proper division of labor among sciences, the connection between brain and mental activity would have to be studied explicitly. It is clear that cognitivists do not actually intend to study the brain or its connection with mental activity:

> Of course, brain activity can be studied physiologically, but cognitive psychologists use a different approach. Since the brain activity of interest cannot be directly observed (for example, we have no idea what happens in the brain when a person remembers a grandmother), we must infer the existence of these processes and then describe the processes in abstract language. (Ellis & Hunt, 1983, p. 7)

In summary, mental activity can be thought of as nonspatiotemporal activity, in which case it steps outside of science altogether. It may be thought of as a brain activity, but then psychologists sometimes act as if we need not explain how the structure of this activity itself came to be. There is a third way to view "mental activity," however—as behavior. This is the view taken by radical behaviorism, to which we now turn.

Mental Activity as Private Behavior

Watson and "Behavior." "Behavior" is commonly taken to refer to a certain subset of organismic action. For example, it is quite typical to hear theorists speak of "thoughts, feelings, and behavior" as if behavior can be easily distinguished from events called "thoughts" or "feelings."

Confusion over this issue can in part be attributed to Watson. Watson's (1925) behaviorism had both methodological and metaphysical components. His methodological behaviorism essentially said that scientists must be behaviorists because science can only deal with the publicly observable. Thus, even though other kinds of human action may exist, we can only deal with behavior because only behavior is publicly observable. This position might be thought of as implicitly dualistic because it recognizes that behavior is only a subset of organismic activity, and encourages a study that is necessarily incomplete since science can only deal with that subset, rather than the entire set, due to rules of proper scientific methodology.

Watson also made a second, somewhat contradictory point. He seemed to say that even if we could solve the problem privacy presents to a scientific analysis, behavior is still all that could be studied because only behavior exists. Although it is possible to read Watson to mean simply that nonspatiotemporal events do not exist, his emphasis on the peripheral locus of such phenomena as thinking (e.g., Watson, 1920, 1925) can also be and was taken to mean that thoughts, feelings, and other private events are not real in their own terms. This position can be termed "Watsonian metaphysical behaviorism."

What is important to note in all of this is that the use of the word "behavior" keeps changing. In Watsonian methodological behaviorism, behavior is viewed as a subset of organismic action that is publicly observable and is therefore subject to a scientific analysis. In Watsonian metaphysical behaviorism, behavior is viewed as the totality of organismic action, but there is the implication that only events that are publicly observable (at least potentially) should be thought of as real.

Radical Behaviorism and "Behavior." Radical behaviorism can be distinguished from these other types of behaviorism in part by the view it takes in regards to "behavior" and the nature of scientific observations (Skinner, 1945, 1963). As in Watsonian metaphysical behaviorism, behavior is taken to be the set of all organismic action. The word "organismic" is important. Actions by suborganismic units (e.g., a single neuron firing) are not usually considered to be the behavior of organisms, but under certain conditions they may if they can conveniently be viewed as the integrated action of a whole organism. For example, the controlled heart rate of a person in a biofeedback training program would probably be thought of as the behavior of an organism, while the beating of a heart removed from the body clearly would not.

Unlike earlier forms of behaviorism, however, radical behaviorism makes no commitment to public observability per se as the defining characteristic of scientifically valid events (Skinner, 1945). Rather, observations are scientifically valid or invalid based on the contingencies controlling these observations. Science is an enterprise that promotes the development of verbal statements of relations between events based on verifiable experience. Scientific verbal behavior thus should be under the control of the subject matter of the science and the value of this verbal behavior is determined through the impact it has on others attempting to come under the control of that same subject matter.

Science attempts to restrict sources of control over scientific observation through the scientific method. Its purpose is to ensure that scientific observations are controlled primarily by events in the relevant subject matter and not by states of deprivation, audience factors, or similar sources of control over verbal behavior (Moore, 1981). Consistent with the "successful working" truth criterion of contextualism, the scientific value of an observation in behavior analysis is ultimately determined by the degree to which it enables prediction and control. The essence of Skinner's (1945) criticism of operationism was thus that public agreement provides no assurance of the proper sources of control over scientific observation, nor of its pragmatic value. Conversely, in principle, observations of private events can be tightly controlled by these events themselves, given the proper history, and can be highly useful. In this sense, observations of private events are no more or less scientific than public events based on their privacy per se. In radical behaviorism, behavior can thus be defined as all observable organismic action, not all publicly observable organismic action (cf. Heidbreder, 1933, and her discussion of the flaws of classical behaviorism). Skinner (1974) has made the point quite clearly:

> [Radical behaviorism] does not insist upon truth by agreement and can therefore consider events taking place in the private world within the skin. It does not call these events unobservable, and it does not dismiss them as subjective. (p. 16)

In this view, then, no objection can be made to talk of events such as thinking or feeling. This talk is not trivialized by insisting it is only the talk itself that is scientifically legitimate (Skinner, 1945). A specific instance of thinking is viewed as a scientifically accessible event—a covert behavior. We may eventually find ways of identifying specific covert behaviors in others. For example, we currently have ways of knowing when reports of private speech are in fact occasioned by the specified private speech (Hayes, 1986).

Mental Causality as Behavior-Behavior Relation

Thoughts as Behavior. One might ask: Why insist that thinking be regarded as covert behavior when the physical properties appear so different from overt behavior? Why not call thinking "mental activity" or even a "brain process"? If "behavior" is defined so broadly, doesn't this make the concept of "behavior" meaningless? Such questions have often been forcefully raised. For example:

> The omission of [mental] states left [Skinner] with an inadequate vocabulary, which he then expanded by moving some stimuli inside the organism ("private stimuli"), and by treating all other aspects of mental states as responses. Seeing became behavior, and imagination became "seeing without the thing seen." But these are assertions, not demonstrated facts. They may serve as the axioms of a parsimonious behavioral system, and that is largely how Skinner used them. But they cannot then also be used as arguments against other systems, or against behavioral systems with augmented axioms, such as the assumption that covert events are sufficiently different from overt ones to deserve separate treatment as a separate category of events. (Killeen, 1984, p. 27)

Skinner himself (1974) is quite clear that the issue is not one of parsimony per se. Asking himself how we could decide between behavior analysis and mentalism, he replies:

> We cannot say that one is simpler than the other . . . [but] accessibility [for use in control] is another matter. No one has ever directly modified any of the mental activities or traits. . . . for most practical purposes they are changed only through the environment. . . . A decision [between the two positions] is perhaps more difficult if we simply want to predict

> behavior. . . . [Traits] are . . . useless in control but they permit us to predict one kind of behavior from another kind. (pp. 208–209)

Behavior-Behavior Relations as Incomplete Accounts. By referring to "mental events" as behavior we do three things. First, we eliminate consideration of "mental events" that cannot be thought of as observable organismic activity, such as purely hypothetical constructs. Second, we emphasize that it is the task of psychology to predict and control these events. And third, we focus on analyses that can accomplish these two goals. If "mental events" are a separate category of events, then they can be used to explain behavioral events and perhaps need not themselves be explained by behavioral scientists. Mental events that cannot be translated into behavioral observations are particularly prone to this problem because by definition they are seemingly a separate category of events from behavior. The problem can be used as an "argument against other systems," but it is not a mere repetition of axioms. It is an identification of possibly mischievous contingencies over the behavior of psychologists, one that the history of psychology gives us every reason to take seriously.

When a radical behaviorist is less than enthusiastic about an account of behavior that predicts that someone will respond in a given way after thinking a particular thought, it should be an absence of enthusiasm resulting from the incompleteness of the account rather than from the reference to a thought. The immediate question then becomes what are the determinants of that thought and (even less obviously) what are the contingencies that lead to a relation between a given instance of thinking and overt responding in this individual.

In behavior analysis, the view that thinking causes overt behavior distills down to the view that one behavior can cause another. In these terms, when we ask such questions as "What role does thinking play in the control of behavior?" we are actually asking about the nature of a behavior-behavior relation. Behavior-behavior relations are very important in behavior analysis in a variety of areas, and they are as worthy of study as is any behavior. No matter how dynamically one behavioral event may be intertwined with other behavioral events within the same individual, however, for a contextualist a behavior-behavior relation is a phenomenon to be explained by appealing to particular contextual arrangements (e.g., contingencies of reinforcement) that might permit prediction and control of the behavior-behavior relation itself. A behavior-behavior relation cannot be a complete explanation of behavior, except to a mechanist, whose worldview does not insist on control as a necessary goal of science. "We may object, first, to the predilection for unfinished causal sequences" (Skinner, 1969, p. 240).

Killeen (1984) has criticized this concern:

> Skinner notes that after we have explained a response in terms of mental states or activities of feeling, we still need to explain the mental state. But

> there is nothing wrong with that. Experimental analysis of one of the links in a causal chain should not necessarily be faulted because it does not include the previous ones; analysis must inevitably stop at some point short of the Ultimate Cause. (pp. 27–28)

For a complete account, however, behavior analysts must take analysis to the point at which prediction and control are directly possible in principle. Behavior of the individual being studied can never satisfy that criterion.

Thus, despite the fact that environment and behavior are always involved in a dynamic interrelation, it is not arbitrary (Bandura, 1978, 1981) to insist that analyses proceed to the environmental level. An environmental cause can in principle be used directly; given the technical ability to manipulate it, effective action can be based on it. A rule pointing to a behavioral "cause" might help locate causal environmental events and relations, but it is also likely, if one is not careful, to stop the search for causes that could permit a complete account. Skinner (1974) has said this explicitly:

> It has been objected that we must stop somewhere in following a causal chain into the past and we may as well stop at a psychic level. . . . It is true that we could trace human behavior not only to the physical conditions which [cause it] but also to the causes of those conditions and the causes of those causes, almost ad infinitum, but there is no point in going back beyond the point at which effective action can be taken. That point is not to be found in the psyche. (p. 210)

Thus, "the *initiating* action is taken by the environment" (Skinner, 1974, p. 73, emphasis added; see also Skinner, 1984). If we explain behavioral events in terms of events that are in the domain of other sciences, we move toward the comprehensive knowledge that we desire. But if we explain behavioral events in terms of other behavioral events of the same individual, then a significant gap is left to be filled. If we will not fill it, who will? If not now, when?

The Effect of Calling Thinking "Behavior." By calling all organismic activity appropriate to psychological study "behavior," we naturally inoculate ourselves to some degree against incomplete accounts. Acceptance of an incomplete analysis is much less likely when all events involved are clearly in the behavioral domain. For example, a researcher may notice that many good Monopoly players are also good poker players. Few of us would be tempted, however, to claim that people play poker well because they play Monopoly well or vice versa. Both of these actions are obviously in the behavioral domain. Events outside of this domain must be found to explain the first behavior, and equally important, to explain the relation between the two behaviors. That is, what actual events lead to good Monopoly playing, good poker playing, and their interrelation? This need seems relatively clear when the two events are obviously from the same domain. Behavior-behavior relations are seldom mistaken for causal analyses adequate for the purpose of prediction and control when they are clearly stated as behavior-behavior relations.

Note, however, that when behavioral events are apparently in different domains, the mistake is readily made. If we observed that good poker players feel self-confident (not "behave self-confidently"), have aggressive personalities (not "behave aggressively"), and are intelligent (not "show intelligent behavior"), we might feel as though we have at least a partial explanation of their skill even though this is in principle identical to the obviously less satisfactory claim that good poker playing comes from good Monopoly playing. To most people feelings, personalities, intelligence, and the like, if not explicitly termed types or qualities of behavior, often seem to be something else. Such things are then easily mistaken for causes of behavior.

Insisting that we call "mental events" by the name "behavior" should not be done to diminish the interest in these so called mental events, any more than calling a public behavior in a behavior-behavior relation by the name "behavior" should be done to diminish interest in public behavior. Behavioral scientists should call events "behavior" to keep clear the fact that it is their job to explain such events and to avoid incomplete accounts based on these events.

A brief summary seems in order. The purpose of this paper has been to place the behavior-analytic rejection of mental causes into the larger context of the goals of science embraced by behavior analysis. Both critics and supporters of behavior analysis seem at times to confuse the various reasons for the behavior-analytic concern with mentalism. Literal dualism is rejected because it is scientifically untenable and because it leaves claimed sources of control over behavior outside the scientific enterprise. This rejection of literal dualism, however, is common to virtually all scientific forms of psychology. The rejection of mentalism on the grounds of the requirements of scientific method, as done by early forms of methodological behaviorism, is not recognized as legitimate by radical behaviorism. Neither is the attempt to define away the independent existence of private events, as in Watsonian metaphysical behaviorism. What, then, is unique about the radical behavioral rejection of mentalism?

Our point has been that the primary radical behavioral objection to mentalism (other than literal dualism) is a metatheoretical one. Nondualistic analyses based on mental causality usually boil down either to pseudophysiologizing, to theorizing based on hypothetical constructs, or to elevating disguised behavior-behavior relations to causal status. The concern with all of these maneuvers is that they interfere with the behavior analytic agenda of predicting and controlling behavior. As we have tried to show, this agenda is not an arbitrary element of behavior analysis. It is a required element for the successful functioning of the perspective. Thus, mental causality is a form of theorizing rejected because its pursuit threatens the successful operation of science as viewed from the standpoint of behavior analysis.

THE SLIPPERY SLOPE OF NONMANIPULABLE CAUSES

We believe that much of the criticism of the behavioral approach arises from a failure to recognize its goals and the reasons for them. Other goals or values make alternative practices and beliefs justifiable, and with these we can have no quarrel, provided only that the researcher honestly states what these goals are. For example, if a particular field of psychology wishes to eschew control as the end product of science, it has the obligation to make that clear to all, whether the person is a psychologist, a client seeking help, a congressman, or a taxpayer helping fund federal research.

We see no relative disadvantage for a radical behavioral approach when prediction and control are being pursued. We do not mean to say, of course, that research generated by nonbehavioral psychologists necessarily results in incomplete analyses as viewed from a contextualistic perspective. See, for example, Ornstein and Naus's (1978) demonstration that recall was increased after the manipulation of environmental events controlling overt rehearsal. We must guard against responding to the quality of language rather than to the quality of the analysis. The issue is not the form of science but its function. It is the quality of the analysis that is at issue rather than an attempt to urge that some simple physical correspondence exists between private and public behaviors.

Examples of the Danger

Behavioral analyses that implicate "covert behavior," rather than "mental events," are equally incomplete if they fail to extend the analysis to environmental variables. Indeed, there are several topics within behavior analysis that share with mentalistic accounts some of the same potential metatheoretical problems of encouraging incomplete accounts.

Self-Rules. There can be little doubt that humans talk to themselves. Presumably, these verbal events can relate in reliable ways to other behavior. To explain other behavior simply in terms of "self-rules," however, is not adequate behavior-analytic explanation. As in the cases discussed earlier, the term "self-rules" does not obviously place these events in the same category as "behavior". "Thus, when talking of a relation between a self-rule and behavior, it is not always obvious that it is a behavior-behavior relation that is at issue. Because it is, we must explain both how external events gave rise to the private talk, and how the private talk came to control the behavior of interest. When this is done, "self-rules" may participate in an overall causal relation, but they should not themselves be seen as causes.

When behaviorists say they have located a "cause," it seems they should have identified a relation that can perform the functions required of a scientific relation within a behavioral perspective, namely, prediction and control. In a sense, causes are not objective independent facts in the world. All events in a thoroughgoing contextualistic system are "events" only because construing them that way serves a purpose. A causal relation can only be tested as a verbal construction, and only when this verbal statement of a relation serves the purposes of science should it be called a "cause." Perhaps when we have finished a complete analysis of a behavior-behavior relation, we could think of the first behavior as a kind of "intermediate cause" (e.g., see Skinner's reluctant agreement on this point, 1984), but it is surely safer not to do so. Some other term is needed. "Controlling behavior" suggests itself because of Skinner's use of the term to serve this function in his analysis of self-control. For example, self-rules might be said to function as controlling behaviors as parts of an overall causal relation. They are not themselves causes, at least not in the behavior-analytically acceptable sense of the word "cause."

Response-Produced Stimuli. At times, behaviorists have used the term "response-produced stimuli" to explain behavior-behavior relations. The apparent effects of private behaviors on other behaviors may be explained on this basis. For example, we may say that a person visualizes one's bedroom, and due to the stimuli produced by this behavior, remembers where the car keys were left. Even if the analysis avoids the idea of an image seen (in favor of the more "behavioral" term "response-produced stimuli") it is troublesome.

Responses obviously usually produce stimuli. For example, all operants, by definition, do so. The concept of response-produced stimuli, however, is usually invoked when there is no possibility of discerning or manipulating the stimuli independently of the behavior itself. The danger is that, because stimuli are apparently in a different class than behavior, explanations based on "response-produced stimuli" will be accepted as complete even when we have in principle no hope of manipulating or even discerning these stimuli independently. Explanations are not complete under these conditions. We move no closer to prediction and control simply by replacing a behavior-behavior relation with a "behavior-response-produced stimuli-behavior" relation unless we have independent access to the stimuli. It is useless to "explain behavior by appealing to independent variables which have been inferred from the behavior thus explained" (Skinner, 1969, p. 264). The radical behavioral objection to hypothetical constructs (when they are used as other than merely a shorthand for behavior) has the same metatheoretical basis as the primary objection to mentalism. In some cases, "response-produced stimuli" can have the status of a purely hypothetical construct.

This objection does not necessarily mean that we should stop using the term "response-produced stimuli." We should distinguish, however, between three types of situations. In the first, the "stimuli" referred to are clearly in the domain in which control is possible in principle. An ordinary operant is an example. A keypeck that produces food is producing food-related stimuli. That is presumably why this behavior occurs in the first place. We could speak of the food as response-produced stimuli. In this case, we are using the term "response-produced stimuli" in a manner totally consistent with the goals of science as seen by behavior analysts because we can manipulate these stimuli independently from the behavior that produced them and discern their effects on behavior.

In the second situation, the stimuli cannot currently be controlled due to technical limitations, but control is possible in principle. Analyzing back-scratching in terms of sensory reinforcement may be an example. Here, when we claim that the back scratch is due to response-produced stimuli we are engaging in interpretation, and in the future we may or may not find the interpretation to have provided a complete account. We may ultimately find ways to block the suggested sensory stimulation and to discern the effects of this manipulation.

Finally, there are times when direct control is impossible in principle. A claim that we have unconscious thoughts and that these produce stimuli might be an example. Here, we are using the term "response-produced stimuli" solely to provide a consistent account, but at a considerable cost. We have disguised an analysis that cannot in principle meet all the goals of science from a behavior-analytic viewpoint in the cloak of terminology that suggests these goals can be met.

Behaviors as Self-Reinforcers. Even radical behaviorists sometimes claim that one behavior can be maintained by the person involved providing other behaviors as "self-reinforcers" (e.g., Malott, 1989). The task of behavior analysis must be to explain both behaviors and their relation. When the contexts giving rise to such behavior-behavior relations have been manipulated experimentally, however (e.g., Hayes, Rosenfarb, Wulfert, Korn, & Zettle, 1985), the apparent influence of self-reinforcing behaviors have always resolved into the effects of environmental events (Sohn & Lamal, 1982). An example of an apparently causal behavioral consequence is the Premack principle. Superficially, this principle seems to suggest that one behavior can reinforce another in the same organism. But if the external environment manipulates the opportunity to engage in a particular behavior following another, then this is not a simple behavior-behavior relation. It is really best thought of as a behavior-environmental restriction behavior relation.

The examples of self-rules, response-produced stimuli, and self-reinforcement show that behavior analysts are also susceptible to the tendency to dress up behavior-behavior relations in the cloak of nonbehavioral events and then to forget that they have done so. The cost of this action is the same as the cost of mentalistic talk or pseudophysiological talk in complete analyses are inappropriately accepted as complete and a resultant gap in knowledge is produced.

CONCLUSION

An embrace of mentalism is not a sure road to an appreciation of the richness of private phenomena, and trivialization is not the necessary result of behavioral translation. Behavior analysts should reject mentalistic terms precisely in order to study the actual phenomena associated with them in a more thorough way and in a way more satisfying to the goals of science as viewed by behavior analysts. Allowing behavioral causes made seemingly less incomplete by calling them "mental" ultimately tends to stop causal analysis before the point at which effective action is possible. We need to understand the actual phenomena pointed to by mentalistic terms, or terms such as self-rules or self-reinforcement for that matter. The analytic discipline supplied by the assumptions inherent in radical behaviorism is needed most in exactly such difficult endeavors, not in order to pursue analytic discipline for its own sake, but in order to develop a more thoroughly adequate explanation of human behavior.

REFERENCES

Bandura, A. (1978). The self system in reciprocal determinism. *American Psychologist, 33*, 344–358.

Bandura, A. (1981). In search of pure unidirectional determinants. *Behavior Therapy, 12*, 30–40.

Catania, A.C. (1973). The psychologies of structure, function, and development. *American Psychologist, 28*, 434–443.

Dawkins, R. (1982). *The extended phenotype*. San Francisco: Freeman.

Ellis, H.C., & Hunt, R.R. (1983). *Fundamentals of human memory and cognition* (3rd ed.). Dubuque, IA: W.C. Brown.

Ericsson, K.A., & Simon, H.A. (1984). *Protocol analysis: Verbal reports as data.* Cambridge, MA: MIT Press.

Harris, M. (1979). *Cultural materialism: The struggle for a science of culture*. New York: Random House.

Hayes, S.C. (1986). The case of the silent dog: Verbal reports and the analysis of rules. A review of Ericsson and Simon's "Protocol analysis: Verbal reports as data." *Journal of the Experimental Analysis of Behavior, 45*, 351–363.

Hayes, S.C., & Reese, H.W. (in press). A review of S.C. Pepper's "World Hypotheses: A Study in Evidence." *Journal of the Experimental Analysis of Behavior.*

Hayes, S.C., Hayes, L.J., & Reese, H.W. (1988). Finding the philosophical core: A review of Stephen C. Pepper's "World Hypotheses: A Study in Evidence." *Journal of the Experimental Analysis of Behavior, 50*(1), 97–111.

Hayes, S.C., Rosenfarb, S.C., Wulfert, E., Korn, Z., & Zettle, R.D. (1985). Self-reinforcement procedures: Another way to set social standards? *Journal of Applied Behavior Analysis, 18*, 201–214.

Heidbreder, E. (1933). *Seven psychologies.* New York: Appleton-Century-Crofts.

Keat, R. (1972). A critical examination of B.F. Skinner's objections to mentalism. *Behaviorism, 1*, 53–70.

Killeen, P.R. (1984). Emergent behaviorism. *Behaviorism, 12*, 25–39.

Locke, J. (1690). *An essay concerning human understanding*. London: Awnsham, Churchill, & Manship.

Malott, R.W. (1989). The achievement of evasive goals: Control by rules describing indirect acting contingencies. In S.C. Hayes (Ed.), *Rule-governed behavior: Cognition, contingencies, and instructional control* (pp. 269–322). New York: Plenum.

Martin, M. (1978). Interpreting Skinner. *Behaviorism, 6*, 129–138.

Moore, J. (1981). On mentalism, methodological behaviorism, and radical behaviorism. *Behaviorism, 9*, 55–77.

Ornstein, P.A., & Naus, M.J. (1978). Rehearsal processes in children's memory. In P. A. Ornstein (Ed.), *Memory development in children* (pp. 69–99). Hillsdale, NJ: Erlbaum.

Pepper, S.C. (1942). *World hypotheses: A study in evidence*. Berkeley: University of California Press.

Reese, H.W. (May, 1984). *Historical and philosophical analysis of causality*. Paper presented at the meeting of the Association for Behavior Analysis, Nashville.

Skinner, B.F. (1945). The operational analysis of psychological terms. *Psychological Review, 52*, 270–276.

Skinner, B.F. (1953). *Science and human behavior*. New York: Free Press.

Skinner, B.F. (1963). Behaviorism at fifty. *Science, 134*, 566–602.

Skinner, B.F. (1969). *Contingencies of reinforcement: A theoretical analysis*. New York: Appleton-Century-Crofts.

Skinner, B.F. (1974). *About behaviorism*. New York: Knopf.

Skinner, B.F. (1984). Reply to Catania. *The Behavioral and Brain Sciences, 7*, 718–719.

Sohn, D., & Lamal, P.A. (1982). Self-reinforcement: Its reinforcing capability and its clinical utility. *The Psychological Record, 32*, 179–203.

Watson, J.B. (1920). Is thinking merely the action of language mechanisms? *British Journal of Psychology, 11*, 87–104.

Watson, J.B. (1925). *Behaviorism*. New York: Norton.

Wessells, M.G. (1981). A critique of Skinner's views on the explanatory inadequacy or cognitive theories. *Behaviorism, 9*, 153–170.

Wessells, M.G. (1982). A critique of Skinner's views on the obstructive character of cognitive theories. *Behaviorism, 10*, 65–84.

ARTICLE 6

ANALYTIC GOALS AND THE VARIETIES OF SCIENTIFIC CONTEXTUALISM

From Hayes, S.C. (1993). In S.C. Hayes, L.J. Hayes, H.W. Reese, & T.R. Sarbin (Eds.), *Varieties of scientific contextualism* (pp. 11–27). Reno, NV: Context Press.

Contextualism is being looked to as a framework within which psychology may advance, stripped of needless mechanism and needless philosophical inconsistencies. An examination of contextualistic writings leads quickly to two conclusions, however, both of which present problems for this progressive construction of the current situation. First, contextualism is not new. American psychology began with a very heavy contextualistic emphasis due to the early influence of James, Pierce, Dewey, and others. Second, there are many contextualistic approaches, each with very different perspectives. It is not yet clear that these different contextualists can even talk with each other effectively.

The first point is troubling because it suggests that our past may be our future. The current wave of interest in contextualism may be doomed to failure. The second is troubling because it suggests that there are many contextualistic paths leading from the present, not all of which are likely to succeed, or—worse—that there is no coherent contextualistic position to be pursued at all.

In this chapter I argue that the ultimate failure of American pragmatism within scientific psychology was due to a subtle but crucial problem, beginning with James himself. I also argue that the varieties of scientific contextualism make sense when this problem is identified and solved. Contextualism can indeed serve as a coherent philosophy of science, despite the diversity of approaches that emanate from it.

THE MODELS OF STABLE TRUTH

Each of Pepper's four world views can be distinguished on the basis of its truth criteria. What may be obvious to most—but was not to me for quite a while—is that the truth criteria are not arbitrarily related to their underlying root metaphors. They are built into the root metaphors themselves.

Formism emerged early in the history of philosophical thought, and for a good reason: its truth criterion is inherent in language itself. If all events are instances of specifiable forms, then the purpose of analysis is to know these forms and to name them. To name or describe an event is to specify a relation between a term or sentence and an occurrence. The formists' simple correspondence is nothing more than the "truth" of common sense language, and it is built into the root metaphor. If I say there is an apple in my hand, the truth of the statement is assessed by examining my hand. If the apple is there, I spoke truthfully. Formism is the philosophy of naming, and the truth criterion is the criterion of that common sense activity.

Mechanism is, in a sense, an elaborated type of formism and its truth criterion is an elaborated form of simple correspondence. Because the mechanist assumes the presence of a world organized *a priori* into events, relations, and forces, truth is to be found in the way ever more ambitious verbal formulae correspond reveal the assumed organization of the world. If one assumes that there is a single way that the world is organized, it makes sense to test verbal formulae by applying them to new phenomena, and thus predictive verification is the primary truth criterion of the mechanist. Again, the truth criterion is built into the root metaphor.

The coherence of the organicist is superficially like the truth sought by a story-teller: many specific elements are integrated into a coherent whole. But the story teller knows that the story can be told many different ways, while the organicist takes a more passive and exclusive view. The coherence of the organicist is more like the coherence of a reader. If the story is well written and well understood, every element will be seen to have its place. The organicist assumes that there is a grand story evolving, in which all apparently contradictory elements will be found in the end to be part of the evolving whole. The truth criterion of the organicist is just the application of this root metaphor. Truth is the removal of all apparently contradictory elements so that they are seen in the end to be part of the evolving whole: in a word, coherence. The truth criterion is built into the root metaphor itself.

In all three of these world views the analyst views the job of analysis to be one of discovery—literally, a matter of "taking the cover off" what is already there.

THE FLUID MODEL: TRUTH AND CONSEQUENCES

Contextualists take a local and pragmatic perspective on truth. Again, this truth criterion is not arbitrarily related to the root metaphor: it is instead an application of it. An act-in-context is a common sense historical act, alive and in the present. As such, it is purposive, not causally, but descriptively (more about this later). Acts like "going to the restaurant for lunch" have what Pepper calls a satisfaction (what behavior analysts might call a consequence or a reinforcer). When we apply this root metaphor to the action of the analyst, it too is related to a consequence. Achieving that consequence is the truth criterion of contextualism: it is built into the root metaphor.

Pepper uses many terms for this truth criterion, and distinguishes among these terms for reasons of interest to professional philosophers, but in my view "successful working" is the clearest term for our purposes. Etymologically, work is related to a word meaning simply "activity." Successful working, in its broadest sense, is just successful activity. Indeed, effective action is commonly used as a synonym for successful working.

What is important is the word "successful." Success is an outcome concept: it is a matter of reaching a goal, fulfilling a purpose, or producing a desirable consequence. The terms "goal," "purpose," or "desirable consequence" all suggest that the important issue is not simply the presence or absence of *any* consequence, but the degree to which the consequence produced was part of the original activity. A behavior analyst might say that the question is the degree to which the consequence produced is part of the function of the operant.

In physics "work" is defined as effort times distance. Distance can only be measured in terms of a direction—from somewhere to somewhere. Similarly, workability as a truth criterion requires direction. We have to measure workability from somewhere to somewhere.

Pepper says it this way:

> Serious analysis for [the contextualist] is always either directly or indirectly practical. . . . If from one texture you wish to get to another, then analysis has *an end, and a direction*, and some strands have relevancy to this end and others do not, and . . . the enterprise becomes important *in reference to the end.* (Pepper, 1942, pp. 250–251, emphasis added)

Note that Pepper uses the term "wish." This suggests that the consequence of importance must be present, even before it is contacted, to be useful as a guide to analysis. An analysis is true to the extent that it reaches the end, or takes one in the direction that was important *before the action of analysis*.

This is a crucial point, because it means that "successful working" is not foundational in contextualism—you cannot start from successful working and proceed from there. What is foundational is a consequence, end, purpose, goal, direction, intention, value, outcome, or metric in terms of which the truth criterion of successful working can be applied.

I will argue that these consequences must also be *verbally* present, as part of the extended present of the original analytic activity. Successful working is a matter of achieving *specified* consequences—of accomplishing that which was there to be accomplished.

Verbal and Non-Verbal Time

The conceptual units familiar to animal behaviorists have to do with change in an experiential sense, or what we might call non-verbal time (see Hayes, L. J., 1992). Consider a simple situation with a pigeon. First there was an observed green light, then a peck on a key, then food eaten. Later, there was an observed green light, then a peck on a key, then food eaten. Still later, there was an observed green light, then a peck on a key, then food eaten. A bird exposed to such a set of experiences has experienced an orderly process of change from one act to another. If these events come together to form an operant class, pecks on the green key is "purposeful" in the sense that a past history of change is present when the light appears. The bird pecks "in order to get food" in the sense that there has been an orderly sequence between pecking and food. Thus, terms like "purpose" when they have to do with non-verbal time are referring to defining qualities of operant or instrumental behavior—not as a source of this behavior but as a way of speaking about the historical role of consequences in present actions.

Verbal time, and thus verbal purpose, is different, however (Hayes, S. C., 1992). I have argued in several places that the essence of verbal behavior is the derivation of relations among events under contextual control not based simply on the form of the relata. Temporal change in a verbal sense is a class of arbitrarily applicable change relations: cause-effect, if . . . then, before-after, and the like. If we are told that "right after *A* comes *B*," we derive that "right before *B* comes *A*." Similarly, if we are taught directly that "right after *A* comes *B*" and "right after *B* comes *C*," we can derive that "shortly after *A* comes *C*" or that "shortly before *C* comes *A*." If *B* has functions (for example, if *B* is an intense shock), other stimuli may have functions based on their derived relations with *B*. For example, *A* may now elicit great arousal, while *C* may lead to calm. The verbal relation of time is brought to bear by contextual cues, not simply by the form of the relata. Thus, construction of a verbal purpose involves relating the present action to consequences not simply because these consequences have been experienced following these actions in the past, but also because a history of deriving change relations is brought to bear on the current situation.

My point is this: verbal time is not the same as non-verbal time, and thus concepts like purpose, goal, or intention must differ in the two domains. But verbal time concepts are also not mental events that "cause" behavior to occur. Verbal time concepts are enabled by the action of deriving an arbitrarily applicable relation between an event and some change. When we then act affirmatively with regard to such derived relations, we are behaving purposefully in a verbal sense. In other words, verbally purposeful actions are rule-governed, and the rule that is involved is a temporal one.

Why Successful Working Must Be Verbal

Truth is not a non-verbal concept. Truth is something that applies to the verbal actions of verbal organisms.

It would be nonsense to say that the actions of a dog or a cat are "true" or "false." For example, suppose a cat tries to open a door by purring. In the past, purring may have led to doors opening because owners have acted on the basis of the purring—that change relation has been directly contacted by the cat and it is the basis upon which we can say that the purring is "purposeful." It is part of an operant class of "opening-the-door behavior." But today the cat's owner is not at home. The failure of the door to open may mean that purring is currently ineffective, but it does not mean that purring is "false." Purring has worked to open the door in the past, and at the moment that the cat purrs it does so based on a history of "successful working" in a non-verbal sense.

This example shows that successful working cannot be allowed to refer solely to non-verbal purpose because, when one does so, *all purposeful actions become "true" because organisms do what has worked in the past.*

One could solve this conundrum by claiming that truth actually has to do with the literal future. The cat's action may be false in the sense that, at the moment it purrs with the owner gone it will be found to be an unworkable means of opening the door. Purring has been true, but now it is false.

This solution reduces truth criteria to non-criteria, because we can never assess the truth of any statement except based on something that has not yet happened. Even if a given action has led to horrific consequences, we cannot rule out that these consequences may change. Asked about the truth value of anything we could only say, "I do not know. Let's wait and see."

My conclusion is this:

1. If successful working has to do with non-verbal time it is applicable but we always find that all present activity is true;
2. If it has to do with the literal non-verbal future, it is never applicable;
3. Therefore, successful working cannot refer solely to non-verbal time.

Truth is a verbal concept, applicable only to verbal events. Statements can be true or false; actual histories cannot.

A verbal analysis can have many consequences:

- To experience the harmony of events
- To experience connections among events
- To produce a consistency of beliefs

- To understand and make sense of the world
- To predict events
- To postdict or interpret the world
- To have a verbal place for everything
- To feel personally satisfied
- To manipulate and control phenomena
- To survive as a species/culture/individual
- To look intelligent
- To have fun
- To give talks
- To speak nonsense
- To confuse your friends
- To get girls
- To get put into a mental hospital

These are all workings. Each could be a goal of a given statement. Successful working, to be a useful truth criteria, must help us sort out verbal statements into true and false categories. Since it cannot do so if it involves only directly contacted and unanalyzed consequences, as I have just shown, I conclude that successful working *must be a matter of contacting verbally specified consequences*. We must say which of these many consequences I have just listed, or many others, is of importance to a speaker.

Unlike its non-verbal variant, successful working that is limited to a verbal sense of "working" can be applied to actions, and it does not always yield the same answer. Suppose a person is engaged in scientific action x. As a contextualist I ask this person "is this working?" or "is this effective?" as a means of assessing the truth value of this activity. If the referent of "working" is totally non-verbal, the answer must always be "in the past, yes; in the future, I do not know." But if "working" is a matter of reaching specified consequences, I must first ask "toward what are you working?" Only when I have a clear answer may I usefully ask "is this working?" in the sense of "is this moving you toward your specified consequence?" Even very richly reinforced behavior can fail such a test.

In short, to be mounted as a truth criterion, successful working first requires a goal, *and that goal must be stated verbally*. A verbal goal is simply the statement of a consequence of interest (for the rest of the paper when I refer to goals I mean verbal goals). Once we have a goal, we can assess the degree to which analytic practices have helped us achieve this goal in the past, or the degree to which they are likely to do so in the future, based on an even verbal broader history that is involved in the verbal construction of a future.

Implicit goals are not very useful for these purposes, because we can always construct a verbal description of our direct operant history. That is, we can always tell a story, post hoc, that would make sense of current behavior in terms of past consequences. Only explicit, stated, specific, *a priori* goals can make successful working a trustworthy guide to analysis.

Why Goals Cannot Ultimately Be Justified

I have just argued that there is no way to apply successful working usefully without a goal. If so, since successful working is the means by which contextualists evaluate events, it must be the case that goals themselves cannot ultimately be evaluated or justified, only stated. To evaluate a goal via successful working would require yet another goal, but then that second goal could not be evaluated.

At times we do have hierarchies of goals. For example, we may have process goals that are linked to outcome goals—we seek goal x because we believe that goal y will then be more likely to be reached. In such a case, goal x can be evaluated in terms of its contribution to the achievement of goal y. In this case, however, goal y cannot be justified or evaluated.

Thus, *ultimate analytic goals are foundational in contextualism*. Such goals must simply be stated—naked and in the wind—they cannot be justified.

THE COMMON ERROR OF CONTEXTUALISTS: DOGMATISM

Dogmatism is a matter of cognitive claims that go beyond the cognitive evidence. If my analysis is sound, without an explicit goal, all cognitive claims by contextualists are dogmatic. Furthermore, all attempts to justify or objectify ultimate goals are dogmatic.

The purpose of a truth criterion is to provide a means to evaluate the cognitive basis for claims. It follows that the cognitive basis for any claim must be inadequate if the truth criterion itself is inadequately or improperly applied. In absence of explicit goals the claims made by contextualists are being made without basis—they are dogmatic.

James: The First Contextualistic Dogmatist

William James is acknowledged by all as the father of contextualistic thought. Building on the pragmatism of Charles Pierce, he was an extremely popular figure in his time. His lectures and books were attended and read not just by philosophers or psychologists, but by the educated public.

What most fascinated the public was his view of truth, and the implications of that view. Here are a few statements about truth from James' 1907 book *Pragmatism*:

> Truth is one species of good. (p. 37)
>
> The true is the name of whatever proves itself to be good in the way of belief, and good, too, for definite, assignable reasons. (p. 37)

> True ideas are those we can assimilate, validate, corroborate and verify. False ideas are those that we cannot. That is the practical difference it makes to us to have true ideas. (p. 92)
>
> The connexions and transitions come to us from point to point as being progressive, harmonious, satisfactory. This function of agreeable leading is what we mean by an idea's verification. (p. 93)
>
> To "agree" in the widest sense with a reality can only mean to be guided either straight up to it or in its surroundings, or to be put into such working touch with it as to handle either it or something connected with it better than if we disagreed. (p. 96)

What is noticeable about these quotes is the almost complete lack of concern over the purposes of analysis. Good things must be good for "definite, assignable reasons" but these presumably can be assigned post hoc. As I have already discussed, however, post hoc analysis of consequences does not enable meaningful distinctions to be made.

In my opinion, James missed the point for a reason: theism. A deeply religious man, James was intensely troubled by Darwin. He was fascinated by Darwinian thought, and was too intellectually honest to dismiss it, but he was horrified at its implications for religious belief. One of the main reasons James was so widely followed by the public was the relief he provided to believers from the relentless onslaught of materialistic science.

In the book *Pragmatism*, a series of public lectures given by James, his analysis of truth builds to a climax that is captured in this quote:

> On pragmatistic principles, if the hypothesis of God works satisfactorily in the widest sense of the word, it is true. Now whatever its residual difficulties may be, experience shows that it certainly does work, and that the problem is to build it out and determine it so that it will combine satisfactorily with all the other working truths. (p. 133)

Of most direct interest is the phrase "experience shows that it certainly does work." The questions fairly shouts out: *work towards what?* James never states that question nor its answer—brushing the issue aside by claiming that the workability of religion is *obvious*. In James' hands, religion is true simply because people enjoy the belief. But this non-explicit sense of workability cannot withstand scrutiny.

In my opinion, James' mixture of religious belief and pragmatism was dogmatic, not because all religious beliefs must be so, but because he *refused to state his analytic goals clearly and explicitly*. Had he stated his goals, religious belief would have had to compete with all other forms of analysis assessed in terms of these same goals.

Skinner: More Contextualistic Dogmatism

I have argued elsewhere that Skinner is best viewed as an implicit contextualist (e.g., Hayes, Hayes, & Reese, 1988). Skinner was certainly explicit about his embrace of a pragmatic truth criterion:

> [Scientific knowledge] is a corpus of rules for effective action, and there is a special sense in which it could be "true" if it yields the most effective action possible. . . . (A) proposition is "true" to the extent that with its help the listener responds effectively to the situation it describes. (Skinner, 1974, p. 235)

This quote could have easily been written by James himself. But, once again, there is no sensitivity to the goals of the analysis, and no attempt to distinguish specified from merely contacted consequences.

When Skinner did talk about the consequences of science he did so as descriptions of the world, not as goals.

> What we call the scientific conception of a thing is not passive knowledge. Science is not concerned with contemplation. When we have discovered the laws which govern a part of the world about us, and when we have organized these laws into a system, we are then ready to deal effectively with that part of the world. By predicting the occurrence of an event we are able to prepare for it. By arranging conditions in ways specified by the laws of a system, we not only predict, we control: we "cause" an event to occur or to assume certain characteristics. (1953, p. 14)
>
> To predict and control the behavior of the individual organism. This is our "dependent variable"— the effect for which we are to find the cause. (1953, p. 35)

When Skinner says that science is not contemplative, he is claiming this as a matter of fact. In his hands, it is also a matter of fact that the purposes of science are prediction and behavioral influence.

This is another type of dogmatism. If a contextualist says "the goal is x" how is this claim to be evaluated? Viewing goals as statements of facts that emerge from analysis creates an infinite regress: the adequacy of the analysis can only be evaluated against still other goals. What were Skinner's analytic goals against which we can assess the truth of the statement that prediction and control are the purposes of science? Viewed as a contextualist, Skinner should have said "*My* goals are to predict and control behavior." This is absolutely Skinner's privilege.

What is wrong with both Skinner and James is that they are appealing to the nature of the world, not to their own values. They refuse to stand naked in front of us and declare their intentions. Both of their positions are dogmatic for that reason.

How to Avoid Dogmatism

I have argued that contextualism cannot mount its truth criterion non-dogmatically without the statement of a goal, for without it there is no non-dogmatic basis for the evaluation of the "success" part of successful working. And there can be no contextualistic grounds for evaluating these goal—to do so only delays the inevitable. Contingency-shaped behavior does not qualify: by this criterion, any action is successful working, from suicide to Hitler's Germany.

If one's goal is to make contextualism more workable as a scientific philosophy that helps foster systematic development of a line of thought, then some specific recommendations can be made:

1. Avoid implicit goals. These types of goals give a free range to dogmatism, and tend to move analysis toward the parochial and primitive.
2. Avoid vague goals or goals that cannot be assessed. Both types of goals weaken the workability of successful working itself.
3. Avoid incompatible goals. It is difficult to move in two directions at once.
4. Avoid using solely short term goals. Extremely short term goals change frequently by their very nature. This is not good for science if your goal is systematic development of a perspective or point of view.
5. Avoid extremely long term goals, without medium and short term goals. If goals are too long term, the evaluation of their accomplishment is indefinitely delayed, and thus their usefulness as a guide is lost. What seems to be needed if systematic development is important, are goals at various levels, all in harmony.
6. Avoid rapidly changing goals. This is not really a problem as long as you state your goals clearly as they change.
7. Compare performance to goals. There is no point in having a criterion that is never used as such.
8. Compare courses of action and modify your behavior accordingly. It is not enough to show that your activities move in the direction of a goal. If one truly values the goal, then one values efficiency in reaching it. Thus, we must be concerned with the *relative* performance of various courses of action.

THE TWO CONTEXTUALISMS

Understanding the importance of goals to contextualism helps us understand why there are different contextualistic theories. I believe these can be divided, currently, into two loose groupings: descriptive contextualism and functional contextualism.

Descriptive Contextualism

Descriptive contextualists have a fairly personal purpose of analysis: they seek an appreciation of the whole by the examination of its participants. This purpose is a kind of coherence goal, but it differs from the coherence criterion of the organicist in several ways. First, there is no assumption that there is any ultimate analysis. An analysis that works at one time may not work at another; one that works for me, may not work for you. Second, advances in one area need not imply advances in another—to understand what it is like to get older does not mean that we understand phobias. Both of these differences come from the dispersive quality of contextualism. Third, the coherence sought is intensely personal—descriptive contextualists seek an active appreciation of the quality of an event by situating it in its various contextual strands.

A Model: History. A ready way to understand descriptive contextualists and their goal is to compare their enterprise to that of history (as, indeed, they themselves do, e.g., L.J. Hayes, 1992). History involves constructing and reconstructing the story behind historical records or "facts." The word "facts" must be in quotes, because the story changes the actual quality of the facts themselves: as context changes, quality changes, and vice versa. For example, the launching of the American civil war can be interpreted as a fight over slavery, or a fight over the economic subjugation of the South by the North. The purpose of the construction of the story is to appreciate the quality of the event—to see how the civil war came to be and what it meant. What the war was changes as the story changes.

The difficulty faced by history is that it is difficult to know when knowledge has truly advanced. Are we moving ahead or falling behind? A contextualist approaching history as an area of study is struck both by the extreme dispersiveness of knowledge, and by its tie to the personal history of the analyst. So extreme may this sense be that one is tempted to deny the progressivity of knowledge entirely.

In Psychology. A descriptive contextualist in the world of psychology approaches the study of a whole organism interacting in and with a historical and situational context much as a historian. A narrative is created that reveals the multiple historical strands and current context of a psychological action. Such a story can attempt to be sensitive to the actual features that participated in the event for the doer, but the descriptive contextualist readily admits that he or she cannot escape the effects of personal history and that no interpretation is ultimate or final. Knowledge is personal, and necessarily somewhat ephemeral. Dramaturgy, hermeneutics, field theoretical, interbehavioral, and narrative approaches are instances of this type of contextualism (e.g., see Rosnow & Georgoudi, 1986).

Strengths and Weaknesses. The strength of descriptive contextualists is that they can more readily stay true to the underlying root metaphor of contextualism. Their purposes do not threaten a holistic perspective, or so it seems. Their problem is three-fold.

First, it is difficult to assess and to share the accomplishment of their goal. When have we told the story well enough? And how can you share a personal experience of coherence? It is difficult to build a progressive science based on a descriptive contextualism. In fact, many descriptive contextualists specifically eschew the possibility. But the more forcefully that argument is made, the fewer reasons they can give to others to listen to them.

Second, while the explicit goal of descriptive contextualists may be an appreciation of the whole through examination of the participants, it is difficult to cordon off other, more directly practical goals. But what grounds are there to argue that an experience of coherence will lead to practical benefits? Descriptive contextualists can resolve this by suggesting that their experience of coherence comes from their greater appreciation of reality which ultimately must be of practical benefit, but to do so is to lean perilously close to organicism. One safe step seems to be to deny that any practical benefits will necessarily flow from analysis, but this is an argument that one may win intellectually only to lose politically. Another approach is to attempt to demonstrate practical benefit, but to do so requires the use of methods—especially experimental ones—that challenge the holistic perspective. It is not easy for descriptive contextualists to use traditional empirical methods (other than naturalistic observational methods), and yet its own methods are either poorly developed or not oriented toward the evaluation of practical impact.

The final problem is a difficult one to explain: the purpose of the descriptive contextualist is subtly contradictory. To appreciate the whole by the examination of its participants does not mean to start with the whole: this is analytically impossible. To say anything about the whole, one must at least have the talk about the whole and the talked about whole: that is, there must be two. This obvious contradiction has a negative impact on analysis *per se*. Like a monk on a mountaintop, there is a tendency as one appreciates more and more to say less and less. The contradiction is lessened, however, when we start instead with the "event" and this is the path taken by contextualistic academics (as compared to mystics). But the event is not the whole, and descriptive contextualists are constantly threatened by a never-ending whirlpool, on both ends of analysis.

On the one hand, to see that the event we seek to understand is but a tiny, arbitrarily abstracted part of the whole leads inexorably to an interest in ever larger units, until one is dealing with the undivided experience of now, about which nothing can honestly be said (L.J. Hayes, 1992). If we lose the event, we lose our voice. On the other hand, even if the descriptive contextualist hangs on tight to the event, appreciating the participants in the event also takes us in ever widening circles: "The analysis of an event consists in the exhibition of its texture, and the exhibition of its texture is the discrimination of its strands, and the full discrimination of its strands is the exhibition of other textures . . . and so on from event to event as long as we wish to go, which would be forever or until we got tired" (Pepper, 1942, p. 249). What saves contextualists from these whirlpools is practical action: "Serious analysis for [the contextualist] is always either directly or indirectly practical (Pepper, 1942, p. 250). But the practical purpose of the descriptive contextualist is ethereal: it is difficult to state, share, or measure. To admit this is to risk a cacophony; to deny it is to risk a collapse into organicism.

Functional Contextualism

Functional Contextualists have an intensely practical purpose for analysis: the prediction-and-influence of events. Influence is a better word than "control," not just for political reasons but also because "control" refers to the elimination of behavioral variability in an absolute sense. To accomplish a particular end I may need to eliminate some forms of variability, but that does not mean that action without variability in an absolute sense is better "understood." The issue is not elimination of all variability, but rather in psychology it is the production of specified response functions, and thus "influence" is a better term (Biglan, 1993).

A Model: Engineering. A ready way to understand functional contextualists and their goal is to compare their enterprise to that of engineering (as, indeed, they themselves do). Engineers are interested in ways of speaking about the physical world that lead to the prediction-and-influence of events. The goal is hyphenated because purely predictive knowledge would be of little use without an ability to change the course of events. Simply to know that a bridge will fail is not enough—we must know how to make it not fail.

Engineers have little use for knowledge in the abstract: when physicists argue about the degree to which string theory can capture the nature of reality, the engineer might remind them that there is no difference that does not make a difference. Because of their practical goals, however, engineers do not just seek practical outcomes on a trial and error basis, much as a craftsman might. Experience has shown that in the long run it is more practically beneficial to have verbal rules with sufficient precision and scope to allow some outcomes to be predicted and influenced. Thus, it is for *practical* reasons that the engineer has an interest in parsimonious knowledge that coheres. It is easier to have a small set of principles than a large one. But the engineer will make do with whatever works, even if that means that principles in one domain do not apply to another, while a third domain has no good principles at all. In other words, the engineer would prefer that knowledge be tight-knit and comprehensive, but is willing to accept whatever approximations exist. The preference for comprehensive principles is not an ontological statement but a practical one.

In Psychology. A functional contextualist in the world of psychology approaches the study of a whole organism interacting in and with a historical and situational context much as an engineer and as a physicist interested in engineering (the actual field of engineering can stand on physics, but psychology cannot, so psychologists must be interested in both roles). Functional contextualists have an interest in both applied psychology on the one hand, and theory of behavior change on the other. An analysis is constructed that points to features of the historical strands and current context of a psychological action that can effectively guide the behavior of the scientist/engineer. The functional contextualist readily admits that he or she cannot escape the effects of personal history and that no interpretation is ultimate or final, but knowledge can be shared and practical when principles emerge that effectively guide the actions of other analysts. Because the best way to test the general utility of principles that involve behavior change is controlled experimentation, this method is often embraced. While generally applicable rules of action are sought, the functional contextualist is willing to accept whatever approximations exist. The preference for comprehensive principles is not an ontological statement but a practical one.

Strengths and Weaknesses. The strength of functional contextualists is that they can readily assess and share the accomplishment of their goals. They know when they have constructed an analysis well enough—when they can predict-and-influence behavior with adequate precision and scope. While admitting that knowledge may not be progressive, they are happy to take order where they find it.

The weakness of functional contextualism is that its methods threaten its root metaphor. Contextualists can borrow mechanistic methods in the services of their goals, but they can in turn be swayed by the implicit values of these methods and become mechanists. Accomplishing practical outcomes requires the division of the whole into parts. Most especially, if one becomes interested in behavioral influence, one must distinguish between events that are—at least in principle—manipulable and those that are not. To influence another's action one must manipulate context—it is never possible to manipulate action directly (Hayes & Brownstein, 1986).

It is not just that it is impossible to manipulate the totality—the descriptive contextualist's looming whole is not the functional contextualists problem; rather even the simplest event must be subdivided. A person goes to the restaurant to buy lunch. If I seek to influence this event I must temporarily act as if "going to the restaurant to buy lunch" is the action, while the restaurant, the time of day, the money used to buy the food, and so on, are abstractable from this event. I do this so that I can manipulate events that might alter the likelihood of going to the restaurant.

This action immediately presents three problems. First, functional contextualists define stimuli functionally. But when I divide an event into pieces and distinguish verbs from manipulable nouns, I am beginning to treat context as a mechanical object: I am only a short step away from mechanism. A second problem is closely related. If I am manipulating stimuli, and stimuli are functions, and these functions are response functions, how can I distinguish "responses" from "stimuli?" Suppose I turn the clock back to 11 a.m. and find that the person I am studying does not go to the restaurant for lunch. Surely it is not the clock that had this effect—it is the person *seeing* the clock. But if so, what of my practical distinction between manipulable and non-manipulable events? It begins to seem that all knowledge is indirect. I can manipulate only that which does not truly interest me: there is a gap in knowledge that cannot be closed. There is a final problem related to the first: what of the analyst? When I divide action and context, even for pragmatic purposes, am I not standing apart from the analysis, as if the contextual features I identify are not an aspect of *my* interaction with the world? When I "change the clock" am I not speaking of an event that I know through my interaction with the world? Thus, the functional contextualist faces another kind of whirlpool—one in which the practical purposes of analysis within a contextualistic root metaphor leads to distinctions that are practically useful and thus fulfill the contextualistic truth criterion but are incomprehensible within the root metaphor. A functional contextualist must either tolerate permanent ambiguity of this kind, resolve the matter by abandoning behavioral influence as a goal, or resolve the matter by abandoning contextualism.

GOALS AND THE FORMS OF CONTEXTUALISM

The strength of descriptive contextualism is the ease with which the root metaphor can be maintained, but the weakness is the difficulty of mounting the truth criterion. The strength of functional contextualism is the ease with which the truth criterion can be mounted, but its weakness is the difficulty of maintaining contact with the root metaphor. Descriptive contextualists are tempted by organicism when their coherence goal hardens into its own truth criterion; functional contextualists are tempted by mechanism when the methods used harden into analytic assumptions.

While both forms of contextualism have problems, both are both truly contextualistic. The choice of a goal in contextualism is *arbitrary*—not in the sense that it makes no difference (it makes an enormous difference) but in the sense that the choice is pre-analytic. It is a metric for analysis, not the result of analysis. Thus, neither descriptive nor functional contextualists can claim that their goal is the "right" goal or only goal one might choose. Conversely, no one may claim that, for example, functional contextualists are wrong to have behavioral influence as a goal.

Choosing a goal has consequences for the types of research that are likely to be done and thus contextualistic positions can differ dramatically while remaining contextualistic. It is my argument that, when the goals of analysis are recognized, these contextualistic positions present themselves as a family of positions. As a functional contextualist, I can agree heartily with the assumptions held by descriptive contextualists and still not *be* one, simply because my goals are different. Descriptive contextualists are not the enemies of functional contextualists, and there are no causes for disagreement with their purposes. At times, the issues descriptive contextualists face will be of direct relevance to me, but other times they will not.

Whatever Happened to American Pragmatism?

I began this chapter with two the curious facts: (a) that early American psychology was frequently contextualistic, but modern day psychology is not, and

(b) contextualism seems to mean so many things. I have attempted to account for both of these facts. It should be clear by now why there is a diversity of contextualistic positions, but whatever happened to the psychology of James, Dewey, Angel, and the like? If modern contextualists cannot give a coherent answer, the recent renewed interest in contextualism may be the beginning of another trend going nowhere.

I believe that the present discussion points to the critical error that was made: the early contextualists did not specify their analytic goals clearly and self-consciously. Because the earliest contextualists were largely descriptive, they could avoid noticing the problem this creates. It cannot be by accident that James, Dewey, Kantor, and the like were more philosophers than experimental scientists—they were descriptive contextualists. As such, they hung on to the root metaphor, but the lack of a clear guide to the use of their truth criterion undermined a sense of progressivity to their knowledge.

American psychology gradually turned away in frustration, looking for a more "empirical"—especially a more experimental—approach. Experimentation is difficult for descriptive contextualists: it is not a method that fits their purpose. The students of Dewey and James, and their students, became experimental psychologists, but in so doing, they gradually lost contact with the contextualistic root metaphor. As a result, the functionalists gradually moved toward other positions, especially mechanism.

Thus the same central issue that explains the current diversity within contextualism, also explains why the original pragmatists were so easily and quietly swallowed up. Contextualism permits many analytic goals, but it eventually exiles those who are not clear about their goals.

As pragmatism emerges again, it seems critical to me that the original error not be repeated. I have identified two main types of contextualism, though I admit there could be many more. It doesn't matter how many types there are or which type is dominant. What does matter is an appreciation of the centrality of analytic goals to all forms of contextualism. If contextualists are to avoid the error of dogmatism, in my view, they need both a firm grasp on their root metaphor, and a firm grasp on the outcomes they will use as an analytic metric.

REFERENCES

Biglan, A. (1993). A functional contextualist framework for community interventions. Chapter in S. C. Hayes, L. J. Hayes, H. W. Reese, & T. R. Sarbin (Eds.), *Varieties of scientific contextualism* (pp. 251–276). Oakland, CA: Context Press / New Harbinger Publications.

Biglan, A.,& Hayes, S.C. (1996). Should the behavioral sciences become more pragmatic? The case for functional contextualism in research on human behavior.

Hayes, L.J. (1992). The psychological present. *The Behavior Analyst, 15*, 139–146.

Hayes, S.C. (1992). Verbal relations, time, and suicide. In S.C. Hayes & L.J. Hayes (Eds.), *Understanding verbal relations* (pp. 109–118). Reno, NV: Context Press.

Hayes, S. C. & Brownstein, A. J. (1986). Mentalism, behavior-behavior relations and a behavior analytic view of the purposes of science. *The Behavior Analyst, 9*, 175–190.

Hayes, S.C., Hayes, L.J., & Reese, H.W. (1988). Finding the philosophical core: A review of Stephen C. Pepper's *World Hypotheses. Journal of the Experimental Analysis of Behavior, 50*, 97–111.

James, W. (1907; reprinted in 1981). *Pragmatism.* Indianapolis, IN: Hackett

Pepper, S.C. (1942). *World hypotheses: A study in evidence.* Berkeley: University of California Press.

Rosnow, R., & Georgoudi, M. (1986). (Eds.), *Contextualism and understanding in behavioral science.* New York: Praeger.

Skinner, B.F. (1953). *Science and human behavior.* New York: Free Press.

Skinner, B.F. (1974). *About behaviorism.* New York: Knopf.

ARTICLE 7

BEHAVIORAL EPISTEMOLOGY INCLUDES NONVERBAL KNOWING

From Hayes, S.C. (1997). In L.J. Hayes & P. M. Ghezzi (Eds.). *Investigations in behavioral epistemology* (pp. 35–43). Reno, NV: Context Press.

Psychology has sometimes been called the "queen of the sciences" because any form of scientific knowledge is based on the psychological activity of scientists. This fact creates some difficulty for psychologists themselves, however, particularly because psychologists are responsible for understanding processes of knowing. When psychologists know something in their discipline, the very process by which they know whatever is known is itself, in principal, part of their disciplinary content domain. I will term this the "paradox of verbal knowing" in which knowing about knowing is both a *process* of knowing and an *object* of knowledge simultaneously.

Contemporary behavior analysts are particularly sensitive to this issue. That is because behavioral analysis takes an inherently contextualistic approach to scientific knowledge (S. C. Hayes, Hayes, & Reese, 1988). As such, a behavior analytic approach is part of the larger tradition of American pragmatism.

Pragmatic schools of thought adopt a truth criterion of "successful working" or one of its variants. In this approach to truth, verbal formulations are not "true" because they correspond with some known real world but because the verbal formulation at issue helps humans accomplish their analytic ends. The pragmatic approach to verbal knowledge is an inherently psychological and a-ontological position. The inherently psychological quality of behavioral epistemology makes the paradox of verbal knowing especially acute for behavior analysts. When the behavior analyst claims to "know something" it is impossible to forget that this "knowing" is assessed by the ability of the knower to do something with the "knowledge." Said another way, the contingencies influencing the behavior of the scientist are necessarily included in any knowledge claim made by contemporary behavioral psychologists. As a result, the paradox of verbal knowing is inescapable and is built right into the analytic units of the behavior analytic position itself.

In the present chapter I take as my task identifying what it means to "know" something and furthermore identifying what it means to say that a "person" knows something. We will build out the paradox of knowing I have already described, and will seek a kind of "solution" to the paradox.

DISTINGUISHING VERBAL AND NONVERBAL KNOWING

There has been a good deal of confusion in both psychology and philosophy between verbal and nonverbal forms of "knowing." This confusion becomes especially mischievous when it is further confused with the process of scientific knowing—an inherently verbal process—that is being applied to verbal and nonverbal knowing as distinct content domains. In other words, verbal knowledge about knowing can be about either kind: verbal or nonverbal. This mix of processes and different types of content—all of which involve "knowing"—can create a morass from which it is nearly impossible to escape. Many behavior analysts sense this problem and avoid it by refusing to speak of knowing at all. That, however, does not solve the paradox of verbal knowing, which does not come from mere terminological confusion, or from a willingness to use loose terms such as "knowing." It is a problem fundamental to any truth claim including those within behavior analysis itself.

It is instructive that in English, as well as other similar languages, the word "know" comes from two etymological roots. In Latin the word *gnocere* meant to "know by the senses" whereas the word *scire* meant "to know by the mind." The similar meanings and similar sounds lead in English to a single word: "know." Many of the important terms that we need to consider in behavioral epistemology come from one or the other of these roots. For example, both the word "science" and the word "consciousness" come from *scire*. These two senses of knowing are reflected in modern behavior analytic distinctions between verbal and nonverbal domains (S. C. Hayes & Wilson, 1993).

Nonverbal Knowing

Nonverbal knowledge has been described by philosophers as "know how." That is, it is the kind of knowledge that is direct and experience based. Nonverbal knowledge is a name for the organism's behavioral repertoire that has been built and elaborated through contact with contingencies, and through forms of generalization built upon the evolutionary history of contact with contingencies by a particular biological species. The field of animal learning is the very field of nonverbal knowing.

For example, through operant conditioning a pigeon might learn to peck a red key because such pecks are followed by food. The pecks on the key are due to the organism's direct contact with the relationship between antecedent and consequent events and this behavioral activity. Based on this direct history the animal may now also peck an orange key, though perhaps at a lower rate or less consistently. Pecking the orange key is not due to the direct history of the individual, but rather on the evolutionary history of birds and their interaction with the visual spectrum. Light is organized along a quantifiable physical dimension. Normal variations in, say, red edible seeds are more likely to include orange seeds than, say, blue seeds. Biological organisms sensitive to the visual spectrum evolved in contact with such contingencies and thus red is more "formally similar" to orange. Such processes as operant or classical conditioning, or of stimulus and response generalization based on the formal properties of events in this evolutionary sense, are the domain of nonverbal knowledge.

Who "knows" when we are speaking only of this kind of knowledge? The nonverbal "self" can be categorized in a number of meaningful ways. A nonverbal knower can be thought of as a kind of behavioral stream: a total history of behavioral interactions. One can think of the nonverbal self as a biological locus of particular behavioral activities. Or the two can be combined, as seems most common in behavioral psychology.

Verbal Knowing

Verbal knowing and the verbal self is a different matter entirely. First we need to consider what it means to "know something" verbally or "cognitively" (cognition, oddly enough, comes from *gnocere*, or "knowing by the senses"—do cognitive psychologists know this?). I have argued that the essence of verbal behavior is derived and arbitrarily applicable stimulus relations (S. C. Hayes & Hayes, 1989, 1992; S. C. Hayes & Wilson, 1993). A detailed presentation of this material is unnecessary given that it is available elsewhere, but a brief summary is needed.

A stimulus relation is responding to one stimulus in terms of another. Operant and classical conditioning involve stimulus relations in that sense. Derived stimulus relations occur when one stimulus is responded to in terms of another not because of direct training with the stimuli of interest, nor because of generalization based on formal properties, but because of a generalized history of responding in particular ways to one stimulus in terms of another. When derived stimulus relations are brought under the control of contextual cues and can be applied to arbitrary sets of events, we can speak of arbitrarily applicable relational responding. Because there are a variety of ways to respond to one stimulus in terms of another, there are a variety of arbitrarily applicable relational responses. Particular types we term "relational frames."

Stimulus equivalence is an example of what we have called a "frame of coordination" and it reveals their general properties. Relational frames are bidirectional and combinatorial: stimulus equivalence specifically shows symmetry and transitivity. The stimulus functions of events framed relationally can be transformed: stimulus equivalence specifically shows the transfer of functions from one event in the relation to another. These processes are quite basic to human functioning. Children as young as sixteen months have acquired derived stimulus relations (Lipkens, Hayes, & Hayes, 1993). By at least age two not only do children know that a novel name probably refers to the novel object, but they will also begin to call the novel object by that name without additional training (Lipkens et al., 1993). Also by age two bidirectional relational frames can be combined to form networks of relations (Lipkens et al., 1993).

In our conception, the ability to construct extended stimulus networks increases over time, as does the kinds of derived relations involved. Children are taught relational frames of cause and effect, opposition, comparison, time, and many others. The behavioral functions of the increasingly verbal world they live in are transformed accordingly. For example, novel contingencies can be described to even very young children. As a result, present behavior becomes verbally related to increasingly abstract, derived, remote, and probabilistic consequences.

The nature of self is expanded when verbal relations are considered. In addition to self as a behavioral stream, self as a physical organism, or their combination, we add three more. The *self as the object of verbal knowledge* occurs because humans can derive relations between their own on-going unified stream of behavior and a panoply of verbal categories. This is the sense of self that is involved when a person lists their attributes, relates their history, or describes their propensities. *Self as the on-going process of verbal knowledge* refers to the degree to which persons are "self-aware" or "mindful" as events occur. This is similar to the first category, but is not evaluative or ossified, and focuses more on the action of relating events verbally, than the referential objects of that activity.

The final category is *self as the experiential locus of knowledge*. This category is important to the present argument and thus a more extended analysis will be made. The core argument is that in order to have the ability to report events verbally, it is necessary to develop a sense of perspective or point of view (see S. C. Hayes, 1984 for a more extended discussion).

From a behavioral point of view, self-awareness is responding to ones' own responding. Skinner (1974) used the example of seeing. Most nonhuman animals see, but humans also see that they see.

> There is a . . . difference between behaving and reporting that one is behaving or reporting the causes of one's behavior. In arranging conditions under which a person describes the public or private world in which

he lives, a community generates that very special form of behavior called knowing. . . . Self-knowledge is of social origin. (Skinner, 1974, p. 30)

Supposedly this happens dominantly through language. As we learn to answer such questions as "What happened to you yesterday? What did you see? What did you eat?" and so on, there emerges a generalized tendency to respond verbally one's own behavior. This is important to the social/verbal community because it gives indirect social access to events occurring elsewhere. As Skinner says, "It is only when a person's private world becomes important to others that it is made important to him" (Skinner, 1974, p. 31).

In order to have the ability to report events verbally in a sophisticated manner, however, it is necessary to develop a sense of perspective or point of view and to distinguish this from others. For example, we may need to learn to report what we ate this morning but also what someone else ate. We must learn to report what we see but also to suppose what it is that others may see. This process of learning to take a perspective is amplified by verbal terms such as "here" and "there" which are defined in relation to a perspective or locus.

When people are asked many, many questions about their history or experience, the only thing that will be consistent is not the *content* of the answer, but the *context* or perspective from which the answer occurs. "I" in some meaningful sense *is* the location that is left behind when all of the content differences are subtracted out. For example, notice what is consistent in answers to the questions "What happened to you yesterday? What did you see? What did you eat?" We will answer "I did such and such," "I saw so and so," and "I ate this and that." The "I" that is referred to is not just a physical organism; it is also a locus, place, or perspective. "Pure consciousness," "being," "spirituality," and "observer self" are among the many terms that have been used to describe this sense of self. It has these qualities, because consciousness is not thing-like for the person being conscious. One can be conscious of the limits of everything except one's own consciousness. For that reason, this sense of perspective or self as a place from which things occur does not change once it emerges in early childhood.

Summary

If verbal and nonverbal forms of knowing are crossed with the locus and nature of knowing, a two by two table results. In the nonverbal column the locus of knowing is not itself a psychological event and is not reflexive. The nature of knowing is defined by direct processes such as operant and classical conditioning. Conversely in the verbal column the locus of knowing is the conscious "I." We have just argued that this quality is itself a psychological event; a side effect of language defined by the learned sense of perspective or point of view. The nature of knowing is, in the verbal column, arbitrarily applicable relational responding.

VERBAL KNOWLEDGE AND THE TRUTH CRITERION OF CONTEXTUALISM

We return now to the implications of this kind of distinction between verbal and nonverbal knowing for behavioral epistemology and the paradox of verbal knowing. Psychology as a functional contextualist system is a social enterprise that has as its purpose the generation of increasingly organized statements about whole organisms interacting in and with their historical and current situational environment that allow those interactions to be predicted and influenced with precision, scope, and depth (Biglan & Hayes, 1996). I have argued elsewhere (S. C. Hayes, 1993) that pragmatic positions must clearly specify, as this definition does, both the content domain and analytic goals of their science.

The accomplishment of goals within a domain constitutes the truth criterion of contextualistic approaches. When behavior analysts show (using concepts and analyses with precision, scope, and depth) an ability to predict and influence the actions of individuals interacting with their environment, the "truth" of these analyses is demonstrated. All "truth" in pragmatism is local—it is not ultimate truth—but that does not mean that truth may not be shared. Indeed, if our goal is a scientific analysis with scope (horizontal breadth of application within a domain) and depth (vertical consistency across domains), then only concepts that have shared value are considered to be useful.

The "successful working" goal of contextualism does not remove the researcher from contact with the paradox of verbal knowing, however. Consider what happens if a skeptical inquirer asks the pragmatist "How do you know that it works?" This question is a very tricky one to answer. It seems to demand an analysis or justification of the scientific act of knowing. In that case, scientific knowing is now an object of verbal knowledge, and the scientist is being asked to engage in a scientific process of knowing with regard to that object. Barnes and Roche (1997) have successfully applied Relational Frame Theory to this moment. They point out that the scientist is being asked simultaneously to be here (analyzing) and there (analyzed). The inability simultaneously to respond in terms of here and there is at the very heart of the paradox of verbal knowing.

The normal response to the question "How do you know that it works?" is to point to the objects of verbal knowledge that are taken to be signs of "working." But if this tact is taken we are turning a pragmatic truth criterion into another form of correspondence (L. J. Hayes, 1993). For pragmatists, it is ultimately impossible to justify knowledge claims by pointing to "facts" that fit in with the claim. Successful working is the truth criterion for all "facts" from a pragmatic perspective. To explain and justify a claim that something works by pointing to factual evidence, one would have to show that treating these facts as facts also works, and there we are, back to the original question "How do you know that treating these facts as facts works?"

Using facts to bolster knowledge claims, if taken too far, has a second and more insidious effect. If the comparison between facts and knowledge claims is the ultimate source of knowledge about workability, then correspondence between a workability claim and factual evidence is the source of workability. At that point, the pragmatic truth criterion has been defended by being dismantled because a correspondence truth criterion has been used as its ultimate proof.

The Two by Four Solution

The verbal senses of "self" discussed earlier establish the paradox of verbal knowing. Normally, verbal statements are not self reflexive. They are made, they guide behavior, and the behavior is maintained or not maintained. "There is food in the refrigerator" leads to going to the refrigerator where food is found (or not) and if found leads to eating. Questions about "how" we know are self referential, however. If a person saying "There is food in the refrigerator" is asked the "how" question, the self is now one object of verbal knowledge (knowing "how" is one object), the process of knowing is the second object (statements about the refrigerator as a process of knowing), and knowing about these two objects of analysis is to occur from a locus or point of view (the "I" who knows). As the person enters into the analysis of "objects" one and two, the process of knowing about these objects (these two processes) will contain the same processes. A self amplifying loop is constructed, in which "here" is moved over "there" to examine it, only to find that there is another "here" from which "there" is being examined (Barnes and Roche, 1997).

This loop cannot be avoided so long as all knowledge is verbal knowledge. If "knowing" includes both verbal knowing and nonverbal knowing, however, then the paradox disappears. I have tried to explain what I mean through this metaphor: when someone says "How do you know that it works?" the proper solution is for the analyst to say "How did you know this?" and then promptly reached for a long two by four and hit the skeptical inquirer firmly on the head. I'm not saying that we can or should punish the quizzical nature of our skeptical inquirer. Rather, I am pointing toward a phenomenon. It is not one that I can fully describe, because to do so is to treat it entirely as a verbal event. Nevertheless, I *will* describe it (though please promptly forget that I did): Both verbal and nonverbal functions are experienced by conscious verbal organisms.

A student of mine (Kelly Wilson) cast the situation this way: A philosopher is lying on the floor with an extremely heavy refrigerator having fallen upon him so that he is unable to move. A psychologist comes by and asks the person if they would like to have help in removing the refrigerator. The philosopher answers, "Indeed I would but I have a significant problem." "What's that?" asks the psychologist. The philosopher replies, "Well I have been thinking and I realize that I do not have any way of knowing, if you remove the refrigerator, whether or not it has really been removed." To that the psychologist replies, "Then you also have no way of knowing that there is a refrigerator on you" at which point the psychologist simply leaves.

The adequacy of the two by four solution to the paradox of verbal knowing depends upon a meaningful link between verbal and nonverbal repertoires. Experientially, the link between nonverbal and verbal repertoires is "I": the conscious self as a locus, perspective, or context. There is a sense in which we can be conscious of even nonverbal functions. For example, if I open my eyes and see a light it is not just "me" as a behavioral system or "me" as a biological organism that views the light, it is also "me" as a locus or point of view from which verbal reports have been made that "sees the light." This process is difficult to describe verbally but it is readily available for anyone who has experimented with meditative techniques. It is possible to observe the contents of one's own "mind" in the same way that one observes a tree or a flower. In these meditative states, "I" (as a sense of locus or context) am aware a wide variety of behavioral functions, not all of which are verbal. This sense of awareness is not itself verbal in the sense of derived stimulus relations, though it is a product of a verbal history. Indeed, becoming verbally aware of this very process immediately stops the process.

I am simply claiming that it is possible to be conscious of nonverbal functions without directly turning these functions into verbal functions. Let us go back to the poor unfortunate who has been hit by a two by four after repeatedly asking "How do you know?" As the person is struck by a two by four she may duck or flinch or wince. The person will "know" that she has been struck. That "knowing" is both verbal and nonverbal. If our skeptical inquirer were to stubbornly claim "I do not know that I was just struck" the wise contextualist should challenge that claim by striking the person firmly with a two by four yet again. If the person cannot distinguish between being struck and not being struck there should be no basis for complaint. Conversely, if the person *can* distinguish between these two states, then the person's direct nonverbal contact with that experience should be evidence for the person's capacity for such knowledge. The person "knows" that they have been hit and they "know" that it hurts. If the person was given a way to avoid being hit the person would "know" that the hitting had stopped.

This knowledge is both verbal and nonverbal and must remain so. If the person hit by the two by four suddenly now saw through the paradox of verbal knowing, and wished to communicate or explain that understanding, the paradox of verbal knowing would immediately reappear. "I see it! I know I was hit!" says our poor hapless former skeptic. Another skeptic walking by comes over and says, "How do you know that you were hit?" The former skeptic dare not respond (unless a stick is handy) because the paradoxical loop will begin anew. Thus, one must hold this point lightly. We can find knowledge in our direct experience of workability but we cannot verbally justify that experience without entering into yet another unproductive loop.

The utility criterion can be conceptualized as a known condition of reinforceability or, less technically, a condition in which a particular function would be valued. These behavioral functions cannot be 100% verbal because human behavior is itself not 100% verbal. It is whole organisms that have and that accomplish goals. Such organisms have histories and repertoires that include both verbal and nonverbal domains. The workability criterion requires this, and when goals are set that are very dominantly verbal (e.g., "understanding"), it has a harder time being used without a paralyzing sense of paradox.

We "know" solutions in the same way that we "know" problems: as whole organisms with multiple response systems. We always end up the same way. To claim that the utility criterion leads inevitability to a correspondence criterion thus can be true only if all forms of knowledge are themselves based upon correspondence. It is only a verbal trick, an illusion that seems to lead to the necessity of correspondence. If one insists that all knowledge claims must be "justified" and "explained" (which can only occur within a verbal knowledge system) then utility claims will ultimately dissolve into correspondence claims. However, there is nothing in our psychological knowledge base—indeed there is much to the contrary—that demands that all knowledge be restricted to verbal knowledge.

If a person unaware of Godel's theorem demands that symbolic systems be entirely internally consistent and not begin with postulates or assumptions that go outside of that symbolic system, then only gibberish can result because such systems do not exist. In a similar fashion, human organisms begin as nonverbal organisms and only over time acquire the repertoires that define themselves as verbal. If nonverbal knowledge is based upon function and if all verbal functions are based to some degree on nonverbal functions, then it is not internally inconsistent to allow organisms to have goals and to evaluate the accomplishment of those goals when what is had and what is evaluated goes beyond verbal behavior per se.

CONCLUSION

Contextualism is always threatened by a looming silence. An act in context is knowable only within a context and so on ad infinitum. This infinite regress is avoided by starting and ending in the situated activity of conscious organisms who have both verbal and nonverbal response repertoires. Out of a totality, that includes events I cannot know verbally, I come to care about a particular goal or a state of affairs. Said another way, I have a problem and I wish to solve it. Science provides a means to generate verbal solutions which, if followed, may change that state of affairs. My knowledge of the changed state of affairs comes from the same exact source as my knowledge of the original problem. If I grasp that too tightly and demand that my own verbal repertoire (my "mind") be the beginning and ending of all knowledge, I will necessarily collapse either into silence or into infinite tail-chasing. But this is all an illusion. I begin and end as a human being living in and with the one world. That I have problems is experientially evident in the purposive quality of action as I take a breath, reach for a drink, seek out food, or take a nap. This awareness is not a verbal *justification* of knowledge. Rather as one situates knowledge experientially, the paradox of verbal knowing simply disappears. It does not disappear rationally and that is precisely the point. I have pushed the refrigerator off me and I am free.

REFERENCES

Barnes, D., & Roche, B. (1997). A behavior-analytic approach to behavioral reflexivity. *The Psychological Record, 47*, 543–572.

Biglan, A., & Hayes, S. C. (1996). Should the behavioral sciences become more pragmatic? The case for functional contextualism in research on human behavior. *Applied and Preventive Psychology: Current Scientific Perspectives, 5*, 47–57.

Hayes, L.J. (1993). Reality and truth. In S.C. Hayes, L.J. Hayes, H.W. Reese, & T.R. Sarbin (Eds.), *Varieties of scientific contextualism* (pp. 35–44). Reno, NV: Context Press.

Hayes, S.C. (1984). Making sense of spirituality. *Behaviorism, 12*, 99–110.

Hayes, S.C. (1993). Analytic goals and the varieties of scientific contextualism. In S.C. Hayes, L.J. Hayes, H.W. Reese, & T.R. Sarbin (Eds.), *Varieties of scientific contextualism* (pp. 11–27). Reno, NV: Context Press.

Hayes, S.C., & Hayes, L.J. (1989). The verbal action of the listener as a basis for rule-governance. In S.C. Hayes (Ed.), *Rule-governed behavior: Cognition, contingencies, and instructional control* (pp. 153–190). New York: Plenum.

Hayes, S.C., & Hayes, L.J. (1992). Verbal relations and the evolution of behavior analysis. *American Psychologist, 47*, 1383–1395.

Hayes, S.C., Hayes, L.J., & Reese, H.W. (1988). Finding the philosophical core: A review of Stephen C. Pepper's *World Hypotheses. Journal of the Experimental Analysis of Behavior, 50*, 97–111.

Hayes, S.C., & Wilson, K.G. (1993). Some applied implications of a contemporary behavior-analytic account of verbal events. *The Behavior Analyst, 16*, 283–301.

Lipkens, G., Hayes, S.C., & Hayes, L.J. (1993). Longitudinal study of derived stimulus relations in an infant. *Journal of Experimental Child Psychology, 56*, 201–239.

Skinner, B.F. (1974). *About behaviorism*. New York: Knopf.

Section 2

Principles and Strategies

COGNITION, ASSESSMENT, AND PSYCHOPATHOLOGY

Basic Behavioral Principles and Applied Model

Fredrick Chin and Steven C. Hayes
University of Nevada

Section 2 of the volume is about basic principles and the creation of an applied model. There are three major articles in this section: one was published in the 1980s and two in the 1990s. These articles address the nature of human language and cognition, the extension of functional contextual thinking into assessment, and the core of the psychological flexibility model of psychopathology.

Article 8—Verbal Relations and the Evolution of Behavior Analysis. This article (Hayes & Hayes, 1992) appeared in an issue of the *American Psychologist* on B.F. Skinner's work. It lays out the foundational ideas in Relational Frame Theory, showing that an extension of behavioral thinking can provide exciting new ways forward in the analysis of human cognition. Prior to RFT, behavior analysts had long lists of areas in language research with essentially no empirical methods available. Beginning with the phenomenon of stimulus equivalence, RFT adds the powerful concept of relational operants: arbitrarily applicable derived relational responding as learned patterns of operant behavior. Relational framing is control by two distinct kinds of contextual control: control over the relations among events and control over the functions of related events that are transformed through relational networks. When the two come together, responding to a phrase like "cold, refreshing glass of milk" contains some of the same perceptual features as contact with the actual glass of milk even if the only physically present stimuli are ink marks on a page. This article was written a decade after the earlier conceptual work on rule-governed behavior (Article 1 in the first section), and those concepts of functional forms of rule following have by now been integrated into RFT. The suggestion is that following such rules inflexibly and rigidly could be responsible for psychopathological behaviors, which in turn sets up psychological flexibility as an applied target.

Article 9—The Treatment Utility of Assessment: A Functional Approach to Evaluating Assessment Quality. There is a vast literature on the quality of psychological assessment, but 99% of that literature has no established empirical relationship to treatment outcome. In essence, "quality" is defined structurally rather than functionally. This article (Hayes, Nelson, & Jarrett, 1987) shows that it is possible to imagine an entire system based instead on treatment utility: the establishment of better treatment outcomes produced by assessment outcomes or processes. Indeed, if some of the value of assessment to outcome is due to the process of assessment itself, it is even possible to have treatment utility without the accomplishment of classical test validity and reliability.

Article 10—Experiential Avoidance and Behavioral Disorders: A Functional Dimensional Approach to Diagnosis and Treatment. In much the same way that the field mindlessly relies on structural properties of assessment, it relies on syndromal classification of psychopathology to organize knowledge despite the known lack of treatment utility for that approach. This article (Hayes, Wilson, Gifford, Follette, & Strosahl, 1996) argues for a contextualistic functional dimensional approach as an alternative, in which problematic "behaviors are organized by functional processes that are thought to have produced and maintained them" (Hayes et al., 1996, p. 1153). Such a model would lead directly to targets of intervention. In a CBS approach, the psychological flexibility model has become an example of such a system, but that model began with this article, which presents experiential avoidance (EA) as an example of a functional diagnostic dimension. The article links EA to several maladaptive patterns of behavior and ties the idea of experiential avoidance back to RFT, demonstrating the functional utility of a co-evolution of basic and applied sciences. Experiential avoidance is presented as a specific pattern of inflexible rule-governed behavior, one that is ubiquitous among humans as a by-product of verbal behavior. Evidence to support the pathological nature of EA is presented from basic experimental science (e.g., thought suppression, coping styles), as well as applied research (e.g., research on process and outcome variables in psychotherapy). The definition of EA is quite broad in this article, and some of the work done by this concept is now carried by the closely related concept of psychological flexibility.

REFERENCES

Hayes, S. C. & Hayes, L. J. (1992). Verbal relations and the evolution of behavior analysis. *American Psychologist, 47*, 1383–1395. doi: 10.1037/0003-066X.47.11.1383

Hayes, S. C., Nelson, R. O., & Jarrett, R. B. (1987). Treatment utility of assessment: A functional approach to evaluating the quality of assessment. *American Psychologist, 42*, 963–974. doi: 10.1037/0003-066X.42.11.963
Hayes, S. C., Wilson, K. W., Gifford, E. V., Follette, V. M., & Strosahl, K. (1996). Experiential avoidance and behavioral disorders: A functional dimensional approach to diagnosis and treatment. *Journal of Consulting and Clinical Psychology, 64*, 1152–1168. doi: 10.1037/0022-006X.64.6.1152

ARTICLE 8

VERBAL RELATIONS AND THE EVOLUTION OF BEHAVIOR ANALYSIS

From Hayes, S. C., & Hayes, L. J. (1992). *American Psychologist, 47*, 1383–1395.

The viability of research paradigms is not decided on entirely rational grounds. The history of science is littered with approaches that died not as a result of their intellectual inadequacy, but by virtue of their failure to develop new and exciting research questions. A scientific area not busy being born is busy dying.

Behavior analysis has long been on many psychologists' list of dead or dying areas in psychology. Few would deny that for the last 30 years basic behavioral perspectives have been muscled off the center stage of psychology. Yet behind the scenes, out of view of all but the most behaviorally oriented, the Skinnerian tradition has evolved. It has identified new and exciting research questions and has witnessed an explosion of research interest in these areas. While some key assumptions have come into question, the core of the position seems remarkably intact. It shows every sign of an area that is busy being born.

EARLY BEHAVIOR ANALYTIC RESEARCH WITH HUMANS AND THE PROBLEM OF INSTRUCTIONAL CONTROL

It wasn't long after the onset of behavior analysis as a distinct area that researchers began to turn their attention to human subjects (e.g., Holland, 1958; Hutchinson & Azrin, 1961). Much of this work was predicated on a core assumption of behavior analysis: the continuity assumption. Behavior analysts assumed that principles identified with nonhumans would apply, more or less in whole cloth, to the actions of human organisms. This assumption justified the research program of behavior analysis, which relied heavily on studies with nonhuman organisms. Skinner made clear from the beginning (1938) that he was not so much interested in animal behavior in its own right as he was interested in it as a convenient and potentially worthwhile preparation for the identification of basic processes common to human behavior.

The continuity assumption invited criticism from outside the field in part because it was not clear to others that this assumption was strategic and not fundamental (S. C. Hayes, 1987). There is nothing in evolutionary or behavioral theory that ensures continuity of this sort.

Evolutionary continuity might be expected in the sense that "new contains old" but it is not necessarily true that "old contains new." Evolutionary continuity moves forward in time, not backward. Nonhuman species are not older versions of humans. Investigations across phyla are examinations of tips of branches, not rungs of a ladder. As such, these investigations always involve connections both from new to old (from the present to common ancestors) and from old to new (from common ancestors to the present). Similarity of psychological processes across species thus cannot be assumed.

The continuity assumption was an issue of research strategy, however. Skinner and his followers bet that the same basic processes would prevail across species, and that they would be revealed more readily by studying relatively "simple" nonhuman behavior in relatively "simple" environments, than by studying human complexity directly. We will term this strategy the *continuity strategy*. If the continuity strategy had turned out to be fruitless behavior analysis could still have continued more or less intact—empirical examinations could simply have proceeded with the human species as the focus. Behavior analysts were always aware that the strategy might turn out to be useless in particular areas (Skinner, 1938, p. 442; cf. Skinner, 1957).

The continuity strategy turned out to be even more useful than expected. In many situations humans respond very similarly to nonhumans. Perhaps most important at the time was the great success of practical interventions based on basic behavioral principles. This success buoyed the behavior analytic community, and strengthened their commitment to the continuity strategy.

From the beginning, however, research in the basic laboratory with humans presented problems for behavior analysts. Although humans often behaved similarly to nonhumans, it was also true that human behavior often did *not* show the same effects of behavioral manipulations (e.g., effects due to simple schedules of reinforcement) despite the fact that these effects were nearly ubiquitous in the rest of the animal kingdom (e.g., Leander, Lippman, & Meyer, 1968; Lippman & Meyer, 1967; Weiner, 1964, 1965, 1969).

In addition, powerful effects were shown for a variable that could not be studied with nonhumans in any obvious fashion: instructions. For example, Lippman and Meyer (1967) examined the effects of instructions on performance on a fixed-interval (FI) 20 seconds schedule. Some subjects were told that reinforcement depended merely on the passage of time; others were told that the consequences were response produced. Subjects given the time instructions responded at low rates. Subjects given the response instructions showed high rates of performance on the task. Subjects given minimal instructions responded with one or the other of these two patterns, but not the FI performance characteristic of nonhumans.

Weiner (1970) examined the effects of instructions during extinction. Some subjects were told they could earn up to 700 pennies in the experiment, others that they could earn 999 pennies, while others were told nothing about the pennies they could earn. After 700 pennies had been earned all subjects were exposed to a 2-hour extinction period. Responding in extinction was greatest for those subjects given no instructions, was less for those subjects told they could earn 999 pennies, and was the least for those subjects told they could earn only 700 pennies.

Some behavioral researchers seemed surprised at the powerful effects of instructions, especially when compared to direct contingency control. Early reports termed these effects "remarkable" (Kaufman, Baron, & Kopp, 1966). Others explained instructional effects as simple instances of stimulus control (e.g., Ayllon & Azrin, 1964). The dominant view seemed to be that the effects of instructions were based on remote sources of control in the history of the individual that were inaccessible to the experimenter. They were not perceived by behavior analysts to threaten the continuity strategy. Most notable by its absence was the failure to consider instruction following as an essentially *verbal* event, despite occasional references to its unique features (e.g., Schoenfeld & Cumming, 1963).

Skinner's Approach to the Listener

This approach to instructions was heavily influenced by Skinner's approach to verbal behavior. Skinner formulated his analysis of verbal behavior from the point of view of the speaker rather than the listener in a speaker-listener interchange. He defended this action on multiple grounds, among which were that a complete account of the speaker implies an account of the listener, that an analysis of the listener is unlikely to be empirically productive, and perhaps most importantly, that "the behavior of a man as listener is not to be distinguished from other forms of his behavior" (Skinner, 1957, p. 34). That is, in Skinner's view the behavior of the listener is ordinary operant behavior under the discriminative control of speech (for a more complete review of the plausibility of Skinner's three claims about the listener, see S. C. Hayes & Hayes, 1989). This idea did not ascribe any special importance to the analysis of instructional control, and it explicitly rejected the idea that instructional control was a type of verbal event.

Skinner later drew a useful distinction between contingency-shaped behavior and rule-governed behavior, but his analysis of the listener limited the utility and clarity of this distinction (Parrott, 1987a, 1987b). Skinner defined rule-governed behavior as behavior controlled by contingency-specifying stimuli (1966, 1969). He never defined what he meant by "specify." Instead, he simply provided examples. Recently some behavior analysts have read "specify" to mean "specify verbally" but Skinner himself did not say this until shortly before his death, and then apparently not in writing. The closest he came was in a draft chapter Skinner wrote for a book edited by the first author (S. C. Hayes, 1989b) in which he described rule-governed behavior as "verbal stimulus controlled behavior." He later edited it out, but its appearance shows that he was beginning to deal with how rules could be defined as "verbal rules" within his system. In his early presentations of the concept of rule-governed behavior, Skinner did not distinguish between verbal rules and regularities drawn from other complex antecedents, such as modeling stimuli (e.g., see Skinner, 1969, p. 163).

These characteristics made it difficult at first for behavior analysis to deal effectively with the topic of verbal rules. Based on Skinner's analysis, the concept of "verbal rules" is incomprehensible because he had no behaviorally sensible account of verbal stimuli. For Skinner, a "verbal stimulus" was merely the stimulus product of verbal behavior (Skinner, 1957, p. 34). In this usage, a "stimulus" is an object or entity, not a psychological function. In most behavior analytic accounts, including those provided by Skinner, categories of stimuli (discriminative, eliciting, reinforcing, etc.) are organized in accordance with the functional relations they sustain with behavior. Given Skinner's analysis of verbal stimuli, it makes about as much sense to view control by verbal rules as a distinguishable category of stimulus control as it would to claim that a pigeon responding to an electric light was engaging in "Edison-governed behavior." Without a functional category to examine, behavior analysis was delayed in its attempts to deal with instructional control.

VERBAL CONTROL AND CONTEMPORARY BEHAVIOR ANALYSIS

Basic human operant research entered a period of stagnation in the late 1960s and most of the 1970s. Much of the research continued to be driven by the continuity strategy, and discussion sections focused largely on the similarities between human and nonhuman performances, not on process accounts of the increasing number of identified differences. A basic analysis of instructional effects was not pursued.

Non-behavioral authors often argued that instructional effects undermined the validity of behavior analytic principles as applied to adult humans.

In a well-known chapter entitled "There Is No Convincing Evidence for Operant or Classical Conditioning in Adult Humans" Brewer (1974) attacked the idea of conditioning in adult humans when it is defined as an entirely automatic and unconscious process—that is, a process without significant verbal involvement. For example, effects due to the self-formulated hypothesis "Every time the red light comes on I get shocked," were held by Brewer to be a function of cognitive processes (1974, p. 2), not conditioning. The various behavior analytic studies showing the overriding effects of instructions were, in his eyes, clear evidence for cognitive theory.

The behavior analysts' failure to provide a process account of the impact of verbal rules may be partially explained, then, by two major sources. First, the continuity strategy mitigated against it, especially when combined with the idea that verbal control was simply a complex form of ordinary stimulus control. Based on Skinner's continuity strategy, if a researcher wanted to study stimulus control, it would make little sense to study the impact of a complex stimulus (e.g., instructions) on a complex organism with an unknown history. Second, the rise of cognitive psychology and its ready explanation of instructional effects via process concepts like awareness and insight may have further dampened behavior analysts' enthusiasm for a basic analysis of verbal control.

In the late 1970s things began to change. Some behavioral researchers began to conclude that some of the differences between human and nonhuman performances could be traced to the effects of verbal events on human action: the so-called "language hypothesis" (Lowe, 1979). Skinner's concept of rule-governed behavior provided an avenue for this hypothesis, in part because of his lack of clarity about it. Skinner himself had entertained the possibility that verbal events involved new principles: "The only differences I expect to see revealed between the behavior of rat and man (aside from enormous differences in complexity) lie in the field of verbal behavior" (1938, p. 442).

Human research began to assume a new role within basic behavior analysis. No longer simply a means of confirming the generality of findings with nonhumans, it has become a means for constructing an empirically based behavior analytic account of verbal behavior itself. This change has had a profound effect on basic behavior analysis. For example, its flagship journal, *The Journal of the Experimental Analysis of Behavior*, has gone from a small fraction of human studies in the early 1970s, to nearly an even split in the current volume. The new human research tradition has led to an increasing openness to new principles, preparations, and findings, and to more diversity within the field on the question of the continuity strategy. It has also yielded an interesting collection of empirical findings and theoretical suppositions that are both relevant to other versions of human psychology (e.g., cognitive psychology) and virtually unknown outside of behavior analysis.

Schedule Control

The role of verbal behavior is being studied, identified and explained in a variety of ways. A popular preparation, early in the move toward more human research, was the FI schedule. This schedule was of particular interest because it is a well-established finding that human FI performance differs significantly from that of other organisms (e.g., Leander, Lippman & Meyer, 1968; Lippman & Meyer, 1967; Weiner, 1964, 1965, 1969). There are ways, however, to reduce this effect and they all seem to turn on the issue of verbal behavior.

For example, human temporal schedule performance is more like that of nonhumans when steps are taken to reduce counting. Procedures have included concurrent verbal tasks such as mental math or reading aloud (e.g., Laties & Weiss, 1963; Lowe, Harzem, & Hughes, 1978) or a response-produced clock (Lowe, Harzem, & Bagshaw, 1978; Lowe et al., 1978).

Similarly, if verbal events are involved in schedule control differences, then pre-verbal humans should show patterns more characteristic of nonhumans. Lowe, Beasty, and Bentall (1983) tested responding on FI schedules with two human infants, ages 9 and 10 months, respectively. Their performances were more like those of nonhuman subjects than like those of adult humans. Developmental studies have shown a gradual transition (especially from about age 2 to age 6 or 7) in performance from the animal-like performances of infants to the pattern of adults, both in schedule performance (e.g., Bentall, Lowe, & Beasty, 1985) and in the effects of self-instructions (Bentall & Lowe, 1987).

Research on verbal rules has examined whether instructed subjects respond differently than uninstructed subjects to changes in environmental contingencies. In general, instructions alter the impact of contingency manipulations. For example, Shimoff, Catania, and Matthews (1981) compared shaped to instructed performance with interval and ratio schedules, each with a superimposed differential reinforcement of low rate (DRL) contingency. For both schedules when the DRL contingency was relaxed, response rate increased for most subjects whose original behavior was shaped but not for those who were instructed. Shimoff et al. concluded that this type of insensitivity is a "defining property" of instructional control (p. 207). Other researchers have since shown that this effect diminishes with time (Michael & Bernstein, 1991) and that instructions can produce more control by programmed contingencies than no instructions under some circumstances (S. C. Hayes, Brownstein, Zettle, Rosenfarb, & Korn, 1986; Joyce & Chase, 1990).

The changes in responding to programmed contingencies produced by verbal instructions result from at least two different effects (S. C. Hayes, Zettle, & Rosenfarb, 1989): (a) Instructions alter the range of responding available to make contact with programmed contingencies, and (b) instructions establish additional socially mediated contingencies for responding in accord with verbal rules. Several studies have shown these separate influences (e.g., Barrett, Deitz, Gaydos, & Quinn, 1987; S. C. Hayes, Brownstein, Haas, &

Greenway, 1986; S. C. Hayes, Brownstein, Zettle, et al., 1986; Joyce & Chase, 1990; Shimoff, Matthews, & Catania, 1986; see S. C. Hayes, Zettle, & Rosenfarb, 1989 for a review). For example, S. C. Hayes, Brownstein, Haas, & Greenway (1986) had subjects press buttons to move a light through a matrix according to a multiple fixed ratio (FR) 18 / DRL 6 s schedule to earn chances on money prizes. These schedules were chosen because they control different rates of responding (high rate with the FR and low with the DRL). An instruction to "Go Fast" was associated with one of the lights presented to the subject and "Go Slow" with a different light. In one condition, only the Go Fast light was on; in a second condition, only the Go Slow light was on; and in a third, the lights alternated within each component of the multiple schedule. Thus, in all cases the instruction light in each condition was accurate only half of the time, but the accuracy/inaccuracy was distributed differently across the three groups. Those who always saw "Go Fast" earned points in the FR component, but not the DRL component. In the "Go Slow" condition, the reverse was true. Those who had the instruction lights rapidly alternated contacted the contingencies in both components.

While the instruction lights were lit the subjects behaved according to them regardless of the actual schedule. For half the subjects the instruction lights were then unexpectedly turned off. Subjects with alternating instructions immediately showed schedule-appropriate behavior. Subjects with consistent instructions generally did not, since the restricted range of behaviors produced by these instructions did not foster contact with the actual contingencies in both components. Implicit social contingencies maintained instructional compliance while the instructional lights were lit, but when they were turned off, only subjects with alternating instructions emitted a range of behaviors that effectively contacted the underlying schedule. Thus, instructions either increased or decreased schedule-appropriate behavior, depending upon the specific instructions and specific schedules.

The general findings in behavior analytic studies of this kind are remarkably consistent (see S. C. Hayes, 1989b for a review): On one hand, verbal rules or instructions interact with many common behavioral procedures and preparations to produce behavioral patterns in humans not commonly seen in nonverbal organisms. On the other, when unexplained differences between human and nonhuman performances are studied carefully they often seem to resolve into differences produced by the impact of verbal rules.

In effect, some of the conclusions reached by Brewer (1974) now make sense within a behavior analytic account, but with a twist. Verbal processes often interact with other basic behavioral processes in normal adults and it is indeed difficult to obtain unequivocal evidence for operant or classical conditioning uncontaminated by verbal involvement. Rather than abandon concepts like operant or classical conditioning, though, behavior analysts are busy examining the nature of these verbal (or one might say, "cognitive") processes from a behavioral point of view.

CONTEMPORARY BEHAVIOR ANALYTIC RESEARCH ON DERIVED STIMULUS RELATIONS

It is one thing to document the involvement of verbal events in complex human behavior. It is another to explain why verbal events have these effects, or even more basically, to explain what verbal events are. While Skinner did not have a functional definition of verbal stimuli, behavior analysts are identifying functional processes that seem to provide one.

This area of research is among the most rapidly developing in the behavioral analytic tradition. Although there are several preparations of importance to the issues involved, by far the most researched is that of stimulus equivalence.

Stimulus Equivalence

When humans are taught a series of related conditional discriminations, the stimuli that enter into those discriminations can often become connected to each other in new ways, not explicitly taught. The phenomena involved are typically investigated in a matching to sample format. Suppose a person is taught, given a novel visual form (the sample—call it *X1*), to choose another visual form from an array (the comparisons—call them *Y1*, *Y2*, and *Y3*). We could say that the person learns "given *X1* pick *Y1*, not *Y2* nor *Y3*." The person is then taught to select another unfamiliar visual form from another array of forms, given the same sample, or "given *X1* pick *Z1*, not *Z2* nor *Z3*." So far we have two simple discriminations. In the presence of other samples, however, what was correct is now incorrect and vice versa. For example, the person would learn "given *X2* pick *Y2*, not *Y1* nor *Y3*." In the typical study, all comparisons are correct and incorrect equally often but the discriminations involved are conditional: A given comparison is correct only given a certain sample (in the rest of the paper we will describe discriminations of this kind with the shorter phrase "given *X1*, pick *Y1*" but it should be remembered that we are speaking of conditional discriminations). With this kind of training, the person probably will select *X1* from an array of comparisons (not *X2* nor *X3*), given *Y1* or *Z1* as samples, and *Y1* (not *Y2* nor Y3) from an array given *Z1* as a sample, and *Z1* (not *Z2* or *Z3*) given *Y1* as a sample (e.g., Sidman, 1971; Sidman, Cresson, & Willson-Morris, 1974). The same performances would be seen for the "2s" and the "3s." While the relation between, say, *X1* and *Y1* is directly trained, that between *Y1* and *X1* is *derived*. It has no direct history of training within the experiment and yet emerges only after the trained relations have been established.

This set of phenomena is called "stimulus equivalence." The basic phenomenon was acknowledged by the ancient Greeks, and has had several incarnations in modern psychology. S-R learning theory struggled with the topic from the 1930s (e.g., Hull, 1934) until its disintegration in the 1960s (e.g., Osgood, 1953; Jenkins & Palermo, 1964). Indeed, part of the reason for the collapse of S-R psychology was the failure of S-R models of response and stimulus mediation (Jenkins & Palermo, 1964). In its modern behavior analytic incarnation, however, the concept is associated both with a more robust experimental methodology, and with behavioral theorizing unburdened by S-R associationism and mediationalism.

In contemporary treatments, an equivalence class is usually said to exist if the trained stimulus-stimulus relations show the three defining derived properties of reflexivity, symmetry, transitivity, and combinations of these (Sidman & Tailby, 1982). In matching-to-sample procedures, *reflexivity* is usually inferred from generalized identity matching. For example, without explicit training, given *X1* the person picks *X1* and not *X2* nor *X3* from an array. *Symmetry* refers to the functional reversibility of a trained relation: When "given *X1* pick *Y1*" is trained, "given *Y1* pick *X1*" emerges in the absence of direct reinforcement (Sidman, Rauzin, Lazar, Cunningham, Tailby, & Carrigan, 1982). To evaluate *transitivity*, at least three stimuli in two linked relations are required. If after "given *X1* pick *Y1*" and "given *Y1* pick *Z1*" have been taught, "given *X1* pick *Z1*" emerges without additional training, transitivity has been demonstrated. Although it is somewhat confusing, the derived relation "given *Z1* pick *X1*" is often termed simply an *equivalence relation* (Fields, Verhave, & Fath, 1984) and is viewed as evidence that the trained relations have the properties of symmetry and transitivity. These defining properties of stimulus equivalence are shown in Figure 8.1.

Stimulus Equivalence as a Working Model of Semantic Relations

A major source of interest in stimulus equivalence is the apparent correspondence between the stimulus equivalence phenomenon and language phenomena. For example, in normal verbal training, word-object relations are symmetrical. If a child of sufficient verbal abilities is taught to point to a particular object among several given a particular written word, the child may, when later given the object, point to the specific word among an array of words without specific training to do so. Natural examples can readily be given for transitivity as well.

Such preparations have been used in several studies, and stimulus equivalence has readily emerged (e.g., M. H. Dixon & Spradlin, 1976; Sidman, 1971; Sidman, Kirk, & Willson-Morris, 1985; Sidman & Tailby, 1982; Spradlin & Dixon, 1976; Yamamoto, 1986). Some behavior analytic researchers have established successful language training or reading programs using equivalence and equivalence-like procedures exclusively (e.g., de Rose, de Souza, Rossito, & de Rose, 1992). This kind of overlap suggests that the equivalence phenomenon may provide a new avenue for the empirical investigation of verbal events. For some behavior analysts, it has become a kind of working empirical model of semantic relations (e.g., S. C. Hayes & Hayes, 1989).

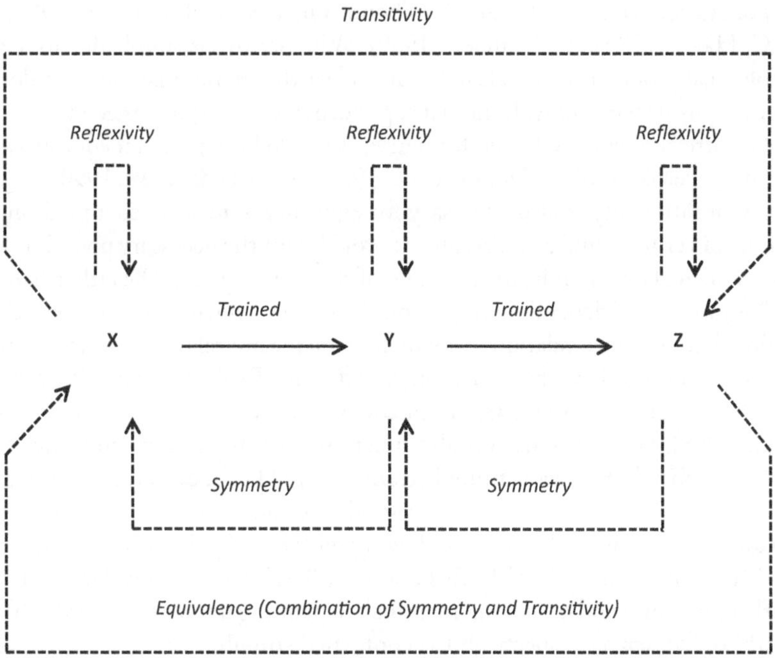

Figure 8.1 A Diagrammatic Presentation of the Trained and Derived Relations in a Typical Stimulus Equivalence Network

If stimulus equivalence provides a preliminary behavior analytic model of verbal stimulation, one would expect to see it emerge readily in humans, but not so readily (or perhaps not at all) in nonhumans. This expectation assumes only that humans have a relative facility with verbal behavior and thus, if equivalence is in some way a model of verbal stimulation, humans should also have a facility with equivalence. This has turned out to be the case. Stimulus equivalence has been shown with a wide variety of human subjects using a wide variety of stimulus materials (e.g., L. S. Dixon, 1977; M. H. Dixon & Spradlin, 1976; Gast, VanBiervliet, & Spradlin, 1979; L. J. Hayes, Tilley, & Hayes, 1988; Mackay & Sidman, 1984; Sidman, 1971; Sidman et al., 1974; Sidman & Tailby, 1982; Spradlin, Cotter, & Baxley, 1973; Spradlin & Dixon, 1976; VanBiervliet, 1977; Wulfert & Hayes, 1988). Even children as young as two years old will display such performances (Devany, Hayes, & Nelson, 1986). Stimulus equivalence has not been shown with nonhuman organisms, however. While conditional discriminations are readily demonstrated in a large variety of animals, including dolphins (e.g., Herman & Thompson, 1982), rats (e.g., Lashley, 1938), and monkeys (e.g., Nissen, 1951), these have not resulted in stimulus equivalence. To date, no unequivocal demonstration of stimulus equivalence in nonhumans has been shown (D'Amato, Salmon, Loukas, & Tomie, 1985; Dugdale & Lowe, 1990; Kendall, 1983; Sidman et al., 1982; Lipkens, Kop, & Matthijs,

1988. As for McIntire, Cleary, & Thompson, 1987 and Vaughan, 1988, see S. C. Hayes, 1989a and Saunders, 1989). Whether this is simply due to methodological problems is not clear, but it is clear that nonhumans at least do not show equivalence readily. In humans, performance on equivalence tasks seems to be correlated with verbal performance, as would be expected if equivalence is a type of verbal relation (Devany et al., 1986; Dugdale & Lowe, 1990).

Conditionality is also necessary for equivalence to serve as a preliminary model of verbal stimulation, because it provides for the necessary precision seen in language. For example, the meaning of the word *gay* could be either "happy" or "homosexual," depending in part on the context in which it occurred. Conditional equivalence relations, in which elements are related to others only in certain contexts, have been demonstrated (e.g., Bush, Sidman, & de Rose, 1989; Gatch & Osborne, 1989; Kennedy & Laitinen, 1988; Wulfert & Hayes, S.C., 1988). Words themselves also function as contexts in which equivalence class membership is reconstituted (Kohlenberg, Hayes, & Hayes, 1991). This corresponds nicely to natural language. For example, compare the different meanings of the word *bat* in the following sentences: "Babe Ruth held the bat" and "Dracula held the bat." In this example, "bat" is in an equivalence relation with a piece of wood or a flying mammal, depending upon other words ("Babe Ruth" or "Dracula," respectively) as contextual stimuli.

The Challenge of Stimulus Equivalence

To understand why stimulus equivalence is having a major impact on behavioral researchers one should note that it is not readily predicted from a direct contingency formulation. If an organism selects *Y1* over *Y2* given *X1*, and selects *Y2* over *Y1* given *X2*, the probability of reinforcement for selecting *Y1* is greater in the presence of *X1* than in the presence of, say, *X2*. We would say that *X1* is functioning as a conditional discriminative stimulus in the presence of which *Y1* is functioning as a discriminative stimulus for a selection response.

This does not mean, however, that the probability of reinforcement for selecting *X1* is greater in the presence of *Y1* than in its absence. Consider a natural example. A monkey may look for and find a snake (and not, say, a cloud) given a rustling sound, but not listen for a rustling rather than some other sound given a snake. We could think of this as a trained relation: given rustle find snake. Such a contingency arrangement provides few grounds to suppose that reversing the functions of the stimuli will be reinforced: given snake find rustle.

In the natural environment of nonverbal organisms, trained sequential or other relations between two events cannot be assumed to reverse. Most commonly, if the functions *were* reversed the consequences would be neutral. Often they would be negative or even life-threatening. Thus it is not clear why operant contingencies should be functionally reversible. Respondent conditioning also provides a no clear process to account for the equivalence results, especially when we move beyond simple symmetry (S. C. Hayes & Hayes, 1989).

The development of theoretical accounts of stimulus equivalence is still in its infancy in behavior analysis. Some researchers view stimulus equivalence as a primitive which cannot be analyzed into component processes (e.g., Sidman, 1990). In behavior analysis, primitives such as reinforcement or stimulus control can only be described in terms of the conditions in which they are seen. They are not "explained" psychologically. If more of an explanation is demanded, usually only an evolutionary one will be attempted. For example, it has been said that conditional discriminations may lead to equivalence in humans (at least) simply because humans have evolved that way (Sidman, 1990).

A second alternative has been to explain equivalence on the basis of verbal mediation (e.g., Dugdale & Lowe, 1990; McIntire et al., 1987), much as earlier S-R learning theorists did. These analyses have so far either failed to be demonstrated empirically (e.g., see S. C. Hayes, 1989a) or appeal to derived relations between stimuli and names that are of the same sort as the derived stimulus relations they mean to explain.

Another alternative, the relational frame account, has appealed to the historical development of relational responding (S. C. Hayes, 1991; S. C. Hayes & Hayes, 1989). This view will be discussed in some detail for three reasons. First, it shows how fairly traditional behavior analytic concepts are leading to quite different views of verbal events. Second, it will be important for other reasons later on to argue that equivalence might itself be learned, and relational frame theory describes one plausible way this might happen. Finally, the analysis shares obvious similarities with contemporary cognitive network theories of meaning, and thus might be of more general interest to non-behavioral readers.

Arbitrarily Applicable Relational Responding

The relational conception of stimulus equivalence starts from a fairly conservative stance: How can equivalence be explained via traditional contingency concepts? Relational frame theory draws upon two central ideas. First, a variety of experimental findings (for example, transposition, Reese, 1968) show that humans and nonhumans can respond to *formal* or *non-arbitrary* relations between stimuli. Perhaps some organisms can take an additional step and bring relational responding under the control of context rather than the form of the relata. Such abstracted relational responding would then be *arbitrarily applicable* to any events, needing only contextual cues to do so. Second, the behavior analytic account of generalized imitation (e.g., Gewirtz & Stengle, 1968), grammatical frames (Skinner, 1957), and other phenomena draws upon the idea that organisms can learn overarching behavioral classes containing virtually unlimited numbers of members. Although equivalence and similar phenomena seem to show novel performances, perhaps this performance is in actuality learned. That is, the action of relating two arbitrary stimuli itself has a history.

Take the case of a young child learning the name of an object. A child is oriented toward several objects. The parent points to one and asks "What's that?" At first parents do not expect a response and after a pause, they say the name. If the child shows any sign of acknowledgment (e.g., a smile when the name is given), the child is tickled, praised, or otherwise rewarded. Sometimes incorrect names will be said deliberately, and the child will be expected to show that it is not correct. Later only actual correct vocalizations by the child are rewarded. Incorrect responses result in additional prompting of the name.

Eventually, the child learns "given object *X*, say name *X*, not name *Y*" (object → name.) But the child is also asked "Where is (name)?" Picking the named object from among others is rewarded with tickles, play, or verbal consequences ("That's right! That's the (name)"). We can say that the child learns "given name *X*, point to object *X* not object *Y*" (name → object). Bi-directional training of this kind occurs only in certain contexts. There are a variety of cues to indicate that this is a naming context, including the use of phrases such as "What's that?" and the juxtaposition of objects and words.

As with generalized imitation, we might suppose that with enough instances of such training the child will begin to learn to derive name → object given only object → name and vice versa. In short, with enough instances of directly trained bi-directional stimulus relations in a given context, bi-directional responding of a more general sort may arise in that context. The process here might be similar to that discussed by Skinner in explaining the speaker's ability to mand events never before manded (1957). On the basis of a history of reinforcement for specific mands, the speaker is thought to learn the mand relation as a frame into which novel events may be incorporated. The capacity to abstract the frame in the case of the mand, or with the kind of stimulus relations we are discussing, may simply require a sufficient history of bi-directional training or it may also require that a particular species be involved (i.e., humans). Beyond such an historical or evolutionary appeal, behavior analytic theory does not ordinarily attempt an account of such processes, either for the present topic or in other areas such as generalized imitation.

Once abstracted from a particular history, the derivation of stimulus relations is not based solely on the formal properties of the relata. It is arbitrarily applicable in the sense that it may be brought to bear on any stimuli in the presence of appropriate contextual cues. If, for example, a person is told "$X = Y > Z$" the bi-directional relations between all possible pairs of *X*, *Y*, and *Z* (e.g., $Z < X$) can be stated, not based on the form of these related events, but on the arbitrarily specified and derived relations among them brought to bear by cues such as = and $<$.

Arbitrarily applicable relational responding involves responding to one event in terms of the other and vice versa based on contextual cues to do so. As such it is a pattern of the transformation of stimulus functions. It has three characteristics (S. C. Hayes, 1991; S. C. Hayes & Hayes, 1989):

Mutual Entailment. If X is related to Y in a given context, then Y is related to X in that context. The specific relations involved need not be literally identical. If X is better than Y, then Y is worse than X. The second relation is entailed by the first—it is not possible to have a relation of "better" without one of "worse." We may describe mutual entailment this way:

$$C_{rel} \{X \, r_x \, Y \, ||| \, Y \, r_y \, X\}$$

That is: when a contextual event brings to bear upon the current situation a history of a particular kind of relational responding (C_{rel}), such that a relation of a particular kind (r_x) is specified between two events X and Y, then a second relation (r_y) is necessarily entailed (|||) between Y and X.

Combinatorial Entailment. If in a given relational context X is related in a particular way to Y and Y is also related to Z, then some kind of relation must be entailed from X to Z and from Z to X. More formally:

$$C_{rel} \{X \, r_x \, Y \text{ and } Y \, r_z \, Z \, ||| \, X \, r_p \, Z \text{ and } Z \, r_q \, X\}$$

Combinatorial entailment differs from simple mutual entailment in more than mere complexity. In mutual entailment, the specified relation between X and Y entails a relation between Y and X at the same level of precision. In the formula above, however, the X-Z and Z-X relations ("r_p" and "r_q") may not be specified to the same degree as that between X and Y, and Y and Z ("r_x" and "r_z"). For example, if X is different than Y and Y is different than Z, we cannot say what the relation is between X and Z and between Z and X. This lack of precision, however, is *specified* by the nature of the relation of "difference" that applies to X and Y, and to Y and Z. We can say that we cannot say what the relation is. This is part of what distinguishes a psychological from a merely logical or mathematical relation. A verbal relation of "no relation" is a relation psychologically speaking because it requires responding to one event in terms of another. It is not a logical or mathematical relation, however, which are more limited subsets of psychological stimulus relations.

Transfer of Functions. It is this last characteristic of arbitrarily applicable relational responding that provides the general psychological importance of such events. If an event X has a psychological function, and that event is placed into a relation with another event Y, under certain conditions Y may acquire a new psychological function based on the function of X and the relations between X and Y. Because if *all* functions of one stimulus transferred to another and vice versa, there would no longer be two separate psychological stimuli, which functions transfer must be under contextual control. We can represent the transfer of functions this way:

$$C_{func} [C_{rel} \{Xf_1 \mid\mid\mid Yf_2r \text{ and } Zf_3r\}]$$

That is, given the presence of contextual cues that select particular psychologically relevant, non-relational stimulus functions ("C_{func}"), that adhere in event *X* ("f_1"), events *Y* and *Z* will show these functions, transformed in terms of the derived relations between these events and event *X*, ("Yf_2r" and "Zf_3r"). Because the transfer of functions is thought to be under contextual control, under some conditions with some functions no transfer may be seen. In the relational frame conception, however, all arbitrarily applicable stimulus relations *enable* some forms of such transfer.

Transfer of functions is a definitional aspect of relational frames in part to denote their psychological nature, but it is more than that. Mutual entailment and combinatorial entailment are themselves interpretable as transfer of functions in a limited sense. For example, in the traditional equivalence study done using a conditional discrimination procedure, the trained conditional function of a sample transfers to the related comparison if symmetry is shown—by definition. Is it possible for only relational stimulus functions to transfer and for no non-relational stimulus functions to transfer? It seems unlikely. For example, suppose a person learns a relation between *X* and *Y* and is then asked to "picture what is related to *Y*." If the person has derived a strong relation between *Y* and *X*, then presumably at least the perceptual functions of *X* will be available to some degree with regard to *Y*. That is, the person will probably picture *X*. Transfer of these perceptual functions is enabled by the property of mutual entailment, but it is distinct from it. Thus, transfers of functions seem to be a definitional aspect of relational frames. Arbitrarily applicable relations are patterns of the mutual transformation of both relational and non-relational stimulus functions.

As a practical example of a transfer of functions, suppose a child is trained that the written word *dog* is called "dog" and that the word *dog* goes with actual dogs. We may say that the child has had two relations directly trained: *dog* → dog and *dog* → "dog." Later the child plays with a dog for the first time and enjoys it. We may say that dogs have directly acquired various functions by virtue of the play. Now, upon hearing his mother say "dogs" from another room the child may smile and go to the other room even though a dog is not visible and the child has no direct history of reinforcement for any of these activities in response to the word *dog*. Based on the relational frame account, we might say that dogs have become discriminative stimuli for approach or eliciting stimuli for emotional responding directly through play. The word *dog* has acquired similar functions not through a direct history, but indirectly through its participation in a derived relation with dogs.

The literature on the transfer of functions across equivalence relations would support the basic outlines of such an analysis. Transfer of discriminative functions have been shown across simple equivalence relations(e.g., S. C. Hayes, Brownstein, Devany, Kohlenberg, & Shelby, 1987; Kohlenberg et al., 1991), and conditional equivalence relations (Wulfert & Hayes, S.C., 1988), and across symmetrically related stimuli (e.g., Catania, Horne, & Lowe, 1989; de Rose, McIlvane, Dube, Galpin, & Stoddard, 1988; Gatch & Osborne, 1989; Lazar, 1977; Lazar & Kotlarchyk, 1986). In much the same way, consequential functions transfer through equivalence relations (S. C. Hayes et al., 1987; S. C. Hayes, Kohlenberg, & Hayes, 1991), as do conditioned emotional responses (Augustson & Dougher, 1991).

Relational Frame. The term *relational frame* was coined to designate particular kinds of arbitrarily applicable relational responding (S. C. Hayes & Hayes, 1989). A relational frame is a type of responding that shows the contextually controlled qualities of mutual entailment, combinatorial entailment, and transfer of functions; is due to a history of relational responding relevant to the contextual cues involved; and is not based on direct non-relational training with regard to the particular stimuli of interest. If a relation is a pattern of mutual transformation of stimulus functions, a relational frame is the name for that particular pattern. It is a noun because the structure of English demands it, but it is a situated action. A relational frame is always "framing relationally."

In a relational frame view, stimulus equivalence is a special case of arbitrarily applicable relational responding based on a "frame of coordination" or sameness (S. C. Hayes & Hayes, 1989). A variety of evidence fits with the relational frame view of equivalence (see S. C. Hayes, 1991; S. C. Hayes & Hayes, 1989), and it makes several predictions that differ from most other accounts (e.g., derived relations should show developmental trends, equivalence is only one of many such phenomena, equivalence relations can be reconstituted in ever more subtle ways based on cues to do so, new kinds of relations can be trained, conditional discrimination procedures are only one of many that should lead to derived stimulus relations). The strongest support for the theory so far has been the demonstration that a variety of relations can be applied to arbitrary matching-to-sample tasks, and give rise to equivalence or non-equivalence depending upon the relations applied (Steele & Hayes, 1991). In the Steele and Hayes experiments subjects' responses to three non-arbitrary stimulus relations (sameness, oppositeness, or difference) were first brought under contextual control. For example, given a contextual cue (background color on a computer screen) for "same," a subject shown a short line as a sample earned points for picking a short line from a set of comparisons. Given a contextual cue for "opposite" and the same sample, picking a long line was rewarded. Given the "different" context, selecting any comparison other than one identical to the sample was reinforced. Subjects were then exposed in the presence of these same contextual cues to matching-to-sample training in which the trained stimulus relations were between arbitrary visual forms that reliably shared no formal properties. In two experiments it was shown that derived performances were consistent with relational responding brought to bear by the contextual cues. In contexts relevant to the relation of sameness, stimulus equivalence emerged. Other kinds of relational networks emerged in the other contexts. For example, when arbitrary stimuli were related in the presence of the opposite cue, derived relations of sameness and oppositeness alternated with each interceding stimulus (e.g., an opposite of an opposite was treated as the same, but an opposite of an opposite of an opposite was treated as opposite).

Why Equivalence May Involve a New Behavioral Principle

The behavior analytic work on the derivation of stimulus relations seems to be opening up behavior analysis to a new behavioral principle. Behavioral principles are admitted into the armamentarium only very slowly within behavior analysis, but both of the major interpretations of stimulus equivalence and similar phenomena seem to lead to it.

On the one hand, equivalence may be a primitive process which cannot be analyzed into component processes (e.g., Sidman, 1990). If this is true, equivalence instantiates a new behavioral principle by definition, since what is meant by a behavioral principle is a basic process. The transfer of functions through equivalence classes would also be considered a new phenomenon, if only because it is based on this new behavioral processes.

Conversely, equivalence and other derived stimulus relations may be learned. The relational frame account is one such learning-based interpretation, but others seem possible. In this case, neither equivalence per se nor higher-order concepts such as relational frames involve new behavioral principles because the processes appealed to are known. At most they are new behavioral outcomes, much as generalized imitation may be a new behavioral outcome.

If the derivation of stimulus relations is learned, however, the transfer of functions through such relations apparently instantiates a new behavioral principle. Behavior analysts distinguish between stimulus functions on the basis of history and current context. For example, conditioned and unconditioned reinforcers are distinguished on the basis of the particular histories that give rise to each. When, as in the example earlier, the child approaches upon hearing the word *dog*, we cannot say that *dog* is a discriminative stimulus. A discriminative stimulus is a stimulus in the presence of which there has been a greater probability of reinforcement for a given behavior than in its absence. In the example (and in actual studies of such phenomena, e.g., Kohlenberg et al., 1991), there is no such history for the word *dog*. Its function is only *discriminative-like*, based on a transfer of control through a derived stimulus relation. In behavior analytic accounts the control exerted by any given discriminative stimulus is learned, but discriminative control per se is not. If the discriminative-like functions of *dog* are based on a learned pattern of the derivation of stimulus relations, then this seems to be a new kind of stimulus control in which the underlying process responsible for the effect is itself learned. The same conclusion would be reached for all the other functions that transfer through derived relations (reinforcing, eliciting, establishing, and evocative).

It may still be possible to interpret equivalence and similar relational phenomena in a way that does not suggest a new behavioral principle. If our logic above is correct, though, such an interpretation would require both that equivalence is learned and that transfer of functions through equivalence does not depend on the learned nature of equivalence. It is not obvious how that could be done.

If there is a new behavioral principle, it is not clear what it should be called. Although it may cause confusion because of its broad use both in lay language and psychology, we (S. C. Hayes & Hayes, 1989) have previously used the word *verbal* as a technical term to qualify functions that depend upon derived stimulus relations. We have argued that verbal events are simply those that involve relational frames. Thus, the new general principle might be termed *verbal control* and the specific terms could include such things as *verbal reinforcers* (e.g., stimuli with reinforcing functions based on the transfer of functions through derived stimulus relations), verbal antecedents, *verbal motivation*, and so on. Unfortunately, the term *verbal* is often used to refer to events based on their form and not their function. For example, if the word *good* increases behavior when it is used contingently as a consequence, some may call it a *verbal reinforcer* simply because it is a "word," not because of any specific psychological processes that led to its reinforcing functions. If behavior analysts concluded (as is suggested by our analysis) that verbal functions are distinct at the level of psychological process, perhaps this topographical use would cease, to be replaced by functional distinctions such as the ones we are making. If not, perhaps *relational control, relational reinforcers, relational antecedents*, and so on, could provide an alternative.

Linking Control by Verbal Rules to Derived Stimulus Relations

Previous behavioral analyses of verbal meaning and of rule control have attempted to reduce these phenomena to outcomes of simple and direct operant and classical conditioning preparations. The analyses that have resulted seem cumbersome and have had a difficult time accounting adequately for verbal effects.

The literature on semantic generalization and conditioned meaning provides a useful illustration. Staats and Staats (1957), for example, directly paired nonsense words with emotionally laden words and found a transfer of emotional functions to the nonsense words as measured by a semantic differential even in subjects "unaware" of the stimulus relation. Applying this model of verbal meaning to everyday language runs afoul of two difficulties. First, it is difficult to suppose a history of repeated pairings in most or all such circumstances in the natural linguistic environment. Secondly, Staats and Staats' conclusions do not explain why there was a correlation between measures of verbal awareness of the stimulus relation and the emotional ratings given to the nonsense words (e.g., Cohen, 1964). From a relational frame point of view, such a correlation should be expected, not because verbal awareness is necessary to conditioning, but because when a subject can describe a stimulus relation it is certain to have been derived (cf., Skinner, 1945, 1966).

Similarly, early behavioral accounts of rule-governance appealed to direct processes of discriminative control (e.g., Galizio, 1979). This account too supposed a history that is difficult to imagine, in which the discriminative effects of all verbal rules must be learned directly.

The behavior analytic literature on derived stimulus relations provides alternatives both for the meaning of verbal formulae and for their effects as rules. A detailed analysis of these issues would take us too far afield (see S. C. Hayes & Hayes, 1989 for some of our efforts in these areas), but a brief outline might help show how the research on derived stimulus relations opens up new ways of approaching old problems and how it is reflecting back on the literature on instructional control and rule-governance.

Verbal Meaning. The literature on derived stimulus relations suggests that when a person hears a word, some of the functions of that word may depend on the derived stimulus relations sustained between it and other events. When a sentence is presented, a variety of new relations may be derived, under the contextual control of the words themselves, their sequence, the nonverbal context, paralinguistic cues, and other events.

Verbally understanding the meaning of a word or sentence might thus be a psychologically distinct action that is based on the act of a listener deriving stimulus relations (e.g., forming equivalence relations, relations of difference, if . . . then relations, and so on). For example, I may "understand" the word *fire* in the sense that its functions depend in part upon derived relations between it and other events (e.g., words like *hot* or *oxidation*). This would represent a different kind of "understanding" than that based on functions of the word that are directly trained (e.g., if *fire* had reliably preceded being burned and thus elicited emotional reactions via classical conditioning). These two types of meaning—verbal meaning and direct meaning—seem based on different psychological processes.

The same kind of interpretation could be applied to the meaning of a sentence. Suppose a person is told "When the bell rings, there is a fire." While the verbal meaning of *bell* or *fire* may be based on pre-existing equivalence relations, the sentence provides cues for the listener to derive an additional dependency relation (if . . . then) between the bell and fire. This network of stimulus relations and their resulting functions could be considered the verbal meaning of the sentence. This view differs markedly from Skinner's view (1957) in which the verbal meaning and direct meaning of a sentence are not distinguishable at the level of psychological process—both are simply forms of stimulus control. Skinner developed this analysis before equivalence had been incorporated into behavior analysis, which may account for much of the difference between his view and ours.

Rule-Following. When defined this way, following a rule as a rule requires an understanding of it (although more than that is involved: see S. C. Hayes et al., 1989). A dog might be taught to get slippers when the master says "slippers" but the command is not functioning as a rule for the dog, since it has no verbal meaning. Rather, the evocative functions of the word depend solely on direct training. Conversely, consider a person who is told "When the bell rings, there is a fire" and now runs at the sound of the bell. In this case, the action of running could be interpreted as a form of rule-following that is dependent upon derived stimulus relations. *Fire* might have some of the functions of actual fires via a transfer of such functions through of relations of coordination, and now *bell* has acquired the function of an actual fire about to happen. Because *bell* has these functions and is in a coordination relation with actual bells, when the bell rings, the person may run, much as would have occurred had an actual fire been seen.

This interpretation of rule-following is speculative, but does not stray far from what is already known. Even if relational frame theory is incorrect, the empirical phenomenon of equivalence alone would support much of the analysis above.

The Properties of Derived Stimulus Functions and Verbal Rules. If rule-governance is dependent upon derived stimulus relations and the non-relational functions that transfer through them, then the findings in the instructional control literature make sense behaviorally. Derived stimulus relations seem to be *specific, indirect*, and *arbitrary*, among other characteristics (S. C. Hayes & Hayes, 1989; Parrott, 1984), and the qualities of behavior guided by verbal rules seems to correspond with these properties.

There seems to be a difference in the *specificity* of derived stimulus functions, one that may come from their relative independence from form as a source of behavioral functions. A normal discriminative stimulus cannot easily come to control a specific response and *only* that response for two reasons. First, the form of the stimulus establishes some functions directly. A key light, for example, is not only a stimulus in the presence of which pecking is reinforced, it is also a stimulus that allows the bird to look at things in an otherwise darkened chamber; it may elicit an orienting response; it may provide sensory stimulation for glances in its direction; it may make eye movements more likely; and so on. It cannot "mean" just one specific thing. Second, all co-present or proximal events are potentially relevant to a non-arbitrary stimulus function. Thus, it is difficult to avoid multiple stimulus functions otherwise present in the environment from adhering to any part of that environment.

When arbitrary stimuli gain their functions based on their relations to other stimuli and not to their forms, these stimulus functions can be narrowed and broadened by the network of derived relations, without significant contamination from functions based upon formal properties or co-present events. Such verbal stimuli "mean" the transformed functions of events that participate in derived relations with them. This also prevents intrusions in meaning from random event sources. For example, if a person heard "I'll meet you next Wednesday at noon" and shortly thereafter stepped on a tack, the phrase would be unlikely to become a powerful cue for careful walking.

Much of the impact of verbal rules is due to a change in the range of behaviors available to contact with the world (S. C. Hayes, Brownstein, Haas, et al., 1986; Joyce & Chase, 1990). If derived stimulus functions are more specific than direct stimulus functions it would help to explain how such a change can be produced and manipulated.

Because of the *arbitrariness* of derived stimulus relations the verbal community can alter the derivation of stimulus relations via social convention. For example, if the verbal community agrees that a given event is "good" or "bad," the derived relation between that event and these evaluations may significantly alter the function of these events for members of the verbal community. This may help explain the sensitivity of rule-governed behavior to social context (e.g., Barrett et al., 1987).

We have already explained how the stimulus functions that transfer through equivalence relations are *indirect*. This might help explain how rules can compete with control by programmed contingencies. For example, a person might have been taught to relate sex to "immorality." The direct effects of sexual contact may differ completely from the indirect effects that come from this relation. Perhaps it is *sensitivity* to such indirect effects that helps produce the apparent "insensitivity" to the direct effects of events that is seen in the rule-governance literature (S. C. Hayes, S.C., 1989b).

CONCLUSION

Skinner rejected the notion that "certain basic linguistic processes [are] common to both speaker and listener" (Skinner, 1957, p. 33) but this is precisely the position we are led to consider when we try to extend the equivalence literature into the areas of verbal meaning and rule-governance. Ideas present in the mind, however, are not the common ground between speaker and listener. In the present view, derived stimulus relations sustained by social convention constitute that ground.

The trend in behavior analysis to grapple with derived stimulus relations suggests a merger of behavioral and cognitive research areas and interests. Although equivalence and relational frames do not seem to have a place in the cognitive literature as yet, the phenomena involved seem central to contemporary cognitive interests in such areas as stimulus class formation or semantic meaning. Other types of derived stimulus relations, such as those involved in stimulus exclusion, are being actively studied both by behavior analysts (e.g., McIlvane, Kledaras, Munson, King, de Rose, & Stoddard, 1987) and by cognitive psychologists (e.g., Markman & Wachtel, 1988). The network theory of meaning implied by relational frame theory overlaps considerably with contemporary cognitive theories of meaning (e.g., Reese, 1991). If the underlying relational frame conception is correct, many of the cognitive findings shown with semantic networks (e.g., priming effects) should apply to equivalence classes (or other relational networks) and vice versa. In short, behavior analysis is now a field actively studying "cognition."

What, then, is the difference between the present kind of analysis and mainstream cognitive psychology? In part, the answer is to be found in the most fundamental premises of the two positions. While much of cognitive psychology—especially that driven by computer metaphors—seems mechanistic, the present analysis is self-consciously contextualistic (S. C. Hayes, Hayes, & Reese, 1988). One implication of this philosophical difference is that cognitive psychologists are interested in developing models that correspond to the real world and are assessed by predictive verification, while contextualistic behavior analysts focus on theories that help accomplish their pragmatic goals of prediction and control. As a result, while cognitive theories embrace mediational accounts on the grounds that they model mental machinery well, behavior analysts reject them on the grounds that they are unhelpful to their goals (S. C. Hayes & Brownstein, 1986). Deriving stimulus relations, for example, is conceptualized in relational frame theory as historically and contextually situated actions of whole organisms, not as a mediational process or mechanism occurring in the brain or mind. Some within the cognitive tradition have begun to argue for a similar approach (e.g., Watkins, 1990).

An explosion of research in stimulus equivalence and rule-governance has occurred since the late 1970s. Too little time has passed for the assimilation of these new data into characterizations of the behavioral perspective by those outside that perspective—indeed, the assimilation within behavior analysis is still underway. It is clear, however, that behavior analysis is actively studying many topics that were once considered outside its purview. It is also clear that although the position is evolving and some of Skinner's theoretical suppositions are being abandoned or transformed, it is still behavior analysis—alive and doing well.

REFERENCES

Augustson, E., & Dougher, M.J. (1991, November). *Transfer of a conditioned emotional response via stimulus equivalence.* Paper presented at the meeting of the Association for Advancement of Behavior Therapy, New York.

Ayllon, T., & Azrin, N.H. (1964). Reinforcement and instructions with mental patients. *Journal of the Experimental Analysis of Behavior, 6*, 327–331.

Barrett, D.M., Deitz, S.M. Gaydos, G.R., & Quinn, P.C. (1987). The effects of programmed contingencies and social conditions on response stereotypy with human subjects. *Psychological Record, 37*, 489–505.

Bentall, R.P., & Lowe, C.F. (1987). The role of verbal behavior in human learning. III: Instructional effects in children. *Journal of the Experimental Analysis of Behavior, 47*, 177–190.

Bentall, R.P., Lowe, C.F., & Beasty, A. (1985). The role of verbal behavior in human learning. II: Developmental differences. *Journal of the Experimental Analysis of Behavior, 43*, 165–181.

Brewer, W.F. (1974). There is no convincing evidence for operant or classical conditioning in adult humans. In W.B. Weimer & D.S. Palermo (Eds.), *Cognition and the symbolic processes* (pp. 1–48). Hillsdale, NJ: Erlbaum.

Bush, K.M., Sidman, M., & de Rose, T. (1989). Contextual control of emergent equivalence relations. *Journal of the Experimental Analysis of Behavior, 51*, 29–45.

Catania, A.C., Horne, P., & Lowe, C.F. (1989). Transfer of function across members of an equivalence class. *The Analysis of Verbal Behavior, 7*, 99–110.

Cohen, B.H. (1964). Role of awareness in meaning established by classical conditioning. *Journal of Experimental Psychology, 67*, 373–378.

D'Amato, M.R., Salmon, D.P., Loukas, E., & Tomie, A. (1985). Symmetry and transitivity of conditional relations in monkeys (Cebus apella) and pigeons (Columba livia). *Journal of the Experimental Analysis of Behavior, 44*, 35–47.

de Rose, J.T., de Souza, D.G., Rossito, A.L., & de Rose, T.M.S. (1992). Stimulus equivalence and generalization in reading after matching to sample by exclusion. In S.C. Hayes & L.J. Hayes (Eds.), *Understanding verbal relations* (pp. 69–82). Reno, NV: Context Press.

de Rose, J.T., McIlvane, W.J., Dube, W.V., Galpin, V.C., & Stoddard, L.T. (1988). Emergent simple discrimination established by indirect relation to differential consequences. *Journal of the Experimental Analysis of Behavior, 50*, 1–20.

Devany, J.M., Hayes, S.C., & Nelson, R.O. (1986). Equivalence class formation in language-able and language-disabled children. *Journal of the Experimental Analysis of Behavior, 46*, 243–257.

Dixon, L.S. (1977). The nature of control by spoken words over visual stimulus selection. *Journal of the Experimental Analysis of Behavior, 27*, 433–442.

Dixon, M.H., & Spradlin, J.E. (1976). Establishing stimulus equivalences among retarded adolescents. *Journal of Experimental Child Psychology, 21*, 144–164.

Dugdale, N., & Lowe, C.F. (1990). Naming and stimulus equivalence. In D.E. Blackman & H. Lejeune (Eds.), *Behavior analysis in theory and practice: Contributions and controversies* (pp. 115–138). Hillsdale, NJ: Erlbaum.

Fields, L., Verhave, T., & Fath, S. (1984). Stimulus equivalence and transitive associations: A methodological analysis. *Journal of the Experimental Analysis of Behavior, 42*, 143–157.
Galizio, M. (1979). Contingency-shaped and rule-governed behavior: Instructional control of human loss avoidance. *Journal of the Experimental Analysis of Behavior, 31*, 53–70.
Gast, D., VanBiervliet, A., & Spradlin, J. E. (1979). Teaching number-word equivalences: A study of transfer. *American Journal of Mental Deficiency, 83*, 524–527.
Gatch, M. B., & Osborne, J. G. (1989). Transfer of contextual stimulus function via equivalence class development. *Journal of the Experimental Analysis of Behavior, 51*, 369–378.
Gewirtz, J. L., & Stengle, K. G. (1968). Learning of generalized imitation as the basis for identification. *Psychological Review, 5*, 374–397.
Hayes, L. J., Tilley, K., & Hayes, S. C. (1988). Extending equivalence class membership to gustatory stimuli. *The Psychological Record, 38*, 473–482.
Hayes, S. C. (1987). Upward and downward continuity: It's time to change our strategic assumptions. *Behavior Analysis, 22*, 3–6.
Hayes, S. C. (1989a). Nonhumans have not yet shown stimulus equivalence. *Journal of the Experimental Analysis of Behavior, 51*, 385–392.
Hayes, S. C. (Ed.). (1989b). *Rule-governed behavior: Cognition, contingencies, and instructional control.* New York: Plenum.
Hayes, S. C. (1991). A relational control theory of stimulus equivalence. In L. J. Hayes & P. N. Chase (Eds.), *Dialogues on verbal behavior* (pp. 19–40). Reno, NV: Context Press.
Hayes, S. C., & Brownstein, A. J. (1986). Mentalism, behavior-behavior relations and a behavior analytic view of the purposes of science. *The Behavior Analyst, 9*, 175–190.
Hayes, S. C., Brownstein, A. J., Devany, J. M., Kohlenberg, B. S., & Shelby, J. (1987). Stimulus equivalence and the symbolic control of behavior. *Mexican Journal of Behavior Analysis*, 13, 361–374.
Hayes, S. C., Brownstein, A. J., Haas, J. R., & Greenway, D. E. (1986). Instructions, multiple schedules, and extinction: Distinguishing rule-governed from schedule controlled behavior. *Journal of the Experimental Analysis of Behavior, 46*, 137–147.
Hayes, S. C., Brownstein, A. J., Zettle, R. D., Rosenfarb, I., & Korn, Z. (1986). Rule-governed behavior and sensitivity to changing consequences of responding. *Journal of the Experimental Analysis of Behavior, 45*, 237–256.
Hayes, S. C., & Hayes, L. J. (1989). The verbal action of the listener as a basis for rule-governance. In S. C. Hayes (Ed.), *Rule-governed behavior: Cognition, contingencies, and instructional control.* (pp. 153–190). New York: Plenum.
Hayes, S. C., Hayes, L. J., & Reese, H. W. (1988). Finding the philosophical core: A review of Stephen C. Pepper's *World Hypotheses. Journal of the Experimental Analysis of Behavior, 50*, 97–111.

Hayes, S.C., Kohlenberg, B.K., & Hayes, L.J. (1991). Transfer of consequential functions through simple and conditional equivalence classes. *Journal of the Experimental Analysis of Behavior, 56*, 119–137.

Hayes, S.C., Zettle, R.D., & Rosenfarb, I. (1989). Rule following. In S.C. Hayes (Ed.), *Rule-governed behavior: Cognition, contingencies, and instructional control* (pp. 191–220). New York: Plenum.

Herman, L.M., & Thompson, R.K. (1982). Symbolic, identity and probe-delayed matching of sounds in the bottle-nosed dolphin. *Animal Learning and Behavior, 10*, 22–34.

Holland, J.G. (1958). Counting by humans on a fixed-ratio schedule of reinforcement. *Journal of the Experimental Analysis of Behavior, 1*, 179–181.

Hull, C.L. (1934). The concept of the habit-family hierarchy and maze learning: Part I. *Psychological Review, 41*, 33–52.

Hutchinson, R.R., & Azrin, N.H. (1961). Conditioning of mental-hospital patients to fixed-ratio schedules of reinforcement. *Journal of the Experimental Analysis of Behavior, 4*, 87–95.

Jenkins, J.J., & Palermo, D.S. (1964). Mediation processes and the acquisition of linguistic structure. In U. Bellugi & R. Brown (Eds.), *The acquisition of language. Monographs of the Society for Research in Child Development, 29* (Serial No. 92).

Joyce, J.H., & Chase, P.N. (1990). Effects of response variability on the sensitivity of rule-governed behavior. *Journal of the Experimental Analysis of Behavior, 54*, 251–262.

Kaufman, A., Baron, A., & Kopp, R.E. (1966). Some effects of instructions on human operant behavior. *Psychonomic Monograph Supplements, 1*, 243–250.

Kendall, S.B. (1983). Tests for mediated transfer in pigeons. *Psychological Record, 33*, 245–256.

Kennedy, C.H., & Laitinen, R. (1988). Second-order conditional control of symmetric and transitive stimulus relations: The influence of order effects. *Psychological Record, 38*, 437–446.

Kohlenberg, B.S., Hayes, S.C., & Hayes, L.J. (1991). The transfer of contextual control over equivalence classes through equivalence classes: A possible model of social stereotyping. *Journal of the Experimental Analysis of Behavior, 56*, 505–518.

Lashley, K. S. (1938). Conditional reactions in the rat. *Journal of Psychology, 6*, 311–324.

Laties, V.G., & Weiss, B. (1963). Effects of concurrent task on fixed-interval responding in humans, *Journal of the Experimental Analysis of Behavior, 6*, 431–436.

Lazar, R. (1977). Extending sequence-class membership with matching-to-sample. *Journal of the Experimental Analysis of Behavior, 27*, 381–392.

Lazar, R.M., & Kotlarchyk, B.J. (1986). Second-order control of sequence-class equivalences in children. *Behavioural Processes, 13*, 205–215.

Leander, J.D., Lippman, L.G., & Meyer, M.M. (1968). Fixed interval performance as related to subjects' verbalizations of the reinforcement contingency. *The Psychological Record, 18*, 469–474.

Lipkens, R., Kop, P.F.M., & Matthijs, W. (1988). A test of symmetry and transitivity in the conditional discrimination performances of pigeons. *Journal of the Experimental Analysis of Behavior, 49*, 395–409.

Lippman, L.G., & Meyer, M.M. (1967). Fixed interval performance as related to instructions and to subjects' verbalization of the contingency. *Psychonomic Science, 8*, 135–136.

Lowe, C.F. (1979). Determinants of human operant behavior. In M.D. Zeiler & P. Harzem (Eds.), *Advances in analysis of behavior: Vol. 1. Reinforcement and the organization of behavior* (pp. 159–192). Chichester, England: Wiley.

Lowe, C.F., Beasty, A., & Bentall, R.P. (1983). The role of verbal behavior in human learning: Infant performance on fixed interval schedules. *Journal of the Experimental Analysis of Behavior, 39*, 157–164.

Lowe, C.F., Harzem, P., & Bagshaw, M. (1978). Species differences in temporal control of behavior. II: Human performance. *Journal of the Experimental Analysis of Behavior, 29*, 351–361.

Lowe, C.F., Harzem, P., & Hughes, S. (1978). Determinants of operant behavior in humans: Some differences from animals. *Quarterly Journal of Experimental Psychology, 30*, 373–386.

Mackay, H.A., & Sidman, M. (1984). Teaching new behaviors via equivalence relations. In P. Brooks, R. Sperber, & C. McCauley (Eds.), *Learning and cognition in the mentally retarded* (pp. 493–513). Hillsdale, NJ: Erlbaum.

Markman, E.M., & Wachtel, G.F. (1988). Children's use of mutual exclusivity to constrain the meanings of words. *Cognitive Psychology, 20*, 121–157.

McIlvane, W.J., Kledaras, J.B., Munson, L.C., King, K.A., de Rose, J.C., & Stoddard, L.T. (1987). Controlling relations in conditional discrimination and matching by exclusion. *Journal of the Experimental Analysis of Behavior, 48*, 187–208.

McIntire, K.D., Cleary, J., & Thompson, T. (1987). Conditional relations by monkeys: Reflexivity, symmetry, and transitivity. *Journal of the Experimental Analysis of Behavior, 47*, 279–285.

Michael, R.L., & Bernstein, D.J. (1991). Transient effects of acquisition history on generalization in a matching-to-sample task. *Journal of the Experimental Analysis of Behavior, 56*, 155–166.

Nissen, H. (1951). Analysis of complex conditional reaction in the chimpanzee. *Journal of Comparative and Physiological Psychology, 7*, 449–516.

Osgood, C.E. (1953). *Method and theory in experimental psychology*. New York: Oxford University Press.

Parrott, L.J. (1984). Listening and understanding. *The Behavior Analyst, 7*, 29–39.

Parrott, L.J. (1987a). Reply to Vaughan. In S. Modgil & C. Modgil (Eds.), *B.F. Skinner: Consensus and Controversy* (pp. 265–276). Sussex, England: Falmer Press.

Parrott, L.J. (1987b). Rule-governed behavior: An implicit analysis of reference. In S. Modgil & C. Modgil (Eds.), *B.F. Skinner: Consensus and Controversy* (pp. 265–276). Sussex, England: Falmer Press.

Reese, H.W. (1968). *The perception of stimulus relations: Discrimination learning and transposition*. New York: Academic Press.

Reese, H.W. (1991). Mentalistic approaches to verbal behavior. In L.J. Hayes & P.N. Chase (Eds.), *Dialogues on verbal behavior* (pp. 151–177). Reno, NV: Context Press.

Saunders, K.J. (1989). Naming in conditional discrimination and stimulus equivalence. *Journal of the Experimental Analysis of Behavior, 51*, 379–384.

Schoenfeld, W.N., & Cumming, W.W. (1963). Behavior and perception. In S. Koch (Ed.), *Psychology: A study of a science* (Vol. 5, pp. 213–252). New York: McGraw-Hill.

Shimoff, E., Catania, A.C., & Matthews, B.A. (1981). Uninstructed human responding: Sensitivity of low rate performance to schedule contingencies. *Journal of the Experimental Analysis of Behavior, 36*, 207–220.

Shimoff, E., Matthews, B.A., & Catania, A.C. (1986). Human operant performance: Sensitivity and pseudosensitivity to contingencies. *Journal of the Experimental Analysis of Behavior, 46*, 149–157.

Sidman, M. (1971). Reading and auditory-visual equivalences. *Journal of Speech and Hearing Research, 14*, 5–13.

Sidman, M. (1990). Equivalence relations: Where do they come from? In D.E. Blackman & H. Lejeune (Eds.), *Behaviour analysis in theory and practice: Contributions and controversies* (pp. 93–114). Hillsdale, NJ: Erlbaum.

Sidman, M., Cresson, O., & Willson-Morris, M. (1974). Acquisition of matching-to-sample via mediated transfer. *Journal of the Experimental Analysis of Behavior, 22*, 261–273.

Sidman, M., Kirk, B., & Willson-Morris, M. (1985). Six-member stimulus classes generated by conditional-discrimination procedures. *Journal of the Experimental Analysis of Behavior, 43*, 21–42.

Sidman, M., Rauzin, R., Lazar, R., Cunningham, S., Tailby, W., & Carrigan, P. (1982). A search for symmetry in the conditional discriminations of rhesus monkeys, baboons and children. *Journal of the Experimental Analysis of Behavior, 37*, 23–44.

Sidman, M., & Tailby, W. (1982). Conditional discrimination versus matching to sample: An expansion of the testing paradigm. *Journal of the Experimental Analysis of Behavior, 37*, 5–22.

Skinner, B. F. (1938). *Behavior of organisms*. New York: Appleton-Century-Crofts.

Skinner, B. F. (1945). The operational analysis of psychological terms. *Psychological Review, 52*, 270–276.

Skinner, B.F. (1957). *Verbal behavior*. New York: Appleton-Century-Crofts.

Skinner, B.F. (1966). An operant analysis of problem solving. In B. Kleinmuntz (Ed.), *Problem-solving: Research, method, and theory* (pp. 225–257). New York: Wiley.

Skinner, B.F. (1969). *Contingencies of reinforcement: A theoretical analysis*. New York: Appleton-Century-Crofts.

Spradlin, J.E., Cotter, V.W., & Baxley, N. (1973). Establishing a conditional discrimination without direct training: A study of transfer with retarded adolescents. *American Journal of Mental Deficiency, 77*, 556–566.

Spradlin, J.E., & Dixon, M. (1976). Establishing a conditional discrimination without direct training: Stimulus classes and labels. *American Journal of Mental Deficiency, 80*, 555–561.

Staats, C.K., & Staats, A.W. (1957). Meaning established by classical conditioning. *Journal of Experimental Psychology, 54*, 74–80.

Steele, D.L., & Hayes, S.C. (1991). Stimulus equivalence and arbitrarily applicable relational responding. *Journal of the Experimental Analysis of Behavior, 56*, 519–555.

VanBiervliet, A. (1977). Establishing words and objects as functionally equivalent through manual sign training. *American Journal of Mental Deficiency, 82*, 178–186.

Vaughan, W. (1988). Formation of equivalence sets in pigeons. *Journal of Experimental Psychology: Animal Behavior Processes, 14*, 36–42.

Watkins, M.J. (1990). Mediationism and the obfuscation of memory. *American Psychologist, 45*, 328–335.

Weiner, H. (1964). Conditioning history and human fixed-interval performance. *Journal of the Experimental Analysis of Behavior, 7*, 383–385.

Weiner, H. (1965). Conditioning history and maladaptive human operant behavior. *Psychological Reports, 17*, 935–942.

Weiner, H. (1969). Human behavioral persistence. *Psychological Record, 20*, 445–456.

Weiner, H. (1970). Instructional control of human operant responding during extinction following fixed ratio conditioning. *Journal of the Experimental Analysis of Behavior, 13*, 391–394.

Wulfert, E., & Hayes, S.C. (1988). The transfer of conditional sequencing through conditional equivalence classes. *Journal of the Experimental Analysis of Behavior, 50*, 125–144.

Yamamoto, J. (1986). Establishing stimulus equivalence in autistic children (in Japanese with English summary). *Japanese Journal of Behavior Analysis, 1*, 1–2.

ARTICLE 9

THE TREATMENT UTILITY OF ASSESSMENT

A Functional Approach to Evaluating Assessment Quality

From Hayes, S. C., Nelson, R. O. & Jarrett, R. (1987). *American Psychologist, 42*, 963–974.

Clinical assessment is an important and fertile area of psychology, and yet there is general agreement that it has not been in a state of continuous and healthy growth (e.g., Bersoff, 1973; Korchin & Schuldberg, 1981; Rorer & Widiger, 1983). Compared to the early days of clinical psychology there has been a decline in the emphasis on clinical assessment both in training and in practice (Garfield & Kurtz, 1973, 1976; Levitt, 1973; Shemberg & Keeley, 1970).

One reason may be that clinical assessment has not yet proven its value in fostering favorable treatment outcome. As clinical psychologists have devoted more and more time to treatment activities, the practical value of assessment has come under closer scrutiny (McReynolds, 1985). Unfortunately, experienced clinicians have not always found assessment data to be useful in treatment (Adams, 1972; Daily, 1953; Meehl, 1960; Moore, Bobbitt, & Wildman, 1968). Even the proponents of clinical assessment admit that they "do not believe that the current [high] status of testing is due to its demonstrated value" (Kaplan, Colarelli, Gross, Leventhal, & Siegel, 1970).

The lack of empirical evidence on the practical value of assessment has long been noted. In 1959 Meehl pointed out that even if an assessment procedure is reliable and valid, a clinician might "be seriously in error if he concluded therefrom that his tests were paying off in practice. On this question there is . . . no published empirical evidence" (p. 117). Twenty-two years later Korchin and Schuldberg could still worry that "clinical assessment may not provide the kind of information needed by therapists. Objective evidence is slim" (1981, p. 1154). Recently, McReynolds asked, "Are tests helpful to the therapist? Amazingly, there has been little research on this crucial question" (1985, p. 10). The purpose of the present article is to consider how to make better progress on understanding the role of assessment in successful treatment.

Any lack of evidence on the clinical value of assessment is not caused by a lack of appreciation for its ultimate practical purposes. Korchin (1976, p. 124) has defined clinical assessment as "the process by which clinicians gain understanding of the patient necessary for making informed decisions." Thus the "basic justification for assessment is that it provides information of value to the planning, execution, and evaluation of treatment" (Korchin & Schuldberg, 1981, p. 1154). Wiggins said, "Although measurement and prediction may be evaluated by formal psychometric criteria, such as reliability and validity, the outcomes of [assessment] decisions must be evaluated in terms of their utilities for individuals and institutions within our society" (1973, p. 272, emphasis in original). Meehl phrased it this way: "In what way and to what extent does this . . . information help us in treating the patient" (1959, p. 117). He called this question "ultimately the practically significant one by which the contributions of our [assessment] techniques must be judged" (1959, p. 116).

DEFINITION OF THE TREATMENT UTILITY OF ASSESSMENT

The impact of clinical assessment on treatment outcome has been discussed under a wide variety of labels. Among other terms, it has been viewed as a matter of incremental validity (Mischel, 1968), concurrent validity (Meehl, 1959), construct validity (Edwards, 1970), predictive validity (Lord & Novick, 1968), discriminative efficiency (Wiggins, 1973), and utility (Cronbach & Gleser, 1965). There is considerable confusion about the concepts relevant to the measurement of pragmatic clinical value.

We propose to use the phrase *the treatment utility of assessment* to refer to the degree to which assessment is shown to contribute to beneficial treatment outcome. Earlier (Nelson & Hayes, 1979), we used the term treatment validity. Although utility issues can indeed be considered to be an aspect of validity, the present term seems more direct. An assessment device, distinction, or strategy has this kind of utility if it can be shown that treatment outcome is positively influenced by this device, distinction, or strategy. The treatment utility of assessment deserves to be termed a type of utility because it relates closely to the functional thrust of that psychometric term. The need to qualify "utility" with the adjective "treatment" is justified by two facts. First, utility has been almost exclusively evaluated in terms of personnel decisions (e.g., Wiggins, 1973). The issues and methods involved in demonstrating the impact of assessment on treatment outcome differ significantly from the methods appropriate to the analysis of personnel decisions. Second, in personnel matters the concept of utility has come to refer primarily to the cost-benefit ratio of assessment strategies. This is why it was originally distinguished from predictive validity (Mischel, 1968). The treatment utility of assessment is not primarily a matter of cost-benefit analysis but of the demonstration of a particular type of benefit.

BARRIERS TO RESEARCH ON THE TREATMENT UTILITY OF ASSESSMENT

Theorists have long believed that research on the treatment utility of assessment should be feasible: "It is well within the capacity of available research methods and clinical facilities to determine what, if any, is the pragmatic advantage of a personality assessment" (Meehl, 1959, p. 125). Why then does there continue to be so little research?

Several possibilities present themselves. Because of conceptual confusion about the psychometric concepts relevant to the treatment utility of assessment, little has been written about the kinds of methods appropriate to these questions. The present paper presents a taxonomy of treatment utility methods in hopes of alleviating this problem.

In addition, "clinical psychologists . . . often make a sharp cleavage between their roles as diagnostician and therapist" (Blatt, 1975, p. 336). Assessment is often not integrated into the therapy process. When the two are disconnected, the value of assessment seemingly turns on the question "Is this diagnosis correct?" not "Is this assessment useful in treatment?" Some clinicians even fear that the assessment process is negatively intrusive on the therapeutic alliance. By focusing on the contribution of assessment to treatment outcome, treatment utility provides an approach for the testing of such concerns, and may itself help integrate assessment and treatment roles.

Another part of the problem may lie in the belief that complete psychometric purity is necessary before the treatment utility of assessment can be shown or even examined. Wiggins, who has emphasized the practical importance of assessment more than most psychometric theorists, noted this possibility: "Concern with the technical problems of measurement . . . has resulted in a relative neglect of the broader context in which such problems arise, namely, the optimal assignment of men to jobs or treatments" (1973, p. 272). As we show later, there seems to be little reason to delay treatment utility research until psychometrically perfect devices are developed.

Finally, research on the treatment utility of assessment did not have a proper intellectual context until the last few years. Two trends in particular have now come together to make such research both possible and important: the increased specificity of treatment and of assessment, and the emphasis on more theoretically oriented therapy research.

Treatment and assessment specificity. In earlier eras of clinical psychology, most psychotherapists practiced according to general schools of therapy. When clinicians apply the same general approach to most clients, assessment data can have few treatment implications (e.g., Wallen, 1956). With the arrival of more specific interventions, however, the need for guidance by assessment data becomes more obvious. Paul's (1969) well-known admonition that we should seek to identify which treatment works best for whom now carries a sense of contemporary urgency: "Compared to the early days of clinical psychology, today there are literally hundreds of competing types of psychosocial interventions . . . what qualities of this person, or aspects of his or her life situation and environment, recommend that he or she be seen in what type of therapy, with what kind of therapist, using what kind of technique? This is the question facing us today" (Korchin & Schuldberg, 1981, p. 1155).

Similarly, the early eras of clinical assessment tended to emphasize more global measures of personality. The treatment implications of such measures are often correspondingly vague, especially because general personality characteristics may be apparent to the clinician without an elaborate assessment process. This may be one reason that traditional assessment rarely alters the diagnostic judgments of clinicians, much less their treatment plans (Adams, 1972). Many contemporary assessment devices, however, are now quite specific, measuring specific behavior patterns, specific cognitions, and so on. With specific assessment devices, more specific treatment implications can be explored.

Theory-oriented treatment research. Psychotherapy researchers now agree that simply showing that therapy works is relatively uninteresting. The renewed emphasis on the role of theory in therapy research (e.g., Forsyth & Strong, 1986) enhances the importance of the treatment utility of assessment. In addition, there seems to be agreement that "future psychotherapy outcome research should, at a minimum, . . . [explore] the relative advantages and disadvantages of alternative treatment strategies with different specific psychological and behavioral difficulties" (VandenBos, 1986, p. 175), moving away from "undifferentiated treatment [as] the status quo" (Miller & Hester, 1986; see also McLean, 1981; Shaw, 1981). Thus, the field may now be intellectually ready to tackle the treatment utility of assessment.

Several Beginning Examples

The questions that can be asked about the treatment utility of assessment span the range of those relevant to assessment in general. Several short examples may serve as an introduction to the flexibility of the approach.

Target Behaviors and Classification. Research on the treatment utility of assessment can address which target behaviors should be the focus of treatment in specific patient subtypes. In one empirical example, patients with social skills problems were divided into those with apparent skills deficits and those with apparent suppression of skills because of social anxiety (Trower, Yardley, Bryant, & Shaw, 1978). This had been a popular distinction in the social skills literature (e.g., Hersen & Bellack, 1977), but the relationship between identifying skills deficits or social anxiety and finding differential treatment outcome had not been shown. Trower et al. (1978) showed that socially deficient patients improved more with social skills training than with systematic desensitization, while socially anxious patients improved as well under either treatment. Thus, the assessment distinction between skills deficits and social anxiety can be said to have a degree of treatment utility, but only for the skills deficit group.

Note that in studies of this type, treatment utility is based on a nexus of assessment devices, theoretical distinctions, and treatment approaches. An assessment distinction can originally have no treatment utility, but may acquire it when theories and treatments that make effective use of the distinction are later developed. Thus, the treatment utility of assessment reflects not just on the assessment device, but on its theoretical and practical context. Mischel noted this point clearly: "It is hard to separate the validity of a test from the validity of the personality construct it supposedly measures. The utility of statements about . . . constructs of psychodynamic theory, for example, depends on the value of the predictions and treatment decisions to which they lead in the individual case. The utility of the results reflects both on the theoretical constructs and on the test procedures from which these results are generated" (1968, p. 104).

Devices and Instruments. Another question that could be addressed from a treatment utility approach is whether given assessment devices are useful. Apparently, no studies have yet been conducted that are designed to measure directly the treatment utility of given devices, but in principle the strategy seems straightforward. For example, suppose we wished to assess the treatment utility of using self-monitoring to guide treatment planning, above and beyond that provided by questionnaires. All subjects could complete both questionnaires and self-monitoring, but the self-monitoring data for only half of the subjects would be made available to therapists designing their treatment programs. If these subjects improved more than those whose treatment plans were based on questionnaires alone, then the treatment utility of using self-monitoring data would be established for this particular disorder. In a similar fashion, the treatment utility of interviews, role-plays, projective tests, and other devices could be evaluated.

Strategies. The treatment utility of general assessment strategies can also be assessed. For example, the treatment utility of a functional analysis of the individual client's problems can be determined by comparing the progress of clients with individually designed treatment programs to those receiving a standard treatment package for a given disorder. A host of similar questions can be asked in the same way. Does objective assessment aid in effective treatment more so than projective assessment? Does the use of single subject evaluation designs improve treatment more than not using such designs? Is the use of psychometrically pure instruments generally more valuable in treatment planning than the use of other instruments? Many of the most central questions in clinical assessment are of this type and yet often the field has generated virtually no data directly relevant to them. Research on the treatment utility of assessment provides a method for answering them.

The Theoretical Impact of Treatment Utility Research

Treatment utility research sets the stage for important theoretical development, in part because it points out differences that are functionally important and thus require theoretical explanation. For example, there are undoubtedly many functionally distinct subtypes of patients currently mixed together in popular diagnostic systems. Yet even when we think we have reliably identified a distinct subtype, we do not know if the distinction is trivial until its treatment utility is established. Indeed, differential response to treatment is itself a good way to identify important patient subtypes in the first place.

Until the sources of treatment utility are identified, however, practices can have treatment utility and still not have much theoretical significance. Suppose, for example, that repeated assessment throughout the course of treatment can be shown to have some degree of treatment utility. We would then have to identify the variables that control or maximize the contribution that repeated assessment makes to treatment effectiveness. We might examine whether it increases the probability that the clinician will engage in other behaviors (e.g., praising improvements), which in turn produce the therapeutic advantages. We might see if the repeated assessment increases a client's contact with relative improvements, serving as an incentive for effective action. Thus over time treatment utility research should fuel conceptual as well as technological progress as the processes responsible for treatment benefits are identified.

The advantage of treatment utility research in this regard is twofold. First, it naturally guides the field toward theorizing based on non-trivial differences (i.e., those that actually make an impact on treatment outcome). Second, researchers examining a particular link between assessment and treatment usually will have some theoretical analysis that leads them to believe that there might be such a link. If it is found, the viability of the theoretical construction increases incrementally. If not, that too is revealing. The few available treatment utility studies already suggest that our previous conceptualizations are often only partially confirmed (e.g., Trower et al., 1978), or fail to be confirmed at all (e.g., Keller, 1983). Thus, in addition to enhancing treatment outcome, treatment utility research can improve our understanding of behavior and contribute to clinical science.

Psychometric Criteria and Treatment Utility

As noted earlier, the slow pace of research on the treatment utility of assessment may be due in part to the belief that such questions cannot be asked until all psychometric hurdles are cleared. Psychometrics is based fundamentally on the concepts of reliability and validity. Reliability refers to the consistency of scores obtained by the same persons when examined with a given assessment device under systematically changing circumstances (e.g., different times, different items, different examiners, different internal divisions of the test). Validity refers to what an assessment device measures and how well it does so (Anastasi, 1982). To put it another way, reliability deals with relations among scores on the same device, while validity deals with relations among scores on different devices (Campbell & Fiske, 1959). Generalizability theory (Cronbach, Gleser, Nanda, & Rajaratnam, 1972) more systematically categorizes the various types of reliability and validity as universes of generalization (e.g., across scores, item, time, setting, or method).

Reliability and validity are thus based on the consistency of measurement. Classical psychometrics views consistency as the hallmark of a good assessment device. In psychometric theory, an observed score is a composite of the true value plus measurement error. Often, the true score is taken to be a hypothetical entity, which is typically assumed to be enduring and stable because it supposedly reflects an enduring, stable, internal entity or trait. Classical test theory (Lord & Novick, 1968) avoids the Platonic connotations of "true scores," but still translates quality assessment into an issue of the degree of underlying consistency.

Many types of consistency seem orthogonal to the issue of the treatment utility of assessment. For example, a measure could readily have treatment utility without internal consistency. Suppose we measure the number of environmental stressors present in a client's life. There is no reason in general to suppose that clients who, say, just lost a spouse will also have, say, just been fired. Thus, high internal consistency should not necessarily be expected. This does not mean that clients with high degrees of environmental stress will not respond differently to treatment than clients with low levels of environmental stress. Many kinds of psychometric criteria are not sufficient, and at times may not even be necessary, for treatment utility.

To take this point to its logical extreme, it is useful to recognize that there may even be times when an assessment process could have treatment utility without the assessment report having any reliability or validity whatsoever. Because all psychometric evaluations are of assessment results (e.g., reports, diagnoses, scores, profiles), not of the actual process of conducting an assessment (e.g., giving the test, watching the patient respond to it), if this assessment process can have treatment utility then some tests or procedures may be psychometrically invalid and still have treatment utility on that basis. This controversial claim can perhaps be seen in the belief, common among many clinicians, that projective techniques may still be useful even if their reliability and validity are not readily established (Blatt, 1975; Zubin, Eron, & Schumen, 1965). Suppose that clinicians varied widely in the way they interpreted a particular projective test. Such a test could not have reliability or validity. If only the actual test report was at issue, the test also could not have treatment utility because the same test performance would lead to different scores, diagnoses, or profiles and thus to different treatment recommendations. Even so, the process of giving this "unreliable" test could have treatment utility. For example, in giving the test and in watching the client respond the clinician may unwittingly learn more about the client's personality. The clinician might then behave more effectively in treatment even though unable to verbalize the relation between the test, the client's personality, and the clinical decisions. In some ways, this possibility seems to match what many clinicians say about the use of projective devices in experienced clinical hands. Whether the claim could be supported is an empirical matter, but it is one that traditional psychometric evaluation cannot determine. It is a treatment utility question that could be addressed using a manipulated assessment study.

What this shows is that the relation between psychometric criteria and treatment utility is often open to question. Thus, there seems to be little reason to insist in principle that treatment utility must always be the last step in the evaluation of a given assessment device, distinction, or approach. Treatment utility is shown by a well-designed study, regardless of the state of previous psychometric evaluations.

This is not to say that reliability and validity should be ignored in treatment utility research. Suppose a clinician devised a test, proceeded directly to an assessment of its treatment utility, and failed to find any. The failure could be due to poor reliability of various kinds, the lack of appropriate treatment, a lack of treatment integrity, or a host of other possible problems other than the practical uselessness of the dimension the clinician was trying to measure. Thus, psychometric evaluations certainly limit the possible sources of a failure to find treatment utility. It also seems reasonable to expect measures with good reliability and validity to be more likely to have treatment utility, though this is largely an empirical question. Further, it is impossible to build a science of assessment totally on treatment utility alone. Knowing the effect on treatment outcome itself requires assessment, and that means that ultimately treatment utility must be based on measures that are themselves not validated in this manner.

Once an aspect of assessment (e.g., a device, approach, or distinction) has been shown to have treatment utility, it is also then possible to use traditional psychometric evaluations to expand the value of the finding. For example, suppose that a given measure has been shown conclusively to distinguish two subgroups of patients who respond differently to various treatments. If a second measure separates patients into virtually the same subgroups, then it must also have treatment utility. A problem comes, however, when the relation between the two measures is only moderate. Here the treatment utility of the new measure cannot be assumed because it is not certain that the area of shared variability is itself responsible for the treatment utility shown with the first measure.

Treatment utility is not the only functionally based means by which to evaluate assessment. It is possible for assessment to produce descriptions that currently have no treatment utility, but contribute to our understanding of a given disorder. The degree to which assessment contributes to our knowledge base may be thought of as an issue of the "conceptual utility" of assessment. Treatment utility and conceptual utility are undoubtedly related, but they are distinguishable. For example, a device may contribute to treatment outcome (it has treatment utility), but for theoretically unclear reasons (it does not yet have conceptual utility). Similarly, a device may be theoretically useful and as yet be useless in terms of treatment outcome. For our present purposes, the point is simply that there are other important goals for assessment other than treatment outcome. Treatment utility should not, therefore, be thought of as the only functional grounds for evaluating assessment quality.

SUMMARY

Treatment utility provides the potential for a science of clinical assessment that is built on evidence of successful contributions to treatment. As such, it is an important method of examining the quality of assessment—one in which the word "quality" is directly related to a central function of clinical assessment. To date, the role of treatment utility has been buried by conceptual confusion, poorly articulated methods, and inappropriate linkage to psychometric criteria. The present article was designed to help in these areas. Treatment utility research has also been hindered by non-specific types of therapy, non-specific types of assessment, unnecessary divisions between the role of assessor and therapist, and an overemphasis on technique over conceptual advancement. The trends in the field all seem positive in these areas. Thus, the time now seems ripe for a vigorous expansion of research on the contribution of assessment to treatment outcome. Because treatment utility provides the practical basis for a concern with clinical assessment, it seems important to proceed rapidly to its demonstration.

REFERENCES

Adams, J. (1972). The contribution of the psychological evaluation to psychiatric diagnosis. *Journal of Personality Assessment, 36*, 561–566.

Anastasi, A. (1982). *Psychological testing* (5th ed.). New York: Macmillan.

Bersoff, D.N. (1973). Silk purses into sow's ears: The decline of psychological testing and a suggestion for its redemption. *American Psychologist, 28*, 892–899.

Blatt, S.J. (1975). The validity of projective techniques and their research and clinical contribution. *Journal of Personality Assessment, 39*, 327–343.
Campbell, D.T., & Fiske, D.W. (1959). Convergent and discriminant validation by the multitrait-multimethod matrix. *Psychological Bulletin, 56*, 81–105.
Cronbach, L.J., & Gleser, G.C. (1965). *Psychological tests and personnel decisions* (2nd ed.). Urbana: University of Illinois Press.
Cronbach, L.J., Gleser, G.C., Nanda, H., & Rajaratnam, N. (1972). *The dependability of behavioral measures*. New York: Wiley.
Daily, C.A. (1953). The practical utility of the clinical report. *Journal of Consulting Psychology, 17*, 297–302.
Edwards, A.L. (1970). *The measurement of personality traits by scales and inventories*. New York: Holt, Rinehart, & Winston.
Forsyth, D.R., & Strong, S.R. (1986). The scientific study of counseling and psychotherapy: A unificationist view. *American Psychologist, 41*, 113–119.
Garfield, S.L., & Kurtz, R. (1973). Attitudes toward training in diagnostic testing: A survey of directors on internship training. *Journal of Consulting and Clinical Psychology, 40*, 350–355.
Garfield, S.L., & Kurtz, R. (1976). Clinical psychologists in the 1970s. *American Psychologist, 31*, 1–9.
Hersen, M., & Bellack, A.S. (1977). *Research and practice in social skills training*. New York: Plenum.
Kaplan, M.L., Colarelli, N.J., Gross, R.B., Leventhal, D., & Siegel, S.M. (1970). *The structural approach in psychological testing*. New York: Pergamon.
Keller, K.E. (1983). Dysfunctional attitudes and cognitive therapy for depression. *Cognitive Therapy and Research, 7*, 437–444.
Korchin, S.J. (1976). *Modern clinical psychology*. New York: Basic Books.
Korchin, S.J., & Schuldberg, D. (1981). The future of clinical assessment. *American Psychologist, 36*, 1147–1158.
Levitt, E.E. (1973). Internship versus campus: 1964 and 1971. *Professional Psychology, 4*, 129–132.
Lord, F.M., & Novick, M.R. (1968). *Statistical theories of mental test scores*. Reading, MA: Addison-Wesley.
McLean, P.D. (1981). Matching treatment to patient characteristics in an outpatient setting. In L.P. Rehm (Ed.), *Behavior therapy for depression*. (pp. 197–207). New York: Academic.
McReynolds, P. (1985). Psychological assessment and clinical practice: Problems and prospects. In J.N. Butcher & C.D. Spielberger (Eds.), *Advances in personality assessment* (Vol. 4, pp. 1–30). Hillsdale, NJ: Erlbaum.
Meehl, P.E. (1959). Some ruminations on the validation of clinical procedures. *Canadian Journal of Psychology, 13*, 102–128.
Meehl, P.E. (1960). The cognitive activity of the clinician. *American Psychologist, 15*, 19–27.

Miller, W.R., & Hester, R.K. (1986). Matching problem drinkers with optimal treatments. In W.R. Miller & N. Heather (Eds.), *Treating addictive behaviors: Processes of change* (pp. 175–203). New York: Plenum.

Mischel, W. (1968). *Personality and assessment.* New York: Wiley.

Moore, G.H., Bobbitt, W.E., & Wildman, R.W. (1968). Psychiatric impressions of psychological reports. *Journal of Clinical Psychology, 24*, 373–376.

Nelson, R. O., & Hayes, S. C. (1979). Some current dimensions of behavioral assessment. *Behavioral Assessment*, 1, 1–16.

Paul, G.L. (1969). Behavior modification research: Design and tactics. In C.M. Franks (Ed.), *Behavior therapy: Appraisal and status* (pp. 29–62). New York: McGraw-Hill.

Rorer, L.G., & Widiger, T.A. (1983). Personality structure and assessment. *Annual Review of Psychology, 34*, 431–463.

Shaw, B.F. (1981). Matching treatment to patient characteristics in an inpatient setting. In L.P. Rehm (Ed.), *Behavior therapy for depression* (pp. 209–229). New York: Academic.

Shemberg, K., & Keeley, S. (1970). Psychodiagnostic training in the psychiatric setting: Past and present. *Journal of Consulting and Clinical Psychology, 34*, 205–211.

Trower, P., Yardley, K., Bryant, B.M., & Shaw, P. (1978). The treatment of social failure: A comparison of anxiety-reduction and skills-acquisition procedures on two social problems. *Behavior Modification, 2*, 41–50.

VandenBos, G.R. (1986). Psychotherapy research: A special issue. *American Psychologist, 41*, 111–112.

Wallen, R.W. (1956). *Clinical psychology: The study of persons.* New York: McGraw-Hill.

Wiggins, J.S. (1973). *Personality and prediction: Principles of personality assessment.* Reading, MA: Addison-Wesley.

Zubin, J., Eron, K.D., & Schumen, F. (1965). *An experimental approach to projective techniques.* New York: Wiley.

ARTICLE 10

EXPERIENTIAL AVOIDANCE AND BEHAVIORAL DISORDERS

A Functional Dimensional Approach to Diagnosis and Treatment

From Hayes, S.C., Wilson, K.G., Gifford, E.V., Follette, V.M., & Strosahl, K. (1996). *Journal of Consulting and Clinical Psychology, 64*, 1152–1168.

The process of classification lies at the root of all scientific behavior. It is literally impossible to speak about a truly unique event, alone and cut off from all others, since words themselves are means of categorization (Bruner, Goodnow, & Austin, 1956). Science is concerned with refined and systematic verbal formulations of events and relations among events. Since "events" are always classes of events, and "relations" are always classes of relations, classification is one of the central tasks of science.

The field of psychopathology has seen myriad classification systems (Hersen & Bellack, 1988; Sprock & Blashfield, 1991). The differences among some of these approaches are both long-standing and relatively unchanging, in part because systems are never free from *a priori* assumptions and guiding principles that provide a framework for organizing information (Adams & Cassidy, 1993).

In the present paper we will briefly examine the differences between two core classification strategies in psychopathology—syndromal and functional. We will then articulate one possible functional diagnostic dimension: experiential avoidance. Several common syndromal categories will be examined to see how this dimension can organize data found among topographical groupings. Finally, the utility and implications of this functional dimensional category will be examined.

COMPARING SYNDROMAL AND FUNCTIONAL CLASSIFICATION

While there are many purposes to diagnostic classification, most researchers seem to agree that the ultimate goal is the development of classes, dimensions, or relational categories that can be empirically wedded to treatment strategies (Adams & Cassidy, 1993; Hayes, Nelson, & Jarrett, 1987; Meehl, 1959). Syndromal classification—whether dimensional or categorical—can be traced back to Wundt and Galen, and thus is as old as scientific psychology itself (Eysenck, 1986). Syndromal classification starts with constellations of signs and symptoms in order to identify the disease entities that are presumed to give rise to these constellations. Syndromal classification thus starts with structure and hopes to *end* with utility. Functional classification, conversely, attempts to *start* with utility by identifying functional processes with clear treatment implications. It then works backward and returns to the issue of identifiable signs and symptoms that reflect these processes. These differences are fundamental.

Syndromal Classification

The economic and political dominance of the American Psychiatric Association's *Diagnostic and Statistical Manual* (American Psychiatric Association, 1994) has led to a world-wide adoption of syndromal classification as an analytic strategy in psychopathology. The only widely used alternative, the International Classification of Diseases (ICD) system, was a source document for the original DSM, and continuous efforts have been made to ensure their ongoing compatibility (American Psychiatric Association, 1994).

The immediate goal of syndromal classification (Foulds, 1971) is to identify collections of signs (what one sees) and symptoms (what the client complains of). The hope is that these syndromes will lead to the identification of disorders with a known etiology, course, and response to treatment. When this has been achieved, we are no longer speaking of syndromes but of *diseases*. Because the construct of disease involves etiology and response to treatment, these classifications are ultimately a kind of *functional unit*. Thus, the syndromal classification approach is a topographically oriented classification strategy for the identification of functional units of abnormal behavior.

The link between syndromes (topography of signs and symptoms) and diseases (function) has been notably weak in psychopathology. After over 100 years of effort, almost no psychological diseases have been clearly identified. With the exception of general paresis and a few clearly neurological disorders, psychiatric syndromes have remained syndromes indefinitely.

In the absence of progress toward true functional entities, syndromal classification of psychopathology has several down sides. Symptoms are virtually non-falsifiable, since they depend only on certain formal features. Syndromal categories tend to evolve—changing their names frequently and splitting into ever finer sub-categories—but except for political reasons (e.g., homosexuality as a disorder) they rarely simply disappear. As a result, the number of syndromes within the DSM system has increased exponentially (W. C. Follette, Houts, & Hayes, 1992). Increasingly refined topographical distinctions can always be made without the restraining and synthesizing effect of the identification of common etiological processes.

The DSM system specifically eschews the primary importance of functional processes: "The approach taken in DSM-III is atheoretical with regard to etiology or pathophysiological process" (APA, 1980, p. 7). This spirit of etiological agnosticism is carried forward in the most recent DSM incarnation. It is meant to encourage users from widely varying schools of psychology to use the same classification system. While integration is a laudable goal, the price paid may have been too high (W. C. Follette & Hayes, 1992).

Functional Classification

In a functional approach to classification, the topographical characteristics of any particular individual's behavior are not the basis for classification; instead, behaviors and sets of behaviors are organized by the functional processes that are thought to have produced and maintained them. This functional method is inherently less direct and naive than a syndromal approach, as it requires the application of pre-existing information about psychological processes to specific response forms. It thus integrates at least rudimentary forms of theory into the classification strategy, in sharp contrast with the atheoretical goals of the DSM system.

FUNCTIONAL DIAGNOSTIC DIMENSIONS AS A METHOD OF FUNCTIONAL CLASSIFICATION

There are many problems with classical functional analysis as a functional classification system (Hayes & Follette, 1992). It is sometimes vague, often difficult to replicate and thus to test empirically, and is ideographic in the extreme. It may not adequately specify the relevant behavioral or contextual characteristics to identify, nor which behavioral principles should be applied and in what manner. Because it is vague, it may fall prey to the well-documented errors common to clinical judgment more generally (Dawes, 1994). Perhaps for all of these reasons, functional analysis has hardly progressed from its promising beginning (Salzinger, 1988).

There are several possible solutions to these problems (Hayes & Follette, 1992). One of the most promising is the development of functional diagnostic dimensions. If one performs many individual functional analyses tied to the same dimension, these might then be arranged into a larger category with related assessment methods and treatment recommendations. The guiding principle behind these collections would be the identification of common processes of etiology or maintenance that suggest effective courses of action.

This idea was prevalent early in the behavior therapy movement (e.g., Bandura, 1968; Kanfer & Grimm, 1977), but the suggested categories were too closely tied to a specific set of abstract principles and too little tied to the characteristic forms of behavior that clients display. For example, Kanfer and Grimm's major categories included "behavioral excesses" and "problems in environmental stimulus control." Such categories can, in principle, be applied to every case. Furthermore, the analytic categories themselves were so specific to behavior analysis that they were not useful unless one subscribed to this specific theoretical approach. Functional diagnostic dimensions may be most useful initially when they point to reasonably widely agreed upon pathological processes, without necessitating the adoption of an entire paradigmatic system. Classification based on such dimensions may integrate the contributions of various theoretical perspectives and allow for the validation of pathological processes tied to clear treatment implications. In the remainder of the paper we will develop an example of a functional diagnostic dimension which we argue demonstrates these possibilities.

EXPERIENTIAL AVOIDANCE AS A FUNCTIONAL DIAGNOSTIC DIMENSION

Experiential avoidance is a putative pathological process recognized by a wide number of theoretical orientations. Experiential avoidance is the phenomenon that occurs when a person is unwilling to remain in contact with particular private experiences (e.g., bodily sensations, emotions, thoughts, memories, behavioral predispositions) and takes steps to alter the form or frequency of these events and the contexts that occasion them. In this paper we argue that many forms of psychopathology are usefully viewed as unhealthy methods of experiential avoidance. In what follows, we will outline some of the perspectives and research that supports the concept of such a dimension, and that shows its potential for integrating research across theoretical orientations and specific research areas.

Convergence of Views on Experiential Avoidance

Experiential avoidance has been recognized, implicitly or explicitly, among most systems of therapy. Unlike other paradigms, behavioral and cognitive therapy have generally focused on changing (rather than accepting) private experiences. Traditional behavior therapy fought anxiety with relaxation;

while cognitive therapy challenged irrational beliefs with more rational ones. Essentially, better forms of experiential avoidance were systematically trained as a mode of intervention. Even within these domains, however, emotional and other forms of experiential avoidance have been recognized as a problem, and such recognition appears to be increasing.

Why Would Experiential Avoidance Be So Pervasive?

It appears that a concern with experiential avoidance is ubiquitous across otherwise divergent psychotherapeutic systems. We believe that the theme of experiential avoidance is so pervasive in various theories of psychopathology because it is such a pervasive aspect of human functioning. Experiential avoidance could be analyzed in a number of ways depending upon one's theoretical orientation, but from our own contextual behavioral perspective (Biglan & Hayes, 1996; Hayes, Follette, & Follette, 1995; Hayes & Wilson, 1993) there are several factors that contribute, including the bi-directional nature of human language, inappropriate generalization of control rules, cultural support for emotions and cognitions as causes of behavior, social encouragement, and modeling of experiential avoidance, among others.

Self-knowledge and the Bi-directional Nature of Language

Let us begin an analysis of experiential avoidance with an even more general matter at the opposite end of the psychological continuum: why is self-knowledge important? Following in the Socratic tradition, almost all schools of psychology have emphasized the importance of self-knowledge. For example, B.F. Skinner suggested: "Self-knowledge has a special value to the individual himself. A person who has been 'made aware of himself' is in a better position to predict and control his own behavior" (Skinner, 1974, p. 31). We agree, but argue that the beneficial effect of self-knowledge depends entirely upon the nature of human language (Hayes & Wilson, 1993).

Human verbal behavior is arbitrarily applicable, bi-directional and combinatorial (see Hayes & Hayes, 1992, for a review of the literature supporting these views). In more common sense terms, when a human interacts symbolically with an event, the functions of the referent are partially present in the symbol and vice versa, and can in some circumstances spread from that symbol to others through a network of related terms. Because of the bidirectional quality of human symbolic behavior, when a human interacts symbolically with his or her *own* behavior, the psychological meaning of *both* the verbal symbol and the behavior itself can change as a result. This bi-directional property makes human self-knowledge useful, because it means that changes in how we view our behavior or the situations that occasion it can in turn change the functions of these situations and behaviors. But this same bi-directional property also makes self-knowledge potentially aversive.

Suppose we train a rat to press a one lever for food pellets if it has recently been shocked, and another if it has not recently been shocked. In effect, the rat can "tell" whether or not it recently received an electric shock. This is readily done because while the shock was aversive to the animal, the report of it is not: after all the report leads to food, not to shock. Simply stated, it is not aversive for a nonverbal organism to report an aversive event.

Contrast this with the case for verbally competent humans. In this case the report and the event reported are mutually related and therefore the functions of events are partially available in the symbolic description and vice versa. Because of this, for example, a survivor of trauma may re-experience pain simply in the verbal reporting of that trauma. In our own technical analysis, we refer to this phenomenon as the "bi-directional transformation of stimulus functions," and have contrasted it with the unidirectional nature of normal operant and classical conditioning (Hayes & Hayes, 1992; Hayes & Wilson, 1993). Verbal awareness of one's own experience, can itself change the experiential quality of what is known.

Human emotions provide an example. Human emotions seem to require a verbal label or appraisal as a cognitive component (Lazarus, 1982). These labels may carry with them implications for emotional avoidance. "Anxiety" is not just a fuzzy set of bodily states and behavioral predispositions (as in nonverbal organisms); it is an evaluative and descriptive verbal category that integrates a wide variety of experiences, including memories, thoughts, evaluations, and social comparisons, among others.

The evaluative connotation of emotional labels alters the functions of private experiences that are so labeled. For example, in most contexts anxiety is a "bad" emotion. The bi-directionality of human language can create the illusion that this "badness" is an inherent quality of the emotion itself: we say "This *is* a bad emotion," not "This is an emotion and I am evaluating it as bad." These same referential or relational processes can increase the negativity of experienced events by relating the verbal label to still other verbal events in more complex ways. For example, if anxiety is said to be predictive of "loss of control" and "loss of control" is predictive of "social humiliation" then the aversiveness of felt (and labeled) anxiety could increase greatly since it is verbally related to humiliation. Since humans have been taught a wide variety of strategies for avoiding negative events, it is not surprising that these would be applied to "negative" emotions. Given our verbal abilities, experiential avoidance can function generally as a learned, negatively reinforced behavior (Gifford, 1994).

We are arguing that experiential avoidance is built into human language and is thus to some degree a basic component of the human condition. The very bi-directional relations that make human verbal self-knowledge useful also can make that self-knowledge inherently difficult and actively resisted when its content is undesirable. In this view, psychopathological or maladaptive experiential avoidance is the dysfunctional range of a fairly "normal" behavior, and it is excessive entanglements with or fusion with thoughts that particularly supports the adoption of experiential avoidance strategies.

Other Reasons Experiential Avoidance Is Ubiquitous

There are several other reasons why experiential avoidance occurs so readily. First, the exercise of conscious, planful control strategies can be extremely useful in avoiding many of the hazards life presents. If one drives cautiously in the rain, accidents can be avoided. A program of regular brushing and flossing can help one to avoid the dentist's drill. Because the exercise of such deliberate, verbally guided control strategies is effective in many contexts, it is only natural that we would attempt to use these same strategies with all evaluated targets, including aversive thoughts, emotions, and the like. It is not at first obvious that this is an inappropriate and unnecessary generalization of control rules to a domain in which they are notably ineffective.

Second, there is a great deal of social encouragement and modeling of emotional avoidance. Children are often explicitly trained to suppress emotional responding (e.g., "Stop crying or I will give you something to cry about"). From the perspective of the child, adults seemingly model this same behavior since they do not show emotions as readily. Regulating emotional displays is not the same thing as regulating private experience, however. The child who deliberately stops crying does not necessarily become happy—only silent.

Third, emotions and cognitions are treated as socially valid reasons for behavior. As part of the socialization process, people are required and able to give verbal explanations for their behavior, even if its sources are unknown or obscure (Semin & Manstead, 1985). Thoughts and feelings are commonly used as reasons for behavior, and by extension, emotions and cognitions that "cause" bad behavior should be avoided. Unfortunately, this same process will excuse destructive forms of experiential avoidance itself. For example, an agoraphobic might use anxiety as a socially valid reason for social withdrawal ("I would have been too afraid if I left the house, so I had to stay home").

Finally, the immediate effects of experiential avoidance are often positive, and short-term consequences are much more important than long-term ones. For example, the immediate effect of cognitive distraction or other forms of thought suppression is positive—it is only over time that the increase in avoided thoughts appears (Gold & Wegner, 1995). Thus, experiential avoidance appears to work, even when it does not.

Why Would Experiential Avoidance Be Detrimental?

These factors may explain why experiential avoidance is ubiquitous, but they do not explain why it may result in psychopathology. There are several possible reasons why emotional avoidance may be detrimental, or why its converse—psychological acceptance—may be helpful. These analyses must be tentative, in part because data on these issues is relatively new. Until recently, the importance of psychological acceptance was emphasized in the less empirical traditions such as the humanistic or existential approaches (Greenberg, 1994). Only within the last ten years have a number of empirically based treatment approaches have emerged that are oriented toward different types of psychological acceptance (e.g., Barlow & Beck, 1984; Chiles & Strosahl, 1995; Cordova & Kohlenberg, 1994; Hayes, 1984, 1987; Hayes, Jacobson, Follette, & Dougher, 1994; Hayes & Wilson, 1994; Jacobson, 1991; Koerner, Jacobson, & Christensen, 1994; Kohlenberg & Tsai, 1991; Linehan, 1993; Marlatt, 1994; Strosahl, 1991). Again, the analysis of detrimental effects differs according to theoretical orientation, although the existence of such effects seems widely accepted. Our analysis of the destructive effects of some forms of experiential avoidance centers around certain well established principles of learning, as well as on some emerging analyses of social-verbal contextual factors.

The Process of Deliberate Avoidance Necessarily Contradicts the Desired Outcome

In humans, deliberate avoidance usually involves formulating and following a verbal plan. In some areas of experiential avoidance this is inherently problematic because the verbal regulatory process includes the avoided item. For example, cognitive avoidance is difficult since deliberately trying to rid oneself of a thought involves following the verbal rule that contains the thought. There is a significant and rapidly growing body of evidence that deliberate thought suppression and control may actually be counterproductive, in that an attempt not to think thoughts often creates those very thoughts (e.g., Wegner, Schneider, Carter, & White, 1987; Wegner, Schneider, Knutson, & McMahon, 1991).

The Regulation of Private Events Is Largely Unresponsive to Verbal Control

Many private experiences are classically conditioned, either directly or indirectly. For example, if painful emotional experiences have been associated with a particular event that is either directly present or present indirectly through verbal relations, it is likely that this event will now arouse negative emotions by association alone. In these circumstances, attempts at purposeful control may be relatively ineffective, because the underlying process or history is not readily verbally governed.

The experimental evidence for the harmful effects of emotional suppression is not yet as great as that for thought suppression, but there seem to be many examples of these vicious cycles. For instance, suppose a person is extremely distressed about anxiety and tries to do everything to eliminate it because of its awful meaning and potentially terrible consequences. In this case, a small bit of classically conditioned anxiety may cue both purposeful attempts to avoid and reduce the anxiety, *and* additional anxiety associated with the verbal construction of highly aversive consequences. In essence, the person may become anxious about being anxious. This kind of harmful effect of experiential avoidance is most likely precisely when the seeming need for it is greatest, because it is then that the negative effects of failure would be most closely related to the avoidance strategy and even minor levels of avoided material would be threatening. Panic disorder may be an example of such a phenomenon (Chambless, Caputo, Bright, & Gallagher, 1984; Craske, Sanderson, & Barlow, 1987; Goldstein & Chambless, 1978; Hayes, 1987).

Change Is Possible but the Change Strategy Leads to Unhealthy Forms of Avoidance

Suppose someone tried not to remember a given event. Memories are not simple voluntary behavior—once an event has occurred, remembering it may occur relatively automatically in a wide variety of circumstances. Strategies to avoid memories might include avoiding all situations that might give rise to it, dissociating, or other means. The problem with these strategies is that even if they are successful they create additional problems, such as constricting the person's freedom to be in otherwise valuable situations, or limiting conscious access to life events. This is one of the processes that has been most emphasized in the humanistic tradition: emotional avoidance restricts the wisdom of human beings by diminishing access to one's own history and the "response tendency information" contained therein (Safran & Greenberg, 1988; c.f., Greenberg, 1994).

The Emotion-Laden Event Is Important

Sometimes experiential control is put in the service of managing entirely appropriate reactions to unchangeable events merely because the reaction is not pleasant. For example, a person may take the view "I can't accept that my dad was killed," and use drugs to avoid the grief associated with his death. Grief is a natural reaction to such losses, and no amount of drug consumption will alter either the situation or the loss. No effort to reduce or alter private events is called for here. When an unchangeable loss occurs, the healthy thing to do is to feel what one feels when losses occur.

Healthy Change Produces Painful Experiences

Change can be frightening. At times, what needs to be done is avoided because it is experientially difficult. This suggests a major reason experiential avoidance may lead to psychopathology: it restricts needed change.

We are not arguing that all forms of experiential avoidance are unhealthy. In many instances there is nothing harmful about seeking relaxation or putting off distracting thoughts or avoiding physical pain. Ironically, however, these healthy forms of experiential avoidance apply most clearly when the experiences involved are not intense and clinically relevant. For example, relaxation is much more likely to reduce normal stress than to eliminate panic attacks. In the present paper, we will limit our analysis to experiential avoidance that persists even when it is costly, useless, or life distorting. In these circumstances, experiential avoidance becomes pathological.

EVIDENCE FOR EXPERIENTIAL AVOIDANCE AS A PATHOLOGICAL DIMENSION

A functional approach is explicitly inductive: the phenomena and its context are the focus of interest. Unlike more deductively oriented approaches, where empirical findings are used to argue for and against complex theoretical positions, functional dimensions are organized more humbly around direct observations. Because of this, data from various schools of thought or research areas become relevant to each other.

In the following sections, we will review literatures as diverse as basic experimental analyses of human cognition and emotion, literature on coping styles, experimental psychopathology, clinical process, and psychotherapy outcome research. Although the purposes and orientation of these various researchers are quite divergent, the dimension of experiential avoidance can play an important role in organizing their data in a coherent way. We believe that this tendency to integrate data from both basic and applied research domains is characteristic of functional diagnostic dimensions (Gifford, 1995).

Evidence From Basic Experimental Work

One major source of data relevant to experiential avoidance is from the emerging thought-suppression literature. A number of studies have demonstrated that when subjects are asked to suppress a thought they later show an *increase* in this suppressed thought when compared to subjects who are not given suppression instructions (D. M. Clark, Ball, & Pape, 1991; Gold & Wegner, 1995; Wegner et al., 1987; Wegner et al., 1991).

A number of variations on this research have been done that have implications for an experiential avoidance perspective. For example, normal subjects asked to suppress a particular thought show rebound effects specifically in contexts in which the suppression took place (Wegner et al., 1991). These data suggest that if an individual successfully suppresses some aversive thought or memory in a particular situation, they might find the thought remaining at fairly low levels in contexts not related to suppression, but if they return to the original context they would not only be likely to re-experience the suppressed thought, but would be likely to experience it at an even higher level than before. This suggests that cognitive avoidance is most likely to fail in the precise contexts in which its success is most important and desired.

The paradoxical effects of thought suppression have also been linked to mood. In a study using mood induction, subjects were asked not to think a specific thought while in a specific mood (Wenzlaff, Wegner, & Klein, 1991). In subsequent phases of the experiment, subjects were assigned to either similar or different mood induction procedures. All subjects showed a rebound effect but the subjects who had the same mood induction in the second phase had a significantly higher rebound effect. This suggests that if a person is avoiding a thought that is associated with anxiety, for example, the paradoxical increase produced by suppression is most likely to be seen when the person is anxious: precisely when a person struggling with an anxious thought would least like suppression to fail. Furthermore, a separate experiment showed that the suppressed thought will come to produce the mood that was present during the original suppression (Wenzlaff et al., 1991). Thus, a kind of self-amplifying loop can be created from precisely the kinds of mood, cognition, and suppression components likely to be experienced by those with clinical disorders.

Evidence From the Coping Styles Literature

Research into coping strategies has also demonstrated the detrimental effects of experiential avoidance. One of the most widely used methods of assessing coping strategies is the *Ways of Coping Questionnaire* (WOC; Folkman & Lazarus, 1988). Lazarus and Folkman (1984) have identified two dominant means of coping with stressful situations: problem-focused and emotion-focused coping strategies. Problem-focused strategies involve active attempts to alter distressing situations, such as "I made a plan of action and followed it." Many of the emotion-focused coping strategies, by contrast, clearly involve experiential avoidance as we have defined it here, such as refusing to think about it, supplanting bad thoughts with good ones, looking at the bright side of things, or telling things to oneself to help feel better.

Similarly, factor analysis of another instrument, the *Coping Inventory for Stressful Situations* (CISS), identified task-oriented, emotion-oriented, and avoidance-oriented coping strategies (Endler & Parker, 1990). Items assessing avoidance involve either distraction ("Watch TV") or social diversion ("Phone a friend"). Endler and Parker suggest that although these activities are not focused on emotion per se, they are engaged in as a way to manage emotional responses to stressful situations.

Consistent with an experiential avoidance perspective, both emotion-focused and avoidant strategies, measured using the WOC, CISS, and similar instruments, have been found to negatively predict outcome for a variety of difficulties, including substance abuse (Ireland, McMahon, Malow, & Kouzekanani, 1994), depression (DeGenova, Patton, Jurich, & MacDermid, 1994; Bruder-Mattson & Hovanitz, 1990), and sequela of child sexual abuse (Leitenberg, Greenwald, & Cado, 1992).

Thought suppression as a general style of coping seems to be detrimental. For example, research using *The White Bear Suppression Inventory* (WBSI; Wegner & Zanakos, 1994) has shown that thought suppressors tend toward depression and obsessional symptomatology. The WBSI includes such items as "I often do things to distract myself from my thoughts," and "I always try to put problems out of mind."

Struggling with negatively evaluated emotions is also detrimental. For example, research using the *Depression Sensitivity Scale* (DSS; Zanakos & Wegner, 1993) has shown that emotional avoiders tend toward depressive symptomatology, particularly when combined with thought suppression as a coping strategy (Wegner & Zanakos, 1994). The DSS includes such items as "When I start to feel sad I try to get rid of those feelings as quickly as I can."

Evidence From Psychotherapy Process Research

In a review of 1100 quantitative studies of the relationships between process and outcome variables, Orlinsky and Howard (1986), found that "self-relatedness" was "the most consistently positive correlate of therapeutic outcome" (p. 366). Clients high in self-relatedness were defined as being "in touch with themselves . . . [and] open to their feelings" as contrasted with being "out of touch with themselves" (p. 359).

The Experiencing Scale (Klein, Mathieu, Gendlin, & Kiesler, 1969; Klein, Mathieu-Coughlan, & Kiesler, 1987) is the most widely used process measure in psychotherapy research (Hill, 1990). The Experiencing Scale measures "the extent to which . . . ongoing, bodily, felt flow of experiencing is the basic datum of . . . awareness" (Klien et al., 1969, p. 1). In our terms the Experiencing Scale measures—at least in part—the absence of emotional avoidance. High client level of experiencing has been consistently related to a good outcome in psychotherapy (Greenberg, 1983; Greenberg & Dompierre, 1981; Greenberg & Webster, 1982; Kiesler, 1971; Luborsky, Chandler, Auerbach, Cohen, & Bachrach, 1971; see Greenberg & Safran, 1989, for a review). Emotional willingness is a marker of good outcomes in the treatment of chronic pain (Geiser, 1992), and other disorders (Khorakiwala, 1991; McCurry, 1991)

Evidence From the Literature on Clinical Syndromes

One approach to determining the utility of experiential avoidance as a functional dimension of psychopathology is to see if it provides a useful addendum to current syndromal categories. Many if not most psychopathological classifications include the presence of problems with private experiences, although the relevant features vary across specific syndromal categories. For example, the *form of the avoidance* may vary. A person who drinks to suppress anxiety may be an alcoholic; a person who hides for the same reason may be an agoraphobic. The *avoided experience* may also vary: for example, persons with a panic disorder may struggle with anxiety while those with obsessive-compulsive disorder may struggle with a thought. The *source of the avoided material* may vary. A person with PTSD (post-traumatic stress disorder) suffered a specifiable original trauma, which a person struggling with depression may not.

We will examine this idea in more detail with four diagnostic categories drawn from the current syndromal system: substance abuse, Obsessive-Compulsive Disorder, Panic Disorder with Agoraphobia, and Borderline Personality Disorder. This list is not exhaustive; indeed several other important disorders have been interpreted from an experiential avoidance point of view (e.g., depression, see Zettle, 1984). In each case we will examine evidence of (a) unacceptable and avoided private experiences as a component of this disorder, (b) ineffective avoidance strategies as a component, and (c) treatment implications of an experiential avoidance interpretation of some persons suffering from the disorder.

Substance Abuse and Dependence

Definitionally, substance abuse and dependence is not a complicated syndrome: it is defined by very straightforward behavioral criteria. Why people use drugs is not at issue. The literature suggests, however, that a sub-group of drug abusers are experiential avoiders (cf., Cooper, Russell, Skinner, Frone, & Mudar, 1992; Wanberg, Horn, & Foster, 1977).

Evidence for drug use in ineffective avoidance strategy. There is no doubt that drug use per se is a highly effective short-term strategy for experiential change. Virtually all drugs of abuse have known psychoactive effects. Furthermore, drug abusers believe in these effects more than do others. In the area of alcoholism, for example, alcoholics exceed problem drinkers (with problem drinkers exceeding non-problem drinkers) in their expectancy that alcohol will enhance pleasure and reduce stress (Conners, O'Farrell, Cutter, & Thompson, 1986). Cooper et al. (1992) found that psychological stressors were related to poorer alcohol outcomes only among drinkers high in use of emotional avoidance coping strategies and high in expectancies that alcohol would lessen negative affect.

Evidence for avoided experiences in drug use. Because the effects of drugs are broad, almost any experience from boredom to anxiety attacks to withdrawal sensations can become linked to drug use. Among the private experiences considered important in various theories are expectancies and beliefs, cravings, aversive bodily states, and disagreeable emotions (Beck, Wright, Newman, & Liese, 1993; Childress, McLellan, Natale, & O'Brien 1986; Meyer, 1986). Sanchez-Craig (1984) reported that among 297 drinking episodes described by 70 subjects, nearly 80% of the episodes involved drinking aimed at manipulating various subjective experiences (e.g., social discomfort, attenuation of negative emotions, increasing pleasure, etc.). Childress et al. (1986) demonstrated that emotions such as anxiety, anger, and depression function to trigger subjective experiences of craving and withdrawal among detoxified opiate addicts.

Given this, it is not surprising that substance abuse is frequent among those with affective and anxiety disorders (e.g., Mirin, Weiss, & Michael, 1987; Pashko & Druley, 1987; Stockwell & Bolderston, 1987; Thyer et al., 1986). Researchers have suggested that some "with primary affective or anxiety disorders may abuse drugs in an attempt to alter undesirable mood states or to ameliorate intolerable anxiety" (Mirin et al., 1987, p. 141). Similarly, since unpleasant private experiences seem most likely given aversive histories, it is not surprising that the incidence of substance abuse among individuals with traumatic histories is high (e.g., Druley, Baker & Pashko, 1987; Polusny & Follette, 1995; cf., Khantzian, 1985). Even if drug abusers did not start their patterns of abuse as a method of experiential avoidance, the effects of drugs on dysphoric or withdrawal states that are the result of excessive drug use may help maintain the pattern of abuse (Marlatt, 1985; Sher, 1987).

Treatment implications. The psychological models applied to substance abuse and its treatment vary widely, but almost all are sensitive to the role of the abuser's private experience, either in the development of the addiction or in relapse prevention, or both. Most empirically oriented efforts to date have attempted to change the avoided content—for example, through anxiety management, stress reduction, or pharmacotherapy—and thus reduce the need for drug use as a method of experiential manipulation (e.g., W. R. Miller & Hester, 1986; Stockwell & Bolderston, 1987). Others have tried to add conditioned aversive emotional states that are produced by reaching for, tasting, or imagining drinking alcohol, so that experiential avoidance works for rather than against treatment goals (Rimmele, Miller, & Dougher, 1989). The direct use of acceptance methods in the empirical treatment of drug and alcohol abuse is in its infancy, though 12-step programs, meditative approaches, and others have long encouraged acceptance as a component of treatment (Marlatt, 1994; Wulfert, 1994). No data are currently available on the relative efficacy of acceptance versus control-based methods.

Obsessive-Compulsive Disorder

In this syndrome (Rasmussen & Eisen, 1992; Hollander, 1993) its very name describes both unacceptable experiences and ineffective change strategies designed to avoid them.

Evidence for avoided experiences. By definition, OCD includes various private experiences that the client seeks to escape or avoid. Aversive thoughts intrude into conscious awareness focused on contamination, persistent doubts about whether one has performed some act (e.g., unplugged appliances, locked doors), or about doing some aggressive or socially unacceptable act (e.g., screaming an obscenity, harming one's children), among others. Note that these thoughts usually are highly negatively valenced, and thus are more likely to initiate a cycle of deliberate struggle and avoidance.

Evidence for ineffective avoidance strategies. When such thoughts occur, some obsessive-compulsive individuals may simply try to ignore or suppress the thought, distract themselves, and so on, while others may develop elaborate rituals that are thought to undo the danger and experientially reduce anxiety connected to the intrusive thoughts. These rituals can become quite extended, since the person can always imagine that they did not sufficiently engage in the ritual "undoing" of the problematic thought. OCD clients become disturbed when these methods of experiential escape and avoidance are interrupted. Exposure and response prevention, the treatment of choice for OCD, is sufficiently aversive that McCarthy and Foa (1990) report that 25% of obsessive-compulsives seeking treatment refuse this form.

OCD provides a clear example of an area in which the process of deliberate control may contradict the desired outcome. Deliberately trying to rid oneself of a thought involves following the verbal rule "I must not think thought x" However, such a rule, by specifying "thought x," produces contact with "thought x" and thus thoughts of "thought x." Whether by ritual, distraction, or suppression, experiential avoidance in OCD seems to be more the source of the life-constricting effects of the disorder than unwanted thoughts per se.

Treatment implications. In general, OCD is fairly treatable using psychosocial methods, and those that are effective seem sensible in light of the literature on thought suppression and other forms of experiential avoidance (D. A. Clark & Purdon, 1993; Gold & Wegner, 1995). Using at least 50% improvement as a cut off, approximately 75% to 80% of those suffering with OCD can be treated successfully using response prevention and exposure (Emmelkamp, Hoekstra, & Visser, 1985; Foa, Steketee, Grayson, Turner, & Latimer, 1984; Hoogduin & Duivenvoorden, 1987; Rachman & Hodgson, 1980). From the current perspective, response prevention and exposure may work because these methods indirectly undermine the use of experiential avoidance strategies such as distraction or rituals. If this analysis is correct, it is especially important that clients face avoided psychological material during exposure. Some evidence exists in support of this idea. For example, researchers have found that distraction strategies applied to situational or somatic stimuli during exposure treatments result in reduced anxiety within session, but actually interfere with the long-term effectiveness of treatment (Grayson, Foa, & Steketee, 1982; Foa & Kozak, 1986). Given the present perspective, pure obsessives should be most difficult to treat because their methods of experiential avoidance (e.g., cognitive distraction) are not overt and thus are much more difficult to undermine. Research has shown this to be the case (Salkovskis & Westbrook, 1987).

Panic Disorder With Agoraphobia

Here we have a classification which also emphasizes the experience to be avoided (American Psychiatric Association, 1994).

Evidence for avoided experiences. Agoraphobics become extremely reactive to changes in their physiological state (Barlow, 1988). Small increases in heart rate may be interpreted as catastrophic (Pauli et al., 1991). This catastrophic interpretation has been theorized to result in a "positive feedback loop between internal perceptions and physiological activity [that] can culminate in a panic attack" (Pauli et al., 1991, p. 137; cf., D. M. Clark, 1986; Ehlers, Margraf, Roth, Taylor, & Birbaumer, 1988). Agoraphobics show increases in anxiety in response to both self-detected increases in heart rate (Pauli et al., 1991), as well as to false heart rate feedback (Ehlers, et al., 1988). A wide range of external or internal stimuli may initially trigger symptoms of physiological arousal (e.g., elevated heart rate, dizziness, or shortness of breath). If the anxiety-prone individual misinterprets these sensations as life threatening, an increase in apprehension is generated which itself creates additional arousal (D. M. Clark, 1986; Ehlers et al., 1988).

Evidence for ineffective avoidance strategies. The fear agoraphobics have is not of the places per se, but rather a fear of their potential reactions to those places. This has led some to describe agoraphobia as the "fear of fear" or "fear of panic" (see Barlow, 1988; Chambless, Caputo, Bright, & Gallagher, 1984; Goldstein & Chambless, 1978), and leads to increasingly restricted lifestyles. Avoiding conditions which might give rise to fear or panic leads patients to limit travel or avoid being in the feared environment unless accompanied by a trusted companion.

Other dominant psychological characteristics of this disorder are interpretable from an experiential avoidance point of view. Agoraphobics frequently report thoughts that they will die, lose control, or go crazy (American Psychiatric Association, 1994). Such catastrophic cognitions have been repeatedly shown to be related to poor treatment outcome (Chambless & Gracely, 1988). For example, Keijsers, Hoogduin, and Schaap (1994) found that fear of the effects of panic is a negative predictor of treatment outcome. The need to control emotion in order to control imagined dangerous outcomes in turn leads to scanning, vigilance, generation of escape plans, and so on. All of these can be construed as methods of experiential avoidance. Craske, Miller, Rotunda, and Barlow (1990) found that agoraphobics rated as extensive avoiders tended to develop more additional anxiety disorders over time than did minimal avoiders, although no such differences existed before their subject's first panic episode.

Experiential avoidance strategies cannot work readily in panic disorder in part because any method of avoidance of a danger reconnects the individual with the danger—and anxiety is the natural response to danger, whether it is established directly or cognitively. "The main problem in the anxiety disorders is not in the generation of anxiety but in the overactive cognitive patterns (schemas) relevant to danger that are continually structuring external and/or internal experience as a sign of danger" (Beck & Emery, 1985, p. 15).

Treatment implications. The treatment of panic disorder has improved markedly in recent years with the addition of methods that deliberately expose clients to emotions, bodily sensations, and other previously avoided private experiences. For example, Barlow and his colleagues emphasize an exposure to fear and its interoceptive accompaniments through deliberate hyperventilation, spinning, and so on (Barlow, Craske, Cerny, & Klosko, 1989; Craske & Barlow, 1990).

There is some evidence that these treatments work in part by undermining experiential avoidance strategies (Barlow, 1988). For example, Craske, Street, and Barlow (1989) gave agoraphobics instructional sets to either focus on feared somatic sensations or to engage in distraction tasks. While the distraction group showed greater improvement post-treatment than the focus group, the focus group showed greater improvements at the 6-month follow-up. There seems to be increasing agreement that "to recover [the agoraphobic] must know how to face, accept, and go through panic" (Weekes, 1978, p. 362).

Borderline Personality Disorder

Although borderline personality disorder (BPD) is so broadly defined that some question its discriminant validity (Akiskal, 1994; Tyrer, 1994; Strosahl, 1991), these multi-problem patients face a wide variety of difficult experiences and show notable avoidance patterns.

Evidence for avoided experiences. Emotional distress is a defining feature of BPD. Among other dimensions, BPD clients are characterized by a volatile and chronic depressive state, self-condemnation, emptiness, abandonment fears, self-destructive fantasies, and profound hopelessness (Cowdry, Gardner, O'Leary, Leibenluft, & Rubinow, 1991; Rogers, Widiger, & Krupp, 1995; Southwick, Yehuda, & Giller, 1995), combined with intense and poorly targeted anger (Gardner, Leibenluft, O'Leary, & Cowdry, 1991). As might be expected, patients with these symptoms often report painful and chaotic childhoods (Goldman, D'Angelo, & DeMaso, 1993; Weaver & Clum, 1993; Diamond & Doane, 1994). Borderline patients not only experience chronically high levels of emotional distress, but they also lack the skills required to moderate emotional arousal or to function with distress (Strosahl, 1991).

Evidence for ineffective avoidance strategies. A hallmark of these patients is impulsive, repetitious self-destructive behavior including suicide attempts

(Soloff, Lis, Kelly, Cornelius, & Ulrich, 1994) and self-mutilation (Dulit, Fyer, Leon, Brodsky, & Frances, 1994). Recurrent self-destructive behavior is usually a primary target of clinical treatment, although it is very common to encounter a other problems such as an eating disorder (Koepp, Shicldbach, Schmager, & Rohner, 1993), alcohol and drug addiction (Links, Heslegrave, Mitton, Van Reekum, & Patrick, 1995; F. T. Miller, Abrams, Dulit, & Fyer, 1993) and, in men, spouse or partner battery (Dutton & Starzomski, 1993). The common feature of all of these behaviors is that they have the experiential avoidance properties of addictive behavior (Chiles & Strosahl, 1995; i.e., the behaviors produce emotional escape or relief from negative arousal). This destructive and dysfunctional avoidance and escape behavior represents an extreme solution to the problems of (a) sustained negative over-arousal, and (b) the lack of verbally based methods for modulating the effects of negative private experiences. The functional experiential avoidance role of these repetitive self-destructive behaviors is revealed in several studies. For example, some self-mutilators experience less or no pain during or following self-injury (Russ, Shearin, Clarkin, Harrison, & Hull, 1993). Similarly, some of these patients show lower levels of depression, anxiety, and hopelessness after the index suicide attempt (Strosahl, Chiles, & Linehan, 1992).

The multi-problem patient consistently blurs the distinction between thought and thinker, feeling and feeler (Hayes, Strosahl, & Wilson, 1999). This cognitive and emotional fusion makes negative inner experiences intolerable and unacceptable and leads to depressive "numbing" or splitting as a way of avoiding direct contact with them. Unfortunately, this primary emotional avoidance not only is purchased at great personal cost (emotional numbness and avoidance of self), but it ultimately fails as a method of avoiding feared private experiences.

Treatment implications. Currently, the only empirically validated treatment for borderline personality disorder is Linehan's Dialectical Behavior Therapy (DBT). This treatment model incorporates a strong affect tolerance and experiential acceptance component (Linehan, 1993, 1994), and overall fits very well with experiential avoidance as a functional diagnostic dimension. Since one of the main purposes of functional diagnostic dimensions is to arrive at analyses with treatment utility, the effective of DBT with this difficult population is very promising for the concept of experiential avoidance.

Evidence From the Literature on Non-syndromal Clinical Problems

There is an inherent weakness in the syndromal approach to classification: many areas of applied knowledge cannot be reduced to syndromes. This may be because the area deals with a sub-clinical problem (e.g., routine forms of marital discord), because it is viewed in terms of health rather than disease (e.g., the development of intimacy), because the literature is organized etiologically (e.g., the effects of childhood sexual abuse), or because the problem area is related to many syndromal and non-syndromal conditions (e.g., suicidality). Functional diagnostic dimensions do not necessarily have this problem, since they are in principle relevant to all these areas as well as to syndromes. We will deal with two examples: suicide and child sexual abuse.

Suicide as the Final Ineffective Avoidance Strategy

No human behavior is harder to conceptualize from a traditional categorical or dimensional diagnostic model than suicide. Suicide cannot be explained as the symptom of a mental illness, since as many as half of all victims could not be diagnosed as having a mental illness (Strosahl & Chiles, 1997). Suicidal behavior and ideation is so prevalent in the general population that, unless more than 50% of all people are going to be diagnosed as suffering from a mental disorder, we must conclude that it is a common feature of contemporary existence (Strosahl, Linehan, & Chiles, 1984). Even considering those patients with behavior disorders, suicide is not the province of any particular diagnostic condition. For example, an equal number of suicides are seen among such diverse diagnostic groups as depression, schizophrenia, and the personality disorders (Buda & Tsuang, 1990). Suicide rates rise steadily with age, while no corresponding increase is seen in the prevalence of mental disorders. Men are much more likely to commit suicide, while women are much more likely to be diagnosed with a mental disorder (Chiles & Strosahl, 1995). Paradoxically, those patients who do not have predisposing conditions may be the most likely to commit suicide (Goldstein, Black, Nasrallah, & Winokur, 1991).

Evidence for avoided experiences and suicide as an avoidance strategy. Approached as a method of experiential avoidance, suicide is relatively easy to understand and investigate. In the presence of seemingly bad feelings, distressing thoughts, unwanted memories, or unpleasant bodily sensations, the person formulates an if . . . then verbal relation in which suicide (as verbally conceived) will lead to relief, ceasing of suffering, proof of one's own rightness (or of the wrongness of others), and similarly positive private outcomes (Chiles & Strosahl, 1995; Hayes, 1992). When the motivational conditions involved in suicide are analyzed, more than half of actual or attempted suicides involve an attempt to flee from aversive events (Loo, 1985; Smith & Bloom, 1985), especially states of mind such as guilt and anxiety (Bancroft, Skrimshire, & Simkins, 1976; Baumeister, 1990). Persons who commit suicide evaluate themselves quite negatively, believing themselves to be worthless, inadequate, rejected, or blameworthy (Maris, 1981; Rosen, 1976; Rothberg & Jones, 1987).

Treatment implications. There are two implications for intervening with suicidal behavior as a method of experiential avoidance (Chiles & Strosahl, 1995). First, it may not be necessary to alter the *form* called "suicidal behavior" to change its psychological function. The client does not have to eliminate suicidal thinking or behavior in order to attain "psychological health." Instead, it may be the client's struggle to eliminate suicidal thoughts directly that leads to the sense of "suicidal crisis," which is really a struggle over self-control. Second, there is no need to conceptualize suicidal behavior as "aberrant." Given its population prevalence, it may be construed as relatively normal behavior. For many suicidal patients, the mystery and fear associated with a clear symptom of "mental illness" can be replaced with a focus on alternative methods for either accepting unchangeable private experiences, targeting problem solving efforts on things that can be controlled, or both.

The Sequelae of Childhood Sexual Abuse

The literature on child sexual abuse suggests that it is a major risk factor in the development of a variety of problems, including depression, anxiety, self-mutilation, substance abuse, somatization, interpersonal isolation, sexual dissatisfaction, and risk for re-victimization (see Browne & Finkelhohr, 1986, and Polusny & Follette, 1995, for reviews of this literature).

Evidence for avoided experiences and ineffective avoidance strategies. Sexual abuse results in intensively negative experiences for many individuals. For example, some of the affective responses include guilt, shame, fear, and rage (Polusny & Follette, 1995). Several researchers (Briere & Runtz, 1991, 1993; Polusny & Follette, 1995; Rodriquez, Ryan, & Foy 1992) have described the correlates of child sexual abuse in terms that fit the idea that experiential avoidance is a core intrapersonal variable in the development of sequelae to childhood sexual abuse.

While the diverse outcomes observed in clinical samples of sexual abuse survivors (e.g., dissociation, substance abuse, PTSD, high-risk sexual behavior, self-mutilation) are quite variant in topography, they may actually be relatively consistent in function. For example, the use of avoidant coping strategies among survivors is predictive of such indicators of poor psychological functioning (Leitenberg, Greenwald, & Cado, 1992; Rodreguez, Ryan, & Foy, 1992), even though survivors rate such coping strategies as most effective in the short term (Leitenberg et al., 1992). This fits with the larger literature on trauma, which shows that when trauma victims are assessed shortly after the traumatic event, symptoms such as numbing and avoidance of trauma reminders are far more prevalent among individuals who subsequently develop PTSD than among those who do not (Foa & Riggs, 1995). Similarly, severity of dissociative symptoms better predicts future outcomes than does severity of anxiety (Foa & Riggs, 1995).

Avoidance of close interpersonal relationships may represent another emotionally avoidant coping strategy for the survivor. The context of a close relationship may re-stimulate thoughts and feelings associated with the abuse, or the fear that those feelings would again occur. For example, intrusive images and thoughts of the abuse are frequently observed by survivors while engaging in sexual activity (Herman, Russell, & Trocki, 1986).

Treatment implications. The empirically based treatment literature on survivors of childhood sexual abuse is still quite limited. However, many of the persons diagnosed with traditional syndromes may carry these syndromal labels in part as a result of their abuse history. Thus, the evidence reviewed in earlier sections is relevant here. From an experiential avoidance perspective, however, treatment of abuse survivors should involve in part exposure to previously avoided thought, feelings, memories, and bodily sensations, and the use of methods that help undermine distraction, dissociation, and other forms of experiential avoidance. Some evidence is supportive of these recommendations (V. M. Follette, 1994).

Summary

The core concept of experiential avoidance seems to integrate a wide body of literature drawn from basic experimental, clinical process, styles of coping, experimental psychopathology, and syndromal and non-syndromal areas. This research comes from diverse theoretical backgrounds. The faults of syndromal classification are often noted, but are justified in part because these atheoretical, topographical entities bring together researchers from a variety of traditions and provide an avenue for research effort. But functional diagnostic dimensions may do the same thing, and without etiology and treatment utility. If many forms of psychopathology are forms of experiential avoidance, then we can proceed to the theoretical and empirical analysis of this functional dimension from a wide variety of research and theoretical traditions.

THE TREATMENT IMPLICATIONS OF EXPERIENTIAL AVOIDANCE

The hallmark of functional diagnostic dimensions is the effort to stay close to the pragmatic purposes of classification. For that reason, it is important that there be clear treatment implications for this dimension. We believe that the recent interest in acceptance-based treatment approaches fits directly with the present analysis of experiential avoidance.

In the current view, many forms of psychopathology are not merely bad problems; they are also bad *solutions*, based on a dangerous and ineffective use of experiential avoidance strategies. Instead of encouraging clients to use more clever ways to fight and win this war with their own thoughts, feelings, and bodily sensations, the ubiquity of problems associated with experiential avoidance suggests that it might be safer to help clients step out of this war altogether.

Acceptance-based treatments attempt to alter the impact of emotions and cognitions by altering the struggle with them, rather than attempting to change their form, frequency, or situational sensitivity. In other words, in acceptance-based approaches the client's original aim of controlling their private experiences (emotions, thoughts, cravings, bodily states, and so on) is itself seen as modifiable (see Hayes et al., 1994 for a book length review of some of these acceptance methods).

Psychological acceptance at its lowest level is implicit in any psychotherapy, because at the minimum the client and therapist must admit that there is even a problem to be worked on. At a higher level, it may be possible to change the change agenda itself. Acceptance in this context means actively contacting psychological experiences—directly, fully, and without needless defense—while at the same time behaving effectively. For the agoraphobic, this may mean seeking out the bodily sensations that have heretofore been avoided; for the obsessive it may mean practicing "just noticing" thoughts. An acceptance approach does not abandon direct change efforts: it simply targets them toward more readily changeable domains, such as overt behavior or life situations, rather than personal history or automatic thoughts and feelings (Hayes, 1994). In accord with our analysis of the origins of experiential avoidance, most forms of acceptance-based treatment target the domination of verbal and cognitive functions over other psychological functions. These might include paradox, meditation, just noticing, exercises in verbal flexibility, mindfulness exercises, experiential exercises, and the like.

As we have already noted in several areas, empirical analyses of acceptance methods are creating excitement in many areas (Hayes et al., 1994). For example: Barlow and his colleagues have improved the treatment of agoraphobics by adding greater exposure to emotional and bodily states (Barlow & Craske, 1989; Barlow et al., 1989); Marlatt has worked on the addition of techniques drawn from eastern psychology to promote acceptance of urges (what he calls "urge surfing") as a component of relapse prevention in substance abusers (Marlatt, 1994); Linehan (1993) has improved the treatment of personality disorders by adding mindfulness strategies and work on the acceptance of aversive emotions; mindfulness training—a Buddhist tradition emphasizing emotional acceptance—has also been used successfully with the treatment of chronic pain (Kabat-Zinn, 1991); Jacobson and his colleagues (Jacobson, 1991; Koener et al., 1994) have improved success in behavioral marital therapy by working on acceptance of the idiosyncrasies of marital partners as a route to increased marital satisfaction; Emotion-Focused Therapy (Greenberg & Johnson, 1988) has shown good results with couples by increasing emotional acceptance; Chiles and Strosahl (1995) have added acceptance to the treatment of suicidality; Acceptance and Commitment Therapy (Hayes, 1987, Hayes, & Wilson, 1994, Hayes, Strosahl, & Wilson, 1999) has shown beneficial effects for the additional of emotional acceptance and cognitive defusion to the treatment of depression (Zettle, 1984; Zettle & Raines, 1989), and other disorders.

Thus, although the area is still very new, we now have a growing body of data that points to the importance of psychological acceptance across a wide range of clinical disorders. Interestingly, many of the less empirically oriented treatment strategies have long emphasized forms of acceptance, from psychoanalysis (Freud, 1924) to logotherapy (Frankl, 1975) to Alcoholics Anonymous (Wulfert, 1994). Some empirical clinicians may be worried by this overlap between the more and less empirical sides of psychology, but it could be very healthy for the field if dimensions can be found that cross these boundaries without a loss in scientific integrity.

SUMMARY

Syndromal classification is in many ways foreign to psychology, since it tends to ignore the developmental, functional, contextual approach to behavior that is characteristic of much of our discipline in favor of a more object like, pathological, medical approach (Hayes & Heiby, 1996). It seems extraordinarily unlikely that syndromal classification will go away anytime soon, but the slow progress of a scientific approach to psychopathology suggests that alternative approaches should be fostered and tested.

Functional diagnostic dimensions present such an alternative, of which emotional avoidance is just one example (other possible dimensions might include such examples as poor rule generation, inappropriate rule following, or socially impoverished repertoires, though defense of these dimensions awaits another day). Functional diagnostic dimensions are not traditional disorders, nor are they well-worked-out etiological theories. They are dimensional processes, not all-or-nothing categories, that suggest psychological processes relevant to etiology, that make coherent many topographical forms under a single functional process, and that can be readily linked to treatment. As such they provide a kind of functional middle ground between mere psychological topography on the one hand or well-developed and functional psychological theories of psychopathology on the other.

Functional diagnostic dimensions focus directly and non-prejudicially on the behavior of interest. This allows research from many areas of our disparate field to proceed, but in a manner that is more fitting with psychology and its traditions than the psychiatric nosology we have imported.

REFERENCES

Adams, H. E., & Cassidy, J. F. (1993). The classification of abnormal behavior. In P.B. Sutker & H. E. Adams (Eds.), *Comprehensive handbook of psychopathology* (pp. 3–26). New York: Plenum Press.

Akiskal, H.S. (1994). The temperamental borders of affective disorders. *Acta Psychiatrica Scandinavica, 89*, 32–37.

American Psychiatric Association. (1980). Diagnostic and statistical manual of mental disorders (3rd ed.). Washington, DC: Author.
American Psychiatric Association. (1980). *Diagnostic and statistical manual of mental disorders* (3rd ed.). Washington, DC: Author.
Bancroft, J., Skrimshire, A., & Simkins, S. (1976). The reasons people give for taking overdoses. *British Journal of Psychiatry, 128*, 538–548.
Bandura, A. (1968). A social learning interpretation of psychological dysfunctions. In P. London & D. Rosenhan (Eds.), *Foundations of abnormal psychology* (pp. 293–344). New York: Holt, Rinehart & Winston.
Barlow, D.H. (1988). *Anxiety and its disorders: Nature and treatment of anxiety and panic.* New York: Guilford Press.
Barlow, D.H., & Beck, J.G. (1984). The psychosocial treatment of anxiety disorders: Current status, future directions. In J.B. Williams & R.L. Spitzer, (Eds.), *Psychotherapy research: Where are we and where should we go?* (pp. 29–44). New York: Guilford Press.
Barlow, D. H., & Craske, M. G. (1989). *Mastery of your anxiety and panic.* New York: Graywind.
Barlow, D. H., Craske, M. G., Cerny, J. A., & Klosko, J. S. (1989). Behavioral treatment of panic disorder. *Behavior Therapy, 20*, 261–282.
Baumeister, R.F. (1990). Suicide as escape from self. *Psychological Review, 97*, 90–113.
Beck, A. T., & Emery, G. (1985). *Anxiety disorders and phobias: A cognitive perspective.* New York: Basic Books.
Beck, A. T., Wright, F. D., Newman, C. F., & Liese, B. S. (1993). *Cognitive therapy of substance abuse.* New York: Guilford Press.
Biglan, A., & Hayes, S.C. (1996). Should the behavioral sciences become more pragmatic? The case for functional contextualism in research on human behavior. *Applied and Preventive Psychology: Current Scientific Perspectives, 5*, 47–57.
Briere, J., & Runtz, M. (1991). The long-term effects of sexual abuse: A review and synthesis. In J. Briere (Ed.), *Treating victims of sexual abuse.* San Francisco: Jossey-Bass.
Briere, J., & Runtz, M. (1993). Childhood sexual abuse: Long term sequelae and implications for psychological assessment. *Journal of Interpersonal Violence, 8*, 312–330.
Browne, A., & Finkelhohr, D. (1986). Impact of child sexual abuse: A review of the research. *Psychological Bulletin, 99*, 66–77.
Bruder-Mattson, S.F., & Hovanitz, C.A. (1990). Coping and attributional styles as predictors of depression. *Journal of Clinical Psychology, 46*, 557–565.
Bruner, J.S., Goodnow, J.J., & Austin, G. A. (1956). *A study of thinking.* New York: Wiley.
Buda, M., & Tsuang, M. (1990). The epidemiology of suicide: Implications for clinical practice. In S. Blumenthal & D. Kupfer (Eds.), *Suicide over the*

life cycle: Risk factors, assessment and treatment of suicidal patients (pp. 17–37). Washington, DC: American Psychiatric Press.
Chambless, D.L., Caputo, G.C., Bright, P., & Gallagher, R. (1984). Assessment of fear of fear in agoraphobics: The body sensations questionnaire and the agoraphobic cognitions questionnaire. *Journal of Consulting and Clinical Psychology, 52*, 1090–1097.
Chambless, D.L., & Gracely, E.J. (1988). Prediction of outcome following in vivo exposure treatment of agoraphobia. In I. Hand & H.U. Wittchen (Eds.), *Panic and phobias II: Treatment and variables affecting outcome* (pp. 209–220). New York: Springer.
Childress, A.R., McLellan, A.T., Natale, M., & O'Brien, C.P. (1986). Mood states can elicit conditioned withdrawal and cravings in opiate abuse patients. In L. Harris (Ed.), *Problems of drug dependence* (pp. 137–144), National Institute of Drug Abuse Monograph Series no. 76. Washington, DC: U.S. Government Printing Office.
Chiles, J., & Strosahl, K. (1995). *The suicidal patient: Principles of assessment, treatment & case management*. Washington DC: American Psychiatric Press.
Clark, D.A., & Purdon, C. (1993). New perspectives for a cognitive theory of obsessions. *Australian Psychologist, 28*, 161–167.
Clark, D.M. (1986). A cognitive approach to panic. *Behaviour Research and Therapy, 24*, 461–470.
Clark, D.M., Ball, S., & Pape, D. (1991). An experimental investigation of thought suppression. *Behaviour Research and Therapy, 29*, 253–257.
Conners, G. J., O'Farrell, T. J., Cutter, H. S. G., & Thompson, D. L. (1986). Alcohol expectancies among male alcoholics, problem drinkers, and nonproblem drinkers. *Alcoholism: Clinical and Experimental Research, 10*, 667–670.
Cooper, M.L., Russell, M., Skinner, J.B., Frone, M.R., & Mudar, P. (1992). Stress and alcohol use: Moderating effects of gender, coping, and alcohol expectancies. *Journal of Abnormal Psychology, 101*, 139–152.
Cordova, J., & Kohlenberg, R. (1994). Acceptance and the therapeutic relationship. In S.C. Hayes, N. S. Jacobson, V. M. Follette, & M. J. Dougher (Eds.), *Acceptance and change: Content and context in psychotherapy* (pp. 125–140). Reno, NV: Context Press.
Cowdry, R.W., Gardner, D.L., O'Leary, K.M., Leibenluft, E., & Rubinow, D.R. (1991). Mood variability: A study of four groups. *American Journal of Psychiatry, 148*, 1505–1511.
Craske, M.G., & Barlow, D.H. (1990). *Therapists guide for mastery of your anxiety and panic*. San Antonio, TX: Harcourt Brace & Co.
Craske, M.G., Miller, P.P., Rotunda, R., & Barlow, D.H. (1990). A descriptive report of features of initial unexpected panic attacks in minimal and extensive avoiders. *Behaviour Research and Therapy, 28*, 395–400.
Craske, M.G., Sanderson, W.C., & Barlow, D.H. (1987). The relationships between panic, fear, and avoidance. *Journal of Anxiety Disorders, 1*, 153–160.

Craske, M.G., Street, L., & Barlow, D.H. (1989). Instructions to focus upon or distract from internal cues during exposure treatment of agoraphobic avoidance. *Behaviour Research and Therapy, 27*, 663–672.
Dawes, R.M. (1994). *House of cards: Psychology and psychotherapy built on myth.* New York: Free Press.
DeGenova, M.K., Patton, D.M., & Jurich, J.A. (1994). Ways of coping among HIV-infected individuals. *Journal of Social Psychology, 134*, 655–663.
Diamond, D., & Doane J.A. (1994). Disturbed attachment and negative affective style: An intergenerational spiral. *British Journal of Psychiatry, 164*, 770–781.
Druley, K.A., Baker, S.L., & Pashko, S. (1987). Stress: Alcohol and drug interactions. In E. Gottheil, K.A. Druly, S. Pashko, & S.P. Weinstein (Eds.), *Stress and addiction* (pp. 24–39). New York: Brunner Mazel.
Dulit, R.A., Fyer, M.R., Leon, A.A. Brodsky, B.S. & Frances, A.J. (1994). Clinical correlates of self-mutilation in borderline personality disorder. *American Journal of Psychiatry, 151*, 1305–1311.
Dutton, D.G., & Starzomski, A.J. (1993). Borderline personality in perpetrators of psychological and physical abuse. *Violence & Victims, 8*, 326–337.
Ehlers, A., Margraf, J., Roth, W.T., Taylor, C.B., & Birbaumer, N. (1988). Anxiety induced by false heart rate feedback in patients with panic disorder. *Behavior Research and Therapy, 26*, 1–11.
Emmelkamp, P. M.G., Hoekstra, R.J., & Visser, S. (1985). The behavioral treatment of obsessive-compulsive disorder, prediction of out-come at 3.5 year follow up. In H. Brenner (Ed.), *Psychiatry: The state of the art* (pp. 265–270). New York: Springer.
Endler, N.S., & Parker, J.D.A. (1990). The multidimensional assessment of coping: A critical evaluation. *Journal of Personality and Social Psychology, 58*, 844–854.
Eysenck, H. J. (1986). A critique of contemporary classification and diagnosis. In T. Millon & G. L. Klerman (Eds.), *Contemporary directions in psychopathology: Toward the* DSM-IV (pp. 73–98). New York: Guilford Press.
Foa, E.B., & Kozak, M.S. (1986). Emotional processing of fear: Exposure to corrective information. *Psychological Bulletin, 99*, 20–35.
Foa, E. B., & Riggs, D. S. (1995). Posttraumatic stress disorder following assault: Theoretical considerations and empirical findings. *Current Directions in Psychological Science, 4*, 61–65.
Foa, E.B., Steketee, G., Grayson, J.B., Turner, R.M., & Latimer, P.R. (1984). Deliberate exposure and blocking of obsessive-compulsive rituals: Immediate and long-term effects. *Behavior Therapy, 15*, 450–472.
Folkman, S., & Lazarus, R. S. (1988). *Ways of Coping Questionnaire.* Palo Alto, CA: Consulting Psychologists Press.
Follette, V.M. (1994). Survivors of child sexual abuse: Treatment using a contextual analysis. In S.C. Hayes, N.S. Jacobson, V.M. Follette, &

M.J. Dougher (Eds.), *Acceptance and change: Content and context in psychotherapy* (pp. 255–268). Reno, NV: Context Press.

Follette, W.C., & Hayes, S.C. (1992). Behavioral assessment in the *DSM* era. *Behavioral Assessment, 14*, 323–343.

Follette, W.C., Houts, A.C., & Hayes, S.C. (1992). Behavior therapy and the new medical model. *Behavioral Assessment, 14*, 323–343.

Foulds, G. A. (1971). Personality deviance and personal symptomatology. *Psychological Medicine, 3*, 222–233

Frankl, V.E. (1975). Paradoxical intention and deflection. *Psychotherapy: Theory, Research and Practice, 12*, 226–237.

Freud, S. (1924). *Collected papers*. Vol 1. London: Hogarth Press.

Gardner D.L., Leibenluft, O'Leary, K.M., & Cowdry R.W. (1991). Self-ratings of anger and hostility in borderline personality disorder. *Journal of Nervous & Mental Disease, 179*, 157–161.

Geiser, D. (1992). *A comparison of acceptance-focused and control-focused interventions in a chronic pain treatment center*. Unpublished doctoral dissertation, University of Nevada, Reno.

Gifford, E. V. (1994). Setting a course for behavior change: The verbal context of acceptance. In S. C. Hayes, N. S. Jacobson, V. M. Follette, & M. J. Dougher (Eds.), *Acceptance and change: Content and context in psychotherapy* (pp. 218–222). Reno, NV: Context Press.

Gifford, E. V. (1995). Functional contextualism as a philosophical position for clinical psychology. *The Naturalist, 2*, 15–21.

Gold, D.B., & Wegner, D.M. (1995). Origins of ruminative thought: Trauma, incompleteness, nondisclosure, and suppression. *Journal of Applied Social Psychology, 25*, 1245–1261.

Goldman, S.J., D'Angelo, E.J., & DeMaso, D.R. (1993). Psychopathology in the families of children and adolescents with borderline personality disorder. *American Journal of Psychiatry, 150*, 1832–1835.

Goldstein, A.J., & Chambless, D.L. (1978). A reanalysis of agoraphobia. *Behavior Therapy, 9*, 47–59.

Goldstein, R., Black, D. W., Nasrallah, A., & Winokur, G. (1991). The prediction of suicide: Sensitivity, specificity, and predictive value of a multivariate model applied to suicide among 1906 patients with affective disorders. *Archives of General Psychiatry*, 48, 418–422.

Grayson, J.B., Foa, E.B., & Steketee, G. (1982). Habituation during exposure treatment: Distraction versus attention focusing. *Behaviour Research and Therapy, 20*, 323–328.

Greenberg, L.S. (1983). Toward a task analysis of conflict resolution in Gestalt therapy. *Psychotherapy: Theory, Research and Practice, 20*, 190–201.

Greenberg, L. (1994). Acceptance in experiential therapy. In S. C. Hayes, N. S. Jacobson, V. M. Follette, & M. J. Dougher (Eds.), *Acceptance and change: Content and context in psychotherapy* (pp. 53–67). Reno, NV: Context Press.

Greenberg, L.S., & Dompierre, L.M. (1981). Specific effects of Gestalt two-chair dialogue on intrapsychic conflict in counseling. *Journal of Counseling Psychology, 28*, 288–294.

Greenberg, L. S., & Johnson, S.M. (1988). *Emotionally focused therapy for couples*. New York: Guilford Press.

Greenberg, L. S., & Safran J. D. (1989). Emotion in psychotherapy. *American psychologist, 44*, 19–29.

Greenberg, L.S., & Webster, M.C. (1982). Resolving decisional conflict by Gestalt two-chair dialogue: Relating process to outcome. *Journal of Counseling Psychology, 29*, 468–477.

Hayes, S.C. (1984). Making sense of spirituality. *Behaviorism, 12*, 99–110.

Hayes, S.C. (1987). A contextual approach to therapeutic change. In N. Jacobson (Ed.), *Psychotherapists in clinical practice: Cognitive and behavioral perspectives* (pp. 327–387). New York: Guilford Press.

Hayes, S.C. (1992). Verbal relations, time, and suicide. In S.C. Hayes & L.J. Hayes (Eds.), *Understanding verbal relations* (pp. 109–118). Reno, NV: Context Press.

Hayes, S.C. (1994). Content, context, and the types of psychological acceptance. In S.C. Hayes, N.S. Jacobson, V.M. Follette, & M.J. Dougher (Eds.), *Acceptance and change: Content and context in psychotherapy* (pp. 13–32). Reno, NV: Context Press.

Hayes, S.C., & Follette, W.C. (1992). Can functional analysis provide a substitute for syndromal classification? *Behavioral Assessment, 14*, 345–365.

Hayes, S. C., Follette, W. C., & Follette, V. M. (1995). Behavior therapy: A contextual approach. In A. S. German & S. B. Messer (Eds.), *Modern psychotherapies: Theory and practice* New York: Guilford Press.

Hayes, S.C., & Hayes, L.J. (1992). Verbal relations and the evolution of behavior analysis. *American Psychologist, 47*, 1383–1395.

Hayes, S.C., & Heiby, E. (1996). Psychology's drug problem: Do we need a fix or should we just say no? *American Psychologist, 51*, 198–206.

Hayes, S.C., Jacobson, N.S., Follette, V.M., & Dougher, M.J. (Eds.) (1994). *Acceptance and change: Content and context in psychotherapy*. Reno, NV: Context Press.

Hayes, S.C., Nelson, R.O., & Jarrett, R. (1987). Treatment utility of assessment: A functional approach to evaluating the quality of assessment. *American Psychologist, 42*, 963–974.

Hayes, S.C., Strosahl, K., & Wilson, K.G. (1999). *Acceptance and Commitment Therapy: An experiential approach to behavior change*. New York: Guilford Press.

Hayes, S.C., & Wilson, K.G. (1993). Some applied implications of a contemporary behavior analytic account of verbal behavior. *The Behavior Analyst, 16*, 283–301.

Hayes, S.C., & Wilson, K.G. (1994). Acceptance and commitment therapy: Altering the verbal support for experiential avoidance. *The Behavior Analyst, 17*, 289–303.

Herman, J.L., Russell, D. E. H., & Trocki, K. (1986). Long-term effects of incestuous abuse in childhood. *American Journal of Psychiatry, 143*, 1293–1296.
Hersen, M., & Bellack, A. S. (1988). *DSM-III* and behavioral assessment. In A. S. Bellack & M. Hersen (Eds.), *Behavioral assessment: A practical handbook* (pp. 38–70). New York: Pergamon.
Hill, C.E. (1990). Exploratory in-session process research in individual psychotherapy: A review. *Journal of Consulting and Clinical Psychology, 58*, 288–294.
Hollander, E. (1993). *Obsessive-compulsive related disorders.* Washington, DC: American Psychiatric Press.
Hoogduin, C.A.L., & Duivenvoorden, H. (1987). A decision model in the treatment of obsessive-compulsive neuroses. *British Journal of Psychiatry, 152*, 516–521.
Ireland, S. J., McMahon, R. C., Malow, R. M., & Kouzekanani, K. (1994). Coping style as a predictor of relapse to cocaine abuse. In L. S. Harris (Ed.). *Problems of drug dependence, 1993: Proceedings of the 55th annual Scientific Meeting* (p. 158). National Institute of Drug Abuse Monograph Series no. 141. Washington, DC: U.S. Government Printing Office.
Jacobson, N.S. (1991, November). *Acceptance and change.* Presidential address delivered to the meeting of the Association for Advancement of Behavior Therapy, New York.
Kabat-Zinn, J. (1991). *Full catastrophe living.* New York: Delta.
Kanfer, F.H., & Grimm, L.G. (1977). Behavioral analysis: Selecting target behaviors in the interview. *Behavior Modification, 1*, 7–28.
Keijsers, G.P.J., Hoogduin, C.A.L., & Schaap, C.P.D.R. (1994). Prognostic factors in the treatment of panic disorder with and without agoraphobia. *Behaviour Research and Therapy, 25*, 689–708.
Khantzian, E. J. (1985). The self-medication hypothesis of addictive disorders: Focus on heroin and cocaine. *American Journal of Psychiatry, 142*, 1259–1264.
Khorakiwala, D. (1991). *An analysis of the process of client change in a contextual approach to therapy.* Unpublished doctoral dissertation, University of Nevada, Reno.
Kiesler, D. (1971). Patient experiencing and successful outcome in individual psychotherapy of schizophrenics and psychoneurotics. *Journal of Consulting and Clinical Psychology, 37*, 370–385.
Klein, M.H., Mathieu, P.L., Gendlin, E.T., & Kiesler, D.J. (1969). *The experiencing scale: A research and training manual* (Vols. 1 and 2). Madison: University of Wisconsin Extension Bureau of Audiovisual Instruction.
Klien, M.H., Mathieu-Coughlan, P.L., & Kiesler, D.J. (1987). The experiencing scales. In L.S. & W.M. Pinsof (Eds.), *The psychotherapeutic process: A research handbook* (pp. 21–71). New York: Guilford Press.
Koepp, W., Shicldbach, S., Schmager, C., & Rohner, R. (1993). Borderline diagnosis and substance abuse in female patients with eating disorders. *International Journal of Eating Disorders, 14*, 107–110.

Koerner, K., Jacobson, N. S., & Christensen, A. (1994). Emotional acceptance in integrative behavioral couple therapy. In S. C. Hayes, N. S. Jacobson, V. M. Follette, and M. H. Dougher (Eds.), *Acceptance and change: Content and context in psychotherapy* (pp. 109–118). Reno, NV: Context Press.

Kohlenberg, R. J., & Tsai, M. (1991). *Functional analytic psychotherapy: Creating intense and curative therapeutic relationships*. New York: Plenum Press.

Lazarus, R. S. (1982). Thoughts on the relations between emotion and cognition. *American Psychologist, 37*, 1019–1024.

Lazarus, R.S., & Folkman, S. (1984). *Stress, appraisal, and coping*. New York: Springer.

Leitenberg, H., Greenwald, E., & Cado, S. (1992). A retrospective study of long-term methods of coping with having been sexually abused during childhood. *Child Abuse and Neglect, 16*, 399–407.

Linehan. M.M. (1993). *Cognitive behavioral treatment of borderline personality disorder*. New York: Guilford Press.

Linehan, M.M. (1994). Acceptance and change: The central dialectic in psychotherapy. In S. C. Hayes, N. S. Jacobson, V. M. Follette, & M. J. Dougher (Eds.), *Acceptance and change: Content and context in psychotherapy* (pp.73–86). Reno, NV: Context Press.

Links, P.S., Heslegrave R.J., Mitton, J.E., Van Reekum, R., & Patrick, J. (1995). Borderline personality disorder and substance abuse: Consequences of comorbidity. *Canadian Journal of Psychiatry—Revue Canadienne de Psychiatrie, 40*, 9–14.

Loo, R. (1985). Suicide among police in federal force. *Suicide and Life-Threatening Behavior, 16*, 379–388.

Luborsky, L., Chandler, M., Auerbach, A.H., Cohen, J. & Bachrach, H.M. (1971). Factors influencing the outcome of psychotherapy. *Psychological Bulletin, 75*, 145–185.

Maris, R. (1981). *Pathways to suicide: A survey of self-destructive behaviors*. Baltimore, MD: Johns Hopkins University Press.

Marlatt, G.A. (1985). Relapse prevention: Theoretical rationale and overview of the model. In G.A. Marlatt & J.R. Gordon (Eds.), *Relapse prevention: Maintenance strategies in the treatment of addictive behaviors* (pp. 3–70). New York: Brunner/Mazel.

Marlatt, G.A. (1994). Addiction and acceptance. In S.C. Hayes, N.S. Jacobson, V.M. Follette, & M.J. Dougher (Eds.), *Acceptance and change: Content and context in psychotherapy* (pp. 175–197). Reno, NV: Context Press.

McCarthy, P.R., & Foa, E.B. (1990). Obsessive-compulsive disorder. In M.E. Thase, B.A. Edelstein, & M. Hersen (Eds.) *Handbook of outpatient treatment of adults: Non psychotic mental disorders* (pp. 209–234). New York: Plenum.

McCurry, S.M. (1991). *Client metaphor use in a contextual form of therapy*. Unpublished doctoral dissertation, University of Nevada, Reno.

Meehl, P.E. (1959). Some ruminations on the validation of clinical procedures. *Canadian Journal of Psychology, 13*, 102–128.
Meyer, R.E. (Ed.). (1986). *Psychopathology and addictive disorders*. New York: Guilford Press.
Miller, F. T., Abrams, T., Dulit, R., & Fyer, M. (1993). Substance abuse in borderline personality disorder. *American Journal of Drug & Alcohol Abuse, 19*, 491–197.
Miller, W.R., & Hester, R.K. (1986). The effectiveness of alcoholism treatment: What research reveals. In W.R. Miller & N. Heather (Eds.), *Treating addictive behaviors: Processes of change* (pp. 121–172). New York: Plenum Press.
Mirin, S.M., Weiss, R.D., & Michael, J. (1987). Psychopathology in substance abusers: Diagnosis and treatment. *American Journal of Drug and Alcohol Abuse, 14*, 139–157.
Orlinsky, D. E., & Howard, K. I. (1986). Process and outcome in psychotherapy. In S. L. Garfield & A. E. Bergin (Eds.), *Handbook of psychotherapy and behavior change* (pp. 311–383). New York: Wiley.
Pashko, S., & Druley, K.A. (1987). Anxiety and control issues in substance abusing veterans. In E. Gotthiel, K.A. Druley, S. Pashko, & S.P. Weinstein (Eds.), *Stress and addiction* (pp. 197–208). New York: Brunner/Mazel.
Pauli, P., Marquardt, C., Hartl, L., Nutzinger, D. O., Hölzl, R., & Strain, F. (1991). Anxiety induced by cardiac perceptions in patients with panic attacks: A field study. *Behaviour Research and Therapy, 29*, 137–145.
Polusny, M.A., & Follette, V.M. (1995). Long-term correlates of child sexual abuse: Theory and review of the empirical literature. *Applied and Preventive Psychology, 4*, 143–166.
Rachman, S., & Hodgson, R.J. (1980). *Obsessions and compulsions*. Englewood Cliffs, NJ: Prentice Hall.
Rasmussen, S.A., & Eisen, J.L. (1992). The epidemiology and differential diagnosis of obsessive compulsive disorder. *Journal of Clinical Psychiatry, 53*, 4–10.
Rimmele, C.T., Miller, W.R., & Dougher, M.J. (1989). Aversion therapies. In R.K. Hester & W.R. Miller (Eds.), *Handbook of treatment approaches: Effective alternatives* (pp. 134–147). New York: Pergamon Press.
Rodriquez, N., Ryan, S.W., & Foy, D.W. (1992, October). *Tension reduction and PTSD: Adult survivors of sexual abuse*. Paper presented at the annual meeting of the International Society for Traumatic Stress Studies, Los Angeles.
Rogers, J.H., Widiger, T.A., & Krupp, A. (1995). Aspects of depression associated with borderline personality disorder. *American Journal of Psychiatry, 152*, 268–270.
Rosen, D.H. (1976). Suicide behaviors: Psychotherapeutic implications of egocide. *Suicide and Life-Threatening Behaviors, 6*, 209–215.
Rothberg, J.M., & Jones, F.D. (1987). Suicide in the U.S. Army: Epidemiological and periodic aspects. *Suicide and Life-Threatening Behaviors, 17*, 119–132.

Russ, M.J., Shearin, E.N., Clarkin, J.F., Harrison, K., & Hull, J.W. (1993). Subtypes of self-injurious patients with borderline personality disorder. *American Journal of Psychiatry, 150*, 1869–1871.

Safran, J. D., & Greenberg, L. S. (1988). The treatment of anxiety and depression: the process of affective change. In P. Kendall & D. Watson (Eds.), *Anxiety and depression: Distinctive and overlapping features* (pp. 455–489). Orlando, FL: Academic Press.

Salkovskis, P. M., & Westbrook, D. (1987). Obsessive-compulsive disorder: Clinical strategies for improving behavioural treatments. In H. Dent (Ed.) *Clinical psychology: Research and developments* (pp. 200–213). London: Croom Helm.

Salzinger, K. (1988). The future of behavior analysis in psychopathology. *Behavior analysis, 23*, 53–60.

Sanchez-Craig, M. (1984). *A therapists' manual for secondary prevention of alcohol problems: Procedures for teaching moderate drinking and abstinence.* Toronto: Addiction Research Foundation.

Semin, N., & Manstead, A. (1985). *Social accountability*. Cambridge, England: Cambridge University Press.

Sher, K.J. (1987). Stress response dampening. In H. T. Blaine & K. E. Leonard (Eds.), *Psychological theories of drinking and alcoholism* (pp. 227–264). New York: Guilford Press.

Skinner, B.F. (1974). *About behaviorism*. New York: Vintage Books.

Smith, G.W., & Bloom, I. (1985). A study of the personal meaning of suicide in the context of Baechler's typology. *Suicide and Life-Threatening Behavior, 15*, 3–13.

Soloff, P.H., Lis, J.A., Kelly, T., Cornelius, J., & Ulrich, R. (1994). Risk factors for suicidal behavior in borderline personality disorder. *American Journal of Psychiatry, 151*, 1316–1323.

Southwick, S.M., Yehuda, R., & Giller, E.L. (1995). Psychological dimensions of depression in borderline personality disorder. *American Journal of Psychiatry, 152*, 789–791.

Sprock, J., & Blashfield, R. K. (1991). Classification and nosology. In M. Hersen, A. E. Kazdin, & A. S. Bellack (Eds.), *The clinical psychology handbook* (pp. 329–344). New York: Pergamon.

Stockwell, T., & Bolderston, H. (1987). Alcohol and phobias. *British Journal of Addiction, 82*, 971–979.

Strosahl, K. (1991). Cognitive and behavioral treatment of the personality disordered patient. In C. Austad & B. Berman (Eds.), *Psychotherapy in managed health care: The optimal use of time and resources* (pp. 185–201). Washington, DC: American Psychological Association.

Strosahl, K., & Chiles, J. (1997). The suicidal patient: Assessment, crisis management, & treatment. In D. L. Dunner (Ed.), *Current psychiatric therapy* (pp. 499–503). Toronto: W.B. Saunders.

Strosahl, K., Chiles, J., & Linehan, M. (1992). Prediction of suicide intent in hospitalized parasuicides: Reasons for living, hopelessness and depression. *Comprehensive Psychiatry, 33,* 366–373.

Strosahl, K., Linehan, M., & Chiles, J. (1984). Will the real social desirability please stand up? Hopelessness, depression, social desirability and the prediction of suicidal behavior. *Journal of Consulting and Clinical Psychology, 52,* 449–457.

Thyer, B.A., Parrish, R.T., Himle, J., Cameron, O.G., Curtis, G.C., & Nesse, R.A. (1986). Alcohol abuse among clinically anxious patients. *Behaviour Research and Therapy, 24,* 357–359.

Tyrer, P. (1994). What are the borders of borderline personality disorder? *Acta Psychiatrica Scandinavica, Supplementum, 379,* 38–44.

Wanberg, K.W., Horn, J.L., & Foster, F.M. (1977). A differential assessment model for alcoholism: The scales of the alcohol use inventory. *Journal of Studies on Alcohol, 38,* 512–543.

Weaver, T.L., & Clum, G.A. (1993). Early family environments and traumatic experiences associated with borderline personality disorder. *Journal of Consulting & Clinical Psychology, 61,* 1069–1075.

Weekes, C. (1978). Simple, effective treatment of agoraphobia. *American Journal of Psychotherapy, 32,* 357–369.

Wegner, D.M., Schneider, D.J., Carter, S.R., & White, T.L. (1987). Paradoxical effects of thought suppression. *Journal of Personality and Social Psychology, 53,* 5–13.

Wegner, D.M., Schneider, D.J., Knutson, B., & McMahon, S.R. (1991). Polluting the stream of consciousness: The effect of thought suppression of the mind's environment. *Cognitive Therapy and Research, 15,* 141–151.

Wegner, D. M., & Zanakos, S. I. (1994). Chronic thought suppression. *Journal of Personality, 62,* 615–640.

Wenzlaff, R.M., Wegner, D.M., & Klein, S.B. (1991). The role of thought suppression in the bonding of thought and mood. *Journal of Personality and Social Psychology, 60,* 500–508.

Wulfert, E. (1994). Acceptance in the treatment of alcoholism: A comparison of Alcoholics Anonymous and social learning theory. In S.C. Hayes, N.S. Jacobson, V.M. Follette, & M.J. Dougher (Eds.), *Acceptance and change: Content and context in psychotherapy* (pp. 203–217). Reno, NV: Context Press.

Zanakos, S.I., & Wegner, D. (1993). *The Depression Sensitivity Scale.* An unpublished scale available through the authors at the Department of Social Psychology, University of Virginia, Charlottesville.

Zettle, R.D. (1984). *Cognitive therapy of depression: A conceptual and empirical analysis of component and process issues.* Unpublished doctoral dissertation, University of North Carolina, Greensboro.

Zettle, R.D., & Raines, J.C. (1989). Group cognitive and contextual therapies in treatment of depression. *Journal of Clinical Psychology, 45,* 438–445.

Section 3

Clinical Methods and Developmental Vision

ACCEPTANCE AND COMMITMENT THERAPY, RELATIONAL FRAME THEORY, AND A CONTEXTUAL BEHAVIORAL SCIENCE APPROACH

Fredrick Chin and Steven C. Hayes
University of Nevada

Section 3 of the volume is about ACT, RFT, and CBS as developed systems. These articles bring together the strands of the early work into a more mature applied approach, positioning ACT among other similar approaches, comparing and contrasting it with Buddhism, and examining its processes, procedures, and evidence. The section ends with a statement about the nature of Contextual Behavioral Science itself. There are four articles in this section: three after 2000 and a final article after 2010.

Article 11—Acceptance and Commitment Therapy, Relational Frame Theory, and the Third Wave of Behavioral and Cognitive Therapies. This article is a presidential address for the Association of Behavioral and Cognitive Therapy. In it (Hayes, 2004), the three waves of behavioral and cognitive therapy are described, and the third wave is characterized. The context for the rise of the third wave is discussed, including a growing number of empirical anomalies in traditional cognitive behavioral models and methods, as well as changes in philosophical assumptions and zeitgeist that challenge the mechanistic assumptions that are often inherent in some aspects of first-wave behavior therapy and particularly second-wave cognitive behavior therapy. A brief review of ACT assumptions, processes, and methods is provided—primarily to allow the reader to see the shift in assumptions and strategies that are characteristic of third-wave interventions more generally.

Article 12—Buddhism and Acceptance and Commitment Therapy. ACT was not modeled after Buddhist principles, but there are clear parallels between the two. This article (Hayes, 2002) highlights these similarities. They include views of the ubiquitous nature of pain, and the reduction in suffering that comes with accepting such pain, and letting go of psychological attachments to problematic cognitions. The Buddhist tradition of living and doing along the Eightfold Path is analyzed from a behaviorally consistent perspective, and issues of self are examined. The paper argues that while there may be clinical utility in the incorporation of wisdom traditions within psychological approaches, the value added needs to be examined from an empirical and scientific perspective, not a religious one.

Article 13—Acceptance and Commitment Therapy: Model, Processes, and Outcomes. This paper (Hayes, Luoma, Bond, Masuda, & Lillis, 2006) presents the psychological flexibility model and evaluates the data on ACT processes, components, and outcomes. The literature review on the efficacy of ACT includes component studies, correlational studies, randomized clinical trials, and mediational studies. The data suggest that the psychological flexibility processes are powerful predictors of psychopathology; that they can be changed by ACT (and somewhat more powerfully than most comparison interventions); that when they are changed, they are at least partly responsible for observed outcome changes; and that ACT does produce good outcomes across a diverse range of problems, ranging from everyday problems to more functionally debilitating conditions. This review was fairly comprehensive as of 2005 but the literature has exploded since then. Over 75% of the randomized controlled trials have appeared since 2010. The value of this article is more in showing how ACT researchers approached evaluation, 15 years after the model was fully presented in book form.

Article 14—Contextual Behavioral Science: Creating a Science More Adequate to the Challenge of the Human Condition. This article (Hayes, Barnes-Holmes, & Wilson, 2012) is designed to be a comprehensive statement of the assumptions, goals, and strategies of contextual behavioral science as of 2012. It appeared in the inaugural issue of the *Journal of Contextual Behavioral Science* and was deliberately designed to echo similar articles in the early days of behavior therapy and behavior analysis. Some of the tricky aspects of CBS and those that distinguish it from mainstream cognitive behavior therapy and behavior analysis are given special treatment. For example, while traditional behavior analysis is a bottom-up strategy (basic behavior analysis develops the principles that practitioners apply), CBS has a reticulated model in which both basic and applied researchers are asked to be responsible for the whole enterprise, allowing basic science and application to evolve in an interconnected and pragmatic manner. The role of middle level terms and of theory is addressed, very much in a manner that will be understandable to readers of the present volume. The functional contextualistic nature of CBS is explicated, and the reasons that any theory or model utilizing this approach must specify directly manipulable causal variables are given. The majority of these issues are ones that were repeatedly addressed in the present set of canonical papers, so this paper brings together many strands from earlier in the volume. One strand that was not covered earlier is the need to nest CBS inside the evolution sciences as examined from a multilevel, multidimensional perspective. In essence this argues that evolution science itself can be thought of from a functional contextual point of view, and when it is, the long hoped-for alliance of behavioral and evolutionary perspectives is relatively easy to build. The article also emphasizes, however, that CBS is a living tradition, and its long-term nature and future are up to younger researchers and practitioners.

REFERENCES

Hayes, S. C. (2004). Acceptance and Commitment Therapy, Relational Frame Theory, and the third wave of behavioral and cognitive therapies. *Behavior Therapy, 35*, 639–665. doi: 10.1016/S0005-7894(04)80013-3

Hayes, S. C. (2002). Buddhism and Acceptance and Commitment Therapy. *Cognitive and Behavioral Practice, 9*, 58–66.

Hayes, S. C., Barnes-Holmes, D., & Wilson, K. G. (2012). Contextual behavioral science: Creating a science more adequate to the challenge of the human condition. *Journal of Contextual Behavioral Science, 1*, 1–16. doi: 10.1016/j.jcbs.2012.09.004

Hayes, S. C., Luoma, J., Bond, F., Masuda, A., and Lillis, J. (2006). Acceptance and Commitment Therapy: Model, processes, and outcomes. *Behaviour Research and Therapy, 44*, 1–25. doi: 10.1016/j.brat.2005.06.006

ARTICLE 11

ACCEPTANCE AND COMMITMENT THERAPY, RELATIONAL FRAME THEORY, AND THE THIRD WAVE OF BEHAVIORAL AND COGNITIVE THERAPIES

From Hayes, S. C. (2004). *Behavior Therapy*, 35, 639–665.

Over the last several years quite a number of behavior therapies have emerged that do not fit easily into traditional categories within the field. Examples include Dialectical Behavior Therapy (DBT; Linehan, 1993), Functional Analytic Psychotherapy (FAP; Kohlenberg & Tsai, 1991), Integrative Behavioral Couples Therapy (IBCT; Jacobson & Christensen, 1996), and Mindfulness Based Cognitive Therapy (MBCT; Segal, Williams, & Teasdale, 2002), among several others (e.g., Borkovec & Roemer, 1994; Marlatt, 2002; Martell, Addis, & Jacobson, 2001; McCullough, 2000; Roemer & Orsillo, 2002). No one factor unites these new methods, but all have ventured into areas traditionally reserved for the less empirical wings of clinical intervention and analysis, emphasizing such issues as acceptance, mindfulness, cognitive defusion, dialectics, values, spirituality, and relationship. Their methods are often more experiential than didactic; their underlying philosophies are more contextualistic than mechanistic.

Acceptance and Commitment Therapy (ACT, said as one word, not as letters; Hayes, Strosahl, & Wilson, 1999) is another of this group. ACT is hard to categorize. The traditional distinctions (e.g., behavioral versus Gestalt; behavioral versus cognitive) seem to be more confusing than clarifying. Theoretically speaking, ACT is rigorously behavioral, but yet is based on a comprehensive empirical analysis of human cognition (Relational Frame Theory, or RFT; Hayes, Barnes-Holmes, & Roche, 2001). Based in clinical behavior analysis, ACT nevertheless seriously addresses issues of spirituality, values, and self, among other such topics. Such categorical ambiguity is shared with the majority of these new methods. For example, while ACT is supposedly "behavioral" and MBCT is supposedly "cognitive," the two seem much more closely allied than either are to, say, Beck's cognitive therapy on the one hand or to desensitization on the other.

When sets of anomalous events co-occur that are difficult to categorize using well established distinctions, sometimes the field itself is reorganizing. Behavior therapy has already lived through periods of reorganization in a disciplinary lifetime that now enters its fifth decade. Now may be such a time. The purpose of this paper is to explain ACT and to show how it relates to the intellectual and practical evolution that seems to be underway within behavior therapy.

THE WAVES OF BEHAVIOR THERAPY

Behavior therapy can be roughly categorized into three waves or generations (except where more specificity is needed, we will use the term "behavior therapy" to refer to the entire range of behavioral and cognitive therapies, from clinical behavior analysis to cognitive therapy). What I mean by a "wave" is a set or formulation of dominant assumptions, methods, and goals, some implicit, that help organize research, theory, and practice.

The First Wave

The first wave of behavior therapy was in part a rebellion against prevailing clinical conceptions. Early behavior therapists believed that theories should be built upon the bedrock of scientifically well-established basic principles, and that applied technologies should be well-specified and rigorously tested. In contrast, existing clinical traditions had a very poor link to scientifically established basic principles, vague specification of interventions, and weak scientific evidence in support of the impact of these interventions. Franks and Wilson (1974) showed this dual metatheoretical and empirical concern when they defined behavior therapy in terms of "operationally defined learning theory and conformity to well established experimental paradigms" (p. 7).

The objections to existing clinical traditions were shared by both of the major streams within behavior therapy at the time, neo-behaviorism and behavior analysis, and for that reason what united early behavior therapists over-rode for a time the substantial differences among them. Both of these traditions were strongly scientifically based, and thus could unite against the obvious metatheoretical and empirical weakness of competing clinical paradigms.

The core of the objections to analytic and humanistic conceptions was metatheoretical and empirical, but the specific arguments were substantive. For example, Freud's case of Little Hans (1928/1955) was skewered by early behavior therapists, who ridiculed the amazing flights of psychoanalytic fancy the case study contained (Bandura, 1969, p. 11–13; Wolpe & Rachman, 1960). Freud argued that Little Hans was failing to leave home as a means of avoiding Oedipal feelings and resulting castration anxiety. The convoluted reasoning that led to this conclusion included claims that a horse going through a gate is similar to feces leaving the anus, a loaded cart is like a pregnant woman, and that "the falling horse was not only his dying father but also his mother in childbirth" (Freud, 1928/1955, p. 128). Behavior therapists (Wolpe & Rachman, 1960) had a far simpler explanation. Since Little Hans had seen a horse drawn cart fall over amidst the cries and screams of riders (among several other horse-related frightening events), it was more plausible that he avoided going outside because he had a learned fear of horses. Behavior therapists poked fun at the complexity of psychoanalytic theorizing by showing experimentally that simple contingencies could readily produce behavior that would occasion bizarre psychoanalytic interpretations (e.g., Ayllon, Haughton, & Hughes, 1965).

Behavior therapy focused directly on problematic behavior and emotion, based on conditioning and neo-behavioral principles. The goal would not be to resolve the hypothesized unconscious fears and desires of Little Hans and others like him—the goal would be to get him to go out of the house and going to school. Psychoanalysts ridiculed this approach (e.g., Bookbinder, 1962; Schraml & Selg, 1966) on the grounds that symptom substitution would far outstrip superficial behavioral gains, or that unconscious desires would overwhelm necessary defense mechanisms. But this claim itself was an object of behavioral criticism (e.g., Yates, 1958), and while it seemed possible from a behavioral point of view (Bandura, 1969, pp. 48–49), as an empirical matter it proved to be much less of a problem than psychoanalysts supposed (Nurnberger & Hingtgen, 1973).

With a direct change focus came also a certain narrowing of vision, however. The rejected analytic and humanistic concepts were clinically rich. They generally were designed to address fundamental human issues, such as what people want out of life or why it is hard to be human. Unfortunately, as vague concepts were rejected, their underlying purposes also became relatively unfashionable.

The Second Wave

In the late 1960s, neo-behaviorists began to abandon simple associative concepts of learning in favor of more flexible mediational principles and mechanistic computer metaphors. The new cognitive psychology established a much more liberal theoretical approach that appealed to hypothesized internal psychological machinery.

The failure of S-R learning theory was paralleled by Skinner's (1957) failure to provide an empirically adequate analysis of language and cognition.

This failure is especially poignant because "radical" behaviorism overthrew the Watsonian restriction against the direct scientific analysis of thoughts, feelings, and other private events. Skinner did so (1945) on the grounds that a behavioral analysis of scientists themselves was necessary (thus the word "radical") and when that analysis was made it was clear that scientific objectivity depended not on the target or location of analyzed events but on the nature of the contingencies controlling the observations of them. Objectivity could occur in the analysis of private events, and scientifically unacceptable subjectivity could occur in the analysis of publicly observed events (or vice versa). That fundamental break with the Watsonian tradition (under the entirely inappropriate label of "radical" behaviorism) was not appreciated for what it was because Skinner's analysis of language and cognition led him to conclude that while a scientifically valid study of thoughts and feelings was possible, it was not needed to understand overt behavior. Language and cognition was conceived of as simple operant behavior and as such it added nothing fundamentally new to the contingency stream surrounding other behaviors. Thus, a door was opened by Skinner, but few behavior analysts walked through it or would have had any reason to do so.

Behavior therapists knew they needed to deal with thoughts and feelings in a more direct and central way. In the context of the failure of both associationism and behavior analysis to provide an adequate account of human language and cognition, the seeds planted by early cognitive mediational accounts of behavior change (e.g., Bandura, 1969) quickly flowered into the cognitive therapy movement (e.g., Beck, Rush, Shaw, & Emery, 1979; Mahoney, 1974; Meichenbaum, 1977). Methodological behaviorism provided a ready means for the transition from the first to the second wave of behavior therapy: "One can study inferred events or processes and remain a behaviorist as long as these events or processes have measurable and operational referents" (Franks & Wilson, 1974, p. 7). Some neo-behaviorists objected that cognition had been dealt with all along (e.g., Wolpe, 1980), but this objection was ignored because what was more at issue was the centrality of cognition and the flexibility needed to deal with it in a more natural way. Early cognitive behavior therapies addressed cognition from a direct, clinically relevant point of view. Certain cognitive errors seemed characteristic of patient populations, and research proceeded directly to the identification of these errors and the methods needed to correct them.

Some of the central themes of the first wave of behavior therapy were carried forward into the second, including the focus on content changes, or what has been called "first-order" change. In the second wave, irrational thoughts, pathological cognitive schemas, or faulty information processing styles would be weakened or eliminated through their detection, correction, testing, and disputation, much as anxiety was to be replaced by relaxation in the first wave. Beck, for example, said: "Although there have been many definitions of cognitive therapy, I have been most satisfied with the notion that cognitive therapy is best viewed as the application of the cognitive model of a particular disorder with the use of a variety of techniques designed to modify the dysfunctional beliefs and faulty information processing characteristic of each disorder" (Beck, 1993, p. 194).

Some leaders of the second wave therapies meant to present an alternate model to both psychoanalysis and first wave of behavior therapy. Beck was particularly clear about this, asking the rhetorical question "Can a fledgling psychotherapy challenge the giants in the field–psychoanalysis and behavior therapy?" (1976, p. 333). Despite that rhetoric, behavior therapy expanded to absorb the innovation. Most therapists within organizations like the Association for Advancement of Behavior Therapy seemed to resolve the tension between the two waves by taking a very large step in the direction of cognitive therapy, but stopping just short of abandonment of the first wave sensibilities through the use of the "cognitive-behavior therapy" (CBT) label. Behavioral principles were given much less emphasis, and cognitive principles were given much more, but nothing seemed to prohibit the use of empirically supported first-order change methods aimed at overt behavior, emotion, *and* cognition, depending on the specific situation and preferences of the analyst. In that way, the second wave largely assimilated the first.

Contexts Supporting a New Wave of Behavior Therapy

When a discipline is markedly successful, it tends to continue in the same direction for a time without a serious examination of its assumptions because adherents have interesting work to do and rewards for doing that work. Eventually, however, these assumptions themselves begin to be examined. Anomalies gradually emerge that undermine the dominant paradigm. Younger members of disciplinary paradigms are less bound to previous assumptions and are thus more prone to question them. Earlier battles and divisions that were never resolved can reemerge if previous minority views once again regain a foothold.

When basic assumptions and models begin to be questioned, the discipline enters into a creative but slightly disorienting time in which new formulations emerge and compete with older ones without a broad consensus about the value of these new approaches. The behavioral and cognitive therapies seem to be in such a stage. There are a multiple reasons, but two will be described here.

Anomalies. According to the traditional narrative of the second wave, the limitations of previous behavioral methods and conditioning models were largely corrected by the addition of cognitive change methods and models. While giving cognitive variables increased weight is generally acknowledged to have been a step forward, various anomalies are forcing a reexamination of certain aspects of this traditional narrative, particularly the core idea that direct cognitive change is a necessary or primary method of clinical improvement in most cases. A large component analysis study (Gortner, Gollan, Dobson, & Jacobson, 1998; Jacobson et al., 1996) showed that with depression "there was no additive benefit to providing cognitive interventions in cognitive therapy" (Dobson & Khatri, 2000, p. 913; cf. Zettle & Hayes, 1987). The explicitly contextualistic "behavioral activation" model that has emerged from this work (Martell et al., 2001) has the potential to be more readily disseminated than cognitive therapy (Hollon, 2001). The response to traditional cognitive therapy often occurs before the presumptively key features have been adequately implemented (Ilardi & Craighead, 1994). There are a variety of possible reasons for this (Tang & DeRubeis, 1999), but on balance this disturbing finding is not yet adequately explained (Ilardi & Craighead, 1999; Wilson, 1999). Support for the hypothesized mediators of change in cognitive therapy is uneven (e.g., Burns & Spangler, 2001; Morgenstern & Longabaugh, 2000), particularly in areas that are causal and explanatory rather than descriptive (Beck & Perkins, 2001; Bieling & Kuyken, 2003). Finally, well-supported learning accounts of major disorders have arisen to challenge traditional cognitive accounts, but while still recognizing the important role of cognition (e.g., Bouton, Mineka, & Barlow, 2001).

Philosophy of Science Changes. The majority of well-known cognitive and behavioral therapies in the first and second wave are relatively mechanistic. This is most obvious in models that literally appeal to computers as a working metaphor, but it is true of other models as well. From a mechanistic point of view, human complexity is thought to be built up of elementary parts, relations, and forces (e.g., in the nervous system or in cognitive mechanisms) and the goal of science is to model those elements in a comprehensive way. Suppose a particular thought is argued to be associated with an undesirable life adjustment (e.g., a particular thought may supposedly be leading to aversive emotions or ineffective actions). In second wave interventions, the content of this thought is usually directly targeted: the logical flaws inherent in its content might be pointed out; the truth of the thought might be tested; or alternative reconstructions might be trained. All of these presuppose that the form, frequency, or situational sensitivity of the thought itself leads directly to emotional and behavioral effects—an inherently mechanistic assumption.

The rise of constructivism and similar post-modernist (and post-post-modernist) theories, have weakened the idea that scientific theories identify discrete parts of reality that can then be organized into comprehensive models (Hayes, Hayes, Reese, & Sarbin, 1993). These changes in philosophy of science have gradually weakened the assumptive base of both the first and second wave of behavioral and cognitive therapies and their underlying theories (e.g., Jenkins, 1974) in favor of a more instrumentalist and contextual approach (Moore, 2000). Changes within the thinking of earlier proponents have sometimes revealed that same process (e.g., compare Beck et al., 1979, with Emery & Campbell, 1986, or Mahoney, 1974 with Mahoney, 2002).

A broader, more contextual focus was also supported by weakening of the FDA (Food and Drug Administration) model that coincided with and heavily influenced the second wave, particularly through federal funding linked to the treatment highly specified syndromes. Over time it has become clear that the vast majority of treatments (whether pharmacological or psychotherapeutic) have broad effects, and pathological processes tend to be similarly broad in their prevalence and impact. As these data were absorbed, some research clinicians began to think in terms of more general models and treatment approaches, which set the stage for an empirical analysis of second-order, not merely first-order, change strategies.

Factors such as these can set the stage, but change requires new ideas and innovations. These have come, and from all corners of behavior therapy. From the more behavioral side, exposure-based therapies began to focus more on contact with internal events (Barlow, 2002), seeking to alter the function of these events, not necessarily their form per se. This, along with other findings (e.g., Adler, Craske, & Barlow, 1987) gradually led to a more contextual rather than simple eliminative approach (e.g., Bouton, Mineka, & Barlow, 2001). The positive outcomes for DBT (Linehan, 1993; see Hayes, Masuda, Bissett, Luoma, & Guerrero, 2004 for a recent outcome review) provided strong support for the role of both acceptance and change and for the value of mindfulness in behavior therapy (Hayes, Follette, & Linehan, 2004; Hayes, Jacobson, Follette, & Dougher, 1994). In the cognitive wing, attentional and metacognitive perspectives (e.g., Wells, 1994) began to shift attention from first-order cognitive change. This shift undermined the idea that the form or frequency of specific problematic cognitions were key, focusing instead on the cognitive context and coping strategies related to these specific thoughts. More emphasis began to be given to contacting the present moment (e.g., Borkovec & Roemer, 1994), similarly shifting attention from first-order change to the psychological context in which cognition occurs. Finally, mindfulness-based cognitive therapy (Teasdale et al., 2002) provided dramatic evidence that it was possible to alter the function of thoughts without first altering their form.

ACT is in line with these same changes. In the next section I will describe ACT—its theoretical and philosophical base; its techniques; and a smattering of data relevant to it. In so doing, I do not wish to imply any primacy for ACT in the changes that seem to be occurring. Nevertheless, the discussion of ACT will be useful for our final task: characterization of the new wave of the behavioral and cognitive therapies.

THE THEORETICAL AND PHILOSOPHICAL BASIS OF ACT

ACT is neither from the first wave of behavior therapy, nor the second, although it builds upon both. In this section, we will describe the philosophical and theoretical underpinnings of ACT. Because of its shorthand nature, this summary is necessarily dense—more complete explications can be found in book form elsewhere (e.g., Hayes et al., 1999; Hayes et al., 2001).

ACT Philosophy: Functional Contextualism

Although it is clearly post-Skinnerian, ACT is part of the behavior analytic tradition and thus is linked to radical behaviorism. "Radical behaviorism" is a poor umbrella term for ACT, however, both because it is a name that begs for misunderstanding, and because ACT is based on only one of two fundamentally distinct philosophies that continue to co-occur under the "radical behavioral" label.

A substantial amount of philosophical work was done to clarify the philosophical basis of ACT—clarifications that help define it as an approach that is neither first nor second wave behavior therapy. ACT (and, arguably, much of behavior analysis itself) is based on a variety of pragmatism known as functional contextualism (Biglan & Hayes, 1996; Hayes, Hayes, & Reese, 1988; Hayes et al., 1993). The core analytic unit of functional contextualism is the "ongoing act in context." The core components of functional contextualism are (a) focus on the whole event, (b) sensitivity to the role of context in understanding the nature and function of an event, (c) emphasis on a pragmatic truth criterion, and (d) specific scientific goals against which to apply that truth criterion. ACT conceptualizes psychological events as a set of ongoing interactions between whole organisms and historically and situationally defined contexts. Removal of a client's problematic behaviors from the contexts that participate in that event (e.g., merely analyzing manifested behavioral symptoms themselves) is thought to miss the nature of the problem and avenues for its solution. Reductionism of all kinds is resisted, whether that be reduction across levels of analysis (e.g., biological reductionism) or within the psychological domain (e.g., physicalistic definitions of behavior or contextual events).

The truth criterion of all forms of contextualism is successful working (Hayes et al., 1988). What is considered "true" is what works. In order to know what works, however, one must know what one is working toward: there must be the clear *a priori* statement of an analytic goal (Hayes, 1993). In contextualism, ultimate goals enable analysis (that is, they allow a pragmatic truth criterion to be applied)—they are not themselves the results of analysis. This means that while ultimate goals are foundational in contextualism, they can only be stated, not justified. There are two major types of contextualism, organized in terms of their goals (Hayes, 1993): descriptive contextualism (e.g., hermeneutics, dramaturgy, narrative psychology, feminist psychology, social constructionism, and the like), which seeks an appreciation of the participants in a whole event, and functional contextualism (e.g., behavior analysis), which seeks the prediction and influence of ongoing interactions between whole organisms and historically and situationally defined contexts. Analyses are sought that have precision (only certain terms and concepts apply to a given phenomenon), scope (principles apply to a range of phenomena), and depth (they cohere across scientific levels of analysis, such as biology, psychology, and cultural anthropology).

In functional contextualism, "prediction and influence" is seen as a unified goal (analyses should help accomplish both simultaneously), and for that reason functional contextual analyses always include contextual variables. Accomplishing a goal of influencing behavior requires successful manipulation of events, and only contextual variables can be manipulated directly (Hayes & Brownstein, 1986). Stated another way, analyses that deal *only* in psychological dependent variables (e.g., emotion, thought, overt action) can never be fully adequate as measured against the pragmatic purposes of functional contextualism. Thus, the environmentalism of behavior analysis is not dogmatic, but pragmatic.

Fully explicating the implications of functional contextualism as a philosophy of science is not possible in the present article (see Biglan & Hayes, 1996; Hayes et al., 1993; Hayes et al., 1988), but three features are worth mentioning here because they are echoed in ACT itself and because they provide a contrast to the mechanistic mainstream. First, functional contextualism is a realistic philosophy that nevertheless, on epistemological grounds, rejects ontology. ACT and RFT are not trying to find what is objectively true or real because we know the world only through our interactions in and with it, and these interactions are always historically and contextually limited. Instead, ACT and RFT are theories and interventions designed to make a particular difference, and they are "true" only to the degree that they do so. In a parallel way, ACT clients are encouraged to abandon any interest in the literal truth of their own thoughts or evaluations, and instead to embrace a passionate and ongoing interest in how to live according to their values. Second, functional contextualism is holistic and context focused—no event affects another in a mechanical way. In ACT there is a conscious posture of openness and acceptance towards all psychological events even if they are formally "negative," "irrational," or even "psychotic"—the issue is not the presence of any particular event, but in its contextually established function and meaning. Finally, the foundational nature of goals in contextualism is reflected in the ACT emphasis on chosen values as a necessary component of a meaningful life (and indeed a meaningful course of treatment).

Basic ACT Theory: Relational Frame Theory

The single biggest failure of the first wave of behavior therapy was failing to deal adequately with cognition. This was not the fault of behavior therapy so much as S-R learning theory and behavior analysis, which had both stumbled in this domain. The second wave dealt with the topic, but did so either by adopting a more clinically based approach, which undermined the link between behavior therapy and basic theory, or by embracing a relatively a mechanistic cognitive psychology (based on "information processing" and computer metaphors) which emphasizes the arrangement of dependent variables that enable prediction rather than differentially emphasizing those contextual variables that can be directly manipulated in the service of psychological change.

ACT takes a third and entirely new path. ACT is built on a functional contextual program of basic research on language and cognition: Relational Frame Theory (Hayes et al., 2001). The presence of such a research program allows a new, post-Skinnerian approach to language and cognition that attempts to provide manipulable basic principles for all forms of cognitive intervention.

According to RFT, the core of human language and cognition is the ability to learn to relate events under arbitrary contextual control. Non-arbitrary stimulus relations are those defined by formal properties of related events. If one object looks the same as another, or bigger than another, a wide variety of animals would be able to learn that relation and then show it with new objects that are formally related in the same way (Reese, 1968). Human beings seem especially able to abstract the features of such relational responding and bring them under contextual control so that relational learning will transfer to events that are *not* necessarily related formally but rather are related on the basis of these arbitrary cues ("arbitrary" in this context means "by social whim or convention"). For example, having learned that "x" is "smaller than" "X," humans may later be able to apply this stimulus relation to events under the control of arbitrary cues (such as the words "smaller than"). A very young child will know, say, that a nickel is bigger than a dime, but a slightly older child will learn that a nickel is "smaller than" a dime by attribution, even though in a formal sense it is not.

There are three main properties of this kind of relational learning. First, such relations show mutual entailment or "bi-directionality." If a person learns that A relates in a particular way to B in a context, then this must entail some kind of relation between B and A in that context. For example, if a person is taught that hot is the same as boiling, that person will derive that boiling is the same as hot. Second, such relations show combinatorial entailment: if a person learns in a particular context that A relates in a particular way to B, and B relates in a particular way to C, then this must entail some kind of mutual relation between A and C in that context. For example, if by attribution a nickel is smaller than a dime and a dime is smaller than a quarter, then it will be derived that a quarter is bigger than a nickel and a nickel is smaller than a quarter. Finally, such relations enable a transformation of stimulus functions among related stimuli. If you need to buy candy and a dime is known to be valuable, it will be derived that a nickel will be less valuable and a quarter will be more valuable, without necessarily directly purchasing candy with nickels and quarters. When all three features are established with a given type of relational responding, we call the performance a "relational frame."

What makes relational framing clinically relevant is that functions given to one member of related events tend to alter the functions of other members. Suppose a child has never before seen or played with a cat. After learning "C-A-T" → animal and C-A-T → "cat," the child can derive four additional relations: animal → C-A-T, "cat" → C-A-T, "cat" → animal, and animal → "cat." Now suppose that the child is scratched while playing with a cat, cries and runs away. Later the child hears mother saying, "oh, look! A cat." Now the child again cries and runs away, even though the child was never scratched in the presence of the words "Oh, look! A cat." Indeed, in this example, the oral name never was trained in the presence of the animal. Such effects may help explain why, for example, people can have an initial panic attack while "trapped" in a shopping mall, and soon find that they are worrying about being "trapped" in an open field or on a bridge. What brings these situations together is not their formal properties in a simple sense, but the verbal/cognitive activities that relate these events.

For simplicity sake, RFT has been presented here without significant citation but it is one of the most active research areas in basic behavior analysis over the last decade, and scores of studies (reviewed in Hayes et al., 2001) have tested and found support for its basic claims. According to RFT, human language and cognition are both dependent on relational frames. When we think, reason, speak with meaning, or listen with understanding, we do so by deriving relations among events—among words and events, words and words, events and events. Unlike Skinner's verbal operants, what is unique about relational operants is that they alter how direct learning processes themselves work. For example, the transformation of stimulus functions alters how stimulus control operates since now events can acquire functions through indirect, relational (i.e., "cognitive") means. Thus, unlike Skinner's account, according to RFT it is not just possible, it is necessary to analyze cognition in order to understand human behavior. This insight corrects the mistake of the first wave, but provides a contextual way forward that differs from the more mechanistic approach of the second.

Applied ACT Theory: The Implications of RFT

Because RFT is a contextualistic theory of cognition, its clinical implications differ from those drawn from alternative conceptions of cognition. RFT can be used to generate innovative methods meant to accomplish the first-order change goals of traditional CBT (e.g., see Hayes et al., 2001, pp. 228–230), but given the purpose of the present paper, the relevance of RFT to ACT will be emphasized.

RFT points directly to the likelihood of cognitive fusion and experiential avoidance, the danger of suppression and disputation, the importance of cognitive defusion and experiential acceptance, the importance of certain senses of "self," and the centrality of values, among other implications. All of these have been expanded into treatment approaches within ACT. Because of the limited space available, only a few of these implications will be explored here.

Experiential avoidance and the failure of suppression. One of the most pathological processes known is experiential avoidance: the attempt to escape or avoid private events, even when the attempt to do so causes psychological harm (Hayes, Wilson, Gifford, Follette, & Strosahl, 1996). Emotion focused and avoidant strategies predict negative outcomes in depression (DeGenova, Patton, Jurich, & MacDermid, 1994), substance abuse (Ireland, McMahon, Malow, & Kouzekanani, 1994), the sequelae of child sexual abuse (Leitenberg, Greenwald, & Cado, 1992), and many others areas. Deliberate attempts to suppress thoughts and feelings can increase their occurrence and behavioral impact (Cioffi & Holloway, 1993; Clark, Ball, & Pape, 1991; Wegner, Schneider, Carter, & White, 1987), and can greatly complicate exposure based strategies (Feldner, Zvolensky, Eifert, & Spira, 2003).

Although amplified by the culture, RFT suggests that such processes are built into human language and cognition itself. A nonhuman trying to avoid pain can do so readily by avoiding the situations in which it has occurred in the past. A human being does not have this option because relational frames allow pain to occur in almost any situation (via a transformation of stimulus functions) and their arbitrary contextual control prevents the success of purely situational solutions such as those followed by nonhumans. Thoughts of a recently dead spouse might be cued by pictures, depressed mood, a comment in a conversation, a beautiful sunset, or any of myriad other cues. Unable to control pain by situational means, humans begin to try to avoid the painful thoughts and feelings themselves. Unfortunately, many of these means (e.g., suppression) will ultimately themselves come to cue the avoided event because they strengthen the underlying relational frames ("don't think of x" will serve as a contextual cue for "x" and the psychological presences of the actual event it is related to).

Cognitive fusion. Relational networks are extraordinarily difficult to break up, even with direct, contradictory training (Wilson & Hayes, 1996), in part because myriad derived relations are available to maintain and reestablish a given relational network. In practical terms this means that elaborated relational networks rarely really go away—they are simply further elaborated. Detecting that one is deriving coherent relational networks (e.g., learning that one is "right"), or that relating events is leading to effective outcomes (e.g., learning that one has "solved the problem"), and similar processes in essence provide automatic reinforcement for the action of deriving stimulus relations. As a result, it is very difficult to slow down language and cognition once it is well established, despite its originally instrumental nature. This combination of features means that stimulus functions from relational frames typically dominate over other sources of behavioral regulation in humans (what we term "cognitive fusion"), making an individual less in contact with here-and-now experience and direct contingencies and more dominated by verbal rules and evaluations (Hayes, 1989). Through a transformation of stimulus functions, the environment will seemingly "contain" stimulus functions that are dependent on relational frames, without the relational process itself necessarily being evident. The fearful person who constructs a fearful environment, will act is if that fearsomeness has been discovered, not constructed. Since behavior governed by relational networks is notoriously insensitive to contradictory experiences (e.g., Hayes, Brownstein, Zettle, Rosenfarb, & Korn, 1986), very ineffective verbal formulations can continue to create harm even when very little environmental support is provided for them.

These kinds of phenomena are precisely why the cognitive revolution occurred in behavior therapy in the first place, but because of mechanistic assumptions it was thought that an undesirable thought → action or emotion → action relation should be modified by changing the form, frequency, or situational sensitivity of private events themselves. RFT suggests a "third wave" alternative: change the contexts that support a thought → action or emotion → action relation (or an emotion → thought → action relation, and any similar variants). Experiential acceptance and cognitive defusion are prime examples of ACT techniques that attempt to do just that.

ACCEPTANCE AND COMMITMENT THERAPY

The general clinical goals of ACT are to undermine the grip of the literal verbal content of cognition that occasions avoidance behavior and to construct an alternative context where behavior in alignment with one's value is more likely to occur. ACT has been described in book length form (Hayes et al., 1999) and the other articles in this issue will provide additional details. Thus, in the present article we will focus only briefly on the components of ACT, giving the barest of examples of their content and intellectual rationale.

Therapeutic Assumptions and Clinical Stance

ACT assumes that dramatic, powerful change is possible and possible quickly, because it is the general context and purpose of action that is the true problem, not the historically produced and well-conditioned content of life difficulties. What the client is feeling, thinking, remembering, or otherwise experiencing is never assumed to be the core difficulty, even though human beings will initially focus on difficult content as the core of their problems. For instance, "anxiety" is not assumed to be the problem in "anxiety disorders"; "mood" is not assumed to be the problem in "mood disorders"; "thought" is not assumed to be the problem in "thought disorders"; and so on. In ACT, it is the tendency to take these experiences literally and then to fight against them that is viewed as harmful.

ACT therapists assume that it is neither possible nor healthy to attempt to rescue clients from the difficulty and challenge of growth. It is inherently difficult to be a human being. ACT therapists compassionately accept no reasons and stories as "true" if these stories are functionally useless or harmful, regardless of their reasonableness—the issue is workability not reasonableness. This applies as well to ACT itself, and thus it is more important as an ACT therapist to do as you say than to say what to do. For example, if the client is trapped, frustrated, confused, afraid, angry, or anxious the ACT stance suggests that this is not so much a problem as it is an opportunity to work on how powerful events in the here and now can become barriers to growth. In exactly the same way, if the therapist feels trapped, frustrated, confused, afraid, angry, or anxious, it is the therapist's job to open up to these experiences, recognizing the humanizing opportunity they provide to put themselves into the shoes of their clients and to do the same work without avoiding or moving one up. Because of this quality, the therapeutic relationship is important, powerful, and deliberately equal in ACT.

Skepticism about the value of "truth" is pervasive. ACT therapists are cautioned not to argue or persuade. The issue is the client's life and the client's experience, not opinions and beliefs, however well meant. The issue is always the function of events, not their decontextualized form or frequency. The key question is thus "What is this in the service of?" not "Is this true or false?"

The key goal of ACT is to support the client in feeling and thinking what they directly feel and think already, as it *is* not as what it *says it is*, and to help the client move in a valued direction, *with* all of their history and automatic reactions. ACT techniques are simply means designed to find a psychological context from which that is possible. The process of ACT is a cycle of detecting cognitive fusion and avoidance, defusing and letting go (thus establishing new, more flexible functions for these events) and moving in a valued direction in a way that builds larger and larger patterns of effective behavior.

ACT therapists are passionately interested in what the client truly wants, but not necessarily with the means that the culture specifies for achieving these ends. It is this distinction that allows ACT therapists to compassionately confront unworkable agendas without invalidation because the client's experience is respected as the ultimate arbiter. For example, typically an anxiety disordered person wants to get rid of anxiety. It could be experienced as invalidating to refuse to work directly on that desired outcome. At another level, however, the anxious client wants to get rid of anxiety in order to do something such as living a vital human life. Lack of anxiety is not the ultimate goal—it is a means to an end. Since often it has failed as a means, ACT suggests abandoning that means—simply because the client's own experience suggests its unworkability. Furthermore, ACT provides something else that the client can do with these previously avoided or fused events, while moving directly and quickly to the ultimate goal (e.g., establishing relationships, participating, contributing). The larger message thus is validating (trust your experience) and empowering (you can live a powerful life from here, without first winning a war with your own history).

As a general style, ACT relies on relatively non-linear uses of language, since language processes themselves (at least in certain contexts) are thought to be the primary source of rigid and ineffective repertoires. Thus ACT relies heavily on paradox, metaphors, stories, exercises, behavioral tasks, and experiential processes, while logical analysis has a relatively limited role.

Techniques

There are several specific domains of ACT intervention, and each has its own specific methodology, exercises, homework, and metaphors.

Confronting the system. ACT seeks to identify the strategies that the client has employed until this point to "solve the problem" and see whether these methods are working. If they have not been truly solving the problem, ACT therapists ask the client to consider the possibility that maybe the problem is not the techniques but their very purpose. In essence, ACT often begins by challenging the linguistic set that defines both problems and their potential solutions, because that set is itself viewed to be a problem. The "Person in the Hole" metaphor, provides a model of this part of ACT:

> The situation you are in seems a bit like this. Imagine that you're placed in a field, wearing a blindfold, and you're given a little bag of tools. You're told that your job is to run around this field, blindfolded. Unknown to you, in this field there are a number of widely-spaced, fairly deep holes. So you start running around and sooner or later you fall into this large hole. You feel around and there are no escape routes you can find. So you reach into your bag and find a shovel. So you start digging, but pretty soon you notice that you're not out of the hole—the hole is bigger. So you try digging faster, or with big scoops. But it is not working. So you come in to see me thinking "maybe he has a really huge shovel—a gold-plated steam shovel." Well, I don't. And even if I did I wouldn't use it because digging is not a way out of the hole—digging is what makes holes. So maybe the whole thing is a big set up—a rigged game.

Control is the problem. In the world of common sense, if we do not want something, we must figure out how to get rid of it. Controlling strategies are taught repeatedly and in most domains they work quite well. In the world of private events, however, it might work differently because of the nature of relational frames. For example, deliberately not thinking of something usually fails because the rule ("Don't think of x") contains the avoided item. Similarly, if it is essential not to feel anxious, anxiety is something to be anxious about. In this part of ACT a simple idea is put on the table: conscious, deliberate, and purposeful control simply may not work very well with regard to the private experiences the client has been targeting. The *Polygraph Metaphor* provides a model of this part of ACT:

> Suppose I had you hooked up to the world's most sensitive polygraph machine and I told you that I had a very simple task for you to perform: stay relaxed. However, I want you to try hard, so I am going to hold a loaded .44 Magnum to your temple. If you get nervous, I'm sorry but I'm going to have to pull the trigger. What you think might happen here?

In unpacking this metaphor (and similar metaphors or exercises) the client is asked to consider the possibility that a virtually impossible task has been adopted: controlling automatic thoughts, feelings, and memories.

Cognitive defusion and mindfulness. It is difficult to find an alternative to conscious control until the illusion of language is penetrated, because language itself provides conscious control as a method of problem solving. This comedic comment is right on target: "I used to think my mind was my most important organ, until I noticed what was telling me that."

From an RFT perspective, the literal functions of language and cognition are not automatic or mechanical: they are contextual. Because of derived stimulus relations and transformation of stimulus functions, thoughts often function as if they are what they say they are. The thought "I am bad" can seem to mean that the person is dealing with *being* bad, not with thinking "I am bad." CBT has always known this, but the solution has been to challenge, test, or analyze the content of these thoughts. Instead, ACT alters their context.

Cognitive defusion techniques erode the tight verbal relations that establish stimulus functions through relational learning (Hayes et al., 1999; Hayes & Wilson, 1994). A classic ACT defusion technique is the *Milk, Milk, Milk* exercise, first used by Titchener (1916, p. 425). It consists of an exploration of all of the properties of a single word. For example "milk" is white, creamy, and so on. This word is then said out loud by the therapist and client rapidly for about a minute. In the context of rapid repetition, it quickly loses all meaning and becomes just a sound. Often the exercise is repeated with a single word variant of a core clinical concern or troublesome thought the specific client may have (e.g., mean, stupid, weak, etc.). The experiential point is that thoughts do not mean what they say they mean, and while it may not be possible or healthy to experience their referents, it is always possible to experience them as an ongoing process if the context in which they are occurring is changed.

Mindfulness exercises are another means to achieve cognitive defusion and thus to increase behavioral flexibility. Contacting events in the here and now, without buying into evaluative and judgmental language is the very essence of mindfulness (Kabat-Zinn, 1994, p. 4). This requires a weakening of literal language, which cannot be done in a purely logical, analytical, or critical manner. Metaphorically, mindfulness teaches clients to look at thoughts as events in the world, not at the world as structured by thoughts. A variety of mindfulness exercises are used in ACT, such as imagining watching one's thoughts as they float by like leaves on a stream, and watching how this becomes impossible when these thoughts are taken literally.

A transcendent sense of self. Difficult thoughts and feelings create an illusion that they are dangerous. That is precisely why we name our disorders after them (e.g., "anxiety disorders"). It is not realistic to ask clients to experience them without providing a safe place from which that is possible. Language itself provides such a place: the continuity of consciousness that emerges from perspective taking (Hayes, 1984). RFT claims that its source is deictic relational frames such as I-you; here-there; and now-then—a claim that has been tested in young children (Hayes et al., 2001; McHugh, Barnes-Holmes, & Barnes-Holmes, 2004). In one sense of the term, "you" are "from-here-now" and once this perspective is acquired it never changes. The lack of experienced limits or variations in "I-here-now" forms a direct experiential basis for human spirituality (Hayes, 1984). Because "as seen from here, now" never changes (there is no other perspective from which to experience events consciously), and its limits are never consciously contacted (by definition), there is a dimension of human experience that is not thing like (or, as Eastern perspective say it, "everything / nothing").

The *Observer Exercise* (a variant of the "self-identification exercise" developed by Assagioli, 1971, pp. 211–217) is a key "eyes closed" ACT exercise designed to promote experiential contact with this transcendent sense of self. The person is asked to become aware of present sensations, and then is asked to remember something that happened a few months earlier and to become intensely aware of what that experience felt like. Then the person is asked to notice (not as a belief, but as a direct experience) that a person ("you") is here now, and a person experienced those events some months ago. The actual experiential continuity between the person "behind the eyes" is emphasized ("you have been you your whole life"). From this "observer perspective" a variety of domains are examined (e.g., bodily sensations, roles, emotions, thoughts, memories). In each case, the rapidly changing content of experiences is contrasted with the continuity of consciousness itself. For example:

> Now let's go to another area: emotions. Notice how your emotions are constantly changing. Sometimes you feel calm and sometimes tense, sometime joyful and sometimes sorrowful. Sometimes happy. Sometimes sad. Even now you may be experiencing emotions . . . interest, boredom,

> relaxation, fear. The only thing you can count on with emotions is that they will change. And yet while these emotions come and go, notice that in some deep sense the "you" that looks out from behind those eyes does not change. You have been you your whole life. I'm not asking you to believe this—I'm asking you to look at your experience. If your emotions are constantly changing and yet the you that you call you is not, it must mean that while you have emotions you do not experience yourself to simply *be* your emotions. [Leave a brief period of silence]. So just notice your emotions for a moment and as you do so notice also who is noticing them.

After several domains are covered (roles, thoughts, bodily sensations, memories) the punch line is simple: "The things you've been struggling with and trying to change are not *you* anyway." Knowing that there is a unchanging transcendent sense of self (not self as an object, but one that is no-thing) helps provide a safe place from which to experience fearsome psychological content with less concern that psychological harm or even psychological obliteration could result.

Acceptance and willingness. Etymologically, acceptance means "to take what is offered." In ACT, acceptance is not merely tolerance—it is the active non-judgmental embracing of experience in the here and now. Acceptance is not possible without defusion. Literal language is referential and for that reason is always about "there and then"—something else, some other time. Even the word "now" refers to the now just experienced, not the now that exists now. Acceptance means actively experiencing events, as they are and not as what they *say* they are. This means feeling feelings as feelings, thinking thoughts as thoughts, sensing sensations as sensations, and so on, here and now.

Acceptance inherently involves "exposure" and thus ACT connects with all of the exposure-based behavior therapies (a point I will pick up again later) but not for an emotional regulatory purpose. Feeling a feeling to get it to diminish involves a simultaneous process of feeling, and cognitively fused processes of measuring, evaluating, and comparing, such as "I am feeling this much anxiety, which is more (or less) than it was and this is good (or bad)." Acceptance and willingness in ACT lead to a different kind of exposure: experiencing actively and fully in the present, moment by moment, for the purpose of experiencing actively and fully in the present, moment by moment.

Values. The emphasis on values distinguishes ACT from many alternative treatments. It is only within the context of values that action, acceptance, and defusion come together into a sensible whole. Indeed, ACT therapists often do values clarification work before other ACT components for that reason. Values are qualities of action that can be instantiated in behavior but not possessed like an object. ACT therapists ask their clients, "What do you want your life to stand for?" In this phase of treatment a client is asked to list values in different life domains such as family, intimate relationships, health, spirituality, and so on. Various evocative exercises are used to develop more clarity about fundamental values. For example, the ACT therapist may ask the client to write out what he or she would most like to see on his or her tombstone, or the eulogy he or she would want to hear at his or her own funeral. In essence, this focuses verbal processes away from literal truth toward psychological meaning and motivation. When values are clarified, achievable goals that embody those values, concrete actions that would produce those goals, and specific barriers to performing these actions are identified.

Values dignify the need for acceptance of specific painful thoughts and feelings because it is only that they have arisen as barriers that requires that they be embraced. ACT is not about endless emotional wallowing; rather it involves "taking in" what one's history offers in the process of living a valued life.

Commitment. ACT seeks to build larger and larger patterns of flexible and effective responding, both by removing the repertoire narrowing effects of cognitive fusion and experiential avoidance, and by promoting deliberate patterns of action that comport with chosen values. ACT involves learning a generalized strategy of moving forward toward valued ends, dissolving psychological barriers through defusion and acceptance, and situational barriers through direct action. A variety of techniques are used, drawn from the larger armamentarium of traditional behavior therapy: for example, clients may be asked to establish specific goals, to make public and concrete commitments, and to work toward these goals in small steps. As its very name implies, ACT is thus as much a change oriented strategy as an acceptance-oriented one. Similar to DBT, the "acceptance and change dialectic" (Linehan, 1993) is maintained as a central focus throughout ACT work.

ACT EMPIRICAL FINDINGS

A review of ACT (and DBT and FAP) outcomes has recently appeared in this journal (Hayes et al., 2004), so no comprehensive restatement seems necessary. Although clearly preliminary, the ACT outcome literature already seems unusually broad, involving effectiveness studies and efficacy studies in depression, psychosis, substance use disorders, chronic pain, eating disorders, work-related stress, and other problems (see Hayes et al., 2004). The theory underlying ACT explains this breadth. RFT suggests that language itself has created the problems ACT is trying to solve. If so, all verbal human beings are confronting these problematic processes on a daily basis. If ACT targets them effectively, its clinical spread should be very large indeed.

Process research in ACT is also young, but there is some support for the idea that ACT produces an unusually rapid decrease in the believability (but not necessarily the frequency) of negative thoughts (e.g., Bach & Hayes, 2002; Zettle & Hayes, 1986), the opposite of what is usually found in CBT. These decreases in the believability of negative thoughts are specifically associated with positive ACT outcomes (e.g., Bach & Hayes, 2002). ACT also produces an increased willingness to experience negative private events—a process that is also associated with positive ACT outcomes (e.g., Bond & Bunce, 2000). The role of other core ACT processes (e.g., values, transcendent self) has not yet been evaluated experimentally.

From an ACT/RFT perspective it is the repertoire narrowing effects of cognitive fusion and avoidance that are most harmful, because that narrowing prevents new contingency shaped behavior and undermines healthy forms of extinction. It is the acquisition of more flexible and less defensive behaviors in the presence of difficult thoughts, feelings, or sensations that reduces their behavioral regulatory effect. This analysis shares features of other accounts, such as Teasdale et al.'s analysis of the impact of CT and MBCT (Teasdale et al., 2002) and Bouton et al.'s analysis of the mechanisms of conditioning in panic disorder (Bouton et al., 2001). Defusion and acceptance alter the functions of heretofore pathogenic thoughts and feelings and permit the acquisition of more flexible and effective response functions related to them, removing needless "safety behavior" or other forms of avoidance that diminishes extinction. These same steps (treating thoughts as thoughts, undermining avoidance, focusing on new behaviors) are also echoed in Behavioral Activation (Jacobson, Martell, & Dimidjian, 2001), DBT (Linehan, 1993), modern interoceptive exposure methods (Barlow, 2002), and many of the other new behavior therapies. Traditional CBT also helps clients distance themselves from their thoughts (cognitive distancing is one of the first steps in traditional CT approaches) and then to behave in different ways toward them (e.g., for purposes of "hypothesis testing") in the earliest stages of CBT when clinical response is known to be particularly powerful despite the lack of focus on cognitive change per se (Ilardi & Craighead, 1994). Thus, the processes targeted by the third wave may help explain some of the empirical anomalies of the second.

THE THIRD WAVE OF BEHAVIOR THERAPY

This discussion of ACT technology and ACT/RFT processes may orient us toward a few general features of the new generation of behavior therapy that seems to be emerging. Grounded in an empirical, principle-focused approach, the third wave of behavioral and cognitive therapy is particularly sensitive to the context and functions of psychological phenomena, not just their form, and thus tends to emphasize contextual and experiential change strategies in addition to more direct and didactic ones. These treatments tend to seek the construction of broad, flexible and effective repertoires over an eliminative approach to narrowly defined problems, and to emphasize the relevance of the issues they examine for clinicians as well as clients. The third wave reformulates and synthesizes previous generations of behavioral and cognitive therapy and carries them forward into questions, issues, and domains previously addressed primarily by other traditions, in hopes of improving both understanding and outcomes. We will consider major components of this characterization below.

Grounded in an empirical, principle-focused approach. Despite worries in some corners (e.g., Corrigan, 2001), examination of the literature shows that the new wave therapies have maintained a commitment to the empirical roots of behavior therapy (Hayes et al., 2004). This is true not just at the level of outcome, but also at the level of processes and principles. Commitment to theoretical development is notable in most of the new treatments. In both of these areas, the third wave builds on the best of previous waves of development.

Contextual and experiential in addition to direct change strategies, focused on function over form. While not abandoning direct or even didactic change strategies, the most unique characteristic of the third wave interventions is the degree of emphasis on contextual and experiential change strategies, including acceptance, defusion, mindfulness, relationship, values, emotional deepening, contact with the present moment, and the like. The purpose of experiential and contextual strategies of this kind is to rapidly alter the function of problematic psychological events, even if their form or frequency does not change or changes only slowly. Mindfulness-based and acceptance technologies show that focus quite clearly. For example, Segal, Teasdale, and Williams (2004) state: "Unlike CBT, there is little emphasis in MBCT on changing the *content* of thoughts; rather, the emphasis is on changing *awareness of* and *relationship to* thoughts" (manuscript p. 13; emphasis in the original). It is worth noting that this step is being taken both by techniques that are quite behavior analytic and thus philosophically contextualistic in their rationalization (e.g., Behavioral Activation, ICBT, DBT, ACT), and by techniques that are quite cognitive in their rationalization (e.g., MBCT). Indeed, procedures which helped foster the current wave of development in the first place, such as interoceptively oriented exposure-based therapies, have in turn increasingly emphasizing themes central to the third wave interventions more generally (e.g., compare Barlow, 1988 to Barlow, 2002).

Construction of flexible and effective repertoires over elimination of narrowly defined problems. One of the main themes of both the first wave and second wave was a focus on eliminating specific problematic behaviors, thoughts, or emotions as a primary purpose of therapy. The third wave's broad focus on new and sometimes very generally applicable skills (e.g., mindfulness, acceptance, interpersonal deepening, emotional deepening, valuing, commitment) harkens back to the earliest days of behavioral thinking in which the construction of broad and flexible repertoires (Goldiamond, 1974) and an appeal to principles that underlie normal functioning were foundational in the understanding of abnormal behavior. Even with the most severe problems, the new behavior therapies tend to focus more on empowerment and repertoire enhancement than on pathologizing narrowly defined problem behaviors. For example, even persons coping with psychotic symptoms (e.g., Bach & Hayes, 2002) or dually diagnosed persons dealing with both borderline personality disorder and substance use disorder (Linehan et al., 2002) are treated in a skills building, relatively non-pathologizing way.

Emphasizing the relevance of the issues they examine for clinicians as well as clients. The reemergence of the relevance of normal processes can also be found in the relevance of these methods to therapists themselves. MBCT advocates suggest that mindfulness practice should be pursued by therapists; DBT underlines the importance of a peer consultation team to "treat the therapist"; FAP advocates have argued that you "cannot teach what you cannot do"; ACT argues that acceptance and defusion is equally relevant to therapists themselves and it is necessary for effective ACT work; and so on. In part as a result, treatment is often radically non-hierarchical—the therapist and client are thought to be swimming in the same stream.

Synthesizing previous generations. It is very much worth noting that these changes are emerging from every wing of behavior therapy. This is important, because it is not that a behavioral model is becoming re-ascendant or that a cognitive model is waning. What seems to be happening is that the assumptive base of both the first and second wave is weakening, to be replaced by a slightly altered set of assumptions for both. As this occurs, the mainstream itself is changed. In a kind of dialectical synthesis of a previous thesis and antithesis, the new wave therapies seem to be healing old wounds and divisions between behavioral and cognitive perspectives. Evidence for this view can be found in the synergies between technologies across of the spectrum of third wave interventions, and in the ways that each of these new approaches has breadth across these divisions regardless of its home of origin. The third wave interventions are not a rejection of the first and second waves of behavioral and cognitive therapy so much as a transformation of these earlier phases into a new, broader, more interconnected form. Thus, while the implications may be revolutionary, the processes giving rise to these developments are evolutionary—as might be expected in an explicitly empirical tradition.

Dealing with the questions, issues, and domains addressed by other traditions. These new treatments are breaking down some of the previously important distinctions between behavior therapy and older, less scientific traditions. In the current period, the issues and methods of less empirical traditions are actively on the table, but now from a scientific point of view, with an interest in coherent theory, carefully assessed processes of change, and solid empirical outcomes. Issues of spirituality, values, emotional deepening, and the like are now central in a way that was uncommon or even unwelcome before. What is resulting is recognizably part of the behavioral and cognitive therapy tradition, but is nevertheless linked to the issues and concerns of other traditions, including some of those (analytic, Gestalt, humanistic, existential) that were turned away from in the earliest days of behavior therapy.

Improving understanding and outcomes. It is not yet clear that this new wave of behavioral and cognitive therapy will achieve better outcomes. The ACT literature is too young to provide much of a guide, but there are examples that provide hope that these changes will make a difference in the effectiveness of behavior therapy. For example, as Borkovec's treatment protocol for GAD (Generalized Anxiety Disorder) has moved from traditional CBT (Borkovec & Mathews, 1988) to a package that includes such third wave interventions as teaching clients to focus on the present moment, intrinsic values training, and interpersonal and emotional deepening, within-group effect sizes have improved nearly 80% (Borkovec & Sharpless, 2004). Similarly, IBCT seems to be producing results that exceed its second wave progenitor, behavioral marital therapy (Christensen, Sevier, Simpson, & Gattis, 2004; Jacobson, Christensen, Prince, Cordova, & Eldridge, 2000). While these examples are not determinative, the fact that these new therapies have remained committed to the empirical values of the behavior therapy tradition means that it will be clear over time whether these changes are progressive as measured by clinical impact.

At the level of understanding, however, there seems to be growing evidence that these new methods are progressive. They help make sense of previous outcomes, and open up the behavior therapy tradition to new ideas in both basic and applied literatures. They have been driven by empirical developments and scientifically sensible ideas. They are logical next steps (Borkovec & Sharpless, 2004).

CONCLUSION

Behavior therapy has been a great success story. True to its empirical commitments, it has been open to new ideas and willing to follow the data. It has also tended to expand its scope over time. The rise of mindfulness, acceptance, defusion, values, relationship, spirituality, and similar concerns, marks another phase of that expansion of scope that can be characterized in a number of ways. I have pointed to some of the apparent dimensions in the present article (second-order, contextual, constructional, experiential, flexible repertoires, and so on) but regardless of how it may be characterized, the breadth of current change and its deviation from core assumptions of earlier generations suggests that a new generation of behavioral and cognitive therapy has arrived. Whatever the source and ultimate outcome of these changes, it seems to mark a maturing of the behavior therapy tradition. The leading force for an empirical clinical approach over the last 50 years is once again expanding both its models and methods to include an even broader range of clinical issues and procedures under the "behavior therapy" umbrella. In the long run, this seems bound to change not just behavior therapy, but the entire field of mental health, substance abuse, and the psychological aspects of physical disease.

REFERENCES

Adler, C. M., Craske, M. G., & Barlow, D. H. (1987). Relaxation-induced panic (RIP): When resting isn't peaceful. *Integrative Psychiatry, 5*, 94–100

Assagioli, R. (1971). *The act of will.* New York: Viking.

Ayllon, T., Haughton, E., & Hughes, H.B. (1965). Interpretation of symptoms: Fact or fiction. *Behaviour Research and Therapy, 3*, 1–7.

Bach, P., & Hayes, S.C. (2002). The use of Acceptance and Commitment Therapy to prevent the rehospitalization of psychotic patients: A randomized controlled trial. *Journal of Consulting and Clinical Psychology, 70*, 1129–1139.

Bandura, A. (1969). *Principles of behavior modification.* New York: Holt, Rinehart, & Winston.

Barlow, D. H. (1988). *Anxiety and its disorders: The nature and treatment of anxiety and panic.* New York: Guilford Press.

Barlow, D. H. (2002). *Anxiety and its disorders: The nature and treatment of anxiety and panic* (2nd ed.). New York: Guilford Press.

Beck, A.T. (1976). *Cognitive therapy and the emotional disorders.* New York: International Universities Press.

Beck, A.T. (1993). Cognitive therapy: Past, present, and future. *Journal of Consulting and Clinical Psychology, 61*, 194–198.

Beck, A.T., Rush, A.J., Shaw, B.F., & Emery, G. (1979). *Cognitive therapy of depression.* New York: Guilford Press.

Beck, R., & Perkins, T.S. (2001). Cognitive content-specificity for anxiety and depression: A meta-analysis. *Cognitive Therapy & Research, 25*, 651–663.

Bieling, P.J., & Kuyken, W. (2003). Is cognitive case formulation science or science fiction? *Clinical Psychology: Science & Practice, 10*, 52–69.

Biglan, A., & Hayes, S.C. (1996). Should the behavioral sciences become more pragmatic? The case for functional contextualism in research on human behavior. *Applied and Preventive Psychology: Current Scientific Perspectives, 5*, 47–57.

Bond, F.W., & Bunce, D. (2000). Mediators of change in emotion-focused and problem-focused worksite stress management interventions. *Journal of Occupational Health Psychology, 5*, 156–163.

Bookbinder, L.J. (1962). Simple conditioning vs. the dynamic approach to symptoms and symptom substitution: A reply to Yates. *Psychological Reports, 10*, 71–77.

Borkovec, T.D., & Mathews, A.M. (1988). Treatment of nonphobic anxiety disorders: A comparison of nondirective, cognitive, and coping desensitization therapy. *Journal of Consulting and Clinical Psychology, 56*, 877–884.

Borkovec, T.D., & Roemer, L. (1994). Generalized anxiety disorder. In R.T. Ammerman & M. Hersen (Eds.), *Handbook of prescriptive treatments for adults* (pp. 261–281). New York: Plenum.

Borkovec, T.D., & Sharpless, B. (2004). Generalized anxiety disorder: Bringing cognitive behavioral therapy into the valued present. In S.C. Hayes, V.M. Follette, & M. Linehan (Eds.), *Mindfulness and acceptance: Expanding the cognitive-behavioral tradition* (pp. 209–242). New York: Guilford.
Bouton, M.E., Mineka, S., & Barlow, D.H. (2001). A modern learning theory perspective on the etiology of panic disorder. *Psychological Review, 108*, 4–32.
Burns, D.D., & Spangler, D.L. (2001). Do changes in dysfunctional attitudes mediate changes in depression and anxiety in cognitive behavioral therapy? *Behavior Therapy, 32*, 337–369.
Christensen, A., Sevier, M., Simpson, L., & Gattis, K. (2004). Acceptance, mindfulness, and change in couple therapy. In S.C. Hayes, V.M. Follette, & M. Linehan (Eds.), *Mindfulness and acceptance: Expanding the cognitive-behavioral tradition* (pp. 288–309). New York: Guilford Press.
Cioffi, D., & Holloway, J. (1993). Delayed costs of suppressed pain. *Journal of Personality and Social Psychology, 64*, 274–282.
Clark, D.M., Ball, S., & Pape, D. (1991). An experimental investigation of thought suppression. *Behaviour Research and Therapy, 29*, 253–257.
Corrigan, P.W. (2001). Getting ahead of the data: A threat to some behavior therapies. *The Behavior Therapist, 24*, 189–193.
DeGenova, M.K., Patton, D.M., Jurich, J.A., & MacDermid, S.M. (1994). Ways of coping among HIV-infected individuals. *Journal of Social Psychology, 134*, 655–663.
Dobson, K.S., & Khatri, N. (2000). Cognitive therapy: Looking backward, looking forward. *Journal of Clinical Psychology, 56*, 907–923.
Emery, G., & Campbell, J. (1986). *Rapid relief from emotional distress.* New York: Rawson.
Feldner, M.T., Zvolensky, M.J., Eifert, G.H., & Spira, A.P. (2003). Emotional avoidance: An experimental test of individual differences and response suppression using biological challenge. *Behaviour Research and Therapy, 41*, 403–411.
Franks, C.M., & Wilson, G.T. (1974). *Annual review of behavior therapy: Theory and practice.* New York: Brunner/Mazel.
Freud, S. (1928/1955). Analysis of a phobia in a five-year-old boy (little Hans)/Analyse d'une phobie chez un petit garcon de cinq ans. (Le petit Hans.) *Revue Francaise de Psychanalyse, 2*(3). Reprinted in *The complete psychological works of Sigmund Freud.* Translated by James Strachey. Vol 10. London: Hogarth.
Goldiamond, I. (1974). Toward a constructional approach to social problems. *Behaviorism, 2*, 1–79.
Gortner, E.T., Gollan, J.K., Dobson, K.S., & Jacobson, N.S. (1998). Cognitive-behavioral treatment for depression: Relapse prevention. *Journal of Consulting & Clinical Psychology, 66*, 377–384.
Hayes, S.C. (1984). Making sense of spirituality. *Behaviorism, 12*, 99–110.

Hayes, S.C. (Ed.). (1989). *Rule-governed behavior: Cognition, contingencies, and instructional control.* New York: Plenum.

Hayes, S.C. (1993). Goals and varieties of scientific contextualism. In S.C. Hayes, L.J. Hayes, H.W. Reese., & T.R. Sarbin. (Eds.), *The varieties of scientific contextualism* (pp. 11–27). Reno, NV: Context Press.

Hayes, S.C., Barnes-Holmes, D., & Roche, B. (Eds.). (2001). *Relational Frame Theory: A Post-Skinnerian account of human language and cognition.* New York: Plenum Press.

Hayes, S.C., & Brownstein, A.J. (1986). Mentalism, behavior-behavior relations and a behavior analytic view of the purposes of science. *The Behavior Analyst, 1,* 175–190.

Hayes, S.C., Brownstein, A.J., Zettle, R.D., Rosenfarb, I., & Korn, Z. (1986). Rule-governed behavior and sensitivity to changing consequences of responding. *Journal of the Experimental Analysis of Behavior, 45,* 237–256.

Hayes, S.C., Follette, V.M., & Linehan, M. (2004). *Mindfulness and acceptance: Expanding the cognitive-behavioral tradition.* New York: Guilford Press.

Hayes, S.C., Hayes, L.J., & Reese, H.W. (1988). Finding the philosophical core: A review of Stephen C. Popper's World Hypotheses. *Journal of Experimental Analysis of Behavior, 50,* 97–111.

Hayes, S.C., Hayes, L.J., Reese, H.W., & Sarbin, T.R. (Eds.). (1993). *Varieties of scientific contextualism.* Reno, NV: Context Press.

Hayes, S.C., Jacobson, N.S., Follette, V.M., & Dougher, M.J. (Eds.) (1994). *Acceptance and change: Content and context in psychotherapy.* Reno, NV: Context Press.

Hayes, S.C., Masuda, A., Bissett, R., Luoma, J., & Guerrero, L.F. (2004). DBT, FAP, and ACT: How empirically oriented are the new behavior therapy technologies? *Behavior Therapy, 35,* 35–54.

Hayes, S.C., Strosahl, K.D., & Wilson, K.G. (1999). *Acceptance and Commitment Therapy: An experiential approach to behavior change.* New York: Guilford Press.

Hayes, S.C., & Wilson, K.G. (1994). Acceptance and Commitment Therapy: Altering the verbal support for experiential avoidance. *The Behavior Analyst, 17,* 289–303.

Hayes, S.C., Wilson, K.G., Gifford, E.V., Follette, V.M., & Strosahl, K. (1996). Emotional avoidance and behavioral disorders: A functional dimensional approach to diagnosis and treatment. *Journal of Consulting and Clinical Psychology, 64,* 1152–1168.

Hollon, S.D. (2001). Behavioral activation treatment for depression: A commentary. *Clinical Psychology: Science & Practice, 8,* 271–274.

Ilardi, S.S., & Craighead, W.E. (1994). The role of nonspecific factors in cognitive-behavior therapy for depression. *Clinical Psychology: Science & Practice, 1,* 138–156.

Ilardi, S.S., & Craighead, W.E. (1999). Rapid early response, cognitive modification, and nonspecific factors in cognitive behavior therapy for

depression: A reply to Tang and DeRubeis. *Clinical Psychology: Science & Practice, 6*, 295–299.
Ireland, S.J., McMahon, R.C., Malow, R.M., & Kouzekanani, K. (1994). Coping style as a predictor of relapse to cocaine abuse. In L. S. Harris (Ed.), *Problem of drug dependence, 1993: Proceedings of the 55th annual scientific meeting* (National Institute on Drug Abuse Monograph Series No. 141, p. 158). Washington, DC: U.S. Government Printing Office.
Jacobson, N. S., & Christensen, A. (1996). *Integrative couple therapy: Promoting acceptance and change.* New York, NY: Norton.
Jacobson, N.S., Christensen, A., Prince, S.E., Cordova, J., & Eldridge, K. (2000). Integrative behavioral couple therapy: An acceptance-based, promising new treatment for couple discord. *Journal of Consulting and Clinical Psychology, 68*, 351–355.
Jacobson, N.S., Dobson, K.S., Truax, P.A., Addis, M.E., Koerner, K., Gollan, J.K., Gortner, E., & Prince, S.E. (1996). A component analysis of cognitive—behavioral treatment for depression. *Journal of Consulting and Clinical Psychology, 64*, 295–304.
Jacobson, N.S., Martell, C.R., & Dimidjian, S. (2001). Behavioral activation treatment for depression: Returning to contextual roots. *Clinical Psychology: Science & Practice, 8*, 255–270.
Jenkins, J.J. (1974). Remember that old theory of memory? Well, forget it. *American Psychologist, 29*, 785–795.
Kabat-Zinn, J. (1994). *Wherever you go, there you are: Mindfulness meditation in everyday life.* New York: Hyperion.
Kohlenberg, R.J., & Tsai, M. (1991). *Functional analytic psychotherapy: Creating intense and curative therapeutic relationships.* New York: Plenum.
Leitenberg, H., Greenwald, E., & Cado, S. (1992). A retrospective study of long-term methods of coping with having been sexually abused during childhood. *Child Abuse and Neglect, 16*, 399–407.
Linehan, M.M. (1993). *Cognitive-behavioral treatment of borderline personality disorder.* New York: Guilford.
Linehan, M.M., Dimeff, L.A., Reynolds, S.K., Comtois, K.A., Welch, S.S., & Heagerty, P. (2002). Dialectical behavior therapy versus comprehensive validation therapy plus 12-step for the treatment of opioid dependent women meeting criteria for borderline personality disorder. *Drug and Alcohol Dependence, 67*, 13–26.
Mahoney, M.J. (1974). *Cognition and behavior modification.* Cambridge, MA: Ballinger.
Mahoney, M.J. (2002). Constructivism and positive psychology. In C.R. Snyder & S.J. Lopez (Eds.), *Handbook of positive psychology* (pp. 745–750). London: Oxford University Press.
Marlatt, G.A. (2002). Buddhist philosophy and the treatment of addictive behavior. *Cognitive & Behavioral Practice, 9*, 44–49.

Martell, C.R., Addis, M.E., & Jacobson, N.S. (2001). *Depression in context: Strategies for guided action*. New York: W.W. Norton.
McCullough, J.P., Jr. (2000). *Treatment for chronic depression: Cognitive Behavioral Analysis System of Psychotherapy (CBASP)*. New York: Guilford Press
McHugh, L., Barnes-Holmes, Y., & Barnes-Holmes, D. (2004). Perspective-taking as relational responding: A developmental profile. *The Psychological Record, 54*, 115–144.
Meichenbaum, D.H. (1977). *Cognitive-behavior modification: An integrative approach*. New York: Plenum.
Moore, J. (2000). Words are not things. *The Analysis of Verbal Behavior, 17*, 143–160.
Morgenstern, J., & Longabaugh, R. (2000). Cognitive-behavioral treatment for alcohol dependence: A review of evidence for its hypothesized mechanisms of action. *Addiction. 95*, 1475–1490.
Nurnberger, J.I., & Hingtgen, J.N. (1973). Is symptom substitution an important issue in behavior therapy? *Biological Psychiatry, 7*, 221–236.
Reese, H.W. (1968). *The perception of stimulus relations: Discrimination learning and transposition*. New York: Academic Press.
Roemer, L., & Orsillo, S.M. (2002). Expanding our conceptualization of and treatment for generalized anxiety disorder: Integrating mindfulness/acceptance-based approaches with existing cognitive-behavioral models. *Clinical Psychology: Science & Practice, 9*, 54–68.
Schraml, W., & Selg, H. (1966). Behavior therapy and psychoanalysis. *Psyche, 29*, 529–546.
Segal, Z.V., Teasdale, J.D., & Williams, J.M.G. (2004). Mindfulness-based cognitive therapy: Theoretical rationale and empirical status. In S.C. Hayes, V.M. Follette, & M. Linehan (Eds.), *Mindfulness and acceptance: Expanding the cognitive-behavioral tradition* (pp. 45–65). New York: Guilford Press.
Segal, Z.V., Williams, J.M.G., & Teasdale, J.D. (2002). *Mindfulness-based cognitive therapy for depression: A new approach to preventing relapse*. New York: Guilford Press.
Skinner, B.F. (1945). The operational analysis of psychological terms, *Psychological Review, 52*, 270–276.
Skinner, B.F. (1957). *Verbal behavior*. New York: Appleton-Century-Crofts.
Tang, T.Z., & DeRubeis, R.J. (1999). Reconsidering rapid early response in cognitive behavioral therapy for depression. *Clinical Psychology: Science & Practice, 6*, 283–288.
Teasdale, J.D., Moore, R.G., Hayhurst, H., Pope, M., Williams, S., & Segal, Z.V. (2002). Metacognitive awareness and prevention of relapse in depression: Empirical evidence. *Journal of Consulting and Clinical Psychology, 70*, 275–287

Titchener, E.B. (1916). *A text-book of psychology*. New York: MacMillan.
Wegner, D.M., Schneider, D.J., Carter, S.R., & White, T.L. (1987). Paradoxical effects of thought suppression. *Journal of Personality and Social Psychology, 53*, 5–13.
Wells, A. (1994). Attention and the control of worry. In G.C.L. Davey & F. Tallis (Eds.), *Worrying: Perspectives on theory, assessment and treatment* (pp. 91–114). Oxford, England: Wiley.
Wilson, G.T. (1999). Rapid response to cognitive behavior therapy. *Clinical Psychology: Science & Practice, 6*, 289–292.
Wilson, K.G., & Hayes, S.C. (1996). Resurgence of derived stimulus relations. *Journal of the Experimental Analysis of Behavior, 66*, 267–281.
Wolpe, J. (1980). Cognitive behavior: A reply to three commentaries. *American Psychologist, 35*, 112–114.
Wolpe, J., & Rachman, S. (1960). Psychoanalytic "evidence": A critique based on Freud's case of little Hans. *Journal of Nervous and Mental Disease, 131*, 135–148.
Yates, A.J. (1958). Symptoms and symptom substitution. *Psychological Review, 65*, 371–374.
Zettle, R.D., & Hayes, S.C. (1986). Dysfunctional control by client verbal behavior: The context of reason-giving. *The Analysis of Verbal Behavior, 4*, 30–38.
Zettle, R.D., & Hayes, S.C. (1987). Component and process analysis of cognitive therapy. *Psychological Reports, 64*, 939–953.

ARTICLE 12

BUDDHISM AND ACCEPTANCE AND COMMITMENT THERAPY

From Hayes, S.C. (2002). *Cognitive and Behavioral Practice, 9*, 58–66.

The purpose of this paper is to relate Acceptance and Commitment Therapy ("ACT," said as one word, not A-C-T) to a Buddhist view of suffering and its amelioration. ACT was developed over the last twenty years from the confluence of behavior analysis, the human potential movement, and experiential psychotherapies. That development work refined the contextualistic philosophy upon which the therapy is based (e.g., Hayes & Brownstein, 1986; Hayes, Hayes, Reese, & Sarbin, 1993), developed a contextual theory of language and cognition (Hayes & Hayes, 1992; see Hayes, Barnes-Holmes, & Roche, 2001, for a book-length treatment), and generated a working account of relevant forms of psychopathology (e.g., Hayes, Wilson, Gifford, Follette, & Strosahl, 1996), as well as developing ACT as a technological approach (Hayes, Strosahl, & Wilson, 1999). Each of these areas will be touched upon in the present paper.

The ACT work was always closely connected to issues of spirituality (indeed, the first article on this work, Hayes, 1984, was on spirituality) and the parallels between ACT and Buddhist thinking is quite clear in some areas. There was no conscious attempt to base ACT on Buddhism per se, however, and my own training in Buddhism was limited. It is for that very reason that these parallels may cast an interesting light on the current discussion. It is one thing to note how Buddhist philosophy and practices can be harnessed to the purposes of behavioral and cognitive therapy. Others in this issue are much better able to address that topic than I. It is another to note how the development of a behavioral clinical approach has ended up dealing with themes that have dominated Buddhist thought for thousands of years. Such an unexpected confluence strengthens the idea that both are engaging topics that are central to human suffering.

Buddhism is a pre-scientific system and the processes it points to are not scientific concepts when left in their own terms. Thus, while it may sounds sacrilegious, if Buddhist concepts and practice are pragmatically useful it will fall to science, not Buddhism itself, to provide a scientifically valid account of why and when these concepts and practice are useful. The concepts and data underlying ACT may be useful in that regard.

ACT AND BUDDHIST CONCEPTS AND PRACTICES

In considering how ACT connects with Buddhist philosophy and practices I will limit my comments to the following issues: the ubiquity of human suffering, the role of attachment, mindfulness, valued action, and issues of self.

The Ubiquity of Human Suffering and Its Source in Attachment

The Four Nobel Truths begin with the idea that human suffering is ubiquitous. In the first sermon delivered by the Buddha after enlightenment (the *Dhammacakka Sutta*, or *Wheel of Dhamma Discourse*), he said, "Birth is suffering, death is suffering, sorrow, and lamentation, pain, grief, and despair are suffering, association with the unloved or unpleasant condition is suffering, separation from the beloved or pleasant condition is suffering, not to get what one wants is suffering" (as cited in Dhamma, 1997, pp. 17–18). The list given is obviously meant to a partial one, and it is obviously ubiquitous. Kumar (2002, p. 41) says it this way: "suffering is an inalienable part of existence, inflamed by any attempt to contain it."

The source of suffering is attachment or craving. The Buddha said it this way:

> This is the Noble Truth of the origin of suffering: It is craving which produces rebirth, bound up with pleasure and greed. It finds delight in this and that, in other words, craving for sense pleasures, craving for existence or becoming and craving for nonexistence or self-annihilation. (*Dhammacakka Sutta*, as cited in Dhamma, 1997, p. 18)

Kumar (2002) states that according to Buddhism, "suffering is generated by the mental tendency towards essentialism" based on "experiencing thoughts, emotions, behaviors, or self as discrete and unchanging" (p. 41). Another modern Buddhist scholar says it this way: "The real cause of suffering is the reaction of the mind. . . . The reaction is repeated moment after moment, intensifying with each repetition, and developing into craving or aversion. This is what in his first sermon the Buddha called tanha, literally 'thirst': the mental habit of insatiable longing for what is not, which implies an equal and irremediable dissatisfaction with what is" (Hart, 1987, p. 38).

In ACT, suffering is also considered to be an inalienable part of human existence. A specific process is posited as the source of the ubiquity of human suffering: the bi-directionality of human language. Pain is unavoidable for all complex living creatures, due to the exigencies of living, but human beings enormously amplify their own pain through language. Because verbal relations are arbitrarily applicable, any situation can "remind" humans of past hurts of all kinds. In nonverbal organisms only formally similar situations will perform this function. Indeed, because events can be related verbally an infinite number of ways, even situations that have the opposite functions of previous pain can evoke this pain. For example, a person who has experienced a painful death in the family may recall that death when seeing a hearse, but may also recall it on a spectacular spring day, or when seeing a flower, or when seeing a child play with great innocence and joy. Just as a person playing a word association game (such as the television game show "Password") can say "hot" when given the clue "cold," so too a person seeing events that are joyful and full of life can be reminded of painful deaths. Similar effects occur clinically: relaxation-induced anxiety, suicide increases during holidays, depression produced by joyful events, or panic produced by noticing the current absence of anxiety.

The bi-directionality of human language also increases suffering by providing a language for self-knowledge, thus providing an invitation to experiential avoidance. Emotions provide a good example. In nonverbal organisms, events that produce aversive reactions are avoided. In verbal organisms, the reactions themselves become targets of avoidance. Human language allows loose sets of bodily sensations, contextual features, and behavioral predispositions to be verbally constructed into "emotional states." We may learn to call one loose set "depression" and another "anxiety." The aversiveness of these verbally organized events is in turn amplified by verbal evaluation (e.g., anxiety is "bad" and something that "people who are together don't have"), and by constructing verbal futures linked to these emotions that are aversive (e.g., "if I have a panic attack here I would make a complete fool of myself"). These verbal constructions considerably increase the aversive of the emotional event itself.

Human suffering is further increased by human language because of the verbal evaluation systems described earlier. Humans constantly compare the current situation to verbally constructed futures, which increases the dominance of verbal sources of behavioral control (e.g., "I would be able to live if only I could get free of this anxiety"). Furthermore, humans can verbally construct outcomes that have never been experienced. These processes can be painful even when they are literally accurate. For example, everyone "knows" they will die, and educated persons "know" that the universe will either expand infinitely and burn out or will be drawn back together into an infinitely dense pea. In either case, they know that all of human achievement is finite.

Finally, having enormously increased the human exposure to pain, human language suggests solution strategies that work just fine in the external world but are often poisonous when applied to conditioned private events. These include particularly ineffective thought and emotional suppression or avoidance strategies, which increase the frequency of events being avoided, further define the situation as an aversive one, and decrease attention to the current demands of the natural environment and thus decrease instrumental effectiveness.

The Buddhist concept of craving and attachment draws its meaning from lay language. The Buddha considered the source of attachment to be mutli-layered, and he saw his own enlightenment as a kind of pealing of that onion based on his direct experience. He discriminated many steps in the Wheel of Suffering, each based on the next: likes and dislikes, sensations, contact with events through the senses and the mind, the illusion of mind and matter, consciousness, reaction, and ignorance.

The theory underlying ACT provides a process that may help explain the Buddha's insights. For example, consider the idea that attachment comes from likes and dislikes, which in turn come from sensations. Consider the definition of attachment quoted earlier of "longing for what is not here." From an RFT (Relational Frame Theory) perspective, this longing has to do with verbal knowledge of certain events, verbal relations about the past, present and future, and with "frames of comparison" allowing events to be evaluated against one another (Hayes et al., 2001). To put this process in a simple form, consider the sentence "I want X." The word "want" comes from the Old Norse term *vant* meaning literally "missing." The simple verbal act of wanting something thus requires (1) noticing verbally (in the RFT sense of that term) what is present; (2) noticing verbally what is not present, thereby contacting this event through derived relations; and (3) comparing the two. If these verbal functions dominate, the person will become "attached" to a verbally constructed future in which what is not present is present. Scientifically, what is present all along is the process of verbal construction. Domination by a verbal future that minimizes contact with the present (attachment) comes from a verbal comparison of verbally known and evaluated experiences and sensations. The Buddha's insight remains, but a scientifically known process helps fill in the picture.

Acceptance and Mindfulness

For a Buddhist, "the first step toward emerging from such suffering is to accept the reality of it, not as a philosophical concept or an article of faith, but as a fact of existence" (Hart, 1987, p. 38). The second is seeing its source in craving and attachment. The Buddha described the cessation of suffering in his Third Noble Truth as "giving up, renouncing, relinquishing, detaching from craving" (*Dhammacakka Sutta*, as cited in Dhamma, 1997, pp. 18). Giving up a craving is not a deliberate change in the craving. It is a profound type of change at another level. It is a change in the agenda of craving itself, not immediately a change in the form or frequency of a craving. "Letting go of a craving is not rejecting it but allowing it to be itself" (Batchelor, 1997, p. 9).

ACT takes a similar view, but a specific set of psychological processes is posited as the source of transformation. Just as self struggle comes from cognitive fusion, acceptance is a natural result of cognitive defusion. Cognitive behavior therapists have decades of research showing that psychopathology tends to be associated with certain kinds of thoughts. Usually this leads to concrete efforts to change the content thoughts, but the contextualistic qualities of ACT opens a different solution: change the context in which thoughts reduce effective action. All verbal relations, like all behavior in a contextualistic system, are situated. Furthermore, the impact of thoughts, like all relations between psychological events, is also contextually situated. The problem with negative or irrational thoughts, for a contextual point of view, is not the form of the thought but its excessive literal quality. Changing the literal quality by literal intervention (e.g., through cognitive disputation) is fraught with difficulty because the process contradicts the outcome. Conversely, changing the context in which thoughts are taken literally changes its literal quality, even if the thought continues.

Consider the thought "I must be perfect." In normal cognitive behavioral approaches this thought would be targeted, disputed, tested, and changed through direct means. A wide variety of contextual alternatives exist, all of which are components of ACT. For example, the thought could be watched dispassionately, as one watches thoughts while meditating. The thought would be repeated out loud rapidly for a few hundred times, until only its sound remains. The thought could be given a size, shape, color, speed, form, texture, and so on, thus treating it as one treats observations of external objects. The person could thank their minds for such an interesting thought to watch. The person could examine the bodily sensations, emotions, memories, and behavioral predispositions that emerge in association with the thought, and could take time experiencing these events as aspects of an unfolding, changing process of living. The person could label their own cognitive processes (e.g., "Now I am having that thought that I must be perfect."). The person could think the thought very, very slowly, so that each word takes minutes to sound out.

These various procedures are designed to reduce the literality of the thought—weakening the tendency to treat a thought as if it is what it refers to—but without targeting the form of the thought itself. Instead, these methods alter the context in which thoughts of a given form are troublesome.

While these methods were not consciously drawn from Buddhist practices, they have clear parallels there. In Buddhist traditions, Right Mindfulness, part of the Eightfold Path, includes many practical methods of acceptance and defusion. For example, "If one experiences any feelings in the body, whether gross or subtle, one should be aware of them in the present moment . . . if there is liking or disliking, desire, anger, or doubt, these should be taken as meditation objects" (Dhamma, 1997, p. 39). Zazen, following the breath, and the like all seem designed to reduce the domination of the literal meaning of events. Similarly, Zen koans are presented as verbal puzzles but their essence is not that at all. What underlies koans is what is there when the puzzle is no more. As was pointed out by the Zen master Chung-feng, "it cannot be understood by logic; it cannot be transmitted in words; it cannot be explained in writing; it cannot be measured by reason" (as quoted in Kapleau, 1989, p. 77). The dual qualities of openness to experience in the moment, and reduction of the literal dimension when it interferes with that openness, seem characteristic of virtually all Buddhist practices of enlightenment.

The techniques of cognitive defusion reduce the behavioral impact thoughts, at least in ACT. Bond and Bunce (2000), for example, found that positive behavioral and psychological outcomes in ACT were produced by increases in the acceptance of previously avoided private events. Similarly, Bach (2000) found that severely mentally ill patients with hallucinations or delusions treated with ACT showed a 48% reduction in rehospitalization over four months compared to treatment as usual, and that this outcome was produced by a significantly greater decrease in the believability but not the frequency of psychotic symptoms.

Valued Action

Buddhism is sometimes called a religion, but it is at its essence one without dogma or belief (Batchelor, 1997). Even the Four Noble Truths are not so much beliefs as orientations to action: seeing suffering, letting go of attachment, and cultivating wholesome deeds. The bottom line in Buddhism is not belief, but living and doing. The Eightfold Path is intensely behavioral.

As a behavior therapy, ACT takes the same stance. Acceptance and cognitive defusion is not an end in itself—these are means to successful living. What requires acceptance and defusion will be determined by history and purpose. The goal is not to feel all one's feelings, but to feel all those that occur in the context of living a valued life. For example, if raising a family brings a person in contact with painful material, the task is to observe that pain and to raise one's family. This seems entirely compatible with Buddhism. S.N. Goenka, a modern Buddhist teacher, says it this way: "This is holy indifference: neither inaction nor reaction, but real, positive action with a balanced mind" (Hart, 1987, p. 54).

Self

Issues of self provide another relevant point of connection. Three kinds of self are considered in ACT: the conceptualized self, self as an ongoing process of knowing, and the transcendent self. ACT seeks to undermine the conceptualized self—that is, an attachment to a literal conception of who we are—on the same grounds that it seeks to undermine attachment to any specific thought: that such attachment is unnecessary and unhelpful. A phrase used in ACT that characterized its posture toward the conceptualized self is "Kill yourself every day."

Self as an ongoing process of knowing is a fluid, dynamic process of knowing one's own flow of experiences. Enhancing self-as-process is implicitly a goal of various forms of therapy, particularly in humanistic and experiential camps. This kind of self supports ongoing verbal (or "conscious") contact with events, such as feeling feelings, or sensing sensations. That, in turn, can be clinically useful in reducing excessive rule control and enhancing contact with the effects of actions.

This seems very much in line with Buddhist thinking. The self as discrete and unchanging is problematic. It is a form of attachment. The self as a process is what one fosters through mindfulness.

There may be a point of divergence in the third area: a transcendent self. ACT relies on this sense of self to support clients in exposing themselves to feared private events. The transcendent self, or self as context, is theorized to result from deictic verbal relations, such as here/now, I/you, or now/then (Barnes & Roche, 1997; Hayes, 1984), and may be defined as knowing from a locus or perspective. Another term might be "consciousness" per se, as distinct from consciousness *of* something. Some experimental support for this conception has recently been shown in very young children: teaching children deictic verbal relations results in a notable increase in perspective taking—including the ability to take another person's perspective into account (Barnes-Holmes & Barnes-Holmes, 2001).

Consciousness is not thing-like for the person being conscious. One can be conscious of the limits of everything except one's own consciousness. Self as context is present everywhere we have ever been, so far as we know, by definition. This means that one's own experience of a transcendence sense of self is that it has no limits: it is not a thing. Things are not things unless they have limits. In one important sense of the term, self thus is nothing (a word that was originally written "no thing."). So far, this sounds very much in line with Buddhist thought, and perhaps forms the psychological basis of the eastern concept of spirituality, and of God, as "everything/nothing."

There may be a point of divergence, however, because while the person is alive, a sense of perspective is not known by that person to change once it emerges (in the preschool period). Indeed, in ACT this sense of self as context is argued to be critical therapeutically because it means that there is at least one stable, unchangeable, immutable fact about oneself that has been experienced directly and is not just a belief or a hope or an idea. In the context of therapy, this kind of stability and constancy helps a client confront extreme psychological pain and trauma, knowing in some deep way that no matter what comes up, the client's deepest sense of being is not threatened.

I am not sure whether this concept diverges from Buddhist teachings. Speaking of an immutable self from the point of view of a knower seems to conflict with Kumar's statement that "self as . . . unchanging deviates from the natural process of change inherent in all existence" (2002, p. 41). Most Buddhists texts do not speaking of self as context, though an observing self seems to be the implicit background of all knowing. In all likelihood, it is the fear of reification of self-concepts that is at the basis of the relative silence on this issue since after all "everything that arises and passes away is not self" (Snelling, 1998, p. 31).

This topic is subtle and hard to talk about due to the reflective issues involved. It is a particularly difficult issue to frame within a written manuscript. Nevertheless, I will try.

By a "transcendent self" I do not mean the *belief* in such a self or the *belief* in immutability, but the *experience* of from-here-now and the essential continuity it provides for all verbally known events from the point of view of the knower. The claim is simply that all verbal knowing is known "from here now." That experience is an important sense of the word "I"—namely, that in one important sense "I" *am* from-here-now. This sense of perspective is immutable from the point of view of the knowing person. It is not immutable in the sense that it assumes a form that cannot or does not change. It is immutable in the sense that it has no form at all. It has no limits that can be known by the knower, by definition. In that sense it is not a thing, and only things can change. No thing cannot.

It is possible to imagine that a person can experience events from somewhere else, some when else. Some spiritual traditions make such claims (e.g., claims of time travel, multiple planes of existence, or of being in two places at once), but even then, the "somewhere else" would then be "here" and the "some when else" would then be "now" from the point of view of the person doing the experiencing. If that was not true I see no way that the experience could be "known" by the person, since knowing as a process *is* now.

CONCLUSION

Buddhist concepts and practices have proven their human value over the millennia, but the question for cognitive behavior therapists is "what additional value can be obtained by considering these practices from the point of view of cognitive behavioral psychology." Importing Buddhist practices into the technical armamentarium of cognitive behavior therapy is fine, but is not a very ambitious step. These concepts and practices are thousands of years old—they are already doing good in the culture. Buddhism includes traditions of faith, ritual, practice, and community that are designed to support mindfulness and wholesome actions, and short of becoming a religion, no system of psychotherapy will include all of these elements.

A real step forward in empirical clinical practice could come, however, by considering these concepts and practices in scientific terms. That might lead to something new. Scientific psychology is still an adolescent. We do not know how much can be done by approaching ancient sources of wisdom from the point of view of scientific knowing.

In each area we examined, there are clear parallels between ACT and Buddhism. These parallels suggest that there can be a common core of understanding about the nature of human suffering within the religious and scientific domains. They also suggest that issues of acceptance, cognitive fusion and defusion, self, and valued action may be worth exploring as one way that behavior therapists might consider Buddhist concepts and practices from the point of view of modern behavioral psychology.

REFERENCES

Bach, P. (2000). *The use of Acceptance and Commitment Therapy to prevent the rehospitalization of psychotic patients: A randomized controlled trial.* Unpublished doctoral dissertation, available from the University of Nevada, Reno.

Barnes, D., & Roche, B. (1997). A behavior-analytic approach to behavioral reflexivity. *The Psychological Record, 47*, 543–572.

Barnes-Holmes, Y., & Barnes-Holmes, D. (2001). Education. In S.C. Hayes, D. Barnes-Holmes, & B. Roche (Eds.), *Relational Frame Theory: A post-Skinnerian account of human language and cognition* (pp. 181–195). New York: Plenum Press.

Batchelor, S. (1997). *Buddhism without beliefs: A contemporary guide to awakening.* New York: Riverhead Books.

Bond, F.W., & Bunce, D. (2000). Mediators of change in emotion-focused and problem-focused worksite stress management interventions. *Journal of Occupational Health Psychology, 5*, 156–163.

Dhamma, R. (1997). *The first discourse of the Buddha.* Boston: Wisdom.

Hart, W. (1987). *The art of living: Vipassana meditation as taught by S.N. Goenka.* San Francisco: Harper.

Hayes, S.C. (1984). Making sense of spirituality. *Behaviorism, 12*, 99–110.

Hayes, S.C., Barnes-Holmes, D., & Roche, B. (2001) (Eds.), *Relational Frame Theory: A Post-Skinnerian account of human language and cognition.* New York: Academic Press.

Hayes, S.C., & Brownstein, A.J. (1986). Mentalism, behavior-behavior relations and a behavior analytic view of the purposes of science. *The Behavior Analyst, 9*, 175–190.

Hayes, S.C., & Hayes, L.J. (1992). Verbal relations and the evolution of behavior analysis. *American Psychologist, 47*, 1383–1395.

Hayes, S.C., Hayes, L.J., Reese, H.W., & Sarbin, T.R. (Eds.). (1993). *Varieties of scientific contextualism.* Reno, NV: Context Press.

Hayes, S.C., Strosahl, K., & Wilson, K.G. (1999). *Acceptance and Commitment Therapy: An experiential approach to behavior change* New York: Guilford.

Hayes, S.C., Wilson, K. G., Gifford, E.V., Follette, V.M., & Strosahl, K. (1996). Experiential avoidance and behavioral disorders: A functional dimensional approach to diagnosis and treatment. *Journal of Consulting and Clinical Psychology, 64*, 1152–1168.

Kapleau, P. (1989). *The three pillars of Zen: Teaching, practice, and enlightenment*. New York: Anchor.

Kumar, S. M. (2002). An introduction to Buddhism for the cognitive-behavioral therapist. *Cognitive and Behavioral Practice, 9,* 40–43.

Snelling, J. (1998). Buddhist traditions of meditation. In J. Smith (Ed.), *Breath sweeps the mind: A first guide to meditation practice*. New York: Riverhead Books.

ARTICLE 13

ACCEPTANCE AND COMMITMENT THERAPY

Model, Processes, and Outcomes

From Hayes, S. C., Luoma, J., Bond, F. W., Masuda, A., & Lillis, J. (2006). *Behaviour Research and Therapy, 44*, 1–25.

The behavior therapy movement began with two key commitments: (1) empirical validation of well-specified interventions for well-specified problems, and (2) an analysis of problems and treatment in terms of basic psychological processes. Franks and Wilson's well-known early definition of behavior therapy shows that dual commitment clearly, asserting that behavior therapy was based on "operationally defined learning theory and conformity to well established experimental paradigms" (1974, p. 7). Over the 40 years of development of behavior therapy, however, only the first of these two commitments has been firmly kept.

Behavior therapy can be divided into three generations: traditional behavior therapy, cognitive behavior therapy, and the more recent "third wave" of relatively contextualistic approaches (Hayes, 2004). In the first generation of behavior therapy it was possible to keep both commitments because traditional behavior therapists drew on a large set of basic principles drawn from the basic behavioral laboratories. Even in the earliest days, however, authors of behavioral principles texts realized that this base needed to expand beyond operant and classical principles to include those focused on human cognitive processes (Bandura, 1968). Clinicians realized that as well, and this realization was at the core of the second generation of traditional cognitive therapy and cognitive behavior therapy (e.g., A. T. Beck, Rush, Shaw, & Emery, 1979).

Unfortunately, none of the basic cognitive models available at the time were as easy to link to clinical interventions as were learning theory principles. The reasons for this are complex, but they go beyond merely the stage of development of basic analyses at the time. The dominant cognitive models largely were (and remain) either mechanistic information processing approaches or organismic cognitive developmental approaches. For philosophical reasons, both are more focused on the nature and evolution of cognitive acts and their impact on other forms of action than they are on the specific contextual events that regulate these psychological events and relate them one to the other. This feature tends to limit the direct applied relevance of the concepts that result (Hayes & Brownstein, 1986).

A principle like reinforcement is focused on the interface between action and its manipulable context, in effect, unifying both dependent and independent variables into a single unit. When the clinician applies such a concept to change behavior (we will we use the term "behavior" in this paper as a term for all forms of psychological activity, both public and private, including cognition), the independent variables specified by the term can be manipulated and the effect noted. This is not, in the main, true of the cognitive concepts generated by information processing and developmental cognitive perspectives. A concept like cognitive schemas (Piaget, 1964) is focused on the organization of a specific kind of dependent variable but it does not itself specify the contextual variables that alter these variables and their impact on other forms of activity.

Unable to rely fully on basic cognitive accounts, clinicians created their own cognitive models and interventions as Cognitive behavior therapy (CBT) was born. For example, specific patterns of irrational cognitions characteristic of specific forms of psychopathology were defined and measured (e.g., A. T. Beck, Brown, Steer, & Weissman, 1991). The terms used to describe these patterns sometimes were loosely linked to basic cognitive psychology (e.g., schemas), but often they were not (e.g., Ellis, 1962) and in either case the actual content of these cognitive processes (e.g., over-generalization; black and white thinking; emotional reasoning; irrational cognitions, and so on) were of little importance to basic cognitive science. These concepts were "cognitive" in the sense that they were about thinking as understood in commonsense terms— that is, they focused on "thoughts." In the area of treatment, the relationship to basic processes was even more tenuous: cognitive disputation, empirical tests, collaborative empiricism, and so on were not methods of fundamental importance to the basic cognitive science laboratory—they were commonsense practical procedures generated clinically.

The second generation of behavior therapy is now 30 years old, and the result of this approach can be examined. CBT techniques are fairly well validated, but the link between cognitive therapy and cognitive science continues to be weak. Looking at the array of popular techniques developed in cognitive-behavior therapy, none are known to have emerged directly from the basic cognitive science laboratories. The underlying model has also received mixed support. Component analysis studies have generally failed to find support for the importance of direct cognitive change strategies (Gortner, Gollan, Dobson, & Jacobson, 1998; Jacobson et al., 1996; Zettle & Hayes, 1987). Well-known cognitive therapists have been forced to conclude that in some important areas "there was no additive benefit to providing cognitive interventions in cognitive therapy" (Dobson & Khatri, 2000, p. 913). The response to traditional cognitive therapy often occurs before cognitive change techniques have been implemented (Ilardi & Craighead, 1994), a finding that has still not been adequately explained. Support for the hypothesized mediators of change in CBT is weak (e.g., Burns & Spangler, 2001; Morgenstern & Longabaugh, 2000), particularly in areas that are causal and explanatory rather than descriptive (R. Beck & Perkins, 2001; Bieling & Kuyken, 2003).

This overall picture presents an anomaly. On the one hand, most modern psychologists agree that traditional behavior therapy was not adequate and that better methods of dealing with thoughts and feelings were needed. On the other, the core conception of traditional cognitive and cognitive behavior therapy—that direct cognitive change is necessary for clinical improvement—is still not well supported.

There is some indication that the new "third wave" interventions in CBT may have found a way around this conundrum.

Examples of third wave CBT interventions include Acceptance and Commitment Therapy (ACT, said as a single word, not as initials; Hayes, Strosahl, & Wilson, 1999), Dialectical Behavior Therapy (DBT; Linehan, 1993), Mindfulness-Based Cognitive Therapy (MBCT; Segal, Williams, & Teasdale, 2001), and meta-cognitive approaches (Wells, 2000). Rather than focusing on changing psychological events directly through first-order change strategies, these interventions seek to change the function of those events and the individual's relationship to them through second-order change strategies such as mindfulness, acceptance, or cognitive defusion (Teasdale, 2003).

TAKING ANOTHER ROAD: ACT, RFT, AND CONTEXTUAL BEHAVIOR ANALYSIS

Third generation approaches are emerging both within more behavioral and more cognitive wings of CBT, which is part of what justifies thinking of these changes in generational terms. In the present article, however, it is our purpose to characterize ACT and its underlying theory, to summarize the data available, and to begin to contrast ACT with traditional CBT. While ACT is part of current developments it is also distinct in the particular development path it has followed. As the above definition emphasizes, third generation CBT in general is more principles focused. ACT is unique in its attempt to develop the basic laboratory itself so as to generate more adequate basic behavioral principles.

The second generation broke away from the first because operant and classical learning principles were not adequate to account for human cognition. ACT is the applied extension of a 20-year long attempt to create a modern form of behavior analysis more adequate to the challenge of human language and cognition—one that will allow behavioral and cognitive therapy to return more fully to its original vision. ACT is based on the development of a philosophy of science, and a theory of human language and cognition specifically designed with a functional unity of applied and basic psychology in mind.

ACT DESCRIPTION AND BACKGROUND

ACT Philosophical Roots

ACT is rooted in the pragmatic philosophy of functional contextualism (Biglan & Hayes, 1996; Hayes, 1993; Hayes & Brownstein, 1986; Hayes, Hayes, & Reese, 1988), a specific variety of contextualism that has as its goal the prediction and influence of events, with precision, scope, and depth (Hayes, 1993). Contextualism views psychological events as ongoing actions of the whole organism interacting in and with historically and situationally defined contexts. These actions are whole events that can only be broken up for pragmatic purposes, not ontologically. Because goals specify how to apply the pragmatic truth criterion of contextualism (Hayes, Hayes, Reese, & Sarbin, 1993), functional contextualism differs from other varieties that have other goals.

ACT reflects these philosophical connections in several ways. It emphasizes workability as a truth criterion, and chosen values as the necessary precursor to the assessment of workability because values specify the criteria for the application of workability. Its causal analyses are limited to events that are directly manipulable, and thus it has a consciously contextualistic focus. From such a perspective, thoughts and feelings do not cause other actions, except as regulated by context (Biglan & Hayes, 1996; Hayes & Brownstein, 1986). Therefore, it is possible to go beyond attempting to change thoughts or feelings so as to change overt behavior, to changing the context that causally links these psychological domains.

ACT Theoretical Roots

Nearly a decade and a half passed between the earliest randomized trials on Comprehensive Distancing (the early form of ACT, Zettle & Hayes, 1986) and those in the modern era (e.g., Bond & Bunce, 2000). In that interval, the basic theory of human language and cognition underlying ACT, Relational Frame Theory (RFT; Hayes, Barnes-Holmes, & Roche, 2001) was developed into a comprehensive basic experimental research program used to guide the development of ACT itself. RFT has become the most actively researched basic behavior analytic theory of human behavior, with over 70 empirical studies focused on its tenets. According to RFT, the core of human language and cognition is the learned ability to arbitrarily relate events, mutually and in combination, and to change the functions of events based on these relations. For example, very young children will know that a nickel is larger than a dime by physical size, but not until later will the child understand that a nickel is smaller than a dime by social attribution. RFT researchers have shown that such relations as knowing that one event is "larger" than another arbitrarily (a) can be trained as an operant (Barnes-Holmes, Barnes-Holmes, Smeets, Strand, & Friman, 2004; Berens & Hayes, 2007), and (b) will alter the impact of other behavioral processes (e.g., Dymond & Barnes, 1995).

RFT has proven itself successful so far in modeling higher cognition at the behavioral and neurobiological level (Hayes et al., 2001). For example, RFT researchers have successfully modeled analogy and metaphor (Stewart, Barnes-Holmes, & Roche, 2004), and shown that relational frames produce semantic priming (e.g., S. C. Hayes & Bissett, 1998). Neurobiological measures tell the same story. For example, complex RFT tasks generate pre-frontal activation (D. Barnes-Holmes, Regan, Y. Barnes-Holmes, Commins, Walsh, Stewart, Smeets, Whelan, Dymond, 2005) as would be expected based on cognitive research on relational reasoning (Waltz, Knowlton, Holyoak, Boone, Mishkin, de Menezes Santos, Thomas, & Miller, 1999).

ACT/RFT Theory of Psychopathology: Psychological Inflexibility

The literature on an ACT/RFT model of psychopathology is large and growing, so only a thumbnail account can be given here. An overall model is shown in Figure 13.1. Cognitive fusion refers to excessive or improper regulation of behavior by verbal processes, such as rules and derived relational networks (see Hayes, Strosahl, et al., 1999 for further details). In contexts that foster such fusion, people's behavior is guided more by their inflexible verbal networks than by the contingencies of reinforcement in their environment. As a result, they are less able to act in a way that is consistent with what the environment affords for behavior that would foster the person's values and goals.

Thus, from an ACT/RFT point of view, it is not the form, or content, of cognition that is most troublesome, but the contexts that lead this cognitive content to inappropriately, or excessively, regulate human action.

Cognitive fusion supports experiential avoidance, which is the attempt to alter the form, frequency, or situational sensitivity of private events even when doing so causes behavioral harm (Hayes, Wilson, Gifford, Follette, & Strosahl, 1996). Due to the temporal and comparative relations present in human language, so-called negative emotions are verbally predicted, evaluated, and avoided. Experiential avoidance is thus due to the natural effects of human language—a pattern that is then amplified by the culture into a general focus on "feeling good" and avoiding pain. Unfortunately, attempts to avoid

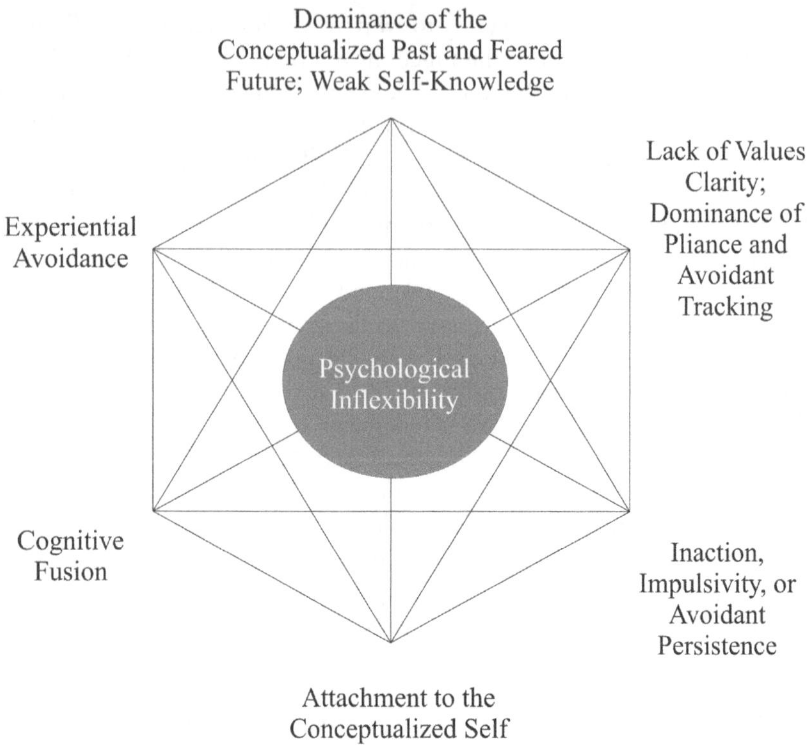

Figure 13.1 An ACT/RFT model of psychopathology

uncomfortable private events tend to increase their functional importance—both because they become more salient and because these control efforts are themselves verbally linked to conceptualized negative outcomes—and thus tend to narrow the range of behaviors that are possible since many behaviors might evoke these feared private events.

The social demand for reason giving and the practical utility of human symbolic behavior draws the person into attempts to understand and explain psychological events even when this is unnecessary or even unhelpful (Hayes, 2002). Contact with the present moment decreases as the person begins to live "in their head." The conceptualized past and future, and the conceptualized self, gain more regulatory power over behavior, further contributing to inflexibility. For example, it can become more important to be right about who is responsible for personal pain, than it is to live more effectively with the history one has; it can be more important to defend a verbal view of oneself (e.g., being a victim; never being angry; being broken; etc.) than to engage in more workable forms of behavior that do not fit that verbalization. Furthermore, since emotions and thoughts are commonly used as reasons for other actions, reason-giving tends to draw the person into even more focus on the world within as the proper source of behavioral regulation, further exacerbating avoidance patterns.

ACT is an approach to psychological intervention defined in terms of certain theoretical processes, not a specific technology. In theoretical and process terms we can define ACT as a psychological intervention based on modern behavioral psychology, including Relational Frame Theory, that applies mindfulness and acceptance processes, and commitment and behavior change processes, to the creation of psychological flexibility.

RESEARCH ON ACT

In this review we will focus primarily on the underlying ACT/RFT model, considering correlational studies, studies of the impact of ACT components, and processes of change studies. We will summarize quantitatively the strength of ACT outcomes as compared to alternative approaches, since processes of change hardly matter if change itself does not occur. We believe that this review references nearly all of the existent literature as of Spring 2005 that directly examines ACT or ACT components. Studies which might have relevance to ACT processes of change (e.g., mindfulness studies outside of ACT per se) but which did not directly attempt to examine ACT or ACT derived components were deliberately excluded from this review since it is hard to know where to draw the line in such a review.

Studies of the ACT Model: Correlational Studies

The correlational studies of the ACT model to date have generally not focused on a single ACT process. The largest body of evidence has used various forms of the Acceptance and Action Questionnaire (AAQ; Hayes, Strosahl, et al., 2004). The AAQ was constructed by having ACT therapists generate an item pool of the kinds of clinical processes targeted by ACT. The resulting instrument measures the degree to which an individual fuses with thoughts, avoids feelings, and is unable to act in the presence of difficult private events. Thus the AAQ, although it is often referred to generically as a measure of experiential avoidance, is actually a more general measure of several ACT processes particularly designed for use in population-based studies.

The individual studies reviewed here are listed in Table 13.1. In order to determine the extent to which the AAQ and psychological outcomes are related, these studies were integrated into a meta-analysis in which correlations established with a greater number of people were given more weight in calculating the average "effect size" using the Pearson product-moment correlation coefficient (*r*) as the metric (Durlak, 1995; Rosenthal & DiMatteo, 2001). The AAQ has been keyed both positively and negatively in the

Table 13.1 Studies included in the meta-analysis that examines the average relationship between the Acceptance and Action Questionnaire (AAQ) or its specific variants (e.g., the CPAQ) and measures of psychopathology and quality of life. Direction is set in all cases so that positive correlations mean *positive for the model* (better scores go with better scores) not literally positive.

Study	Psychopathology and Quality of Life Measures	N	*r*
Batten, Follette, & Aban (2001)	Brief Symptom Inventory (BSI)-Global Severity Index (GSI)	257	.57
	Trauma symptom inventory	257	.55
Begotka, Woods, & Wetterneck (2004)	Trichotillomania severity	436	.24
Bond & Bunce (2000)	Perceived physical health	97	.41
	Affective well-being at work	97	.38
	Job Induced Tension Scale	97	.37
	General Health Questionnaire	97	.32
	Beck Depression Inventory (BDI)	97	.66
Bond & Bunce (2003)	General Health Questionnaire	412	.44
	Performance	412	.34
	Negative affectivity	412	.36
	Job satisfaction	412	.26
Cook (2004)	Symptom Checklist-90-R	154	.56
Donaldson-Feilder & Bond (2004)	General Health Questionnaire	290	.36
	Physical health	290	.32
Dykstra & Follette (1998)	BSI GSI	41	.70
	BDI	41	.72
	Fear Questionnaire (FQ)-Social phobia	41	.55
	FQ-Blood injury phobia	41	.49
	FQ-Agoraphobia	41	.44
Forsyth et al. (2003)	Anxiety Sensitivity Index	94	.71
	Body Sensations Questionnaire—Fear of autonomic arousal	94	.24
	BDI	94	.57
Gold et al. (submitted)	PTSD severity (Posttraumatic Stress Diagnostic Scale)	145	.46
	BDI II	145	.65
	Lesbian Internalised Homophobia Scale	72	.37
	Nungesser Homosexuality Attitudes Inventory	73	.50
Gratz & Roemer (2004)	Deliberate Self-Harm Inventory	357	.20
Greco et al. (2005)	Posttraumatic Stress Checklist	66	.48
	Parenting Stress Inventory	66	.55

Study	Psychopathology and Quality of Life Measures	N	*r*
	Parental Stressor Scale	66	.30
Karekla et al. (2001)	Quality of Life Inventory	381	.40
Karekla et al. (2004)	State-Trait Anxiety Inventory	54	.16
	Subjective Units of Discomfort Scale	54	.17
Marx & Sloan (2005)	PTSD severity	185	.31
	Peritraumatic Dissociative Experiences Questionnaire	185	.24
McCracken (1998)	Depression about pain*	160	.58
	Anxiety about pain*	160	.66
McCracken & Eccleston (2003)	Daily functioning hampered by pain*	230	.47
McCracken et al. (2004)	Medication taken for pain*	235	.24
Pistorello (1998)	BDI-II	51	.60
Plumb et al. (2004)			
Study 1 and 2	BSI GSI	298	.55
	Post-traumatic Diagnostic Scale	298	.37
Study 3	Traumatic stress symptom severity	37	.32
	BDI	37	.50
Polusny et al. (2004)	BDI	304	.51
	SCL-90-R	304	.53
	Alcohol Dependence Scale	304	.15
Roemer, Salters, Raffa, & Orsillo (2005)			
Study 1	Generalized Anxiety Disorder Questionnaire-IV	240	.43
	Penn State Worry Questionnaire	240	.57
Study 2	Depression Anxiety Stress Scales (DASS)—Depression	19	.40
	DASS-Anxiety	19	.47
	DASS-Stress	19	.48
	Penn State Worry Questionnaire	19	.35
Sloan (2004)	Emotional reactivity	62	.24
Stewart et al. (2002)	Anxiety sensitivity index	205	.52
Strosahl et al. (1998)	BDI	419	.36
	Beck Anxiety Inventory	419	.58
Toarmino et al. (1997)	Symptom Checklist-90-R	202	.49
	Beck Anxiety Inventory	202	.35
	Fear of intimacy	202	.33
Tull, Gratz, Salters, & Roemer (2004)	PTSD Checklist	160	.49

(*Continued*)

Table 13.1 (*Continued*)

Study	Psychopathology and Quality of Life Measures	N	*r*
	BSI GSI	160	.55
	BSI Depression	160	.55
	BSI Anxiety	160	.53
	BSI Somatization	160	.49
Woods et al. (2006)	MGH-Hairpulling Scale	25	.59

Note. *r* = Pearson product-moment correlation coefficient representing the relationship between the AAQ and the listed measure. The AAQ has been keyed both positively and negatively in the literature, depending on whether people are speaking in terms of experiential avoidance (so that down is good) or acceptance and flexibility (so that up is good). Outcome measures also are sometimes similarly keyed in different directions. In this summary, the directions are set so that positive correlations comport with the ACT model (e.g., if higher flexibility or acceptance is associated with lower depression the correlation is set to be positive rather than negative. Thus better flexibility/acceptance predicts better depression scores, better quality of life scores, and so on).

literature, depending on whether people are speaking in terms of experiential avoidance (so that down is good) or acceptance and flexibility (so that up is good); outcome measures are that way as well and their labels are sometimes not enough to disambiguate the direction. This is made worse by the use of terms that amount to double negatives (e.g., lower levels of inflexibility) which, when they enter into negative correlations, become very confusing.

In the table and in this summary, directions were set so that in every case *positive correlations mean that the result is positive for the ACT model we have described.*

Twenty-seven studies, involving 5,616 participants, investigated the relationship between the AAQ and various quality of life outcomes, including psychopathology (e.g., depression, anxiety, post-traumatic stress, trichotillomania), stress, pain, job performance, and negative affectivity. Several separate meta-analyses were performed, examining the overall data set and sub-sets, defined by specific problems or common measures.

The overall dataset produced 67 correlations between these two sets of variables. The weighted effect size of these relations was 0.42 (95% confidence interval: 0.40–0.44) showing that this measure of ACT processes had a moderate relationship with psychological outcomes generally. Three studies (Bond & Bunce, 2000, 2003; Donaldson-Feilder & Bond, 2004) showed that higher levels of psychological flexibility (i.e., acceptance and values-based action processes) were associated with a lower probability of having a psychiatric disorder, as measured by the General Health Questionnaire (GHQ; Goldberg, 1978). The relationship between the AAQ and GHQ was of a medium size: 0.40 (95% confidence interval: 0.34–0.45). Finally, results indicated that the GHQ did not predict AAQ scores, one year later. Taken together, these longitudinal findings suggest that levels of psychological flexibility are impacting subsequent mental health, and not the reverse.

Eight studies (Bond & Bunce, 2000; Dykstra & Follette, 1998; Forsyth, Parker, & Finlay, 2003; Gold, Marx, & Heidt, submitted; Pistorello, 1998; Plumb, Orsillo, & Luterek, 2004; Polusny, Rosenthal, Aban, & Follette, 2004; Strosahl, Hayes, Bergan, & Romano, 1998) compared the AAQ with either edition one or two of the Beck Depression Inventory (BDI; Edition I: A. T. Beck, Ward, Mendelson, Mock, & Erbaugh, 1961; Edition II: A. T. Beck, Steer, & Brown, 1996), and when we aggregated these correlations in a meta-analysis, we obtained an effect size of 0.50 (95% confidence interval: 0.46–0.54). Similarly, three studies (Cook, 2004; Polusny et al., 2004; Toarmino, Pistorello, & Hayes, 1997) investigated the association between the AAQ and the Symptom Checklist-90-R (SCL-90-R; Derogatis, 1994), which assesses various indicators of mental ill-health. The aggregated correlations between these variables also produced a large effect: 0.53 (95% confidence interval: 0.47–0.58). Our final meta-analysis, based upon data from four studies (Karekla, Forsyth, & Kelly, 2004; Stewart, Zvolensky, & Eifert, 2002; Strosahl et al., 1998; Toarmino et al., 1997), showed that the AAQ was, overall, significantly related to three well-known measures of anxiety, to a fairly large extent: 0.49 (95% confidence interval: 0.44–0.54). (These three measures were: State-Trait Anxiety Inventory, Spielberger, Gorsuch, Lushene, Vagg, & Jacobs, 1983; Beck Anxiety Inventory, A. T. Beck & Steer, 1993; and the Anxiety Sensitivity Index, Reiss, Peterson, Gursky, & McNally, 1986.) Cohen (1977) notes that finding large effect sizes is unusual in the behavioral sciences.

The AAQ is not just correlated with important measures of psychopathology, however. Research indicates that it is also associated with behavioral effectiveness, in the form of job performance and chronic pain management. Specifically, Bond and Bunce (2003) found that psychological flexibility predicted, to a medium extent, the number of computer input errors that call center workers made over the following year. This measure of job performance did not predict AAQ scores one year later, thus suggesting that it is the AAQ that is determining job performance and not the reverse.

McCracken (1998) found that higher levels of psychological flexibility as measured by a pain-specific variant of the AAQ predicted, to a medium extent, less disability, better work status, and more daily "up-time," among people experiencing chronic pain and did so to a greater degree than actual pain ratings. McCracken, Vowles, and Eccleston (2004) also found that higher levels of this measure amongst chronic pain patients were related, to a medium extent, to fewer pain-related health care visits and fewer classes of prescribed analgesic medications.

Overall, the correlational evidence is fairly supportive of the ACT model as assessed by self-report instruments specifically designed by ACT therapists to measure the range of processes targeted by ACT. A wide range of concepts and measures seem to overlap with the ACT model, and researchers are beginning to explore connections with such concepts as distress tolerance (Brown, Lejuez, Kahler, & Strong, 2002), learned industriousness (Eisenberger, 1992), thought suppression (Wenzlaff & Wegner, 2000), delay discounting (Myerson & Green, 1995), strivings (Sheldon, Ryan, Deci, & Kasser, 2004), mindfulness (Baer, Smith, & Allen, 2004), metacognition (Wells, 2000), decentering (Watkins, Teasdale, & Williams, 2000), and the like.

Experimental Psychopathology and ACT Component Studies

Many current empirically supported treatment protocols are large packages composed of diverse elements. Unless each element is linked to a basic principle and integrated into a larger theory, it is difficult to know how to dismantle these packages because the natural lines of fracture are drawn more from common sense than theory. Small scale dismantling studies tend to be ignored, but large scale studies are expensive and are only conducted with the most widely adopted treatments, and then only many years after scores of clinicians have been trained in and have adopted the model. By that time, dismantling studies may have little immediate impact if they show that favored components are unhelpful, and their results may just be explained away.

ACT researchers are following a different course that is afforded by an inductive, technique-building, principles-focused treatment development approach: conduct micro-studies on each of the key ACT processes to see if each is psychologically active and works in a fashion that accords with the theory. The early published studies have focused largely on acceptance, defusion, and values, but targeted studies are underway or completed on all of the other elements.

The impact of a cognitive defusion technique on negative self-referential thoughts has been examined (Masuda, Hayes, Sackett, & Twohig, 2004) using the Milk-Milk Exercise (Hayes, Strosahl, et al., 1999, pp. 154–155) in which a thought is rapidly repeated aloud until it loses all meaning. In this study the impact of word repetition on the discomfort and believability of self-relevant negative thoughts was investigated as compared to a distraction task (reading about Japan) or to a thought control task involving abdominal breathing training and instructions to shift attention to more pleasant thoughts. In a series of alternating treatments designs ($N = 8$) the cognitive defusion technique was found to reduce both discomfort and believability more so than the comparison approaches. Group control studies suggested that the effect was not due to demand characteristics.

Another study examined the impact of a 90-minute ACT protocol focused on acceptance and defusion on pain tolerance utilizing a cold pressor task (Hayes, Bissett, et al., 1999) as compared to a traditional CBT pain-management condition (training in applying the gate theory of pain) and to an attention placebo condition consisting of discussion of a behavioral approach to pain. The acceptance and defusion protocol addressed the paradoxical effects of emotional control, an attempt to undermine feelings and thoughts as reasons for actions, the workability of emotional control, and defusion of thoughts and feelings from the self. No differences were found in the intensity of pain at post intervention, but participants in the acceptance and defusion condition were able to keep their hand in the cold water significantly longer than the other conditions at post-test. Participants in the acceptance condition also showed lower levels of belief in pain-oriented reasons for action than the other groups.

This cold pressor study was extended by a subsequent study that attempted to determine whether the acceptance and defusion exercises were important or whether it was the rationale itself that made a difference even if more traditional CBT exercises were used (Takahashi, Muto, Tada, & Sugiyama, 2002). An acceptance and defusion rationale was used in each of two active treatment conditions, but one also used the Leaves on the Stream mindfulness exercise (Hayes, Strosahl, et al., 1999, pp. 158–161) and the Physicalizing defusion exercise (Hayes, Strosahl, et al., 1999; pp. 170–171), both of which are designed to undermine the literal impact of difficult private events. The other condition used exercises designed to control pain. Participants (*N* = 28) were randomly assigned to these conditions or to an attention-placebo control. Participants in the acceptance-based condition that included acceptance and defusion exercises but not those in the other two conditions showed positive changes in pain tolerance suggesting that acceptance and defusion exercises were necessary to produce the effect.

Another pain tolerance study (Gutierrez, Luciano, & Fink, 2004) examined the impact of a 20-minute long ACT acceptance, defusion and values intervention using the Card Exercise (Hayes, Strosahl, et al., 1999, p. 162) and Swamp Metaphor (Hayes, Strosahl, et al., 1999, pp. 247–248) as compared to a cognitive and emotional change intervention. Pain levels were systematically raised throughout the study, and the randomly assigned participants (*N* = 40) were paid to persist as long as they could in each condition. ACT participants showed significantly higher tolerance of pain, and significantly greater willingness to persist even after they said the pain levels had reached very high levels.

The effects of ACT acceptance techniques on tolerance of exposure to carbon dioxide (CO2)-enriched air (Felder, Zvolensky, Eifert, & Spira, 2003) was examined with 48 college students who scored high or low on the AAQ. Participants were randomly assigned either to a computerized acceptance-based condition that taught participants to observe and let go of a struggle with feelings during the exposure to CO2-enriched air or a similar condition that instructed participants to suppress their feelings during the CO2 inhalation. In the suppression condition but not the acceptance condition, individuals with high experiential avoidance reported greater levels of anxiety relative to those with low experiential avoidance. Participants with high experiential avoidance in comparison to those with low experiential avoidance reported greater levels of anxiety and affective distress, but not physiological arousal, in the exposure to the CO2.

In a similar study 60 highly anxious females were randomly assigned to a 10-minute acceptance condition (i.e., accepting and mindfully observing feelings; use of a physical version of the Chinese Finger Trap metaphor; Hayes et al., 1999, pp. 104–105), an emotional-control condition (controlling psychological experiences by abdominal breathing), or a no-instruction condition (Eifert & Heffner, 2003). Compared to the control and non-instruction participants, those in the acceptance condition were less avoidant behaviorally and also reported less intense fear and cognitive symptoms. Participants in the acceptance group also reported greater willingness to return to the CO_2-inhalation study than those in comparison groups.

The impact of a brief acceptance method on the exposure to CO_2-enriched air has also been examined using individuals with panic disorder (Levitt, Brown, Orsillo, & Barlow, 2004). Sixty patients were randomly assigned one of three 10-minute audiotaped interventions: acceptance, suppression and distraction. The acceptance-based condition focused on the futile and paradoxical nature of experiential control, and the importance of focusing on behavior change in alignment with own values. The acceptance group showed significantly greater levels of willingness to participate in the biological challenge again and lower level of anxiety than those is comparison groups.

Summary of Component Results. The existing evidence is supportive of acceptance and defusion procedures and their impact comports with the ACT model. Values-based procedures are just beginning to be tested. As of yet other aspects of the ACT model have not been specifically tested in ACT component studies.

Processes of Change

A second method for studying processes of change is to attempt to measure their fluctuation during treatment outcome studies and to examine their relation to treatment condition and outcome. This section reviews several ACT intervention studies that have examined processes of change in ACT, generally focusing either on the AAQ, similar instruments that target a specific domain of experience (e.g., the CPAQ), or on brief rating scales targeting acceptance or defusion.

Quantitative Characterization of the Relative Strength of ACT Outcomes. Understanding processes of change is of no importance unless there is change to begin with. The between condition effect sizes for the ACT outcome literature (including all studies with a direct applied purpose and excluding non-clinical analogue studies) are shown in Table 13.2. Summarizing across this early extant literature on the primary outcome variable targetted, and weighting average effect sizes by the number of cases that produced the effect, ACT has produced between condition effect sizes (using Cohen's *d*) of .74 at post (N = 629) and 1.17 at follow-up (N = 519). Average effect sizes for comparisons between ACT and active, well-specified treatments that were deliberately provided to affect the targetted problem were .58 at post (N = 381) and 1.41 at follow-up (N = 343); for comparisons with wait list, treatment as usual, or placebo treatments the effect sizes were .99 at post (N = 248) and .72 at follow-up (N = 176). Across the dataset, follow-ups, when they occurred, ranged from 8 to 52 weeks with a weighted average of 19.6 weeks.

As these results apply to the ACT model per se it seems worth noting the few studies that have directly compared ACT and traditional CT or CBT (Block, 2002; Branstetter, Wilson, Hildebrandt, & Mutch, 2004; Zettle & Hayes, 1986; Zettle & Rains, 1989). Between condition effect sizes were .73 at post (range: .49 to 1.23) and .83 (range: .79 to .92) at follow-up in favor of the ACT approach on primary outcome measures. The total number of participants in these four studies is still very small however (N = 96 and 39 at post and follow-up, respectively). On primary processes of change measures specified from an ACT model, the between condition effect sizes in these studies were 3.32 at post (N = 96) and .74 at follow-up (N = 39).

These early data provide a possible indication that ACT and traditional CBT impact change processes differently and that ACT may contribute to clinical outcome. Furthermore, although some of these trials have been conducted by A. T. Beck-trained clinicians (Zettle & Hayes, 1986; Zettle & Rains, 1987), these studies are also being conducted by researchers interested in ACT, so bias is possible. Larger scale studies and broader effectiveness trials that those current conducted (Strosahl et al., 1998) will be needed to tease out these issues.

Mediational Studies. This section examines the formal mediational analysis results. Zettle and Hayes (1986) compared an early version of ACT to two variants of cognitive therapy for depressed clients (N = 18) delivered in a 12-week individual protocol. Since the two variants were virtually identical in outcomes, the two groups were combined for the main comparison. ACT was superior to CT on depression outcomes at post and at a 2-month follow-up. ACT and CT did not differ significantly on the Automatic Thoughts Questionnaire (Hollon & Kendall, 1980), which measures depressogenic thought frequency but did if clients were asked to rate the believability of these same thoughts were they to occur (the "ATQ-B")—a measure of cognitive defusion.

At the mid-point of treatment (week six), ACT and CT did not differ significantly in their BDI scores (F (1, 16) = 2.81, p = .12, ACT M = 12.05, SD = 7.15, CT M = 22.86, SD = 13.48, d = 1.00), but they did differ significantly in their ATQ-B scores (F (1, 16) = 8.61, p = .01, ACT M = 49.0, SD = 10.95, CT M = 92.25, SD = 34.77, d =1.68). The mid-point ATQ-B scores were then assessed for their role as a mediator of outcomes on the

Table 13.2 ACT Outcome Literature

ACT as Compared to Structured Interventions Designed to Impact the Problem				**d (N)**	**d (N)**	**F-up**
Study	**Problem focus**	**Primary Measure**	**Comparison condition**	**Post**	**F-up**	**Weeks**
Block (2002)	Social phobia	Speaking time	Group CBT	0.49 (26)		
Bond & Bunce (2000)	Work Stress	GHQ	Workplace Innovation	0.8 (60)	0.72 (60)	12
Branstetter et al. (2004)	End stage Cancer	Distress	CBT	0.9 (31)		
Gifford et al. (2004)	Smoking	Not smoking	Nicotine Patch	0.06 (62)	0.57 (55)	52
Gregg, 2004	Type II Diabetes	Self-management	Diabetes Education		3.63* (78)	8
Hayes, Bissett, et al. (2004)	Stigma and Burnout	Maslach Burnout Inventory	Biological Education	0.74 (59)	0.61 (53)	12
Hayes, Bissett, et al. (2004)	Stigma and Burnout	Maslach Burnout Inventory	Multicultural Training	0.26 (64)	0.57 (58)	12
Hayes, Wilson, et al. (2004)	Polysubstance abuse	Objective UA Opiates	Methadone Maintenance	0.41 (51)	0.95 (43)	24
Levitt et al. (2004)	Agoraphobia	Willingness to do exposure	Suppression	0.67 (40)		
Zettle & Hayes (1986)	Depression	BDI	Cognitive Therapy	1.23 (18)	0.92 (18)	12
Zettle & Rains (1989)	Depression	BDI	Cognitive Therapy	0.53 (21)	0.75 (21)	8
Zettle (2003)	Math anxiety	MARS (Math anxiety)	Systematic Desensitization	–0.55 (24)	-0.12 (18)	
Weighted Average Effect Size for ACT vs. Structured Interventions:				.58 (381)	1.41 (343)	

ACT as Compared to Wait List, Placebo, or General Treatment as Usual				d (N)	d (N)	F-up
Study	**Problem focus**	**Primary Measure**	**Comparison condition**	**Post**	**F-up**	**Weeks**
Bach & Hayes (2002)	Psychosis	Rehospitalization	Treatment as Usual		0.45 (70)	16
Block (2002)	Social phobia	Speaking time	Control	0.52 (26)		
Bond & Bunce (2000)	Work Stress	GHQ	Wait list control	0.72 (60)	0.7 (60)	12
Dahl, Wilson, & Nilsson (2004)	Chronic pain	Sick leave (days)	Treatment as Usual	1.17 (19)	1 (19)	24
Gaudiano & Herbert (2006b)	Psychosis	Clinically large BPRS improvement	Enhanced TAU	1.11 (29)**		
Gratz & Gunderson (2006)	BPD	Self harm	Treatment as Usual	0.98 (22)		
Levitt et al. (2004)	Agoraphobia	Willingness to do exposure	Distraction	0.81 (40)		
Lundgren (2004); Lundgren & Dahl (2005)	Epilepsy	Seizure frequency X duration	Attention placebo	1.43 (27)	1.23 (27)	52
Woods et al. (2006)	Trichotillomania	MGH-HS (Hair pulling)	Wait list	1.72 (25)		12
Weighted Average Effect Size for ACT vs. Wait List, Placebo, or General TAU:				.99 (248)	.72 (176)	
Total Weighted Average Effect Size for ACT vs. All Other Conditions:				.74 (629)	1.17 (519)	

* based on difference scores since pre-scores were different between groups

** the effect size on the raw BPRS scores was .52

post-score BDI, which did reveal a significant difference in outcome (F (1, 16) = 4.61, $p < .05$, ACT M = 4.83, SD = 5.19, CT M = 19.42, SD = 16.01, d = 1.23). All four steps of the mediational model suggested by MacKinnon (2003) were satisfied: (1) a Spearman above .2 between treatment condition and outcome (actual result = .50, p = .033); (2) a significant Spearman between treatment condition and the mediator (actual result = .60, p = .008); (3) a significant Spearman between the mediator and the outcome (actual result = .85, $p < .001$); and 4) a significant regression between the mediator and the outcome after condition is included in the model (*Beta* = .97, t = 7.35, $p < .001$). A similar analysis was then conducted on the follow-up Hamilton scores (HRS-D F-up). The results were similar. Treatment condition correlated significantly with HRS-D F-up (.57, p = .013), and week 6 ATQ-B (reported above), which in turn correlated with HRS-D F-up (.88, $p < .001$). The regression between the week 6 ATQ-B and HRS-F F-up scores was significant after condition was included in the model (*Beta* = .87, t = 5.35, $p < .001$). Thus greater changes in the believability of depressogenic thoughts mediated the superior outcomes achieved by ACT in this study.

A worksite stress reduction study randomly assigned 90 participants to receive 9 hours of ACT, 9 hours of a behavioral program designed to teach workers to remove stressors in the workplace, or to be waitlisted (Bond & Bunce, 2000). At a 3-month follow-up, ACT was significantly better than the other groups on the GHQ, while both active treatment groups were improved in initiating innovative working practices. The study reported that the AAQ mediated ACT versus wait list group GHQ outcomes and workplace innovation at follow-up using follow-up AAQ scores. In a re-analysis done for the present paper all four steps of MacKinnon's (2003) mediation steps were met using post-AAQ scores and follow-up outcome scores. The relation of treatment to the follow-up outcomes and treatment to the post AAQ is reported in the original article. The reanalysis showed a significant Spearman between the mediator and the outcome (GHQ: r = .55, $p < .001$; innovation: r = .35, p = .005); and a significant regression between the mediator and the outcome after condition is included in the model (GHQ: *Beta* = .53, t = 4.76, $p < .001$; Innovation: *Beta* = .41, t = 3.12 p = .007) thus satisfying all four steps in this type of mediational test. Changes in the AAQ did not mediate the significant effects of the behavior therapy program on initiating innovation, showing that this mediational effect was specific to ACT.

Type II diabetes requires emotionally challenging and consistent patterns of self-management, which is traditionally encouraged by detailed diabetes education. ACT plus diabetes education was compared to diabetes education alone in a trial that randomized 81 newly diagnosed poor and primarily minority diabetics to a 1-day workshop for either approach (Gregg, 2004). At 3-month follow-up, ACT outperformed the control condition on changes in self-management behaviors and blood glucose (HbA1C) among those participants with a high HbA1C value. A version of the AAQ that targeted diabetes-related content, the Acceptance and Action Diabetes Questionnaire (AADQ; Gregg, 2004) was used as the mediator. Mediational analyses were conducted using as the steps specified by MacKinnon (2003) and showed that diabetes-related acceptance and action was a mediator of self-management behaviors but not change in HbA1c scores. Self-management changes also did not mediate blood glucose.

A study comparing ACT to Nicotine Replacement Therapy (NRT) for smoking cessation (Gifford et al., 2004) randomized 67 smokers either to NRT or seven individual and seven group sessions of ACT. ACT had significantly better outcomes at one-year follow-up (35% vs. 15%). The Avoidance and Inflexibility Scale (AIS), developed for this study, examined smokers endorsement of the need to avoid smoking related thoughts and feelings in order to maintain abstinence. Mediational analyses showed that the AIS passed all of Baron and Kenny's (1986) steps for mediation.

A study compared ACT, multicultural training (MT), and education about the biology of addiction in terms of their effectiveness in reducing stigma toward clients and burnout among substance abuse counselors (Hayes, Bissett, et al., 2004). Ninety-six counselors were randomized to a day-long, 6-hour workshop in each condition. At follow-up, ACT, but not MT, was superior to the education condition on the frequency of stigmatizing attitudes; ACT was also significantly better than MT on burnout. The Stigmatizing Attitudes Believability Scale (SAB), a measure designed for this study, measured defusion from stigmatizing thoughts towards substance abusing clients, as distinct from their form, frequency, or situational sensitivity. Mediational analyses were conducted using the steps specified by MacKinnon (2003) and found that the SAB mediated both counselor burnout and stigmatizing attitudes in the ACT group but not the MT group as compared to education.

Gaudiano and Herbert (2006a, 2006b) replicated Bach and Hayes (2002) with a better controlled but smaller study focused on coping with hallucinations or delusions among inpatients hospitalized with a primary psychotic disorder or mood disorder with psychotic features (N = 29). In this study, enhanced treatment as usual (ETAU—enhanced so as to control for therapist contact) was compared to three sessions (on average) of ACT plus TAU. At discharge from the hospital, participants in the ACT condition showed significantly greater improvement in affective symptoms, overall improvement, social impairment, and distress associated with hallucinations. Fifty percent of the ACT group showed a two standard deviation improvement on the total score of the BPRS as compared to 7% in the ETAU group, a significant difference. Although four month rehospitalization rates were 38% lower in the ACT group, this difference did not reach statistical significance. A rating of the believability of delusions or hallucinations was used as the process measure in this study. Only the ACT condition was found to result in lower believability ratings at post-intervention. Mediational analyses conducted as specified by Baron and Kenny (1986) found that believability of hallucinations mediated the relationship between frequency of hallucinations and associated distress at post-intervention.

A study of the distress produced by end-stage cancer (Branstetter, Wilson, Hildebrant, & Mutch, 2004) randomly assigned cancer patients either to 12 sessions of ACT or traditional CBT focused on relaxation and cognitive restructuring. Treatment was delivered during chemotherapy or other medical visits. Patients were dying at too high a rate for meaningful follow-up. By session 12 ACT produced significantly greater reductions in distress, anxiety, and depression than traditional CBT. A mediation analysis using Sobel's method (1982) found that the Mental Disengagement subscale of the COPE (Carver, Scheier, & Wientraub, 1989), which includes items like "I go to movies or watch TV, to think about it less," mediated the reduction in distress. Only the ACT condition reduced mental disengagement: this measure actually increased in the CBT condition.

A small randomized trial ($N = 27$) done with poor institutionalized South African epileptics who had seizures that were not well controlled by medication (Lundgren, 2004; Lundgren & Dahl, 2005) tested the impact of an ACT intervention to reduce seizures and stress as compared to an attention placebo control condition. Large and significant reductions in a seizure index (frequency times the duration of seizures) were found at post and at a 6-month and 1-year follow-up (between condition $d = 1.44, 1.27$, and 1.24, respectively). Improvement in overall quality of life using the World Health Organization Quality of Life scale was not found at post, began to improve at 6-month follow-up, and showed large and significant changes by the 1-year follow-up (between condition $d = .28, .51$, and 1.59 across post, 6-month follow-up, and 1-year follow-up, respectively). ACT produced very large improvements at post and both follow-ups (between condition $d = 3.23, 3.76$, and 2.82, respectively) in a specific epilepsy-focused version of the AAQ. Post scores on the epilepsy focused AAQ fully mediated 1-year follow-up outcomes for both seizures and quality of life, using the steps recommended by Baron and Kenny (1986). The quality of life result is particularly important since the post AAQ changes occurred before significant quality of life changes were observed.

Other Studies. Several others studies have reported changes in process variables. Bach and Hayes (2002) compared four 45-minute sessions of ACT to treatment as usual (TAU) in a randomized trial helping inpatients cope with positive psychotic symptoms ($n = 80$). Patients in the ACT condition had half the rate of rehospitalization over a 4-month follow-up period. ACT was found to result in significantly lower believability ratings of psychotic symptoms (e.g., rating whether the delusions/hallucinations were literally true) at the 4-month follow-up. Overall symptom reduction was less in the ACT group than the TAU group. An interesting pattern was found only in the ACT group, where rehospitalization rates for patients who admitted psychotic symptoms were only one-fourth of that than for those who did not. This pattern was interpreted as an indication that ACT undermined denial and thus symptom admission was an indication of greater acceptance in the ACT group. No one in the ACT condition was rehospitalized who both admitted symptoms and viewed them as less believable.

Zettle (2003) compared ACT and systematic desensitization for math anxiety (*N* = 24) and found equivalent reductions in math-related anxiety, but greater change in trait anxiety with systematic desensitization. This is the only study in the literature so far in which effect sizes between ACT and another condition were negative (see Table 13.2). It may be that this was in part due to the relatively healthy population being treated. The study showed some support for this idea since significantly greater reductions in math anxiety were found for ACT participants who had higher initial levels of experiential avoidance as measured by the AAQ, but this was not true with desensitization.

McCracken, Vowles, & Eccleston (2005) reported the effects of a 3- to 4-week residential/inpatient treatment for chronic pain conditions based on ACT (*n* = 108). Significant improvements in emotional, social, and physical functioning as well as lower health care utilization was found following treatment. The CPAQ improved significantly with acceptance-based treatment, and changes in this measure were significantly associated with change in five of nine outcome variables examined, including depression, pain-related anxiety, physical and psychosocial disability, and the ability to stand and sit rapidly in a timed test.

ACT plus habit reversal was compared to a wait list control for the treatment of trichotillomania in a small (*N* = 25) randomized trial reported by Woods, Wetterneck, and Flessner, (2006). Wait list subjects then received the combination treatment. Self-reported and objectively verified hair pulling decreased significantly with treatment, was maintained at a 3-month follow-up and correlated .57 with changes in the AAQ.

Block (2002) conducted a small randomized trial (*N* = 39) comparing ACT, cognitive-behavioral group therapy (CBGT), and a waitlist control. Both active groups were superior to the wait list on most measures. Participants in the ACT condition stayed longer in an arranged public speaking situation than those in the other groups post-treatment, and showed larger reductions in distress during the speech (Cohen's *d* within-condition effect-sizes for distress of 1.37 for ACT, versus .67 for CBGT and –.02 for the wait list). The primary process variable, rated willingness to experience anxiety during exposure, also increased more pre to post for ACT (Cohen's *d* within-condition pre-post effect-sizes for willingness of 1.03, .38, and-.42 for the ACT, CBGT, and wait list conditions, respectively). The pre-differences among groups approached significance, however (ACT participants were generally more severe), so regression to the mean is a possible explanation for these results. Examining only the post-scores on the primary outcome variable (length of time in a public speaking situation), however, the effect sizes were *d* = .49 and .52 for ACT as compared to CBGT and the control, respectively, which is particularly supportive given the trends at pre-assessment.

Another study examined the treatment of polysubstance abusing individuals being maintained on methadone (Bissett, 2001; Hayes, Wilson, et al., 2004). Participants (*N* = 124) were randomly assigned to either ACT, Intensive Twelve-Step Facilitation, or to methadone maintenance only. In the two active treatments, participants received 32 individual and 16 group sessions. At the 6-month follow-up participants in the ACT condition demonstrated a greater decrease in objectively measured (through monitored urinalysis) total drug use than did methadone maintenance alone; and greater decreases in self-reported total drug use than both of the other conditions.

In a small (*N* = 22) randomized trial on self-harm and emotional dysregulation among Borderline Personality Disordered patients, Gratz and Gunderson (2006) compared treatment as usual to a short group consisting of ACT and DBT. About two-thirds of the sessions appeared to have been drawn from ACT. Large between group effects were found at post on measure of self harm (*d* = .98) and emotional dysregulation (*d* = 1.84). Unusually large effects were found on the AAQ (*d* = 3.08) but correlations between process and outcome were not reported.

The impact of an eight session ACT protocol on OCD (Obsessive Compulsive Disorder) has been assessed in a multiple baseline (*N* = 4) by Twohig, Hayes, and Masuda (2006). Large reductions were found in the frequency of obsession and the distress they produced at post (*d* = 2.86 and 3.08, respectively) and at a 3-month follow-up (*d* = 3.24 and 4.63, respectively). Relatively large changes occurred in ACT-relevant processes, including the AAQ (post *d* = .92; follow-up = 2.86).

DISCUSSION

ACT is part of a larger movement in the behavioral and cognitive therapies toward the use of mindfulness and acceptance (Hayes, Follette, & Linehan, 2004). The long delay between the earliest studies on ACT (Zettle & Hayes, 1986) and its publication as a book-length model and manual (Hayes, Strosahl, & Wilson, 1999) allowed time for the development of a theoretical account for these processes based on a comprehensive experimental program in human language and cognition (Hayes et al., 2001).

Reviewing the entire body of evidence suggests that the ACT model seems so far to be working across an unusually broad range of problems, and across a range of severity from psychosis to interventions for ordinary people (e.g., worksite stress interventions). Effect sizes generally seem somewhat larger with more severe problems, and larger at follow-up than immediately post intervention, although the literature is too young to say for sure. The studies conducted so far cover different ethnic groups, classes, and geographic regions, from poor institutionalized native South Africans to behavioral health professionals in the United States, with no indication that outcomes or processes covary in accord with such factors. It appears that the processes targeted by ACT are at least in part responsible for the outcomes ACT produces. It also appears that the processes being targeted seem to work in broadly similar ways across the tested range of settings and populations.

This research program is still very young, despite its nominal chronological age, in part because so much time has been devoted to developing the basic foundation of the approach. As a result, many aspects of the model have received little attention as yet. While beyond the scope of this article, RFT is also developing rapidly and is beginning to model applied processes from the bottom up. In the ideal world these two research programs will merge. For example, if the overall theory is valid it should be possible to create cognitive fusion and then use a variety of techniques to dismantle it—all in the experimental laboratory. These procedures could then be able to be applied and tested directly in the clinic.

In the earliest days of behavior therapy translational research of that kind was both possible and common, but it is rarely seen today. The ACT/RFT program is focused on producing a new contextual behavioral psychology that is more adequate to the challenge of the human condition that is coherent from the most basic study to the most applied. Whether that "back to the future" vision will come to pass only tomorrow will tell. This article shows, however, that there is preliminary empirical support for the ACT model and the processes and components it specifies.

REFERENCES

Bach, P.B., & Hayes, S.C. (2002). The use of Acceptance and Commitment Therapy to present the rehospitalization of psychotic patients: A randomized controlled trial. *Journal of Consulting and Clinical Psychology, 70*, 1129–1139.

Baer, R.A., Smith, G.T., & Allen, K.B. (2004). Assessment of mindfulness by self-report: The Kentucky inventory of mindfulness skills. *Assessment, 11*, 191–206.

Bandura, A. (1968). *Principles of behavior modification*. New York: Holt, Rinehart, and Winston.

Barnes-Holmes, D., Regan, D.,Barnes-Holmes, Y., Commins, S., Walsh, D., Stewart, I., Smeets, P. M., Whelan, R., & Dymond, S. (2005). Relating derived relations as a model of analogical reasoning: Reaction times and event-related potentials. *Journal of the Experimental Analysis of Behavior*, 84(3): 435–451. doi: 10.1901/jeab.2005.79-04

Barnes-Holmes, Y., Barnes-Holmes, D., Smeets, P. M., Strand, P., & Friman, P. (2004). Establishing relational responding in accordance with more-than and less-than as generalized operant behavior in young children. *International Journal of Psychology and Psychological Therapy, 4*, 531–558.

Berens, N.M., & Hayes, S.C. (in press). Arbitrarily applicable comparative relations: Experimental evidence for a relational operant. *Journal of Applied Behavior Analysis*. doi: 10.1901/jaba.2007.7-06

Baron, R.M., & Kenny, D.A. (1986). The moderator-mediator variable distinction in social psychological research: Conceptual, strategic, and statistical considerations. *Journal of Personality and Social Psychology, 51*, 1173–1182.

Batten, S.V., I.B. (2001). Experiential avoidance and high-risk sexual behavior in survivors of child sexual abuse. *Journal of Child Sexual Abuse, 10*, 101–120.

Beck, A.T., Brown, G., Steer, R.A., & Weissman, A. (1991). Factor analysis of the dysfunctional attitudes scale in a clinical population. *Psychological Assessment, 3*, 478–483.

Beck, R., & Perkins, T. S. (2001). Cognitive content-specificity for anxiety and depression: A meta- analysis. *Cognitive Therapy & Research, 25*, 651–663.

Beck, A.T., Rush, A.J., Shaw, B.F., & Emery, G. (1979). *Cognitive therapy of depression*. New York: Guilford Press.

Beck, A. T., & Steer, R. A. (1993). *Beck Anxiety Inventory Manual*. San Antonio: Harcourt Brace.

Beck, A.T., Steer, R.A., & Brown, G.K. (1996). *Beck Depression Inventory manual* (2nd ed.). San Antonio, TX: Psychological Corporation.

Beck, A. T., Ward, C. H., Mendelson, M., Mock, J., & Erbaugh, J. (1961). An inventory for measuring depression. *Archives of General Psychiatry*, 4, 561–571.

Begotka, A. M., Woods, D.W., & Wetterneck, C.T. (2004). The relationship between experiential avoidance and the severity of trichotillomania in a nonreferred sample. *Journal of Behavior Therapy and Experimental Psychiatry, 35*, 17–24.

Bieling, P.J., & Kuyken, W. (2003). Is cognitive case formulation science or science fiction? *Clinical Psychology: Science & Practice, 10*, 52–69.

Biglan, A., & Hayes, S.C. (1996). Should the behavioral sciences become more pragmatic? The case for functional contextualism in research on human behavior. *Applied and Preventive Psychology: Current Scientific Perspectives, 5*, 47–57.

Bissett, R.T. (2001). *Processes of change: Acceptance versus 12-step in polysubstance-abusing methadone clients*. Doctoral dissertation available from the University of Nevada. Dissertation Abstracts International—B, 63/02, p. 1014, Aug 2002.

Block, J.A. (2002). *Acceptance or change of private experiences: A comparative analysis in college students with public speaking anxiety*. Doctoral dissertation, University at Albany, State University of New York.

Bond, F.W., & Bunce, D. (2000). Mediators of change in emotion-focused and problem-focused worksite stress management interventions. *Journal of Occupational Health Psychology, 5*, 156–163.

Bond, F.W., & Bunce, D. (2003). The role of acceptance and job control in mental health, job satisfaction, and work performance. *Journal of Applied Psychology, 88*(6), 1057–1067.

Branstetter, A.D., Wilson, K.G., Hildebrandt, M., & Mutch, D. (2004). *Improving psychological adjustment among cancer patients: ACT and CBT.* Paper presented at the Association for Advancement of Behavior Therapy, New Orleans.

Brown, R.A., Lejuez, C.W., Kahler, C.W., & Strong, D.R. (2002). Distress tolerance and duration of past smoking cessation attempts. *Journal of Abnormal Psychology, 111*(1), 180–185.

Burns, D.D., & Spangler, D.L. (2001). Do changes in dysfunctional attitudes mediate changes in depression and anxiety in cognitive behavioral therapy? *Behavior Therapy, 32*, 337–369.

Carver, C.S., Scheier, M.F., & Weintraub, J.K. (1989). Assessing coping strategies: A theoretically based approach. *Journal of Personality and Social Psychology, 56*, 267–283.

Cohen, J. (1977). *Statistical power analysis for the behavioral sciences.* San Diego: Academic Press.

Cook, D. (2004). *Culture and acceptance and control-based strategies: Predictors of psychological adjustment among Asian Americans and Caucasian Americans.* Unpublished doctoral dissertation, University of Nevada, Reno.

Dahl, J., Wilson, K.G., & Nilsson, A. (2004). Acceptance and Commitment Therapy and the treatment of persons at risk for long-term disability resulting from stress and pain symptoms: A preliminary randomized trial. *Behavior Therapy, 35*, 785–802.

Derogatis, L.R. (1994). *Symptom Checklist-90-R (SCL-90-R): Administration, scoring and procedures manual.* Minneapolis, MN: National Computer Systems.

Dobson, K.S., & Khatri, N. (2000). Cognitive therapy: Looking backward, looking forward. *Journal of Clinical Psychology, 56*, 907–923.

Donaldson-Feilder, E.J., & Bond, F.W. (2004). The relative importance of psychological acceptance and emotional intelligence to workplace well-being. *British Journal of Guidance & Counselling, 32*(2), 187–203.

Durlak, J.A. (1995). Understanding meta-analysis. In L.G. Grimm & P.R. Arnold (Eds.), *Reading and understanding multivariate statistics.* Washington, DC: American Psychological Association.

Dykstra, T.A., & Follette, W.C. (1998). *An agoraphobia scale for assessing the clinical significance of treatment outcome.* Unpublished manuscript.

Dymond, S., & Barnes, D. (1995). A transformation of self-discrimination response functions in accordance with the arbitrarily applicable relations of sameness, more-than, and less-than. *Journal of the Experimental Analysis of Behavior, 64*, 163–184.

Eifert, G.H., & Heffner, M. (2003). The effects of acceptance versus control contexts on avoidance of panic-related symptoms. *Journal of Behavior Therapy and Experimental Psychiatry, 34*(3–4), 293–312.

Eisenberger, R. (1992). Learned industriousness. *Psychological Review, 99*, 248–267.

Ellis, A. (1962). *Reason and emotion in psychotherapy*. Secaucus, NJ: Citadel.

Feldner, M.T., Zvolensky, M.J., Eifert, G.H., & Spira, A.P. (2003). Emotional avoidance: An experimental test of individual differences and response suppression using biological challenge. *Behaviour Research and Therapy, 41*(4), 403–411.

Franks, C.M., & Wilson, G.T. (1974). *Annual review of behavior therapy: Theory and practice*. New York: Brunner/Mazel.

Forsyth, J.P., Parker, J.D., & Finlay, C.G. (2003). Anxiety sensitivity, controllability, and experiential avoidance and their relation to drug of choice and addiction severity in a residential sample of substance-abusing veterans. *Addictive Behaviors, 28*(5), 851–870.

Gaudiano, B.A., & Herbert, J.D. (2006a). Acute treatment of inpatients with psychotic symptoms using Acceptance and Commitment Therapy. *Behaviour Research and Therapy, 44*, 415–437.

Gaudiano, B.A., & Herbert, J.D. (2006b). Believability of hallucinations as a potential mediator of their frequency and associated distress in psychotic inpatients. *Behavioural and Cognitive Psychotherapy, 34*, 497–502.

Gifford, E.V., Kohlenberg, B.S., Hayes, S.C., Antonuccio, D.O., Piasecki, M.M., Rasmussen-Hall, M.L., & Palm, K.M. (2004). Acceptance theory–based treatment for smoking cessation: An initial trial of acceptance and commitment therapy. *Behavior Therapy, 35*, 689–706.

Gold, S.D., Marx, B.P., & Heidt, J.M. (submitted). *Lesbian and gay sexual assault survivors: The relationship between internalized homophobia and psychological sequelae.*

Goldberg, D. (1978). *Manual of the General Health Questionnaire*. Windsor: National Foundation for Educational Research.

Gortner, E.T., Gollan, J.K., Dobson, K.S., & Jacobson, N.S. (1998). Cognitive-behavioral treatment for depression: Relapse prevention. *Journal of Consulting & Clinical Psychology, 66*, 377–384

Gratz, K.L., & Gunderson, J.G. (2006). Preliminary data on an acceptance-based emotion regulation group intervention for deliberate self-harm among women with borderline personality disorder. *Behavior Therapy, 37*, 25–35.

Gratz, K.L., & Roemer, L. (2004). Multidimensional assessment of emotion regulation and dysregulation: Development, factor structure, and initial validation of the difficulties in emotion regulation scale. *Journal of Psychopathology and Behavioural Assessment, 26*, 41–54.

Greco, L. A., Heffner, M, Poe, S., Ritchie, S., Polak, M., & Lynch, S. K. (2005). Maternal adjustment following preterm birth: Contributions of experiential avoidance. *Behavior Therapy, 36*, 177–184.

Gregg, J.A. (2004). *A randomized controlled effectiveness trial comparing patient education with and without Acceptance and Commitment Therapy*. Doctoral dissertation, University of Nevada, Reno.

Gutierrez, O., Luciano, C., & Fink, B.C. (2004). Comparison between an acceptance-based and a cognitive-control-based protocol for coping with pain. *Behavior Therapy, 35*, 767–784.

Hayes, S.C. (1993). Analytic goals and the varieties of scientific contextualism. In S.C. Hayes, L.J. Hayes, H.W. Reese, & T.R. Sarbin (Eds.), *Varieties of scientific contextualism* (pp. 11–27). Reno, NV: Context Press.

Hayes, S.C. (2002). Buddhism and Acceptance and Commitment Therapy. *Cognitive and Behavioral Practice, 9*, 58–66.

Hayes, S.C. (2004). Acceptance and Commitment Therapy, Relational Frame Theory, and the third wave of behavior therapy. *Behavior Therapy, 35*, 639–665.

Hayes, S.C., Barnes-Holmes, D., & Roche, B. (Eds.). (2001). *Relational Frame Theory: A post-Skinnerian account of human language and cognition.* New York: Plenum Press.

Hayes, S.C., & Bissett, R. (1998). Derived stimulus relations produce mediated and episodic priming. *The Psychological Record, 48*, 617–630.

Hayes, S.C., Bissett, R.T., Korn, Z., Zettle, R.D., Rosenfarb, I.S., Cooper, L.D., & Grundt, A. (1999). The impact of acceptance versus control rationales on pain tolerance. *The Psychological Record, 49*(1), 33–47.

Hayes, S. C., Bissett, R., Roget, N., Padilla, M., Kohlenberg, B. S., Fisher, G., Masuda, A., Pistorello, J., Rye, A. K., Berry, K., & Niccolls, R. (2004). The impact of acceptance and commitment training and multicultural training on the stigmatizing attitudes and professional burnout of substance abused counselors. *Behavior Therapy*, 35, 821–835. doi: 10.1016/S0005-7894(04)80022-4

Hayes, S.C., & Brownstein, A.J. (1986). Mentalism, behavior-behavior relations and a behavior analytic view of the purposes of science. *The Behavior Analyst, 9*, 175–190.

Hayes, S.C., Follette, V.M., & Linehan, M.M. (2004) (Eds.), *Mindfulness and acceptance: Expanding the cognitive behavioral tradition.* New York: Guilford Press.

Hayes, S.C., Hayes, L.J., & Reese, H.W. (1988). Finding the philosophical core: A review of Stephen C. Pepper's *World Hypotheses. Journal of the Experimental Analysis of Behavior, 50*, 97–111.

Hayes, S.C., Hayes, L.J., Reese, H.W., & Sarbin, T.R. (Eds.). (1993). *Varieties of scientific contextualism.* Reno, NV: Context Press.

Hayes, S.C., Strosahl, K., & Wilson, K.G. (1999). *Acceptance and Commitment Therapy: An experiential approach to behavior change.* New York: Guilford Press.

Hayes, S.C., Strosahl, K.D., Wilson, K.G., Bissett, R.T., Pistorello, J., Toarmino, D., Polusny, M., A., Dykstra, T.A., Batten, S.V., Bergan, J., Stewart, S.H., Zvolensky, M.J., Eifert, G.H., Bond, F.W., Forsyth J.P., Karekla, M., & McCurry, S.M. (2004). Measuring experiential avoidance: A preliminary test of a working model. *The Psychological Record, 54*, 553–578.

Hayes, S. C., Wilson, K. G., Gifford, E. V., Bissett, R., Piasecki, M., Batten, S. V., Byrd, M., & Gregg, J. (2004). A randomized controlled trial of twelve-step facilitation and acceptance and commitment therapy with polysubstance abusing methadone maintained opiate addicts. *Behavior Therapy, 35*, 667–688. doi: 10.1016/S0005-7894(04)80014-5

Hayes, S.C., Wilson, K.G., Gifford, E.V., Follette, V.M., & Strosahl, K. (1996). Experiential avoidance and behavioral disorders: A functional dimensional approach to diagnosis and treatment. *Journal of Consulting and Clinical Psychology, 64*(6), 1152–1168.

Hollon, S.D., & Kendall, P.C. (1980). Cognitive self-statements in depression: Development of an automatic thoughts questionnaire. *Cognitive Therapy & Research, 4*, 383–395.

Ilardi, S. S. & Craighead, W. E. (1999). Rapid early response, cognitive modification, and nonspecific factors in cognitive behavior therapy for depression: A reply to Tang and DeRubeis. *Clinical Psychology: Science & Practice, 6*, 295–299.

Jacobson, N.S., Dobson, K.S., Truax, P.A., Addis, M.E., Koerner, K., Gollan, J.K., Gortner, E. & Prince, S.E. (1996). A component analysis of cognitive-behavioral treatment for depression. *Journal of Consulting and Clinical Psychology, 64*, 295–304.

Karekla, M., Forsyth, J.P., & Kelly, M.M. (2004). Emotional avoidance and panicogenic responding to a biological challenge procedure. *Behavior Therapy, 35*, 725–746.

Levitt, J.T., Brown, T.A., Orsillo, S.M., & Barlow, D.H. (2004). The effects of acceptance versus suppression of emotion on subjective and psychophysiological response to carbon dioxide challenge in patients with panic disorder. *Behavior Therapy, 35*, 747–766.

Linehan, M.M. (1993). *Cognitive-behavioral treatment of borderline personality disorder*. New York: Guilford Press.

Lundgren, T. (2004). *Psychological treatment of epilepsy*. Unpublished dissertation, Uppsala University, Uppsala, Sweden.

Lundgren, T., & Dahl, J. (2005). *Development and evaluation of an integrative health model in treatment of epilepsy: A randomized controlled trial investigating the effects of a short-term ACT intervention compared to attention control in South Africa*. Association for Behavior Analysis, Chicago.

MacKinnon, D.P. (2003). *Mediator and moderator methods*. Paper presented at the Association for the Advancement of Behavior Therapy meeting, Boston.

Marx, B.P., & Sloan, D.M. (2002). The role of emotion in the psychological functioning of adult survivors of childhood sexual abuse. *Behavior Therapy, 33*, 563–577.

Marx, B.P., & Sloan, D.M. (2005). Peritraumatic dissociation and experiential avoidance as predictors of posttraumatic stress symptomatology. *Behaviour Research and Therapy*, 43(5), 569–583.

Masuda, A., Hayes, S.C., Sackett, C.F., & Twohig, M.P. (2004). Cognitive defusion and self-relevant negative thoughts: Examining the impact of a ninety year old technique. *Behaviour Research and Therapy, 42*, 477–485.

McCracken, L.M. (1998). Learning to live with pain: Acceptance of pain predicts adjustment in persons with chronic pain. *Pain, 74*, 21–27.

McCracken, L.M., & Eccleston, C. (2003). Coping or acceptance: What to do about chronic pain? *Pain, 105*, 197–204.

McCracken, L.M., Vowles, K.E., & Eccleston, C. (2004). Acceptance of chronic pain: Component analysis and a revised assessment method. *Pain, 107*(1–2), 159–166.

McCracken, L.M., Vowles, K.E., & Eccleston, C. (2005). Acceptance-based treatment for persons with complex, long-standing chronic pain: A preliminary analysis of treatment outcome in comparison to a waiting phase. *Behaviour Research and Therapy, 43*, 1335–1346.

Morgenstern, J., & Longabaugh, R. (2000). Cognitive-behavioral treatment for alcohol dependence: A review of evidence for its hypothesized mechanisms of action. *Addiction, 95*, 1475–1490.

Myerson, J., & Green, L. (1995). Discounting of delayed rewards: Models of individual choice. *Journal of the Experimental Analysis of Behavior, 64*, 263–276.

Piaget, J. (1964). Development and learning. In R.E. Ripple and V.N. Rockcastle (Eds.), *Piaget rediscovered* (pp. 7–19). Ithaca, NY: Cornell University Press.

Pistorello, J. (1998). *Acceptance, suppression, and monitoring of personally-relevant unwanted thoughts in women diagnosed with borderline personality disorder.* Unpublished doctoral dissertation, University of Nevada, Reno.

Plumb, J.C., Orsillo, S.M., & Luterek, J.A. (2004). A preliminary test of the role of experiential avoidance in post-event functioning. *Journal of Behavior Therapy and Experimental Psychiatry, 35*, 245–257.

Polusny, M.A., Rosenthal, M. Z., Aban, I., & Follette, V. M. (2004). Experiential avoidance as a mediator of the effects of adolescent sexual victimization on negative adult outcomes. *Violence and Victims, 19*, 109–120.

Reiss, S., Peterson, R. A., Gursky, D. M., & McNally, R. J. (1986). Anxiety sensitivity, anxiety frequency and the predictions of fearfulness. *Behaviour Research and Therapy*, 24, 1–8.

Roemer, L., Salters, K., Raffa, S. D., & Orsillo, S.M. (2005). Fear and avoidance of internal experiences in GAD: Preliminary tests of a conceptual model. *Cognitive Therapy and Research, 29*, 71–88.

Rosenthal, R., & DiMatteo, M.R. (2001). Meta-analysis: Recent developments in quantitative methods for literature reviews. *Annual Review of Psychology, 52*, 59–82.

Segal, Z.V., Williams, J.M.G., & Teasdale, J.T. (2001). *Mindfulness-Based Cognitive Therapy for depression: A new approach to preventing relapse.* New York: Guilford Press.

Sheldon, K.M., Ryan, R.M., Deci, E.L., & Kasser, T. (2004). The independent effects of goal contents and motives in well-being: It's both what you pursue and why you pursue it. Personality and Social Psychology Bulletin, 30, 475–486.

Sloan, D.M. (2004). Emotion regulation in action: Emotional reactivity in experiential avoidance. *Behaviour Research and Therapy, 42*, 1257–1270.

Sobel, M.E. (1982). Asymptotic intervals for indirect effects in structural equations models. In S. Leinhart (Ed.), *Sociological methodology 1982* (pp. 290–312). San Francisco: Jossey-Bass.

Spielberger, C. D., Gorsuch, R. L., Lushene, R., Vagg, P. R., & Jacobs, G. A. (1983). *Manual for the state-trait anxiety inventory*. Palo Alto, CA: Consulting Psychologists Press.

Stewart, I., Barnes-Holmes, D., & Roche, B. (2004) A functional-analytic model of analogy using the relational evaluation procedure. Psychological Record, *54*, 531–552.

Stewart, S.H., Zvolensky, M.J., & Eifert, G.H. (2002). The relationships of anxiety sensitivity, experiential avoidance, and alexithymic coping to young adults' motivations for drinking. *Behavior Modification, 26*, 279–296.

Strosahl, K.D., Hayes, S.C., Bergan, J., & Romano, P. (1998). Assessing the field effectiveness of acceptance and commitment therapy: An example of the manipulated training research method. *Behavior Therapy, 29*(1), 35–63.

Takahashi, M., Muto, T., Tada, M., & Sugiyama, M. (2002). Acceptance rationale and increasing pain tolerance: Acceptance-based and FEAR-based practice. *Japanese Journal of Behavior Therapy, 28*, 35–46.

Teasdale, J.T. (2003). *Mindfulness and the third wave of cognitive-behavioural therapies*. Paper presented at the European Association for Behavioural and Cognitive Therapies Annual Congresses, Prague, Czech Republic.

Toarmino, D., Pistorello, J., & Hayes, S.C. (1997). *Validation of the Acceptance and Action Questionnaire*. Unpublished manuscript.

Tull, M. T., Gratz, K. L., Salters, K. S., & Roemer, L. (2004). The role of experiential avoidance in posttraumatic stress symptoms and symptoms of depression, anxiety, and somatization. *Journal of Nervous and Mental Disease, 192*, 754–761.

Twohig, M. P., Hayes, S. C., & Masuda, A. (2006). A preliminary investigation of Acceptance and Commitment Therapy as a treatment for chronic skin picking. *Behaviour Research and Therapy, 44*, 1513–1522. doi: 0.1016/j.brat.2005.10.002

Waltz, J. A., Knowlton, B. J., Holyoak, K. J., Boone, K. B., Mishkin, F. S., de Menezes Santos, M., Thomas, C. R., & Miller, B. L. (1999). A system for relational reasoning in human prefrontal cortex. *Psychological Science*, 10, 119–125.

Watkins, E., Teasdale, J.D., & Williams, R.M. (2000). Decentering and distraction reduce overgeneral autobiographical memory in depression. *Psychological Medicine, 30*, 911–920.

Wells, A. (2000). *Emotional disorders and metacognition: Innovative cognitive therapy*. Chichester, United Kingdom: Wiley.
Wenzlaff, E.M., & Wegner, D.M. (2000). Thought suppression. *Annual Review of Psychology, 51*, 59–91.
Woods, D.W., Wetterneck, C.T., & Flessner, C.A. (2006) A controlled evaluation of Acceptance and Commitment Therapy plus habit reversal for trichotillomania. *Behaviour Research and Therapy, 44*, 639–656.
Zettle, R.D. (2003). Acceptance and Commitment Therapy (ACT) vs. systematic desensitization in the treatment of mathematics anxiety. *The Psychological Record, 53*, 197–215.
Zettle, R.D., & Hayes, S.C. (1986). Dysfunctional control by client verbal behavior: The context of reason giving. *The Analysis of Verbal Behavior, 4*, 30–38.
Zettle, R.D., & Hayes, S.C. (1987). Component and process analysis of cognitive therapy. *Psychological Reports, 64*, 939–953.
Zettle, R.D., & Rains, J.C. (1989). Group cognitive and contextual therapies in treatment of depression. *Journal of Clinical Psychology, 45*(3), 436–445.

ARTICLE 14

CONTEXTUAL BEHAVIORAL SCIENCE

Creating a Science More Adequate to the Challenge of the Human Condition

From Hayes, S. C., Barnes-Holmes, D., & Wilson, K. G. (2012). *Journal of Contextual Behavioral Science, 1*, 1–16.

As a functional contextualist sees it, the ultimate purpose of behavioral science is to change the world in a positive and intentional way. Science is taken to be an empirical strategy of interacting in and with the world so as to learn how to be more effective in organizing it, speaking about it, measuring it, and changing it. This distinctively pragmatic perspective derives from a focus on the functions of actions in a historical and situational context, and from being willing to apply that same view to the actions of scientists themselves. Some ways of behaving work better than others, and in a precisely parallel way, some ways of conceptualizing the world work better than others given particular analytic purposes. If the bold purpose of intentional positive change is to be embraced, a well thought out plan is essential. This article is about the purpose and plan of an emerging scientific tradition.

From a functional and contextual perspective, scientific analysis is a social enterprise that seeks the development of increasingly organized statements of relations among events that allow analytic goals to be accomplished with precision, scope, and depth, based on verifiable experience. From this perspective on science, the product of science is verbal, like other human activities such as law or literature, but what distinguishes it as a human invention are the conditions under which scientists can speak, and the evaluative criteria applied to what is said. The criterion of precision means that only a limited number of analytic concepts apply to a given case; scope means a given analytic concept applies to a range of cases; and depth means analytic concepts cohere across well-established scientific domains. A bread recipe has precision but no scope; animism has the opposite problem. Science has been especially successful in generating ideas that meet all of these goals simultaneously, and relations such as E = mc^2 are famous because they do so. Limits in precision and scope restrict the practical utility of scientific knowledge; limits in depth restrict its integration. Thus, the importance of the accomplishment of scientific goals with precision, scope, and depth are ultimately a practical matter.

The present article explores the nature and purpose of a contextualistic tradition that adopts this perspective, Contextual Behavioral Science (CBS). CBS is a strategy of scientific and practical development that gathers together a coherent set of philosophical assumptions and strategies of knowledge development and application. This article will examine the assumptions and analytic goals of CBS and their strategic implications.

CONTEXTUAL BEHAVIORAL SCIENCE

It is worth beginning with the ending. *Contextual Behavioral Science (CBS) is a principle-focused, communitarian strategy of reticulated scientific and practical development. Grounded in contextualistic philosophical assumptions, and nested within multi-dimensional, multi-level evolution science as a contextual view of life, it seeks the development of basic and applied scientific concepts and methods that are useful in predicting-and-influencing the contextually embedded actions of whole organisms, individually and in groups, with precision, scope, and depth, and extends that approach into knowledge development itself so as to create a behavioral science more adequate to the challenges of the human condition.* The present article will attempt to make these definitional features more understandable.

CBS AS A DISTINCT EXTENSION OF BEHAVIOR ANALYTIC PSYCHOLOGY

Several articles have been written on the nature of Contextual Behavioral Science and its roots in contextualistic behavioral psychology (e.g., Hayes, Levin, Plumb, Boulanger, & Pistorello, 2013; Hayes, Long, Levin, & Follette, 2013; Levin & Hayes, 2009; Vilaradaga, Hayes, Levin, & Muto, 2009). Among other topics, these articles have described philosophical contextualism and the research program that led to Acceptance and Commitment Therapy (ACT; Hayes, Strosahl, & Wilson, 1999, 2011) and to Relational Frame Theory (RFT; Hayes, Barnes-Holmes, & Roche, 2001).

Confusion between the two is especially difficult for those without quite specific behavioral psychology backgrounds, and furthermore, although CBS and behavior analysis are historically intertwined, in some ways the two areas have diverged over time. Despite its lofty goals (Baer, Wolf, & Risley, 1968) applied behavior analysis has been unable to avoid domination of the field by the narrow topic of developmental disabilities, both in research and practice (Friman, 2010). Basic behavior analysis continues primarily to focus on animal learning rather than on human functioning—a tendency that may even be increasing (Dymond & Critchfield, 2001)—despite the evidence that symbolic behavior constitutes a new and characteristically human behavioral process that cannot be fully modeled using non-human studies. As grant and academic support for animal learning dwindles, basic behavior analysis "proceeds as an academic discipline in an ever-dwindling number of supportive universities" (McIlvane, 2009, p. 279) and for those who view symbolic behavior as central to human functioning that comes as no surprise. Meanwhile, some well-known behavior analysts reject a contextualistic characterization of behavioral psychology (e.g., Marr, 1993; Staddon, 1993).

All of these trends and characteristics are the opposite of those displayed by the CBS tradition, which is broadly focused, centered on human learning and language processes, growing rapidly in popularity in the academy and practical settings alike, and unabashedly contextualistic. We have reached a point in which the new alliances and connections that need to be made and that are being made by CBS (e.g., DeHouwer, 2011; D. S. Wilson, Hayes, Biglan, & Embry, 2014) can no longer be built rapidly from the existing organizational or professional base within behavior analysis.

CLARIFYING ASSUMPTIONS OF CONTEXTUAL BEHAVIORAL SCIENCE

For scientists, the crucial aspect of philosophy of science is the process of explicating and taking responsibility for scientific assumptions. To ensure that theory, data, and methods comport over time, scientific assumptions need to be clear and coherent. If a research program wanders from its assumptions, the work becomes empty or unstable, and soon enough it is not a "program" at all. When the grand learning theories of the 1930's and 40's collapsed, individual research programs became increasingly fractionated, developing narrow ways of speaking that applied to the domain in which they were working, but lacking connection to any integrative theory. Meta-theoretical assumptions are needed to provide answers to such questions as "what is the goal of knowledge" or "How do we know something is true?" These are not empirical questions; rather, the answers to such questions are what permits empirical work to be done in a well-coordinated way.

Drawing from the post-Darwinian functional tradition of American pragmatism (Dewey, 1925/1981, 1938/1981; James, 1907/1981; Pierce, 1878/1983; see Gifford & Hayes, 1999), and its further development within behavior analysis (Skinner, 1945), the philosophy of science that undergirds CBS is functional contextualism (e.g., Barnes-Holmes, 2000; Biglan & Hayes, 1996; Gifford & Hayes, 1999; Hayes, 1993; S. C. Hayes, L. J. Hayes, & Reese, 1988; Hayes & Long, 2013; K. G. Wilson, Whiteman, & Bordieri, 2013). Functional contextualism is a specific variety of scientific contextualism

(Hayes, Hayes, Reese, & Sarbin, 1993), with clear assumptions about the units of analysis, ontology, epistemology, and truth criteria.

Units of Analysis: The Act-in-Context

A functional contextual perspective focuses on the behavior of organisms interacting in and with a context, considered both historically and situationally: the ongoing situated act-in-context. Units drawn from this focus are holistic—the act and its context are not fully separable. For example, consider the act of "going to the store." It implies a place to go from and a place to go to; it implies conditions that establish the importance of going to the store (e.g., lack of food in the cupboard) and consequences of importance to going there (e.g., the food that will be obtained or the party that will be held). No amount of detail about the act itself disconnected from its context (e.g., how the legs move while walking) will make sense of such an act. History, circumstances, and consequences are aspects of the act itself in a functional sense. A person raising a hand to stretch is engaged in a fundamentally different act than a person raising a hand to say hello, even if the muscle movements are identical. The unit is whole, but at the same time aspects of that whole can be examined, much as the sides of a bubble can be examined without supposing that the bubble is assembled like building blocks from its various sides.

The act-in-context occurs not only at the individual level, but also at the group level. Social context and psychological actions blend into actions of groups as the scope of the unit expands into the social, sociological, and anthropological domains. In much the same way, finer grained units emerge as extended actions are examined in a more fine-grained way, or the actions of whole organisms are examined in sub-organismic detail. Examination of the structure of the organism in light of the contributions of specific inheritance streams to a given psychological phenomenon—genetic, epigenetic, behavioral, and symbolic (Jablonka & Lamb, 2006)—extend the psychological analyses of situated actions into biology and the life sciences.

If the same basic formulation is maintained, those extensions of a functional contextual perspective into multiple overlapping units can be done seamlessly. Reductionism and expansionism are rejected because the utility of any explanation needs to be empirically established at its given level of analysis. The psychological level focuses on the situated actions of whole organisms (Hayes, 1993). That level is not explained by analyses at other levels (e.g., neuroscience, anthropology) but it is richly embedded with them, as we will discuss later. The consistency of the formulation of units of analysis (the situated action) and the goal of depth, encourages analysts to weave together what is useful across levels of analysis into an interconnected whole. That is what CBS is trying to do, in cooperation with its sister approaches in other scientific domains.

Evolutionary Epistemology

The idea of an evolving, ongoing act-in-context becomes more complex when this same unit is applied to scientists or practitioners themselves. We appreciate the act by appreciating its context, finding purpose and function amid history and circumstance. But that appreciation is itself an act and it too has a purpose, function, and context. In one sense, Contextual Behavioral Science is just what emerges when evolutionary and selectionist approaches to behavior are applied in a thoroughgoing way to knowledge development itself.

This flexible recursive contextual unit—the act-in-context consistently applied—presents challenges and opportunities scientifically speaking. Living creatures divide up the world by their interactions in and with it, phylogenetically and ontogenetically. Humans do such divisions verbally as well—such divisions are the very substance of science itself. Any behavioral stream can in principle be divided an infinite number of ways, limited only by the creativity of the analyst—what selects among them is the same thing that selects any situated action, namely, its effects. The effectiveness of an analysis, however, does not provide the basis to argue that it was effective *because* divisions contained within that analysis are pre-existing. Such an argument adds nothing to workability itself and thus has no known truth-value. Some use the term "ontology' to refer merely to explicit specification of conceptualizations, and about that no objection can be made. But a thoroughgoing selectivist or evolutionary epistemology cannot sustain ontological statements if one means the more traditional philosophical definition of what categories exist or can be said to exist in the world and the correspondence between analyses and these categories. Functional contextualists maintain a principled disinterest in ontology in that sense, while maintaining an intense interest in the epistemology implied by behavioral pragmatism (Barnes-Holmes, 2000).

The need to abandon an interest in ontology in the sense just described is an initially awkward implication of a naturalistic contextual account. Natural science relies on commonsense linguistic habits that focus on what "is," not on "works in experience" but if that very habit is examined contextualistically, it cannot be taken literally: "If the scientific activity of the behavioral pragmatist is the product of a behavioral history, then he or she can never claim to have found an ontological truth, because a different or more extended history may have produced a different truth" (Barnes-Holmes, 2000, p. 198). Evolutionary epistemology (Radnitzky & Bartley, 1987) has sometimes tried to avoid this implication of a thoroughgoing application of selectivist processes. Campbell (1959) provides an illustrative example of such avoidance by evolutionary psychologists in his "epistemology of the other"—focusing his evolutionary account on how organisms come to know even while "no effort is made to justify 'my own' knowledge processes" (p. 157). Campbell recognized that he was embracing an inconsistency but excused it on the grounds that it avoided solipsism (1959, p. 157), and only years later (1987) acknowledged that a more thoroughgoing pragmatist or contextualistic position is logically implied by a consistent application of evolutionary principles. Pragmatic philosophers also have attempted to dodge the implication. For example, Quine attempted to avoid the problem by the concept of an observation sentence validated by witnesses with similar sensory systems (1974, p. 41). This demands the ontological assumption of relatively static similar sensory systems among humans (Barnes-Holmes, 2000), which inconsistently blends essentialist and pragmatic assumptions. It appears to be a kind of *ad hoc* repair patch arbitrarily glued to contextualism in order to avoid the a-ontological implications of its unit of analysis and truth criterion (Hayes & Long, 2013).

Functional contextualism is based on the bolder and more consistent option taken by Skinner: In order to create a consistent contextualistic science we must include an analysis of the history and context of scientific knowing itself (Skinner, 1945). Our analyses cannot just be focused outwardly on others, as if we can conveniently forget that we too are behaving. When the scientist is included in the analysis we have to be a bit more humble. Language itself begins and ends as nothing but a social behavioral tool, not a passageway to pre-organized reality: "[Scientific knowledge] is a corpus of rules for effective action, and there is a special sense in which it could be 'true' if it yields the most effective action possible. . . . (A) proposition is 'true' to the extent that with its help the listener responds effectively to the situation it describes" (Skinner, 1974, p. 235). We have to test *that* kind of truth by showing that verbal principles help those who use scientific knowledge to respond effectively in and with the world. This is an approach consistent with the original truth criterion of pragmatists such as Pierce: "There is no distinction of meaning so fine as to consist in anything but a possible difference of practice (1878/1983, p. 145); or James: "Truth in our ideas means their power to 'work'" (1907/1981, p. 165).

CBS is intensely interested in pragmatic truth linked to stated goals, and nothing else. The principled disinterest in commonsense "ontological truth" and the enthusiastic interest in pragmatic truth is echoed in clinical procedures in CBS, such as in the emphasis on defusion and workability in ACT. It is also reflected in the willingness to use both technical and non-technical terms in CBS in different contexts for different purposes, which we will discuss later.

The Truth Criterion

If left there, the dispersive nature of individual aims would make it difficult for contextualism to serve as a coherent philosophy of science: One person would seek one kind of knowledge and another would seek a very different kind (cf., Ruiz & Roche, 2007). Science is social enterprise, however, and stating scientific goals publicly allows science to progress cooperatively and in a socially responsible, non-coercive way. CBS properly acknowledges the capacity of others to make their own values-based choices of scientific goals and invites others to choose to work with those who have similar aims and purposes.

Because purposes establish the criterion for pragmatic truth, logically they cannot themselves ultimately be right, correct, or true. They can be nested (smaller into larger; process goals into outcome goals), but they cannot ultimately be justified. If truth is a matter of workability, defending the validity of ultimate purposes is a fool's errand. Justifying a pragmatic purpose would require the statement of still more pragmatic purposes, ad infinitum. Outcome goals and values thus must ultimately be stated naked and in the wind. The importance of this idea is echoed in clinical procedures in CBS, such as in the emphasis on values in ACT as a choice rather than as a reasoned action, which then allows an examination of the workability of behavior. Some goals are merely process goals however (that is means to ends), and these can be justified empirically with reference to outcomes. In ACT that might occur with behavioral goals linked to values (e.g., if X is the value, then it may be an empirical fact that Y would be an effective committed action).

The goal of functional contextualism is to predict-and-influence, with precision, scope, and depth, whole organisms interacting in and with a context considered historically and situationally. This goal brings the definitions of science and psychology into contact with "prediction-and-influence" as a unified goal (we are hyphenating it here when treating the phrase as the goal of functional contextualism to emphasize that as a goal it is viewed as inseverable). That goal is what is most distinctive about functional contextualism as compared to other varieties of scientific contextualism such as the more descriptive contextual approaches labeled constructionism, dramaturgy, hermeneutics, and the like, that seek a personal appreciation of the participants in the whole (Hayes et al., 1993). For that reason, the analyses that emerge from other contextualistic traditions are of unknown usefulness until they are examined by functional contextualists, as measured against their own purposes. It is also different than non-contextualistic positions such as elemental realism (mechanism) that emphasize predictive verification and view influence as an occasional side-benefit of understanding, not as a primary test of it.

As stated in the first sentence of this article contextual behavioral scientists seek to change the world in positive and intentional ways—that is what prediction-and-influence is for. If it is stated as an aspiration rather than a declaration of accomplishment envisioning a behavioral science more adequate to the challenge of the human condition means that CBS is a wing of science that explicitly embraces pro-sociality and human development as a goal of scientific and professional development. This also means that in a CBS approach, minimization—the tendency of scientists to dismiss human complexity as being "merely" this or "just" that, in the absence of broad evidence for these claims—is firmly rejected. Minimization is a kind of intellectual bravado in which further questioning is waived away and further progress is needlessly abandoned. Preventing premature answers from dominating over important questions is seen in the parallel tendency of ACT practitioners to encourage clients to embrace bold questions in living, but to hold any answers lightly.

Monism

The situated action of contextualism is naturalistic and monistic: The word "behavior" refers to *any and all actions of the whole organism*, including those that are private. The monism of functional contextual science is not a matter of emphasizing the physical over the non-physical, but in the assumptive sense of starting with oneness. Behavior and its functions in context are not treated as proxies for inferred processes or hypothetical variables—they are viewed as legitimate levels of analysis in their own right.

One advantage of this approach is that the gap between concepts and the conditions under which they are applied can be kept small. All concepts require auxiliary assumptions and conditions in order to be tested (e.g., they need to be measured). The tendency to blame auxiliaries and conditions for conceptual failures has been the bane of theory falsification (Hayes, 2004b). The small gap between concepts and conditions is a major advantage of a reticulated model that treats behavior and context as legitimate targets of analysis rather than proxies for other things. The conditions under which one can speak of a consequence as a reinforcer, or a set of actions as being an arbitrarily applicable relational response, is so specific, contextually embedded, and available that there is little room to blame auxiliaries and conditions when models relying on such concepts are not supported. That is just not true with our more common psychological concepts such as "self-esteem" or "schemas" or "personality" and the like. Finally, monism is embraced in CBS, not as an ontological assumption, but instead as a strategic assumption. Disinterest in commonsense ontology allows the practical problems of dualism, including the ways that the mental and physical domains in dualism react or are related, to be left behind.

STRATEGIC IMPLICATIONS OF FUNCTIONAL CONTEXTUAL ASSUMPTIONS

Many of the features of CBS as a strategy of scientific development and many aspects of the basic and applied methods that have emerged from a CBS perspective flow from these foundational ideas, assumptions, and goals. We will explore a set of these implications that seem to be especially important and then examine how these implications touch ground in a practical way in a CBS approach.

Environmentalism, Causality, and Experimental Analysis

The hyphenation of the term "prediction-and-influence" is to indicate that the goal of functional contextualism is unified; for that reason, *causal analysis in a functional contextual approach ultimately must extend to the manipulable context of action* (Hayes & Brownstein, 1986). From a CBS perspective, any concept or theory that affords prediction but not influence is not yet known to be "true." Since a person who applies knowledge to behavior is and must be in the domain of the context of that action, knowledge statements meant to produce prediction-and-influence must begin in the manipulable world of history and circumstance. Thoughts, emotions, and overt action cannot be directly manipulated in others—that is why they are "dependent variables" in behavioral science. A gap in knowledge is created (relative to the goal of causal analysis in a functional contextual approach) when psychological variables are treated as causal because the person using this knowledge cannot apply it without a leap into the unknown (e.g., without guessing about how to change contextual events to change these variables or their relationships). Thus, any theory consisting entirely of dependent variables (e.g., thoughts cause emotions which cause overt actions) cannot be fully successful in a CBS approach.

This does not mean that private experiences are rejected, or that organisms are reactive or passive entities. Since public agreement is not used as a foundational criterion for truth in a functional contextual position, there are no barriers to considering private experiences as a legitimate focus of scientific and practical analysis. Furthermore, some actions do commonly relate to others (e.g., thinking may be related to overt actions); and actions alter the environment, not just the other way around. For pragmatic reasons, however, analysis is not complete until the context of psychological events, and the context of the relationship among them (e.g., why thoughts are related to overt behavior), are specified (Hayes & Brownstein, 1986). Strong correlations among behaviors often provide an excellent starting point (but not a good ending point) for experimental analyses focused on context that lend themselves to prediction and influence. The focus on the contexts that strengthen and weaken relations between thoughts, emotions, and actions is echoed in clinical procedures in CBS, such as in the emphasis on acceptance or defusion as contexts that foster response flexibility, and their instigation and modeling in the therapeutic relationship in ACT.

Sometimes theories in science cannot be tested against the criterion of influence for purely technical reasons, of course. For example, experimental tests of cosmological analyses might be theoretically but not practically possible given limits on the ability to generate and direct energy. Interpretation can be of use in these situations but not if they become permanent way stations, beyond empirical analysis. Interpretation is an extension of knowledge meant to create a consistent and testable account. In the physical sciences the principles on which interpretive extensions are based are often well established via experimental manipulation in the laboratory, and in the history of the physical sciences technical barriers to the tests of interpretations are often gradually overcome. That can happen in the behavioral sciences too but only if analyses are based on events that are manipulable *in principle* and are subjected to actual research as soon as possible. CBS embraces that approach. When experimental analysis is not possible for technical reasons (e.g., the analysis of large scale cultural change or language development in situ), smaller scale laboratory manipulations can be emphasized as solutions to the technical barriers are sought. The many demonstration studies in RFT that have manipulated experimental histories to establish complex performances are examples, such as training deictic framing and then examining Theory of Mind skills (Weil, Hayes, & Capurro, 2011) or establishing relational skills and then examining intellectual ability (Cassidy, Roche, & Hayes, 2011)

In a CBS approach non-experimental forms of research, such as correlational, naturalistic, participatory action, and qualitative research, have an important role to play. For example, qualitative and naturalistic research help maintain rich contact with the quality of actions and contexts, allowing possibly key features to be abstracted, as we will note in more detail later. Ultimately, however, from a CBS perspective these ideas need to be tested through experimental analysis. In a sense, the ultimate purpose of research in CBS is the determination of causality, but that does not mean that causes are discovered. *"Cause" is taken to be merely way of speaking that indicates that prediction-and-influence can be accomplished in a particular context based on a particular analysis.*

The Reticulated Development of Principles, Theories, and Practices

The *a priori* commitment to analyses with high precision, scope, and depth that can advance the human condition has over time had a profound effect on the CBS tradition, and it makes sense of the kind of research and practice that it encourages. There is an understandable tendency when faced with human need to abandon basic work in favor of applied technology. Practitioners and social change agents need help, and they need help *now*. The slow but hopefully steady progress of a basic scientific tradition may hold little appeal in that context, as the history of science shows (Kantor, 1963). Conversely, the behavioral forbearers of CBS often approached behavioral science purely as a bottom-up enterprise in which basic principles alone would allow the analysis of human complexity (e.g., Skinner, 1938). Unfortunately, this has three key flaws: First, it can be slow to the point of obstruction of progress; second, there is nothing to ensure that the basic principles needed for applied work are in fact being developed merely by basic scientist indulging their current interests; and third, principles can be too complex to be mastered by front line practitioners for practical use. In the history of behavior therapy and behavior analysis, for example, practitioners often gave up waiting for adequate basic behavioral analyses and tried to move on without further delay. Committed behaviorists (e.g., Azrin, 1977) and those willing to jump to a cognitive position (e.g., Mahoney, 1974) both adopted this strategy, suggesting that the problem of speed was a practical rather than theoretical problem. But as these leaps away from the laboratory were taken, the need for basic principles remained unmet. Behavior analysis tried to proceed with direct contingency analysis as its primary tool kit, even narrowing the field to developmental disabilities and a few other areas if that was what was required to do so; cognitive behavior therapy abandoned the early dream of laboratory behavioral science as a guide to application and instead embraced clinical or even folk psychology theories of cognition and behavior change if that was what was needed to move on (Hayes, 2004a).

CBS has aimed to balance these tensions in a very different way: agreeing that principles are key to the scope of scientific work, but arguing for a reticulated (that is, a web-like) model of scientific and practical development, in which theoretical and technological progress occurs at multiple levels but in an interconnected way, with differing standards of progress appropriate to the particular level of the work given what else is known.

Basic Principles and Analytic Abstractive Theories. The core unit of CBS naturally focuses on environment-behavior relations. Based on careful and systematic observations of action and its context, it is possible to develop ways of speaking about environment-behavior relations that are high in both precision and scope. That is what is meant by the term "behavioral principles" such as principles of reinforcement or stimulus control. These principles need to be embedded in similar contextual analyses that focus on other dimensions and time scales. For example, behavioral principles should be embedded in knowledge about the genetic and epigenetic bases of learning—how they evolved and the conditions under which they apply (Ginsberg & Jablonka, 2010). For that reason, we will at times use the term "contextual principles" to refer to the larger set that apply to the entire body of functional contextual knowledge.

Sets of contextual behavioral principles can be used to unpack the history and situational determinants of complex human actions. In classical behavioral clinical approaches this is done one at a time in the form of functional analyses of individual problems. For *de novo* functional analyses of that kind, practitioners need to master a wide variety of available principles, but when a set of such functional analyses exist in a domain, another possibility exists: to develop ways of speaking about entire sets of functional analyses. That is what a theory looks like in CBS, and it is profoundly different than "theory" in more mainstream approaches (for a useful discussion of some of these differences, see Hineline & Wanchisen, 1989).

Unfortunately, modern psychology largely developed its ideas about theory from the hypothetico-deductive approaches of S-R (Stimulus-Response) learning theory. S-R theorists claimed that if a functional relation is "always the same . . . then we would have no need of theory" (Spence, 1944, p. 51), going so far as to say that theoretical constructs were "guesses as to what variables *other than the ones under the control of the experimenter* are determining the response (Spence, 1944, p. 51, italics added). This turns the practical value of theory on its head. If the goal is prediction-and-influence, only variables under the control of the practitioner could possibly be of applied use. In the hypothetico-deductive view of theory, behavior becomes a mere indicator of inferred theoretical processes supposedly taking place, if anywhere, at other levels of analysis (e.g., such as the "mind/brain") but without being able to abstract these concepts from those other levels considered on their own terms.

CBS takes a different and more pragmatic approach in which "theories" are systematic and generally applicable analyses of classes of observations about action-in-context in a given domain that are stated in terms of coherently related sets of contextual principles, and that allow behavioral phenomena within that class to be predicted-and-influenced as a unified goal (Hayes, 1998b, p. 68). In this more inductive approach, theories are "analytic-abstractive"—they are abstractions from sets of functional analyses. Theories of this kind avoid the classic pragmatic problems of hypothetico-deductive theories (Skinner, 1950) and stay rooted to the contextual features so necessary for the accomplishment of prediction-and-influence when knowledge is applied by practitioners.

Practical Clinical Models and Middle Level Terms. The purely pragmatic approach to knowledge embraced by a CBS approach allows ways of speaking to emerge that are considered in reference to their own purpose and context. Practitioners need models that simplify human complexity without dismissing or minimizing its important qualities and features. It may be unrealistic and unnecessary to expect every practitioner to know the details of behavioral and other contextual principles and to be able to apply them *de novo* to complex situations, but applied methods can be guided by middle-level terms, organized into practically useful models.

The deliberately humble label of "middle-level terms" is meant to underline the fact that not all abstractive concepts need be technical terms (terms with very high precision, scope, and depth). Looser functional abstractions can help orient practitioners to some features of a domain in functional contextual terms so as to produce better outcomes and to facilitate knowledge development (i.e., for treatment and research utility).

The psychological flexibility model that underlies ACT is an example. It encompasses the core concepts of acceptance, defusion, flexible attention to the now, values, self-as-context, and committed action. None of these are technical terms; none of them have the same degree of precision, scope, and depth of classical behavioral principles such as "reinforcement," nor of technical RFT concepts such as "the transformation of stimulus functions," nor of contextual principles drawn from evolution science such as "multi-level selection." Over time the reticulated approach inside CBS may increase the precision, scope, and depth of some middle-level terms, rendering them more technical than they currently are but meanwhile they are designed to orient practitioners to key contextual features of various domains.

In some contexts, very high levels of precision are necessary. In others, little precision is needed. "Turn left at the stop light" may be all the precision necessary to help you navigate a drive to the grocery store. Although we could speak in very precise terms about the relative positions of you and the grocery store in terms of global coordinates, elevation, and such, instructions given in those terms would likely confuse anyone who was not an orienteer. In some contexts, highly precise terms are not functional. Middle-level terms are most coherent in a reticulated approach when they summarize technical knowledge, but in other cases they merely orient listeners toward some aspects of a technical account and we do not currently know if they can be reduced in a point to point way to particular contextual behavioral principles. The converse does not follow. We should work toward a basic analysis of why a middle-level term is useful when it is known to be, including why a lack of precision may be functional under some circumstances.

Multi-level and Reticulated Scientific and Practical Development. The liberal quality of theorizing that emerges when scientific and applied language is viewed exclusively through the lens of effectiveness, is restrained in CBS by the *a priori* goal of analyses with precision, scope, and depth. These three features cannot ultimately be obtained via an "anything goes" cacophony. What works in each area is a pragmatic matter, but if precision, scope, and depth are key, what works in one area needs to influence the search for what works in another. This means that there needs to be a constant effort for middle-level terms to be anchored gradually to more technical accounts. Metaphorically, clinical models need to be developed that are a bit like the operating systems of modern computers. An operating system can help get jobs done even without knowing the technical programming language that enables it to do so—but ultimately an operating system cannot be fully understood without knowing that language and how it was used in the case of a specific operating system. Furthermore, as new basic language methods are developed, better operating systems follow.

An instructive historical example is provided by the analysis of spirituality and self-knowledge (Hayes, 1984). Taken literally, "spirit" is about as far from natural science as one can get, but from a functional contextual perspective "terms are to be understood by identifying the conditions under which they are used and the effects their use has. Literal meaning is part of this picture (because the socially established structure of language must participate in its function) but it is not synonymous with it" (Hayes, 1984, p. 100). The analysis of spirituality lead to a focus on perspective taking and its possible basis in human language, and to the possible clinical role of perspective taking in undermining excessive behavioral regulation by thoughts and feelings.

Both of these implications have been pursued over the years, the former in research in RFT and the latter in research on ACT. The concepts of self-as-context and perspective-taking have fostered a variety of clinical interventions (Hayes, Strosahl, et al., 2011) and have helped explain the impact of methods used by others (e.g., Gestalt exercises, role-playing, self-distancing exercises). At the purely clinical level these concepts are still somewhat vague, however. There is as yet no adequate clinical measure of "self-as-context," and a recent review of laboratory-based tests of ACT components (Levin, Hildebrant, Lillis, & Hayes, 2012) found no studies that had yet tested clinical interventions focused on this sense of self in the laboratory. Only one small randomized trial has provided data relevant to the outcome impact of self-as-context (Williams, 2006).

Because CBS is a reticulated research program, however, much more can be said. Three possible bases were given for the basic processes that develop this sense of self (Hayes, 1984): (1) what we now call deictic relations: "words such as 'here' and 'there' are acquired which do not refer to a specific thing but to a relation to the child's point of view" (p. 102); (2) what we now call Theory of Mind skills, such as being able to apply perspective taking to dolls, other people, and oneself at different points in time and space? (p. 103); and (3) the invariant between perspective taking and self-referential terms (p. 103). The analysis was even applied to the behavior of a behavioral scientist grappling with the functional contextual definition of truth within functional contextualism itself (Barnes & Roche, 1997).

In the years since, a great deal has been learned about deictic relational frames such as I-You, Here-There, and Now-Then, and their relation to Theory of Mind skills. Measures have emerged of deictic relational responding and developmental trajectories plotted (McHugh, Barnes-Holmes, & Barnes-Holmes, 2004), and training is known to improve deictic performance with side benefits in Theory of Mind performance (Weil et al., 2011). This basic progress is beginning to impact other applied areas. For example, studies have shown that deictic responding can illuminate key clinical concepts such as social anhedonia (e.g., Villatte, Monestès, McHugh, Freixa i Baqué, & Loas, 2010), or the developmental delays shown in Asperger's Syndrome (Rehfeldt, Dillen, Ziomek, & Kowalchuk, 2007). Entire books have been written on the progress of a basic analysis of self in RFT and its applied implications (McHugh & Stewart, 2012). Until this is fully extended, the development process will not be complete, but clearly progress is being made and the impact of such research is measurable (Dymond, May, Munnelly, & Hoon, 2010).

Thus, rather than either a bottom-up basic approach, or a top-down clinical approach, CBS has evolved into a reticulated strategy based on the mutual interest between basic and applied workers on common core issues (Hayes, 1998a). Progress can occur at each level using standards appropriate to that level, but the implications need to be explored in an interconnected way with progress in either area influencing the other.

We should not expect RFT labs to provide an account that will apply point to point with existing clinical models. For example, while excellent progress has been made in the deictic basis of sense of self, the same cannot yet be said for acceptance. Fortunately, a reticulated approach does not demand this. As basic findings are extended, entirely new middle-level terms may emerge and existing ones will fall away or be supported only in part. These new basic findings may provide a way to think about the issues engaged by concepts like "fusion" and "defusion" even if there is no point to point correspondence. What makes such a reticulated agenda possible is that the analyses are always contextual and the truth criterion is always the same.

Consilience. Like a fractal, this process of agreeing on core assumptions and goals, and constructing a multi-level reticulated model of theoretical development, applies to each issue, or area, or domain. It has been seen in a gross way in the effort over the last 30 years to co-develop ACT and RFT; and in a more fine-grained way in the similarly lengthy effort to develop a clinical analysis of self and a basic analysis of perspective taking. But it is also being seen in quite different efforts to link RFT to modern work in cognitive science (DeHouwer, 2011; DeHouwer, Barnes-Holmes, & Moors, 2013), or to link ACT and RFT to multi-level selection in evolution science (Hayes & Long, 2013; D.S. Wilson et al., 2014). It is being seen in the effort to link ACT to other contextual forms of cognitive behavior therapy (Hayes, Villatte, Levin, & Hildebrandt, 2011), or to the development of pro-social groups from an evolutionary point of view (D. S. Wilson et al., 2014).

Even if others are not contextualists or functionalists, maintaining a functional position encourages researchers to explore perspectives involving different philosophical assumptions and truth criteria merely to see what might be useful. For example, even if cognitive and functional perspectives are distinct and separate, there is no reason for the researchers involved in the work to remain isolated from each other. What allows a higher level of integration, however, are commonalities among those with a functional contextual approach. Examining behavior in its historical and situational context, and interpreting it based on variation and selective retention (and applying that idea recursively even to knowledge development itself), provides a bridge to selectivist and contextualistic accounts of all kinds, in all areas, and at all levels.

In essence, Contextual Behavioral Science is emerging as a branch of evolution science, provided evolution science itself is viewed in a functional contextual way. Psychology is not subservient to biology, any more than biology is subservient to chemistry, but the concept of "depth" elevates the unity of science to that of an *a priori* analytic goal. As with all such goals, it need not be defended and justified—but it does need to be stated. For the goal of depth to be met, analyses need to be nested in a coherent fashion. The analysis of the behavior of whole organisms is part of the life sciences, and a contextual approach makes that a productive area of reticulated interaction with other areas of the life sciences, not merely a truism. If a unified fabric of science is never obtained, that is unfortunate, but in the meantime it is actively being sought by contextual behavioral scientists as a chosen goal.

The breadth of this perspective can seem overwhelming, but it need not be so. Consilience is an old idea made popular in recent times by E. O. Wilson (1998) but was developed originally by William Whewell as a way of explaining how inductive sciences can come together despite the more narrow focus on particular domains in scientific work (1840). A reticulated approach offers some new possibilities in the promotion of consilience. For one thing, a reticulated scientific tradition can advance even if very few people are working on interconnections between areas, domains, or levels. No one person need work on the enterprise as a whole. What is key is that common assumptions allow developments to apply one area to the other, that the importance of interconnection is understood, and that at least some are able to link these developments and to carry them into the more specific areas of intellectual and practical work (see Hayes, 1998a).

It is worth contrasting this approach with the more common forms of reductionism that are integral to elemental realist perspectives. Perhaps the clearest example of the difference between the multi-level reticulated program of CBS and mainstream psychological science is the role of neuroscience and other biological areas. In the mainstream approach, brain processes are causal (cf., Hineline & Wanchisen, 1989), and when vague psychological terms are examined that are of unknown utility in prediction-and-influence at the psychological level, they are often seemingly explained by the high precision of neurobiological analyses. For example, suppose researchers wished to understand generosity and where it comes from. We might create a self-report measure of generosity and select people who are high or low on our measure. While imaging the brain, we might expose those high or low on this trait to various tasks seemingly involving generosity. If clear differences are found, the headlines around the world will declare the common vision of this approach: "Brain Explains Generosity"; or "Researchers Learn that Generosity is Real"; or "Your Spouse Not Generous? It's in His Head."

All such conclusions are an illusion, in which ignorance at one level of analysis disappears into the very assumptions that establish importance for studies at another level of analysis (Fletcher, Schoendorff, & Hayes, 2010). The only reason the brain images are seemingly important is because generosity is of interest. The study provided no understanding of the history, context, function, and nature of generosity but rather was based on the guesses embedded in the self-report measure and tasks. It was these guesses that enabled the collection of sophisticated neurobiological information. Unfortunately, the ignorance we began with is now packed forever beyond reach into the assumptive base of the imaging study. Readers now *assume* these images have something to do with generosity (otherwise, why do the study?) but the elements of history, context, and function that were missing at the beginning are still missing at the end. They are nowhere to be found in the elegant images that technology has provided. It is a high cost because such variables might tell us how to create more generous schools, workplaces, and communities, as well as fostering a more interesting form of neurobiological knowledge.

Contrast this with a contextual behavioral neuroscience. In this approach, the material state of the brain is never by itself a scientifically adequate cause of psychological action; instead neurobiological evidence relative to psychology examines the depth of psychological accounts and provides a larger scientific context for them. If a behavioral event is understood in terms history, context, and function, nothing should appear at the neurobiological level that contradicts that understanding. If it does, then the analysis fails because it has no depth. If, conversely, relations between precisely defined situated actions and neurobiology are obtained then we have increased our understanding of neurobiology and of behavior, because *all of the factors of history, context, and function known to be important at the behavioral level can now inform our understanding of how the brain develops and functions*. As neurobiological evidence grows based on more adequate behavioral and contextual knowledge, the implications for behavioral science of neurobiological knowledge grow as well.

Skinner long ago provided examples of this approach (Skinner & Heron, 1937) and pointed out what this approach would mean: "What is generally not understood by those interested in establishing neurological bases [of behavior] is that a rigorous description at the level of behavior is necessary for the demonstration of a neurological correlate . . . both must be quantitatively described and shown to correspond in all their properties" (Skinner, 1938, p. 422). As has been pointed out, "In one sense, that is a daunting idea because it means that no one aspect of this integrated research program can sprint ahead while other aspects lag behind. What it promises, however, is, over time, a more integrated and useful knowledge base" (Fletcher et al., 2010, p. 60).

DOMAINS OF CBS RESEARCH AND PRACTICAL DEVELOPMENT

In previous writing on CBS (Hayes, 2008; Levin & Hayes, 2009; Hayes, Levin, et al., 2013; Vilardaga, Hayes, Levin, & Muto, 2009) several key aspects of system building have been delineated. These articles have generally described these items in a way that could apply to any analytic tradition (e.g., arguing that we need to be clear about assumptions, or we need basic principles) and only then describing how CBS per se approaches these issues (e.g., explaining functional contextualism and RFT).

In this paper we will describe the characteristics of CBS in a different way, stating each as a prescriptive agenda for CBS research and then offering a few examples. Any prescriptive statement can appear to be intellectual bullying if it is taken out of context. What prevents it from being so here (we hope) is that we have already described how a small set of core assumptions have guided the nature of CBS theory and practice and lead to certain key recommendations. For example, it may already be clear to the reader why the CBS research program needs to test its applied methods broadly (to test scope), or needs to focus on mediation and moderation (to test processes more precisely), or needs to consider dissemination at every step (to ensure that knowledge leads to effective action), or emphasize component analyses linked to manipulable processes (to make sure that principles and processes have pragmatic implications), and so on. These are the kind of implications we will develop below, primarily expressed as recommendations for action in CBS research and practice.

CBS Research Should Develop Connections With Multi-dimensional and Multi-level Evolution Science

The functional wing of behavioral psychology was always explicitly a form of evolutionary psychology:

> Selection by consequences is a causal mode found only in living things or in machines made by living things. It was first recognized in natural selection, but it also accounts for the shaping and maintenance of the behavior of the individual and evolution of cultures. In all three of these fields, it replaces explanations based on the causal modes of classical mechanics. The replacement is strongly resisted. Natural selection has now made its case, but similar delays in recognizing the role of selection in the other fields could deprive us of valuable help in solving the problems that confront us. (Skinner, 1981, p. 501)

CBS brings additional content to that table. It contains a knowledge base about arbitrarily applicable derived relational responding as the core of human symbolic behavior, and encompasses a focus on human psychological flexibility and pro-sociality. It can establish itself as a new form of evolutionary psychology with a conscious agenda of linking knowledge about behavioral and symbolic development to other dimensions of human inheritance and development, including genetic and epigenetic factors, biological and behavioral developmental plasticity, and cultural extensions of behavioral and symbolic development.

Evolutionary psychology as it has developed is explicitly hostile to behavioral psychology (e.g., Pinker, 2002; Tooby & Cosmides, 1992) due in part to hoary mischaracterizations that are simply irrelevant to CBS (e.g., supposedly behavioral researchers believe that humans are blank slates or black boxes; thoughts cannot be studied directly but must be studied based on inputs and outputs; and so on). Classical evolutionary psychology is relatively gene-centric and is so far unable to accommodate the role of general learning processes (D. S. Wilson et al., 2014). CBS is going to have to forge a new path forward that properly links itself to the contextualistic wings of the life sciences if it is to assume its natural place.

CBS has a broad focus on ontogenic development that can readily be embedded into multi-dimensional and multi-level evolution science. What we mean by "multi-dimensional" is the view that variation and selective retention occurs in multiple strands of mutually interacting events (e.g., genetic, epigenetic, behavioral and symbolic; Jablonka & Lamb, 2006); what we mean by "multi-level" is the view that variation and selection occurs at different levels of organization, with competition and selection occurring both between and within groups.

Multi-dimensionality places CBS concerns into a larger body of scientific work. Gene expression is regulated by an epigenetic system that is an inheritance system in its own right (Morris, 2012), and the epigenetic regulation of genes is massively impacted by environment and behavior (Francis, 2011; Jablonka & Lamb, 2006). There is increasing awareness that developmental plasticity is critical to both gene expression and to genetic evolution itself (West-Eberhard, 2003). Multi-dimensional evolution science considerably increases the relevance of ontogenetic processes at all levels such as the relevant of opponent physiological adjustments to the consequences of long-term use of pharmacotherapy, or the importance of learning and symbolic development as examples of developmental plasticity. Any lack of understanding of the situated actions of whole organisms leaves a hole in the fabric of the life sciences. CBS has an important role to play in this domain. It will be necessary as interconnections are explored for CBS researchers and practitioners to consider data, methods and analytic techniques from the contextualistic life sciences more generally.

Similarly, principles of multi-level selection have profound implications for cooperation and pro-sociality (Nowak, Tarnita, & Wilson, 2010; D. S. Wilson & Wilson, 2007). All forms of selection, both within and between group, are engaged by phenotypes or forms, not directly by genotypes, and behavioral phenotypes are perhaps the most important. The genotype is an important inheritance system that retains some of the effects of selection, but the unit of selection itself is the phenotype, not the genotype.

Multi-level selection applies in principle to everything in CBS. For example, if humans are particularly cooperative because they are eusocial, then it seems likely that relational framing evolved in a social context of cooperation. This could help explain the evolution of relational framing itself (Hayes & Long, 2013). Imagine that teaching an object → sign relation *from the point of view of the speaker* (see object → say "name") and teaching a sign → object relation *from the point of view of the listener* (hear "name" → look for object) eventually helps to establish the frame of coordination. In this case, the frame of coordination as an overarching operant depends in part on the coordination of roles between a speaker and listener who are sharing a common ground of intentional cooperation. The cooperative context thus provides a reason for social training in the first place and as a basis for a continuous process of genetic, behavioral, and cultural evolution in support of symbolic communication of a sort described by RFT. Such an evolutionary process could quickly create a minimally competent social/verbal community that could then shape additional relational frames, modeled on the mutuality of speaker and listener roles but no longer attached to them. For example, comparative frames that involve the derivation of A < B given training in B > A, may involve learning that *from the point of view of* A, B is bigger, but *from the point of view of* B, A is smaller. This changes how we think about relational frames, because it suggests that the non-verbal basis of perspective taking was involved in giving rise to them, and they were, at least in part, originally cooperative acts.

CBS should consider itself that wing of pragmatic behavioral science that is consciously considering these strands of development and their interactions as part of the whole of human behavior considered in a multi-dimensional and multi-level way. As we expect to see CBS research on such topics such as:

- the epigenetic effects of learning, education, psychological flexibility processes, and developmental plasticity generally, and how these effects impact the genetic regulation of structural and behavioral phenotypes;
- exploring how the parameters of general learning processes are modified by genetic evolution in some areas such as has been done with taste aversion;
- considering how preferences for specific environments alters the underlying neurobiological substrate of behavior;
- applying evolution science methods to relational framing, such as studying the implications of eusociality for non-verbal perspective taking or how this may have fed into the evolution of relational framing itself;
- examining the role of behavioral and symbolic development in cultural evolution;
- applying multi-level selection principles to guide the deployment of ACT in groups and organizations, and so on.

Basic Principles and Theories Need to Be Further Developed in Behavior, Language, and the Interaction With Other Inheritance Streams Over Time

The CBS tradition has always aimed to develop principles of organism-environment interactions within the lifetime of the individual. Behavior in context needs to be examined repeatedly and naturalistically, beginning in psychology with the intensive analysis of individuals and scaling to groups as a level of analysis across the behavioral sciences. Contextual behavioral principles include such things as habituation, the adaptation that an organism shows to the repeated presentation of a stimulus that could be potentially threatening or important but can in fact be safely ignored; respondent or

Pavlovian conditioning, or learning to prepare for a meaningful stimulus based upon a signal that typically occurs just beforehand; and operant conditioning, or changing behavior based on the consequences that it produces. Work on such basic behavioral principles of this kind continues, but progress has clearly slowed over the decades and the biggest need for additional contextual principles appears to reside in three major areas: human language and cognition, the interactions among inheritance systems (e.g., between behavioral, symbolic, genetic, and epigenetic development), and the extension of these processes into human culture.

The need for a contextual analysis of human language and cognition is clear to practitioners, who need an account of cognition that provides directly manipulable contextual targets, which is part of what drove the development of RFT. But the need for such an analysis is equally clear to the contextualistic life sciences more generally. While basic learning processes likely date to the Cambrian period, and thus are more than 500 million years old (Ginsberg & Jablonka, 2010), human symbolic relations are far, far younger. Homo sapiens may be as much as 195,000 years old (McDougall, Brown, & Fleagle, 2005), but human symbolic behavior may be only about 100,000 years old (Nichols, 1992). CBS itself has contributed to the evidence that symbolic behavior is a relatively new inheritance stream. Despite the best efforts of some of the finest behavioral researchers over the last 40 years, there still remains no unequivocal evidence for even the simplest symbolic activity as RFT defines it in a non-human species, including the higher primates (e.g., Dugdale & Lowe, 2000). Furthermore, relational learning has been shown in many studies to constitute a dividing line demarked by human language abilities (e.g., Devany, Hayes, & Nelson, 1986), not because language produces relational learning, but because it is itself a form of relational learning.

From an RFT perspective the dividing line is not relational learning per se (since a wide variety of species can learn to relate events non-arbitrarily); it is bringing this learning under arbitrary contextual control. Initially, a young child who learns that A is related to B may not "understand" that B is therefore related to A, and thus the B-A relation also has to be taught directly. If the same relations are taught across a range of other "problems," however, eventually learning about a relation in one direction (X-Y) in a specific context generates a derived relation in the other direction (Y-X). In a sense, the child has learned how to learn about symbolic relations. Although the complexity of the relations may increase dramatically to levels that are potentially almost limitless, the basic process underpinning symbolic learning remains relatively simple—relational responses are selectively strengthened or weakened based on the consequences that the responses produce in the social and physical world of the human organism. In this sense, human language and cognition *evolve* during the lifetime of each individual, given a proper social context, just as it has evolved as an inheritance system in its own right in the form of written language, books, tapes, digital recordings, and the like.

RFT researchers spent many years showing that relational learning was built upon the foundation of operant processes. In essence this program of research created a technical account of an interaction between two inheritance streams, namely, how operant learning helped create symbolic relations.

Very careful additional work will be needed to describe the complexities of human language and cognition in RFT terms, and to map out how genetics, epigenetics, behavior, and symbolic behavior interact and extend over time into cultural practices. Some of these areas will likely result in new contextual principles in their own right. The great advantage of the CBS approach is that the rich, reticulated nature of the research and the focus on manipulable contextual features ensures that practical concerns will enter into the choice of basic problems to study, making it less likely that basic advances will be disconnected from application.

As examples of this domain of CBS research we expect to see CBS research on:

- how relational learning helps explain complex cognitive and behavioral topics such as memory, reasoning, persuasion, emotion, intellectual ability, logic, discourse, reappraisal, problem-solving, goal-setting, and so on;
- how relational learning changes the operation of more primitive learning processes (for example, how symbolic behavior alters the impact of classical conditioning);
- how the transformation of stimulus functions is regulated;
- how relational learning shapes human emotion;
- how perspective taking relates to human emotions such as love, compassion, or empathy;
- how sense of self impacts on pro-sociality or cooperation, and so on.

Reticulated Models and Theories of Domains, Problems, Interventions, and Health Need to Be Developed

Having a set of basic principles and theories is a good start, but in a reticulated approach, it is not enough. Principles are like well-built and highly polished tools: They are beautiful in their own terms but their real value comes when they are used. Behavioral principles, and the additional contextual principles that may emerge regarding the interactions between inheritance streams, dare not remain at the level of polished tools sitting on a shelf. CBS models and theories are needed in all areas of human complexity such as intimate relationships, meaning and purpose, problem-solving, intellectual ability, creativity, spirituality, sexuality, and so on; they are needed in the array of problems in psychopathology; they are needed in intervention, prevention, and health promotion.

Sometimes analytic-abstractive theories can be constructed in which the transition from basic principles, to functional analysis, to classes of functional analyses is seamless. RFT is an example. At other times, middle-levels terms need to be used that cannot yet be fully tied down to basic principles in a point to point way, with models that are built from organized sets of such terms. The psychological flexibility model underlying ACT is a primary current example. Bottom-up strategies are likely to be more precise but can be slow and at times miss the phenomena of interest. Top-down strategies maintain contact with the kind of complexity that needs to be explained but are likely to be more confusing since some middle-level terms will fail to lead to technically or practically adequate accounts. The reticulated model aims to encourage both but keeping them in a dynamic tension designed to ensure the better long-term integrations of applied and basic work.

The bold and broad goals of CBS go far beyond psychopathology and its amelioration, but the same combination of reticulated bottom-up and top-down work that has yielded gains there needs to be applied to other domains. As examples of this domain of CBS research we expect to see such things as:

- theories of human well-being and happiness;
- models of education, prevention, or health development;
- theories explaining the human tendency toward prejudice and stigma and ways to counteract it;
- contextual models of violence, sexual abuse, and child neglect;
- a psychological flexibility account of the therapeutic relationship; and
- new approaches to increase pro-sociality and empowerment of social concern toward social disparities, environmental degradation, global climate change, poverty, child deprivation, and similar matters.

CBS Needs to Develop Theoretically and Technologically in the Area of Measurement of Processes of Change and Behavioral Outcomes

Adequate measures of processes of change and behavioral outcomes are integral to a reticulated approach. In the CBS ideal, practices improve outcomes by changing behavioral processes suggested by contextual principles and models. Measurement of processes of change thus is critical to the success of a CBS approach. Unfortunately, classical test theory is poorly positioned to ensure quality measurement from a CBS point of view.

In classical test theory or more modern item response theory, if a measure samples from the domain, is reliable and internally consistent, and shows positive correlations with measures of similar traits, negative correlations with measures of opposing traits, and zero order correlations with measures of orthogonal traits, the measure is declared valid. These classical views of validity emerge from elemental realist ontological assumptions (Borsboom,

Mellenbergh, & van Heerden, 2003). Good measures are assumed to mirror, imperfectly, the true elements of the world. Particular responses are seen as behavioral manifestations of the underlying concept, which is not subject to direct observation. The consistency of item performance is used to model the latent construct.

In a CBS approach, truth is pragmatic and measures must show treatment or research utility, above and beyond any other property. Treatment utility (Hayes, Nelson, & Jarrett, 1987) means that a measure should tell a practitioner what to do. Change agents with the results of the measure need to be able to (1) better target interventions, (2) change the level of the process, and (3) thereby produce better outcomes with such information than without it. Research utility refers to the measure's ability to model change and its determinants. Some measures of change processes may not prove useful at the level of the individual, but may show broader shifts in population-based studies or in laboratory studies.

Although there are beginnings (Hayes et al., 1987), to date no one has thoroughly examined classical psychometrics and its alternatives from a contextual point of view. It will be difficult because psychometric theory is so universally supported that it has even entered ethical codes as the definition of "quality" assessment. Some parts of psychometrics can be helpful to CBS measurement development, given that utility is primary, because it provides methods to document consistencies in action and in its contextual regulation. Response patterns of individuals on a measure are not an indicator of what is unseen, however; they are patterns requiring a contextual account. Suppose individuals who endorse "I feel sad" at a high level, also tend to endorse "I withdraw from people." We should not assume that this consistency indicates an inferred variable (e.g., depression)—rather we should study the conditions that establish, maintain, or undermine the relationship among these aspects of behavior. ACT studies have repeatedly demonstrated desynchronies among thought, emotion, and action after treatment (e.g., Bach & Hayes, 2002) because ACT, at times, fundamentally alters the social/verbal contexts that maintain the consistent response patterns detected by psychometric methods. If after treatment, self-reports of, say, thinking or emotion no longer correlate with action, this may not indicate that the measure has failed (as would be assumed in classical psychometrics). It may indicate instead that treatment was successful in creating more flexible response patterns; indeed we can imagine conditions in which a reduction of Cronbach's alpha of a well-established measure is itself a measure of treatment success.

It seems important for researchers within CBS to devote resources toward developing specific and compatible measures, in addition to working on contextual assessment theory. Examples of new areas of assessment that seem especially resonant with CBS assumptions are experience sampling (Bolger, Davis, & Rafaeli, 2003) focused on psychological flexibility processes, or measures of the strength or fluency of relational framing, including relational measures of implicit cognition.

Experience sampling involves asking participants several times over the course of a day to respond to questions about activity, mood, and cognition. Once difficult to conduct, the ubiquity of smart phones has made it a broadly applicable clinical and research tool. It is especially resonant with a CBS approach because it embeds assessment in life as it is lived, it allows a large number of repeated measures over time, and items can focus on the direct properties of psychological events.

The development of relational measures of implicit cognition in RFT laboratories is the best developed current example showing why measures borrowed from mainstream psychology may at times be of limited use to CBS and how to go beyond them. Consider, for example, the now ubiquitous implicit association test (IAT; Greenwald, McGhee, & Schwartz, 1998). The test is based, as the name implies, on the assumption that cognition is inherently associative in nature. In a CBS approach, human language and cognition is argued to be relational, not associative (see Hughes, Barnes-Holmes, & DeHouwer, 2011, for an extended discussion). A novel measure of implicit cognition was needed that targeted relating as a behavioral probability rather than the mental construct of associating, and one was found in the Implicit Relational Assessment Procedure (IRAP). Although the work involved in developing the measure was necessarily slow and painstaking and still continues at the time of writing, recent research has begun to show that the IRAP could be extremely useful across a range of applied domains. For example, it has predicted treatment outcome when other mainstream measures fail to do so (Carpenter, Martinez, Vadhan, Barnes-Holmes, & Nunes, in press), and the IRAP appears to predict subtle differences in psychopathology that would be difficult to target using the IAT (Nicholson & Barnes-Holmes, 2012a, 2012b).

We would hope to see CBS assessment research and scholarship in such areas as:

- measures of the fluency of relational framing with children that are appropriate for educational settings;
- tests of the treatment utility of psychological flexibility measures;
- additional implicit measures of psychological flexibility processes;
- IRAP procedures applicable to other existing self-report instruments, allowing implicit measures to cover a wider variety of psychological concepts;
- behavioral measures of response flexibility and other key outcomes;
- measures of values attainment, quality of life, and life functioning that can be customized to fit the individual;
- methods for identifying "functional symbotypes"—patterns of cognition and context with known behavioral functions (see D. S. Wilson et al., 2014);
- studies of how contextual interventions produce or restrain desynchrony among measures and items;

- contextual theoretical analysis of classical psychometrics;
- experience sampling methods focused specifically on psychological flexibility processes, and so on.

Specific Techniques and Components Need to Be Developed and Tested, Linked to Processes and Principles

When CBT broke away from traditional behavior therapy, functional analysis became far less central and attention turned toward packages linked to syndromes. By adding contextual cognitive principles to the mix, CBS affords a new way toward the vision of evidence-based processes linked to evidence-based procedures (Rosen & Davison, 2003). It is a mistake to think primarily in terms of testing packages of methods that contain a large variety of procedures. If some methods are contained in these packages that are inert or even harmful, it could take decades to ferret them out—and even when they are it may be too late to change practices easily. CBT is living through this right now with the loss of confidence in putatively critical cognitive methods (Longmore & Worrell, 2007). Randomized controlled trials of contextual clinical approaches such as ACT are important but in routine applied work it is more natural to use procedures linked to processes. The psychological flexibility model underneath ACT can be used to organize flexible deployment of ACT methods, for example, but it can also be used to bring in procedures from Functional Analytic Psychotherapy (Kohlenberg & Tsai, 1991), Mindfulness-Based Stress Reduction (Kabat-Zinn, 1990), or Compassion Focused Therapy (Gilbert, 2009). Over time, fitting methods to individual needs based on good principles and theory seems destined to constitute the heart of applied work in CBS. Whether that work will mostly be called "ACT" or something else is not as important as whether clinical needs are met by a scientific tradition.

As clinical, educational, and social change procedures come to be based on technical RFT concepts, not just the middle-level terms of psychological flexibility, the inductive functional analytic focus of CBS will likely lead to new techniques and components. The wider range of applied problems CBS is dealing with seems to demand it. RFT research suggests how particular educational problems might be remediated, for example; relational fluency is clearly an important foundation of many intellectual skills and applied extensions of RFT already exist (Cassidy et al., 2011; see Rehfeldt & Barnes-Holmes. 2009, for a book-length treatment). However, more RFT-informed models and methods of learning and education are needed. Similarly, CBS researchers are focusing more on stigma and prejudice, and a number of social change methods suggested by RFT and psychological flexibility have been tested. Clear, testable models of stigma, prejudice, compassion, and cooperation are needed linked to innovative components and procedures.

A recent meta-analysis of 66 laboratory studies examining ACT components (Levin et al., 2012) provides an instructive example of the benefits of a component focus, living under the umbrella of models, theories, principles, and processes. As compared to inactive comparisons, significant positive effect sizes were observed for many of the elements of psychological flexibility: acceptance, defusion, present moment, values, mixed mindfulness components, and values plus mindfulness component interventions. Larger effect sizes were found for theoretically specified outcomes, and for differences between theoretically distinct interventions. Finally, larger effect sizes were found for interventions including experiential methods (e.g., metaphors, exercises) as compared to rationales by themselves. This pattern of results provides support for the psychological flexibility model being applied in a process-focused fashion, helping to free practitioners from linear applications of entire packages.

We would hope to see more research in such areas as:

- developing procedures linked to basic RFT processes—for example, using distinct methods to move cognitive processes that are brief versus those that are elaborated and extended (see Hughes, Barnes-Holmes, & Vahey, 2012);
- developing specific procedures linked to evolution science principles, such as Ostrom's design principles for effective groups (1990);
- developing new strategies for linking functional analysis to intervention components, not just clinically but also in education, prejudice, child development, and other areas;
- learning how to sequence psychological flexibility components for greater impact, based on individual need, and so on.

A Full Range of Research on Processes of Change Needs to Be Deployed, Especially in the Area of Mediation and Moderation

Based on its definition of science and its goal, CBS is fundamentally oriented toward the development of analytically adequate processes of change. Given its broad goals a full range of research on processes of change needs to be deployed. Qualitative research helps ensure that concepts maintain a rich contact with human experience (e.g., Berman, Hill, Liu, Jackson, Sim, & Spangler, 2012). CBS has had a long-term commitment to the inductive and intensive analysis of individuals (e.g., Hayes, Barlow, & Nelson-Gray, 1999) in part because time-series and single-case designs allow the development of principles entirely at the psychological level. Correlational research provides a quick extension of concepts to a population (e.g., Hayes, Luoma, Bond, Masuda, & Lillis, 2006). Naturalistic longitudinal research and experience sampling examine the role of identified processes in the development of pathology or health.

That is particularly true in the area of moderation and mediation, where CBS research has been especially strong. Moderation research provides evidence that functional analytic concepts about individual needs are useful in treatment outcome. Mediation research shows that processes of change are functionally important in the production of positive outcomes. So far moderation and mediation work has been focused on psychological flexibility processes in ACT outcomes (e.g., Hayes et al., 2006), but CBS has a broader range of topics to consider.

Examples of needed CBS research on processes of change might include studies on:

- the degree to which psychological flexibility predicts positive adjustment in the face of environmental stress such as the adjustment of military personnel to deployment or military families to their absence;
- how psychological flexibility processes propagate through social groups;
- the meditational role of changes in implicit cognition in clinical outcomes;
- naturalistic longitudinal studies on the role of relational fluency in child development;
- emotional, cognitive, and overt behavioral flexibility as mediators of exposure interventions, and so on.

We Need Increasing Research on Effectiveness, Dissemination, and Training

In the typical approach to knowledge construction, issues of dissemination, effectiveness, and training can wait until knowledge is well-developed. The mainstream approach envisions a path from the laboratory, to small pilot trials, to open trials, to randomized studies, to multisite studies, to component and process analyses, and finally to effectiveness and dissemination, after the treatment has been thoroughly tested and refined.

The CBS approach is quite different (Hayes & Long, 2013). The utility of knowledge is the very measure of truth we seek. Thus, from the beginning, interventions need to be designed with the streets in mind. There is no reason to delay testing in these settings. Indeed one of the earliest trials of ACT showed that outcomes were improved in a real world setting when clinicians were trained in ACT, even though clinicians were not required to use or implement ACT methods (Strosahl, Hayes, Bergan, & Romano, 1998). Knowing early on that outcomes were good when a high level of control was abandoned and treatment was tested in a more real world way supported the practical importance of the whole development program.

Any disconnect between science and practice slows down practice and undermines the usefulness of science. Clients in clinics are not randomly assigned to treatment conditions, compensated for participation, or regularly assessed by assessors blinded to treatment condition. They are not required to meet diagnostic criteria for one and only one condition. Their therapists are not being recorded, observed by experts, rated, remediated, and required to work within a highly specified protocol. Scientists rightly prize the sort of tightly controlled evidence that emerges from well-crafted efficacy trials, and the CBS tradition embraces such trials as well, but not at the cost of testing the impact of procedures in the hurly burly of applied agencies.

Treatment development ought to occur in rich contact with a range of applications, including a richer variety of provider types and application contexts. A narrow treatment development environment needlessly increases the risk that protocols and concepts will in the end apply narrowly (to specific environments, provider groups, cultures, or treated population) or not at all. High precision/high scope principles reduce this risk, but from a CBS approach, broad testing ought to lead to broadly applicable principles. In a reticulated approach the problem of narrow principles can be reduced by effectiveness studies, the use of practitioners themselves in research collaborations, and program evaluation studies of agencies and organizations using CBS methods.

We would hope to see more research in such areas as:

- learning whether experiential training or use of mindfulness methods in the practitioner's own life helps in the retention and use of ACT methods;
- examining methods of increasing group support among professionals as methods of increasing dissemination;
- testing the use of CBS informed methods by allied health professionals such as nurses, dieticians, occupational therapists, speech therapists, and so on;
- testing new and evolving technologies, such as smart phone applications in well-established areas (e.g., ACT for chronic pain, smoking, or depression);
- whether learning to read psychological flexibility processes in clients increases skill in applying ACT;
- whether FAP (Functional Analytic Psychotherapy) training helps ACT practitioners applying contingent social reinforcement to produce better outcomes;
- testing cultural adaptations of ACT, mindfulness, or compassion-focused treatment;
- rigorous testing of CBS self-help books and websites;
- testing whether increasing basic knowledge (e.g., of RFT, of flexibility principles) facilitates the application of clinical skills, and so on.

Applied Protocols Need to Be Tested Broadly and at Multiple Levels of Analysis

By its nature, CBS is an enormously broad approach, since it is essentially an approach to behavioral science writ large, not just clinical psychology, psychiatry, social work, nursing, education, or any other subarea. The approach is broad also in its focus on common core principles that can be scaled into components and packages to create intentional change.

This means that as applied or basic knowledge is developed, CBS research will attempt to detect the boundary conditions for these principles and processes. You can already see the result in ACT research, which has visited virtually every major applied domain in its short history, but we expect that to continue as other areas in CBS reach the same level of development.

One boundary condition that may prove more difficult is the shift from clinical interventions to prevention programs, school interventions, and similar areas. CBS naturally orients toward such topics as a matter of practical impact, and so far psychological flexibility applies well, but it remains to be seen if new technology needs to be developed to alter these processes in such contexts.

We expect to see more research in a wide variety of areas as:

- behavioral medicine applications;
- addressing so called co-morbidity in an efficient way;
- reaching chronic, severe, and underserved populations;
- resilience training and other prevention approaches;
- applying CBS knowledge to organizations, leadership, businesses, and public policy;
- integration of CBS methods into programs based in schools, churches, or the criminal justice system;
- forensic use of the IRAP, and so on.

CBS IS DEPENDENT ON A DEVELOPMENT COMMUNITY CONSISTENT WITH CBS ITSELF

The explicitly contextual perspective of CBS, and its pro-social goals, demands much of its development community. It makes no sense to understand how to promote pro-sociality and then fail to do so inside the development community itself; it makes no sense to argue that history and situations are critical and then fail to promote a professional community with a diversity of backgrounds. CBS is reflexive; it applies with equal force to researchers and practitioners as it does to research participants and clients. Thus, the development community needs to adopt values-based, communitarian strategies for decision making, consensus building, and organizational development. This is especially important as CBS expands from psychology to other disciplines, and from the developed world to professionals in developing nations. ACBS has been organized in a way that is consciously linked to the psychological flexibility model and to the evolution of pro-social groups. It is not enough merely to *attempt* to do that, however—this connection needs to be actively monitored and modified based on results.

Research in this domain of CBS might include studies on:

- the application of Ostrom's (1990) design principles to the functioning of ACBS special interest groups or chapters;
- the broad application of CBS knowledge through research—practice networks;
- how to form clinical support networks across a diverse variety of settings;
- how to better connect researchers to practitioners, and so on.

Organizationally, ACBS might:

- facilitate translation of materials into a wide variety of languages, especially treatment protocols, assessments, and worksheets;
- provide a centralized forum for dealing with problems and facilitating adaptations to various cultural and language differences;
- cultivate a broader base of professionals from a variety of disciplines, including traditional mental health providers from psychology, social work, and medicine, but also from disciplines that could fit into a contextual evolutionary science, including those from biology, sociology, education, public health, and business;
- cultivate the involvement not just of those professionals working with clinical problems such as psychosis, depression, and anxiety, but those in the workplace, organizations, education, and medical arenas, among others;
- cultivate the development of researchers and trainers who can link these areas;
- cultivate the development of researchers and trainers from across a wide variety of cultures and language groups;
- create free and low cost avenues to training competence, including free access to training protocols and treatment materials, and so on.

SUMMARY AND CONCLUSION

The description we began with should now make much better sense: Contextual Behavioral Science (CBS) is a principle-focused, communitarian strategy of reticulated scientific and practical development. Grounded in contextualistic philosophical assumptions, and nested within multi-dimensional, multi-level evolution science as a contextual view of life, it seeks the development of basic and applied scientific concepts and methods that are useful in predicting-and-influencing the contextually embedded actions of whole organisms, individually and in groups, with precision, scope, and depth, and extends that approach into knowledge development itself so as to create a behavioral science more adequate to the challenges of the human condition.

We have attempted to characterize CBS as a scientific and practical tradition: what it is, where it came from, and where it is going. We have spent time listing areas of needed empirical work that might foster its expansive agenda. We want to reiterate that these are mere examples of areas we need to explore, not comprehensive lists, and furthermore they are seen from the limited point of view of a small number of the developers. Our goal is not to limit this tradition but to empower it. Undoubtedly there are scores of important research areas we have left out of the discussion. Readers seeing holes in this paper are seeing something important and we hope it will inspire actions to fill them.

Contextual Behavioral Science is a new phase in the evolution of contextual thinking. None of its elements are truly new, but they have been brought together into a new form. We do not truly know yet if it will succeed but so far CBS seems progressive as measured by its basic science, applied science, practical extension, and professional growth. The present paper was not a declaration of victory—it was a call to action based on a strategic argument. CBS is a coherent and distinctive knowledge development approach that seems to be creating principles, theories, and methods of use to others. No one knows what the future holds for CBS, but it contains the vision of a reinvigoration of contextualistic perspectives in the behavioral and life sciences. We will likely never reach the day when the behavioral sciences are fully adequate to the challenge of the human condition, but focusing on that goal seems worthy of effort, and any day that brings us a little closer to it is a day well spent.

REFERENCES

Azrin, N.H. (1977). A strategy for applied research: Learning based but outcome oriented. *American Psychologist, 32*, 140–149.

Bach, P. & Hayes, S. C. (2002). The use of Acceptance and Commitment Therapy to prevent the rehospitalization of psychotic patients: A randomized controlled trial. *Journal of Consulting and Clinical Psychology, 70* (5), 1129–1139. doi: 10.1037//0022-006X.70.5.1129

Baer, D. M., Wolf, M. M., & Risley, T.R. (1968). Some current dimensions of applied behavior analysis. *Journal of Applied Behavior Analysis, 1*, 91–97.

Barnes, D., & Roche, B. (1997). A behavior-analytic approach to behavioral reflexivity. *The Psychological Record, 47*, 543–572.

Barnes-Holmes, D. (2000). Behavioral pragmatism: No place for reality and truth. *The Behavior Analyst, 23*, 191–202.

Berman, M.I., Hill, C.E., Liu, J., Jackson, J., Sim, W., & Spangler, P. (2012). Relational events in acceptance and commitment therapy for three clients with anorexia nervosa: What is corrective? In L.G. Castonguay & C.E. Hill (Eds.), *Transformation in psychotherapy: Corrective experiences across cognitive behavioral, humanistic, and psychodynamic approaches* (pp. 215–244). Washington, DC: American Psychological Association. doi:10.1037/13747–012

Biglan, A., & Hayes, S.C. (1996). Should the behavioral sciences become more pragmatic? The case for functional contextualism in research on human behavior. *Applied and Preventive Psychology: Current Scientific Perspectives, 5*, 47–57. Doi: 10.1016/S0962–1849(96)80026–6

Bolger, N., Davis, A., & Rafaeli, E. (2003). Diary methods: Capturing life as it is lived. *Annual Review of Psychology, 54*, 579–616. DOI: 10.1146/annurev.psych. 54.101601.145030

Borsboom, D., Mellenbergh, G.J., & van Heerden, J. (2003). The theoretical status of latent variables. *Psychological Review, 110*, 203–219.

Campbell, D.T. (1959). Methodological suggestions from a comparative psychology of knowledge processes. *Inquiry, 2*, 152–183.

Campbell, D.T. (1987). Evolutionary epistemology. In G. Radnitzky & W. Bartley (Eds.), *Evolutionary epistemology, rationality, and the sociology of knowledge* (pp. 48–89). La Salle, IL: Open Court.

Carpenter, K.M., Martinez, D., Vadhan, N.L., Barnes-Holmes, D., & Nunes, V.E. (in press). Measures of attentional bias and relational responding are associated with behavioral treatment outcome for cocaine dependence. *American Journal of Drug and Alcohol Abuse.*

Cassidy, S., Roche, B., & Hayes, S.C. (2011). A relational frame training intervention to raise intelligence quotients: A pilot study. *The Psychological Record, 61*, 173–198.

DeHouwer, J. (2011). Why the cognitive approach in psychology would benefit from a functional approach and vice versa. *Perspectives on Psychological Science, 6*, 202–209.

DeHouwer, J., Barnes-Holmes, D., & Moors, A. (2013). What is learning? On the nature and merits of a functional definition of learning. *Psychonomic Bulletin and Review, 20*, 631–642.

Devany, J.M., Hayes, S.C., & Nelson, R.O. (1986). Equivalence class formation in language-able and language-disabled children. *Journal of the Experimental Analysis of Behavior, 46*, 243–257. Doi: 10.1901/jeab.1986.46–243

Dewey, J. (1981). The influence of Darwinism on philosophy. In J.J. McDermott (Ed.), *The philosophy of John Dewey* (Vol. 1, pp. 31–41). Chicago: University of Chicago Press. (Original work published 1938)

Dewey, J. (1981). The development of American pragmatism. In J.J. McDermott (Ed.), *The philosophy of John Dewey* (Vol. 1, pp. 41–58). Chicago: University of Chicago Press. (Original work published 1925)

Dugdale, N., & Lowe, F. (2000). Testing for symmetry in the conditional discriminations of language-trained chimpanzees. *Journal of the Experimental Analysis of Behavior, 73*, 5–22.

Dymond, S., & Critchfield, T.S. (2001). Neither dark age nor renaissance: Research and authorship trends in the experimental analysis of human behavior (1980–1999). *The Behavior Analyst, 24*, 241–253.

Dymond, S., May, R.J., Munnelly, A., & Hoon, A.E. (2010). Evaluating the evidence base for Relational Frame Theory: A citation analysis. *The Behavior Analyst, 33*, 97–117.

Fletcher, L.B., Schoendorff, B., & Hayes, S.C. (2010). Searching for mindfulness in the brain: A process-oriented approach to examining the neural correlates of mindfulness. *Mindfulness, 1*, 41–63.

Francis, R.C. (2011). *Epigenetics: The ultimate mystery of inheritance.* New York: W.W. Norton.

Friman, P.C. (2010). Cooper, Heron, and Heward's "Applied Behavior Analysis": Checkered flag for students and professors, yellow flag for the field. *Journal of Applied Behavior Analysis, 43*, 161–174.

Gifford, E.V., & Hayes, S.C. (1999). Functional contextualism: A pragmatic philosophy for behavioral science. In W. O'Donohue & R. Kitchener (Eds.), *Handbook of behaviorism* (pp. 285–327). New York: Academic Press.

Gilbert, P. (2009). *The compassionate mind: A new approach to facing the challenges of life.* London: Constable Robinson.

Ginsberg, S., & Jablonka, E. (2010). The evolution of associative learning: A factor in the Cambrian explosion. *Journal of Theoretical Biology, 266*, 11–20.

Greenwald, A.G., McGhee, D.E., & Schwartz, J.K.L. (1998). Measuring individual differences in implicit cognition: The Implicit Association Test. *Journal of Personality and Social Psychology, 74*, 1464–1480.

Hayes, S.C. (1984). Making sense of spirituality. *Behaviorism, 12*, 99–110.

Hayes, S. C., Hayes, L. J., & Reese, H. W. (1988). Finding the philosophical core: A review of Stephen C. Pepper's *World Hypotheses. Journal of the Experimental Analysis of Behavior, 50*, 97–111. doi: 10.1901/jeab.1988.50-97

Hayes, S.C. (1993). Analytic goals and the varieties of scientific contextualism. In S.C. Hayes, L.J. Hayes, H.W. Reese, & T.R. Sarbin (Eds.), *Varieties of scientific contextualism* (pp. 11–27). Oakland, CA: Context Press/New Harbinger.

Hayes, S.C. (1998a). Building a useful relationship between "applied" and "basic" science in behavior therapy. *The Behavior Therapist, 21*, 109–112.

Hayes, S.C. (1998b). Understanding and treating the theoretical emaciation of behavior therapy. *The Behavior Therapist, 21*, 67–68.

Hayes, S.C. (2004a). Acceptance and Commitment Therapy, Relational Frame Theory, and the third wave of behavior therapy. *Behavior Therapy, 35*, 639–665. Doi: 10.1016/S0005–7894(04)80013–3

Hayes, S.C. (2004b). Falsification and the protective belt surrounding entity postulating theories. *Journal of Applied and Preventive Psychology, 11*, 35–37. Doi: 10.1016/j.appsy.2004.02.004

Hayes, S.C. (2008). Climbing our hills: A beginning conversation on the comparison of ACT and traditional CBT. *Clinical Psychology: Science and Practice, 15*, 286–295.

Hayes, S.C., Barlow, D.H., & Nelson-Grey, R.O. (1999). *The Scientist-Practitioner: Research and accountability in the age of managed care* (2nd ed.). New York: Allyn & Bacon.

Hayes, S.C., Barnes-Holmes, D., & Roche, B. (2001). *Relational Frame Theory: A Post-Skinnerian account of human language and cognition.* New York: Plenum Press.

Hayes, S. C., Barnes-Holmes, D., & Wilson, K. G. (2012). *Journal of Contextual Behavioral Science, 1*, 1–16.

Hayes, S.C., & Brownstein, A.J. (1986). Mentalism, behavior-behavior relations and a behavior analytic view of the purposes of science. *The Behavior Analyst, 9*, 175–190.

Hayes, S. C., Hayes, L. J., & Reese, H. W. (1988). Finding the philosophical core: A review of Stephen C. Pepper's *World Hypotheses. Journal of the Experimental Analysis of Behavior, 50*, 97–111. doi: 10.1901/jeab.1988.50-97

Hayes, S.C., Hayes, L.J., Reese, H.W., & Sarbin, T.R. (Eds.). (1993). *Varieties of scientific contextualism.* Oakland, CA: Context Press/New Harbinger.

Hayes, S.C., Levin, M., Plumb, J., Boulanger, J., & Pistorello, J. (2013). Acceptance and Commitment Therapy and contextual behavioral science: Examining the progress of a distinctive model of behavioral and cognitive therapy. *Behavior Therapy, 44*, 180–198. Doi: 10.1016/j.beth.2009.08.002

Hayes, S.C., & Long, D. (2013). Contextual behavioral science, evolution, and scientific epistemology. Chapter in Dymond, S. & Roche, B. (Eds.). *Advances in Relational Frame Theory: Research and application.* Oakland, CA: New Harbinger / Context Press.

Hayes, S.C., Long, D.M., Levin, M.E., & Follette, W.C. (2013). Treatment development: Can we find a better way? *Clinical Psychology Review. 33*, 870–882.

Hayes, S.C., Luoma, J., Bond, F., Masuda, A., & Lillis, J. (2006). Acceptance and Commitment Therapy: Model, processes, and outcomes. *Behaviour Research and Therapy, 44*, 1–25. doi: 10.1016/j.brat.2005.06.006

Hayes, S.C., Nelson, R.O., & Jarrett, R. (1987). Treatment utility of assessment: A functional approach to evaluating the quality of assessment. *American Psychologist, 42*, 963–974. Doi: 10.1037//0003–066X.42.11.963

Hayes, S.C., Strosahl, K., & Wilson, K.G. (1999). *Acceptance and Commitment Therapy: An experiential approach to behavior change.* New York: Guilford Press.

Hayes, S.C., Strosahl, K., & Wilson, K.G. (2011). *Acceptance and Commitment Therapy: The process and practice of mindful change* (2nd ed.). New York: Guilford Press.

Hayes, S.C., Villatte, M., Levin, M. & Hildebrandt, M. (2011). Open, aware, and active: Contextual approaches as an emerging trend in the behavioral and cognitive therapies. *Annual Review of Clinical Psychology, 7*,141–168. Doi: 10.1146/annurev-clinpsy-032210–104449

Hineline, P.N., & Wanchisen, B.A. (1989). Correlated hypothesizing and the distinction between contingency-shaped and rule-governed behavior. In S.C. Hayes (Ed.), *Rule-governed behavior: Cognition, contingencies, and instructional control* (pp. 221–268). New York: Plenum Press.

Hughes, S., Barnes-Holmes, D., & DeHouwer, J. (2011). The dominance of associative theorising in implicit attitude research: Propositional and behavioral alternatives. *The Psychological Record, 61*, 465–498.

Hughes, S., Barnes-Holmes, D., & Vahey, N. (2012). Holding on to our functional roots when exploring new intellectual islands: A voyage through implicit cognition. *Journal of Contextual Behavioral Science, 1*, 17–38.

Jablonka, E., & Lamb, M.J. (2006). *Evolution in four dimensions: Genetic, epigenetic, behavioral, and symbolic variation in the history of life.* Cambridge, MA: MIT Press.

James, W. (1981). *Pragmatism.* Indianapolis, IN: Hackett. (Original work published 1907)

Kabat-Zinn, J. (1990). *Full catastrophe living.* New York: Delacorte Press.

Kantor, J.R. (1963). *The scientific evolution of psychology* (Vol. 1). Chicago: Principia Press.

Kohlenberg, R.J., & Tsai, M. (1991). *Functional analytic psychotherapy.* New York: Plenum Press.

Levin, M., & Hayes, S.C. (2009). ACT, RFT, and contextual behavioral science. In J.T. Blackledge, J. Ciarrochi, & F.P. Deane (Eds.), *Acceptance and Commitment Therapy: Contemporary research and practice* (pp. 1–40). Sydney: Australian Academic Press.

Levin, M.E., Hildebrandt, M.J., Lillis, J., & Hayes, S.C. (2012). The impact of treatment components suggested by the psychological flexibility model: A meta-analysis of laboratory-based component studies. *Behavior Therapy, 43*, 741–756.

Longmore, R.J., & Worrell, M. (2007). Do we need to challenge thoughts in cognitive behavioral therapy? *Clinical Psychology Review, 27*, 173–187.

Mahoney, M.J. (1974). *Cognition and behavior modification.* Cambridge, MA: Ballinger.

Marr, M.J. (1993). Contextualistic mechanism or mechanistic contextualism? The straw machine as tar baby. *The Behavior Analyst, 16*, 59–65.

McDougall, I., Brown, F.H., & Fleagle, J.G. (2005). Stratigraphic placement and age of modern humans from Kibish, Ethiopia. *Nature, 433*, 733–736. doi:10.1038/nature03258.

McHugh, L., Barnes-Holmes, Y., & Barnes-Holmes, D. (2004). Perspective taking as relational responding: A developmental profile. *The Psychological Record, 54*, 115–144.

McHugh, L., & Stewart, I. (2012). *Self and perspective taking.* Oakland, CA: Context Press/New Harbinger.

McIlvane, W.J. (2009). Translational behavior analysis: From laboratory science in stimulus control to intervention with persons with neurodevelopmental disabilities. *The Behavior Analyst, 32*, 273–280.
Morris, K.V. (2012). *Non-coding RNAs and epigenetic regulation of gene expression: Drivers of natural selection*. Norfolk, UK: Caister Academic Press
Nichols, J. (1992). *Linguistic diversity in space and time*. Chicago: University of Chicago Press.
Nicholson, E., & Barnes-Holmes, D. (2012a). Developing an implicit measure of disgust propensity and disgust sensitivity: Examining the role of implicit disgust- propensity and-sensitivity in obsessive-compulsive tendencies. *Journal of Behavior Therapy and Experimental Psychiatry, 43*, 922–930.
Nicholson, E., & Barnes-Holmes, D. (2012b). The Implicit Relational Assessment Procedure (IRAP) as a measure of spider fear. *The Psychological Record, 62*, 263–277.
Nowak, M.A., Tarnita, C.E., & Wilson, E.O. (2010). The evolution of eusociality. *Nature, 466*, 1057–1062.
Ostrom, E. (1990). *Governing the commons: The evolution of institutions for collective action*. New York: Cambridge University Press.
Pierce, C. S. (1983) How to make our ideas clear (selected excerpts). In M. White (Ed.), *The age of analysis: 20th century philosophers* (pp. 143–153). New York: Meridian. (Original work published 1878)
Pinker, S. (2002). *The blank slate: The modern denial of human nature*. New York: Viking.
Quine, W.V. (1974). *The roots of reference*. La Salle, IL: Open Court.
Radnitzky G., & Bartley, W. (Eds.) (1987). *Evolutionary epistemology, rationality, and the sociology of knowledge*. La Salle, IL: Open Court.
Rehfeldt, R. A., & Barnes-Holmes, Y. (Eds.). (2009). *Derived relational responding: Applications for learners with autism and other developmental disabilities*. Oakland, CA: New Harbinger.
Rehfeldt, R.A., Dillen, J.E., Ziomek, M.M., & Kowalchuk, R.K. (2007). Assessing relational learning deficits in perspective-taking in children with high-functioning autism spectrum disorder. *Psychological Record, 57*, 23–47.
Rosen, G. M., & Davison, G. C. (2003). Psychology should list empirically supported principles of change (ESPs) and not credential trademarked therapies or other treatment pack- ages. *Behavior Modification*, 27, 300–312.
Ruiz, M.R., & Roche, B. (2007). Values and the scientific culture of behavior analysis. *The Behavior Analyst, 30*, 1–16.
Skinner,B.F.(1938).*BehaviorofQrganisms*.NewYork:Appleton-Century-Crofts.
Skinner, B.F. (1945). The operational analysis of psychological terms. *Psychological Review, 52*, 270–276.
Skinner, B.F. (1950). Are theories of learning necessary? *Psychological Review, 57*, 193–216.
Skinner, B. F. (1974). *About behaviorism*. New York: Knopf.

Skinner, B. F (1981). Selection by consequences. *Science, 213*, 501–504.
Skinner, B. F., & Heron, W. T. (1937). Effects of caffeine and benzedrine upon conditioning and extinction. *The Psychological Record, 1*, 340–346.
Spence, K. W. (1944). The nature of theory construction in contemporary psychology. *Psychological Review, 51*, 48–68.
Staddon, J. E. (1993). Pepper with a pinch of psalt. *The Behavior Analyst, 16*, 245–250.
Strosahl, K. D., Hayes, S. C., Bergan, J., & Romano, P. (1998). Does field based training in behavior therapy improve clinical effectiveness? Evidence from the Acceptance and Commitment Therapy training project. *Behavior Therapy, 29*, 35–64.
Tooby, J., & Cosmides, L. (1992). The psychological foundations of culture. In J. H. Barkow, L. Cosmides, & J. Tooby (Eds.), *The adapted mind: evolutionary psychology and the generation of culture* (pp. 19–136). Oxford: Oxford University Press.
Weil, T. M., Hayes, S. C., & Capurro, P. (2011). Establishing a deictic relational repertoire in young children. *The Psychological Record, 61*, 371–390.
West-Eberhard, M. J. (2003). *Developmental plasticity and evolution.* New York: Oxford University Press.
Whewell, W. (1840). *The philosophy of the inductive sciences, founded upon their history*. London: Parker.
Williams, L. M. (2006). *Acceptance and commitment therapy: An example of third-wave therapy as a treatment for Australian Vietnam War veterans with posttraumatic stress disorder*. Unpublished doctoral dissertation, Charles Sturt University, Bathurst, New South Wales.
Wilson, D. S., & Wilson, E. O. (2007). Rethinking the theoretical foundation of sociobiology. *Quarterly Review of Biology, 82*, 327–348.
Wilson, D. S., Hayes, S. C., Biglan, T., & Embry, D. (2014). Evolving the future: Toward a science of intentional change. *Behavioral and Brain Sciences, 37*, 395–416.
Wilson, E. O. (1998). *Consilience: The unity of knowledge*. New York: Knopf.
Wilson, K. G., Whiteman, K., & Bordieri, M. (2013). The pragmatic truth criterion and values in contextual behavioral science. In S. Dymond & B. Roche (Eds.), *Advances in Relational Frame Theory & Contextual Behavioral Science: Research and application* (pp. 27–47). Oakland: New Harbinger.
Vilardaga, R., Hayes, S. C., Levin, M. E., & Muto, T. (2009). Creating a strategy for progress: A contextual behavioral science approach. *The Behavior Analyst, 32*, 105–133.
Villatte, M., Monestès, J. L., McHugh, L., Freixa i Baqué, E., & Loas, G. (2010). Adopting the perspective of another in belief attribution: Contribution of Relational Frame Theory to the understanding of impairments in schizophrenia. *Journal of Behavior Therapy and Experimental Psychiatry, 41*, 125–134.

EPILOGUE

LOOKING TO THE FUTURE OF ACT, RFT, AND CONTEXTUAL BEHAVIORAL SCIENCE

Steven C. Hayes and Fredrick Chin
University of Nevada

The present volume is focused on the work on a single individual, which distorts somewhat the nature of CBS and its components. CBS is a community (and not a small one—as of this writing ACBS has just under 7,500 members worldwide). The community itself is designed to be consistent in its internal operations with the principles of the methods and models the tradition itself has produced: open, accepting, and values based. There are many areas of work in CBS that are not touched on significantly in these 14 articles: implicit cognition, data on educational or other applications of RFT, recent innovations in ACT and its extension to new domains such as health promotion or group effectiveness, the rapidly growing linkage between evolution science and ACT and RFT, the inclusion of applied methods other than ACT or RFT in CBS writ large, and so on.

What the volume shows is that care was taken to build a foundation—philosophically, theoretically, methodologically, technologically—that may be able to sustain the kind of progressive and long-term effort needed to create a psychology more worthy of the challenge of the human condition. If that care was successful, and so far it appears to be relatively adequate, the community itself will determine how progressive CBS will become.

In that context it seems worth a few moments to look ahead. What are the trends that seem likely in the future based on the foundational work we have explored in this volume? We can predict several with relative degrees of confidence. Given space restrictions all we can do, however, is to list these in short paragraphs.

1. *RFT will continue to evolve and will produce robust applied methods.* We see these trends already in the development of RFT-based language training

methods (especially in applied behavior analysis), language assessment devices for children and others, and IQ assessment and training. We can also see the beginnings of the development of RFT as a foundation for a functional diagnostic system, and as a way to produce direct clinical guidance.

2. *RFT will link to mainstream psychology while retaining its character.* RFT is too useful to be ignored just because it is "behavioral." We are already seeing RFT-based methods of assessment of implicit cognition (forms of the Implicit Relational Assessment Procedure) move into mainstream studies. Major cognitive scientists are writing about RFT. It seems likely we will see RFT-based methods in research on mainstream cognitive topics (reasoning, problem solving, memory, and so on) as was a such areas as attitude change, employee screening, assessment of motivation, advertising, voting, and many other areas.

3. *Psychotherapy in CBS will broaden clinically and will become more process and procedure focused.* The early dream of functional analysis is back. As psychological flexibility is combined other theoretical ideas (Elinor Ostrom's design principles; evolution science principles; the flexible connectedness model; and ideas drawn from compassion-focused therapy, mindfulness-based methods, functional analytic psychotherapy, and so on) psychotherapy from a CBS perspective will expand based on principles, processes, models, and methods from areas other than ACT alone. It is not yet clear if this will be called ACT, or clinical CBS, or something else.

4. *Scaling for impact.* ACT and CBS are going into hospitals, organizations, clinics, schools, and communities. There are World Health Organization ACT trials, clinics in the developing world, and ACT being combined with Elinor Ostrom's principles in the PROSOCIAL project in the Evolution Institute. Entire medical clinics are organized around ACT in areas such as pain, weight, diabetes, and so on. This all seems likely to continue.

5. *Indirect intervention.* ACT and other CBS methods are invading the world of apps, online programs, bibliotherapy, and so on. This will increase and expand.

6. *Touching the gatekeepers.* ACT will be doing more with teachers, chaplains, ministers, coaches, and anyone else with access to people in need. ACT will be harnessed more to thriving, not just alleviation of suffering.

7. *Bridge building.* CBS has constructed a strong bridge with evolution science. Expect to see the same with humanistic, analytic, existential, cognitive science, and other perspectives and points of view.

8. *Addressing what people care about.* Expect CBS to be more visible in addressing issues such as art, literature, sport, humor, culture, terrorism, war, and other topics of popular interest and common concern.

9. *Developing and deploying scientific methods more consistent with CBS.* Expect more use of experience sampling, functional definitions of assessment quality, radically pragmatic evaluation strategies (e.g., the manipulated training

method of verifying the utility of CBS ideas), IRAP-based self-report measures, epigenetic measures, developmental neuroscience assessments, and other methodological innovations that are consistent with functional contextual assumptions.

10. *Public footprint.* CBS, RFT, and ACT will be increasingly visible to the community at large.

Taken together it is an exciting future. We shall see.

INDEX

acceptance: based condition 261–2; and change 216; psychological 178, 192–3
Acceptance and Action Questionnaire (AAQ) 255–6, 258–9, 261–2, 266, 268–70
Acceptance and Commitment Therapy (ACT) 62–4, 66–7, 81–2, 207–8, 210–11, 216–31, 239–41, 243–5, 251–3, 255, 262–71, 283–6, 305, 307–8, 319–21; condition 267–70; group 267–9; model 255, 258–60, 262–3, 270–1; processes 208, 255, 258; therapists 6, 223–4, 227–8, 255, 259
Acceptance and Commitment Therapy: Model, Processes, and Outcomes 249–79
agoraphobics 52, 177, 183, 186–7, 192
alcohol 183, 188
analytic goals 5, 40, 65, 75, 100–1, 103, 105–9, 111, 113, 115, 122, 217, 280–1
Analytic Goals and the Varieties of Scientific Contextualism 100–16
anxiety 18–19, 22–3, 25, 174, 176–9, 181, 183–90, 213, 222–3, 225, 227, 241, 257–9, 262, 268; disorders 184, 187, 222, 226, 232; social 164
apparent speaker-mediated consequences 11
applied behavior analysis 281, 320
assessment 53, 129–30, 161–3, 165–8, 252, 303–4, 310, 320; devices 161, 163–4; process 130, 162–3, 166; treatment utility of 130, 160–7
Association for Contextual Behavioral Science (ACBS) 309–10, 319
assumptions, scientific 282
auxiliaries and conditions 39–40, 287
aversive stimulation 11, 16–17
avoided experiences 183, 185–7, 189–90

Barlow, D. H. 186–7, 192
basic cognitive science laboratories 250
Beck, A. T. 26–8, 31
Beck Anxiety Inventory 257, 259
Beck Depression Inventory (BDI) 259
behavior: activation 229–30; analysis 42–3, 46, 86, 88, 95, 117, 213; change 112–13, 213, 262, 290; cognitive 8; components 20, 27–8; controlled 135; controlling 63, 96; control of 65, 92; covert 91, 95; disorders 130, 171; epistemology 5, 117–19, 121–3, 125; events 47, 70, 84, 87–8, 92–4, 296; functions 120, 124–5, 151; governed 15, 52; marital therapy 192, 232; methodology 7–8; modification 40; of organisms 67, 90, 283; outcomes 148, 302; overt 20, 91, 192, 213–14, 252, 288; perspective 43, 79, 95, 153; phenotypes

298–9; point 42–3, 120, 138, 212; positions 79–80; predispositions 48, 174, 176, 241, 243; products of 43; public 94–5; qualities of 94, 151; researchers 134, 136, 142, 297, 300; science 67; sciences 5, 207, 259, 280–1, 286, 288–90, 296, 299, 310–11; scientists 92, 94, 286, 295; self-management 266–7; self-rule-governed 15; shaped 53–4, 229; speaker's 15, 21; structure of 84; system 80, 83, 85–6, 88, 91, 124; target 163; thinking 4, 129, 230
behavioral principles 148, 173, 214, 290, 301; basic 129, 133, 300; contextual 290, 299; new 148–9
behavioral psychology 40, 119, 281–2, 297; modern 247, 255
behavioral stream 119–20, 284
behavior analysis 63–70, 72–5, 78–84, 86, 88, 90–2, 94–5, 132–3, 135–6, 143, 148, 151–3, 208, 217–19, 281–2; basic 136, 208, 220, 281–2; clinical 210–11; elements of 66, 74; evolution of 129, 132; experimental 57, 136
behavior analysts 65–6, 69–75, 78–9, 84, 93, 97–8, 102, 117, 122, 129, 132–6, 138–40, 148–9, 153, 213
behavior-analytic positions 78, 81, 83
behavior-behavior relations 5, 78–9, 81, 83, 85, 87, 89, 91–7, 99
behaviorism 7, 42–4, 85, 89–90; methodological 8, 89, 94, 213
behaviorists 32, 42, 44, 48, 67, 70, 72, 78, 83–6, 89, 95–6, 213; radical 8, 16, 92, 97
behavior therapists 31, 211–13, 247
behavior therapy 7–8, 18, 32, 208, 210–16, 218–19, 222, 229–32, 244, 249–50, 289; first wave of 211, 213–14, 216, 218; movement 174, 249; new 229–30; third wave of 229; tradition 232; traditional 174, 228, 249, 251, 305
believability 228–9, 244, 260, 263, 266–7
borderline personality disorder (BPD) 183, 187–8, 231, 265
Bouton, M. E. 229
BPD *see* borderline personality disorder
Buddhism 207, 239–41, 243–7
Buddhism and Acceptance and Commitment Therapy 207, 239–48
Buddhist concepts 240, 246–7
carbon dioxide (CO_2) 261–2
causality 68, 288–9
causal relations 95–6
CBS *see* contextual behavioral science
CBT *see* Cognitive behavior therapy
children 13–14, 23–4, 44, 46–7, 120, 140–1, 144, 146, 177, 182, 185, 189–90, 219–21, 300, 304
Chiles, J. 192
Chin, Fredrick 3–4, 129, 207–8, 320
classical conditioning 119, 121, 136, 138, 150, 176, 301
clients, depressed 26–7, 263
clinical assessment 160–1, 163, 165, 168
cognition 3–5, 119, 129, 153, 163, 175, 177, 181, 208, 212–16, 218–22, 225, 250–3, 300–1, 304
cognitive-behavioral group therapy (CBGT) 269
cognitive-behavioral interventions 18
cognitive behavioral psychology 246
cognitive behavior therapists 8, 243, 246
cognitive behavior therapy (CBT) 3–4, 7–8, 18, 25, 28, 32, 207–8, 214, 225, 228–30, 246, 249–51, 263–4, 290, 294, 305
cognitive fusion 221–2, 243, 247, 253, 271
cognitive phenomena 8
cognitive psychologists 88, 119, 153
cognitive psychology 70, 88, 136, 153, 219
cognitive restructuring procedures 22
cognitive theories 136, 153
cognitive therapy 17, 21, 27–8, 136, 153, 174–5, 207, 210–11, 213–16, 229–32, 239, 250–1, 263–4, 270
cognitivism 70–1, 84–5
cognitivists 70–1, 84, 87–9
coherence 61, 71, 74, 101, 110
combinatorial entailment 145–7, 219
community, development 309
conceptual categories 57–8
conceptualized self 244–5, 254
conceptual utility 168
conditional discriminations 139, 141, 143
conflicts 57, 59, 69, 73–4, 246
consciousness 118, 121, 242, 245
consequences 9, 11–12, 14, 16–17, 26, 31, 40, 63–4, 70, 101–5, 107–8, 283, 287, 297–8, 300; specified 103, 105
contextual approach, functional 3, 288, 294

contextual behavioral science (CBS) 3, 5, 130, 286–9, 291, 296–7, 299, 301–4, 307–9
Contextual Behavioral Science: Creating a Science More Adequate to the Challenge of the Human Condition 280–318
contextual control 103, 129, 146–7, 150, 219
contextual cues 103, 119, 143–8, 221
contextualism 5, 58–9, 61–4, 66–8, 73–5, 81–3, 85, 100, 102, 109–10, 114–15, 217–18, 252, 285, 287
contextualistic life sciences 298, 300
contextualists 5, 63–74, 82, 85–6, 92, 100–2, 105–6, 108, 110–11, 113, 115, 294
contextual perspective, functional 283, 292
contextual principles 290–1, 302
contingencies 9–11, 14–16, 20, 28, 31, 43–4, 53, 80, 82, 90, 92, 117–19, 137–8, 213; dual 10, 15, 17; natural 12, 15, 17, 21, 27–9; programmed 137, 152; social 15–17
continuity strategy 133–6
contradictions 38, 50, 61, 111
contradictory elements 101
control: behavior 9, 24, 80, 108; behavioral 83, 241; conscious 225; emotional 261; emphasis on 79–80; loss of 176; rules 175, 177; sources of 44, 51, 90; verbal 52, 135–6, 149, 178
coping self-statements 22–5
correlational studies 208, 255
covert behavior 91, 95

defense 6, 39–40, 192–3
depression 26, 28, 182–3, 188–90, 215, 221, 228, 241, 257–8, 268–9, 303, 308, 310; cognitive treatment of 18, 25, 27, 31
derived stimulus relations 119, 124, 139, 143, 147–53, 225
descriptive contextualists 109–11, 113–15
Dialectical Behavior Therapy (DBT) 188, 210, 216, 228–31, 251, 270
disciplines 117, 193, 214, 309–10
discriminative stimuli 10, 82, 142, 146, 148
disorders, obsessive-compulsive 183–4
distress 187, 267–70
dogmatism 78, 106–9, 115, 218
domains, behavioral 93
dualism 44, 51, 54, 287

EA *see* experiential avoidance
education 267, 299, 302, 305–6, 309–10
effective action 65, 93, 98, 102, 108, 165, 243, 285, 297
effect sizes 255, 259, 263, 265, 269–70
Ellis, A. 9, 19–21, 27–8
emotional acceptance 192
emotional avoidance 176–9, 182, 193
emotions 52, 174–7, 180–1, 184, 187, 192, 212, 214, 221–2, 226–7, 240–1, 243, 288, 301, 303; human 176, 301
entity-postulating theories 38–41
environment-behavior relations 290
equivalence relations 140, 142, 147, 150, 152
events 47–50, 58, 62, 64–6, 79–96, 103–6, 110–14, 119–21, 142–6, 149–50, 152, 174–6, 216–21, 241–5, 251–3; biological 67; category of 91–2; mental 87, 92, 94–5, 103; particular 26, 60, 178, 218
events and relations, descriptions of 79
evolution science 209, 291, 294, 319–20
experience events 226, 246
experiential avoidance (EA) 130, 171, 173–83, 185, 187–92, 221, 228, 241, 253, 255, 258, 269; method of 184–6, 189
Experiential Avoidance and Behavioral Disorders: A Functional Dimensional Approach to Diagnosis and Treatment 171–204
explicit goals 106, 111
exposure 25, 185, 187, 191–2, 227, 261–2, 269

falsification 4, 38–40
feelings 5, 7, 9, 45, 47, 89, 91–2, 182, 190–2, 213, 221–3, 225–9, 243–4, 251–2, 261; thoughts and 9, 177, 213, 251–2, 261, 267, 292
Finding the Philosophical Core: A Review of Stephen C. Pepper's World Hypotheses 57–77
foreign concepts 74
formism 58–61, 101
formists 61, 72–3, 101
formulation 14–15, 17, 25, 29–31, 211, 283

functional analyses 43, 164, 173, 290–1, 302, 305–6, 320
functional classification 172–3
functional contextualism 3, 5, 109, 112–14, 217–18, 252, 282, 285–6, 293, 296; goal of 286, 288
functional contextualists 3, 112–14, 280, 284, 286
functional diagnostic dimensions 130, 173–4, 180, 188–9, 191, 193
functional processes 130, 173
functions: nonverbal 123–5; transfer of 120, 145–9

hallucinations 244, 267–8
Herbert, J. D. 51, 267
human behavior 65, 78, 93, 98, 125, 133, 189, 220, 252, 299
human language 129, 175–6, 241–2, 252–3, 292
human symbolic behavior 175, 254, 297, 300

implicit cognition 304, 307, 319–20
Implicit Relational Assessment Procedure (IRAP) 304, 309, 320
impure tacts 17, 28–9, 31
ineffective avoidance strategies 183, 185–7, 190
instructional control 132, 134–5, 137, 150
instructions, effects of 133–4, 136
irrational beliefs 19–22, 175

Kanfer, F. H. 23, 174
Killeen, P. R. 78, 92
knowledge 45–6, 48, 62, 68, 72, 110, 112–13, 115, 117–20, 123–6, 130, 285, 288, 290–1, 307; development of 281, 284, 291, 294, 310; scientific 65, 78, 108, 117, 281, 285

language, and cognition 3–4, 212–13, 219–21, 225, 239, 251–2, 270, 300–1, 304
learning, relational 219, 225, 300–1
life sciences 283, 294, 298, 311
literal dualism 86–8, 94
literal quality 54, 243

Marlatt, G. A. 192
matter/spirit distinction 42, 44, 49, 51
MBCT *see* Mindfulness-based Cognitive Therapy
McCracken, L. M. 259, 269
Meehl, P. E. 4, 38–41, 160–2, 172
mentalism 5, 65, 71, 78–9, 81, 83, 85–7, 89, 91, 93–7, 99
mindfulness 210, 216, 225–6, 230, 232, 240, 242, 245, 251, 255, 260, 270, 308; and acceptance 270
Mindfulness-based Cognitive Therapy (MBCT) 210–11, 216, 229–31, 251
multi-level evolution science 281, 297–8, 310
mutual entailment 145–7, 219

negative self-statements 22–3, 25
negative thoughts 22, 25, 228–9
neo-behaviorists 212–13
nonfunctional definitions 66–7

OCD 185, 270
operating system 292
organicism 58–9, 61, 71, 111, 114
organismic action 89–90
organisms, nonverbal 125, 138, 142, 176, 241
Oxford English Dictionary (OED) 45, 86–7

participants 64, 109, 111, 217, 258, 261–3, 266–7, 269–70, 286, 304
personality 72, 94, 163–4, 287; assessment 162; client's 167; types 72
perspective behavior 49–50
philosophical assumptions 5, 68–9, 73–4, 207, 281, 294
pliance 11, 13–14, 17, 19–21, 23–5, 29–32
potential functions 23, 67
Potential Theoretical Framework 3, 7
pragmatic truth 3, 72–3, 75, 108, 122–3, 217, 252, 285–6
pragmatism 81, 106–7, 115, 122, 217
prediction-and-influence 286, 288–9, 291, 295
private events 7–8, 45, 65, 86, 89, 94, 178–9, 213, 221, 224; observations of 90; situational sensitivity of 222, 253
private world 46, 91, 120–1
process goals 106, 286
psychological events 67–8, 121, 217–18, 230, 243, 250, 252, 254, 288, 304

psychological flexibility 130, 208, 255, 259, 299, 303–9, 320
psychological processes 133, 149–50, 173, 193, 243; level of 149, 151
psychological systems 59, 69, 73
psychologists 63, 68, 73, 89, 92, 95, 106, 112, 117, 124, 132
psychology, evolutionary 297
psychopathology 15, 18–19, 28–9, 129–30, 171–2, 174–5, 177, 179, 182, 191, 193, 253–4, 256–9, 301–2, 304
psychotherapy 20, 52, 54, 130, 182, 192, 246, 320

radical behaviorism 3, 7–8, 81, 85, 87, 89–91, 94, 98, 213, 217; contemporary 7
rational-emotive therapy 18, 20
relapse prevention 184, 192
relational frames 119–20, 146–9, 152, 220–2, 225–6, 253, 293, 299
Relational Frame Theory (RFT) 4, 129–30, 143, 151, 153, 207, 210, 218–22, 242, 251–3, 255, 281, 293–4, 299–300, 319–21
relational framing 5, 129, 220, 298–9, 304
relational measures of implicit cognition 304
relations, trained 139–40, 142
relatively adequate world views 58–9, 63
reliability 130, 161, 166–7
religious beliefs 107
researchers, development of 310
response prevention 185
RFT *see* Relational Frame Theory
Roche, B 122, 210, 239, 252–3, 281, 289
root metaphor 58–61, 81, 101–2, 113–15
rule-governed behavior 3–4, 7, 9–15, 17–19, 21–3, 25, 27–9, 31–2, 129, 135–6; sensitivity of 152
Rule-Governed Behavior: A Potential Theoretical Framework for Cognitive-Behavioral Therapy 7–35
rules 9–17, 19–21, 23–32, 44, 51–4, 80, 89, 104, 129, 135, 150–2, 185, 193, 225, 253; of change 61; control by 51; untestable 27

science, goals of 40, 78–81, 83–6, 94, 97–8, 215
scientific analysis 8, 40, 65, 89–90, 122, 280
scientific contextualism 5, 100, 282, 286
scientific goals 74, 81, 85–6, 217, 281, 286
scientific statements 48, 80
scientists 5, 40, 60, 63–6, 68–71, 80–2, 87–9, 117, 122, 213, 280, 282, 284–6, 308
self-as-context 291, 293
self-control 16, 18, 31, 96, 190
self-knowledge 121, 175–6, 241, 292
self-pliance 17, 29, 31
self-plys 20, 29–31
self-reinforcement 16, 23, 97–8
self-rules 14–17, 19, 24–5, 27–30, 32, 95–8
self-statements 22, 24–6
self-tracking 17
sensations 186, 227, 229, 242; bodily 174, 187, 189, 191–2, 226–7, 241, 243
sense of self 120–1, 245, 293–4, 301
sexual abuse 182, 189–91, 221, 302
short term goals 109
Skinner, B. F. 9–11, 15–16, 129, 134
social context groups 24
soft psychology 38–40
speaker behavior, functional units of 11–12
speaker-mediated consequences 13; control of apparent 11
spirit 42–6, 48–9, 86–7, 173, 292
spirituality 4–5, 42–9, 51, 53–4, 121, 210, 227, 232, 239, 245, 301
stimulus 8, 67, 82, 88, 91, 96–7, 103, 113, 119, 135, 139–40, 142–9, 151–2, 219, 299–300; control 11, 51, 134–5, 143, 149, 151, 220, 290; equivalence 120, 129, 139–43, 147–8, 153; objects 17, 70; response-produced 96–7
stimulus functions 120, 145, 147–8, 151–2, 176, 219–22, 225, 291, 301; derived 151–2; non-relational 146; relational 146
stimulus relations 119, 144, 147, 150–1, 219; derivation of 144, 148–9, 152
stimulus-response theories 70, 85
substance abuse 182–4, 190, 221, 232
successful working 74, 81–2, 102, 104, 117
suicidal behavior 189
suicide 109, 187, 189, 241
suppression, thought 130, 177–8, 181–2, 185, 260
symbolic behavior 282, 300–1

symbolic development 297–9
syndromal classification 172, 191, 193
systematic development 109

third wave interventions 230–2, 251
tracking 12–14, 17, 19, 21, 23–4, 27–9, 32
transcendent self 229, 245
treatment: behavioral 20; condition 262, 266, 307; implications 163, 183–5, 187–9, 191; outcome 130, 160–2, 165, 167–8, 186, 307; utility 130, 162, 164–8, 188, 191, 303–4
Treatment Utility of Assessment: A Functional Approach to Evaluating the Quality of Assessment 160–70
truth criterion 5, 61, 63, 65, 73, 81–2, 100–2, 104–6, 114–15, 117, 122, 217, 283, 285, 294

ultimate goals 172, 217, 223–4
units, functional 9–12, 17, 172

verbal behavior 8, 10, 12–13, 15, 17, 21–2, 27, 30, 32, 44–6, 49, 52–3, 90, 130, 134–7; analysis of 32, 134; essence of 103, 119; human 44, 175; of rational-emotive therapists 20; role of 137
verbal community 15, 43–4, 46, 48, 51, 53, 121, 152
verbal events 95, 104, 123, 134, 136–7, 139–40, 143, 149, 176
verbal goals 105
verbal knowing, paradox of 117–18, 122–4, 126
verbal knowledge 117–18, 120, 122–3, 125, 242; object of 120, 122–3
verbal meaning 149–52
verbal organisms 9–10, 45, 51, 53, 104, 241
verbal rules 40, 112, 135–8, 149–52, 178, 185, 222
verbal stimuli 51, 135, 139, 152

Watsonian metaphysical behaviorism 89–90, 94
Weiner, H. 134
Wessells, M. G. 83
work, scientific 71, 73, 87, 290, 295, 298
workability 6, 102, 107, 109, 123, 125, 223, 252, 261, 284–6
workshop 266–7
world hypotheses 5, 57–9

For Product Safety Concerns and Information please contact our EU representative GPSR@taylorandfrancis.com Taylor & Francis Verlag GmbH, Kaufingerstraße 24, 80331 München, Germany